Sven Quadflieg, Klaus Neuburg, Simon Nestler (eds.)
(Dis)Obedience in Digital Societies

DIGITAL SOCIETY | Volume 37

This publication was made available via Open Access within the framework of the funding project 16TOA002 with funds from the German Federal Ministry of Education and Research.

Bibliographic information published by the Deutsche Nationalbibliothek
The Deutsche Nationalbibliothek lists this publication in the Deutsche Nationalbibliografie; detailed bibliographic data are available in the Internet at http://dnb.d-nb.de

This work is licensed under the Creative Commons Attribution-NonCommercial-NoDerivatives 4.0 (BY-NC-ND) which means that the text may be used for non-commercial purposes, provided credit is given to the author. For details go to http://creativecommons.org/licenses/by-nc-nd/4.0/
To create an adaptation, translation, or derivative of the original work and for commercial use, further permission is required and can be obtained by contacting rights@transcript-publishing.com
Creative Commons license terms for re-use do not apply to any content (such as graphs, figures, photos, excerpts, etc.) not original to the Open Access publication and further permission may be required from the rights holder. The obligation to research and clear permission lies solely with the party re-using the material.

© 2022 transcript Verlag, Bielefeld

Cover layout: Klaus Neuburg, Sven Quadflieg
Cover illustration: Klaus Neuburg, Sven Quadflieg
Typeset: Klaus Neuburg, Sven Quadflieg
Printed by Majuskel Medienproduktion GmbH, Wetzlar
Print-ISBN 978-3-8376-5763-0
PDF-ISBN 978-3-8394-5763-4
EPUB-ISBN 978-3-7328-5763-0
https://doi.org/10.14361/9783839457634
ISSN of series: 2702-8852
eISSN of series: 2702-8860

Printed on permanent acid-free text paper.

(Dis)Obedience in Digital Societies

Perspectives on the Power of Algorithms and Data

Sven Quadflieg
Klaus Neuburg
Simon Nestler (eds.)

[transcript]

Content

06   Sven Quadflieg / Klaus Neuburg / Simon Nestler
         (Dis)obeying Algorithms?
         Introductory Thoughts on the Power
         of Algorithms and the Possible
         Necessity of Resisting it

24   Florian Arnold
         The Dialectics of Dis-Obedience.
         Notes from the Crystal Palace

48   Johanna Mellentin / Francesca Schmidt
         Surveillance, Artificial Intelligence and
         Power

70   Fabian Weiss
         Embodied Algorithmic Optimization.
         How Our Bodies are Becoming a
         Product of Code

102   Carolin Höfler
         The Lock Down City and the Utopian
         Program of Open Interfaces

136   Moritz Ahlert
         Hacking Google Maps

148   Harald Trapp / Robert Thum
         The Algorithmic Construction of
         Space

172   Christina Schlecht
         Torn Between Autonomy and Algorithmic
         Management.
         (Dis)Obedience of Solo Self-Employed
         Working via Digital Platforms

194 Victoria Guijarro Santos
 A Crack in the Algorithm's Facade.
 A Fundamental Rights Perspective on
 "Efficiency" and "Neutrality" Narratives of
 Algorithms

226 Katja Dill
 When Search Engines Discriminate.
 The Posthuman Mimesis of Gender Bias

250 Fabian Lütz
 Discrimination by Correlation.
 Towards Eliminating Algorithmic Biases
 and Achieving Gender Equality

294 Matthias Pfeffer
 The Power of Algorithms and the
 Structural Transformation of the Digital
 Public

318 Lotte Houwing
 Reclaim your Face and the Streets.
 Why Facial Recognition, and Other
 Biometric Surveillance Technology in
 Public Spaces, Should be Banned

342 Bernd Friedrich Schon
 Identity 5.0: How to Fight Algorithms
 Online (Fast).
 Heuristic Compressions of Personality
 Concepts (Dis)Obedient to Algorithmic
 Power—from Film, Television and a Cult
 Classic Novel

372 About the Authors

Sven Quadflieg / Klaus Neuburg / Simon Nestler

(Dis)obeying Algorithms?

Introductory Thoughts on the Power of Algorithms and the Possible Necessity of Resisting it

We live in a time when terms such as digital transformation are constantly being used and in which—as the series in which this book is published also indicates—people often talk about our digital society. Data and algorithms, it seems, have a great influence on social developments and they are often given so much importance that they are described as shaping an era. This is reflected in the title of this book, which also addresses the concept of a digital society and refers to algorithms and data. At the same time—it should be noted at the outset—the technical aspect of this phenomenon is not of significant importance in the following pages. Of course, for reading the subsequent contributions it would be useful to understand how algorithms work and why data has such a great influence on their functionality—but it will not be explained in depth at any point in the book. This is because, instead of technical details, this book only considers the impact of this technical structure on those who consciously or unconsciously interact with it: The humans and the society they form.

In the context of digital transformation, people and computers are entering into a fascinating symbiosis, something which Joseph Carl Robnett Licklider predicted as early as the 1960s, when he said that growing computing capacities would lead to new ways of using computers. The very notion of computer use is exciting here, as we probably associate it with false images; after all, computers are ubiquitously integrated into our physical environment and not even always recognizable as computers. This new kind of computer use is all-encompassing: It affects our private lives as well as major societal developments—computers and the algorithms that work within them have an impact on our lives whose dimension is almost impossible to grasp.

This influence naturally takes up a considerable amount of space in this book—however, the title already indicates that we are most interested in strategies for how individuals, groups, or even civil society in general can break this influence through forms of disobedience. In the title of the book and its implied dichotomy, we want to illustrate the complexity of the topic: Accepting algorithms is automatically a form of obedience—it can only be actively resisted—and every form of obedience should always provoke a debate about disobedience and gathering the power to question it. After all, many of the achievements of today's society are based on active disobedience or resistance.[1] The problem, as Howard Zinn provocatively put it, is not disobedience, but obedience.[2]

Disobedience, or civil disobedience, often has a moral level: For the most part, acts of civil disobedience are called for to remedy an existing injustice or to remove oneself as an active person from a political or social process and thus reduce one's own guilt. For example, Henry David Thoreau coined the term civil disobedience by arguing in his 1849 essay that one should bow to the law of the state only if it is consistent with one's own moral values. Thoreau argued that as a citizen he did not want to be complicit in the war against Mexico and the slavery that followed[3], mitigating his guilt by refusing to pay taxes. Thoreau thus not only shaped the concept of civil disobedience, but also inspired many subsequent civil rights movements and civil rights activists (including Martin Luther King[4])—despite his libertarian stance. Thoreau's theoretical statements are based on his practical actions and experiences—at one point he did in fact refuse to pay a tax payment and was imprisoned for a short period of time. Thus, Thoreau can already be counted as one of numerous examples of applied disobedience (whether his

---

1   David Graeber sets this out impressively: Laws are legitimized—depending on the form of government—by a constitution, which in turn was legitimized by the people. Using the examples of the USA and France, Graeber reminds us that an act of then illegal violence brought the people into the situation of being able to legitimize a constitution in the first place. Laws were formed out of resistance. Cf. Graeber, David: The Democracy Project. A History. A Crisis. A Moment, London 2014, p. 237–239.

2   He writes: "As soon as you say the topic is civil disobedience, you are saying our problem is civil disobedience. That is not our problem ... Our problem is civil obedience. Our problem is the numbers of people all over the world who have obeyed the dictates of the leaders of their government and have gone to war, and millions have been killed because of this obedience. [...] Our problem is that people are obedient all over the world, in the face of poverty and starvation and stupidity, and war and cruelty. Our problem is that people are obedient while the jails are full of petty thieves, and all the while the grand thieves are running the country. That's our problem." Zinn, Howard: The Zinn Reader: Writings on Disobedience and Democracy, New York City 2011, p. 405.

3   In 1849, he wrote for example: "In other words, when a sixth of the population of a nation which has undertaken to be the refuge of liberty are slaves, and a whole country is unjustly overrun and conquered by a foreign army, and subjected to military law, I think that it is not too soon for honest men to rebel and revolutionize." Thoreau, Henry David: Resistance to Civil Government. In: Myerson, Joel (Ed.): Transcendentalism. A Reader. Oxford 2000, p. 546–565. Here: p. 550.

4   Cf. Powell, Brent: Henry David Thoreau, Martin Luther King Jr., and the American Tradition of Protest. In: OAH Magazine of History 9, no. 2, 1995, p. 26–29.

act was actually a justified example of civil disobedience is still a matter of debate[5]). Prominent events followed on different scales: Numerous major political transformations of the 20th and 21st centuries were based on strategies of civil disobedience—for example, the Indian independence movement—and various resistance and protest movements of different kinds—from Solidarność to Otpor!—adopted strategies of civil disobedience to protest against governments (at this point we should also refer to Gene Sharp, whose guidance on nonviolent resistance inspired protest movements all over the world[6]). The moral level of civil disobedience is an important point here that is always a focus of discussion—for example, in John Rawls[7] or Hannah Arendt[8]—and certainly evokes intriguing questions in the context of this book: What legit-

---

5   Cf. Gros, Frédéric: Disobey. The Philosophy of Resistance. London/New York 2020, p. 126–127.

6   Cf. Sharp, Gene: From Dictatorship to Democracy, Boston 2010.
Sharp's influence has already been the subject of extensive media coverage. See, for example: Thumfart, Johannes: Der Demokrator. In: Die Zeit, Nr. 10/2011, https://www.zeit.de/2011/10/Gene-Sharp (April 11, 2021).

7   Vgl. Rawls, John: A Theory of Justice, Cambridge 1999.

8   Vgl. Arendt, Hannah: Ziviler Ungehorsam. In: Id.: In der Gegenwart. Übungen zum politischen Denken II, Edited by Ursula Ludz, München 2000, p. 283–321.

imizes a form of resistance?[9] What can be described as moral justification or even as duty?[10] And what are the limits of this justification?[11]

The questions about legitimizing possible acts of resistance (the dialectic of [dis]obedience is discussed in Florian Arnold's contribution right at the beginning of this book) take on a new quality in times of the digital transformation mentioned at the beginning. This is due to the lack of transparency (which will be discussed later) and requires its own nuanced consideration. In this book, very different perspectives are brought together in order to open up a broad discursive field. This approach is illustrated in the subtitle: *Perspectives on the Power of Algorithms and Data*. The very first word is itself up for debate, as it is not altogether precise: What appears in the following pages represents only an academic, Eurocentric subset of possible perspectives on a topic that is relevant almost everywhere, but is of course evaluated differently

---

[9] It should be noted that groups outside the democratic spectrum also repeatedly invoke morality to legitimize their acts of civil disobedience. In Germany, the Reichsbürger movement could serve as an example here, as could the right-wing extremist Identitarian movement, which has achieved relatively great media attention in German-speaking countries with acts of civil disobedience. In doing so, it repeatedly presents itself as a morally-driven movement on the one hand, and refers to strategies for nonviolent resistance on the other. Martin Sellner, probably the most important leader of the Identitarian movement in German-speaking countries, quotes Gene Sharp or Srdja Popovic, the co-founder of the Serbian protest movement Otpor! in his writings. This illustrates the complexity of moral justification in this context.

[10] These questions naturally also apply to protest in the digital society mentioned above. Prominent and controversial examples include the Internet activist Julian Assange, who uses his platform Wikileaks as a (digital) tool to draw attention to grievances, and the whistleblower Edward Snowden, whose revelations have shaken confidence in digital communication forever. In the public debate, the spectrum of opinions about the aforementioned activists ranges from almost cult-like veneration on the one hand to contempt as "lawbreakers" on the other. Cf. Kleger, Heinz; Makswitat, Eric: Digitaler Ungehorsam. Wie das Netz den zivilen Ungehorsam verändert. In: FJ SB 4/2014, p. 8–17, http://forschungsjournal.de/node/2654 (July 1, 2021).

[11] Defining these limits seems easier when a system of government differs greatly from current values and norms: In totalitarian systems such as National Socialism, resistance becomes, according to contemporary values, a civic duty. In modern societies, on the other hand, democratic mechanisms are generally provided for citizens to engage in critical discourse and civic or political participation, so that resistance to state power is also directed against a democratically legitimized community. The question of justification thus becomes an even more complex one. Cf. Braune, Andreas: Zur Einführung: Definitionen, Rechtfertigungen und Funktionen politischen Ungehorsams. In: Id. (Ed.): Ziviler Ungehorsam. Texte von Thoreau bis Occupy, Stuttgart 2017, p.9–38.

by individuals in other cultural, geographical, or social contexts. Algorithmic power is a global phenomenon and, depending on context and perspective, a global problem, and this book can, of course, only examine a small corner of it. Algorithms are often discriminatory—particularly through the data with which they are trained—and our view of the phenomenon comes from a privileged position in that we are not usually victims of that discrimination. While some contributions at least address discrimination in the context of sexism and perhaps classism (though here not from the perspective of the victim), there is a lack of consideration of discrimination, at least in the context of racism[12], so the perspectives mentioned here are fairly limited. This is particularly relevant because the book aims to demonstrate that algorithmic power does not, of course, act uniformly across society. Rather, it acts as an amplifier of the existing power structure—it repeatedly displays aspects of group-focused enmity when it makes sexist or racist decisions, for example.

But what exactly does power structure mean in the context of this book? As already indicated, algorithms shape human behavior on an individual and societal scale: They influence not only our perception of the world, but also the well-being and social interaction of us as their users. They act in the political context, create social realities, and intervene in concrete social situations—for example, in public spaces. Algorithms are thus not to be regarded as a purely technical structure, but as a social phenomenon. They embed themselves—currently still very subtly and with little transparency—in our political and social system: In digitized contexts, they determine what we read, what we consume, whom we perceive, whom we ignore, what we like, what we hate, whom we love: in short, how we live (and perhaps even how we die—after all, weapons also exist that autonomously kill people based on algorithms[13]). These effects of algorithms on our lives have been the subject

---

12   There are innumerable forms of hostility against groups, so of course other discriminations could be mentioned as well. But racism in particular is of course an important point of discussion in the context of algorithmic discrimination, which is why we highlight it here and elsewhere in the introduction. But of course, racism is also of particular importance in the context of intersectionality. We cannot duly represent an explicitly intersectional perspective with our book either.

13   Only recently a UN report triggered a discussion in the media about whether autonomous weapons had in fact already been deployed. Cf. Merlot, Julia: Autonome Waffe könnte Menschen erstmals eigenständig angegriffen haben. In: Der Spiegel, 2.6.2021, https://www.spiegel.de/wissenschaft/technik/autonome-waffe-koennte-menschen-erstmals-eigenstaendig-angegriffen-haben-a-ad06b93d-191c-4a5f-b4ae-853e7a7a177d (June 26, 2021).

of much discussion: Lev Manovich, for example, outlines the impact of algorithms on our cultural development and their influence on our aesthetic perception by suggesting what we should consume.[14] And without wanting to judge, we obey already because we let them recommend things to us by giving away our data and accepting suggestions based on it.[15] It is difficult to attribute agency to algorithms, since they are first and foremost merely mathematical representations of facts and processes.[16] Nevertheless, they can be seen as a power structure, even if, strictly speaking, it is not algorithms that exercise power—rather, power is exercised with them.[17] We believe, however, a legitimate form of simplification is valid here: Since social actions, following Bruno Latour, are ultimately always embedded in a network of things, and artifacts are always embedded in a network of actions[18], by power structure

14 He writes: "[...] recommendation engines suggesting what we should watch, listen to, read, write, or wear; devices and services that automatically adjust the aesthetic of captured media to fit certain criteria; software that rates the aesthetic quality of our photos, etc." Manovich, Lev: AI Aesthetics, Moscow 2018, p. 19–20.

15 And at the same time, of course, they are changing the nature of cultural creation, because in the context of music, for example, it seems increasingly important that a song be algorithm-compatible.

16 Cf. Reicherts, Jo: Von Menschen und Dingen. Wer handelt hier eigentlich? In: Poferl, Angelika; Schröer, Norbert (Eds.) Wer oder was handelt? Zum Subjektverständnis der hermeneutischen Wissenssoziologie, Wiesbaden 2014, p. 95–120. Here: p. 111–113.

17 In his observations on the phenomena of power, sociologist Heinrich Popitz describes, among other things, a data-setting power through technical action. Even if Popitz does not explicitly refer to algorithms, these observations can be transferred very well: "In changing the object world, we set 'data' to which other people are exposed. We exercise a kind of materialized power, a data-setting power, in which the effect of the powerholder over the power-affected is mediated by objects. This effect can be unintentional, accidental, not predictable, or planned and deliberate." (translation by the authors) Popitz, Heinrich: Phänomene der Macht, 2. Auflage, Tübingen 1992, p. 167.

18 On the role of objects as agents of agency, Bruno Latour has made an interesting contribution with his Actor-Network-Theory: "If action is restricted a priori to what 'intentional,' 'meaningful' people do, it is hard to see how a hammer, a basket, a door closer, a cat, a rug, a mug, a list, or a pendant could act". Latour, Bruno: Reassembling the Social. An Introduction to Actor-Network-Theory, Oxford 2012, p. 71.
This approach becomes even more relevant the more objects are equipped with "intelligent" capabilities. As a result, every everyday object could in future theoretically be part of a larger network, so that our everyday actions will be co-determined by an unknown number of "actors" who make data available or collect it and reuse it in other contexts. These networks are in principle all-pervasive ("evasive"), untransparent ("opaque") and exceed in their complexity what can be realized in the situation. Nevertheless, they structure our actions. Cf. Pranz, Sebastian: Der Berliner

in this context we mean the influence that algorithms exert on individual and social life[19]. This immediately leads to a major problem: algorithms often evade this discussion. It is precisely in the context of the algorithmic *black box* that the question of power urgently needs to be discussed—or, to be more precise, the question of responsibility. Andreas Matthias describes this as a "responsibility gap": We find ourselves in a situation in which autonomous machines based on algorithms make decisions whose decision-making path (also for future decisions) disappears into the deep black of the black box. It thus raises not only the question of who exercises power at this point, but also the moral question of who has the responsibility for this power.[20]

A list of examples of this algorithmic power could almost be endless—our private moments in particular are shaped by it. In a digital and datafied world, algorithms have an influence on our well-being—for example, through social media—and on the way we perceive the world; and it quickly becomes clear that algorithms also have a political dimension. The influence of algorithms on a large scale has been detailed in the context of the 2016 US election campaign[21], but the phenomenon can be described much more broadly. For example, Ivana Bartoletti suggests that the rise of populism can also be seen as a partial victory of algorithms over our information society—she links the electoral successes of Viktor Orbán, Jair Bolsonaro, or Rodrigo Duterte to the influence of algorithms.[22] It can thus be seen as an irony of history that the advancing intelligence of our technology, of all things, also seems to contribute to the political regression prevailing in some countries. Bartoletti concludes that AI has the potential to fundamentally transform our society[23]

Schlüssel. Bruno Latour und die Akteur-Netzwerk-Theorie. In: Döbler, Thomas; Rudeloff, Christian; Spiller, Ralf (Eds.): Schlüsselwerke der Kommunikationswissenschaft. Wiesbaden 2021, in press.

19 Strictly according to Latour, it would probably have to be argued that neither the algorithms, nor the programmers, nor even the users have the power, but that it is distributed dynamically in the network.

20 Cf. Matthias, Andreas: The responsibility gap: Ascribing responsibility for the actions of learning automata. In: Ethics and Information Technology 6, 2004, p. 175–183.

21 Cf. for example: Coeckelberg, Mark: AI Ethics, Cambridge/London 2020, p.100.

22 Cf. Bartoletti, Ivana: An Artificial Revolution. On Power, Politics and AI, London 2020, p. 14.

23 At this point, we must define our criticism clearly: The basic criticism that could be formulated here quickly reaches a limit. An algorithm—regardless of whether it is defined as AI or not—is first simply the subdivision of an action into a sequence of steps with the goal of solving a problem. An algorithm is therefore not per se

and links this to oppression: "And if we can understand how AI is related to oppression, then we can understand how to resist it."[24]

While discussing algorithms, AI is a fascinating term, but it is deliberately omitted from the title of the book, because we include in our considerations both algorithms developed by humans and algorithms developed by computers. Computers can—without going into the many differentiations of this type of learning—develop algorithms, for example, by the computer itself learning[25] with a kind of neural network and a large[26] amount of data. In a very simplified way, the human programs the computer's brain and the computer programs—based on data—a suitable algorithm. In the first case, people determine the behavior of the computer by programming the algorithm; in the second case, they determine this behavior primarily by selecting the data.[27] However, as exciting as the exact functioning of artificial intelligence may now be, there are few concrete implications that can be derived from it for the discourse in the context of this book. This book, as mentioned, is concerned neither with how algorithms work nor how they learn—but with what power structures and dependencies arise through algorithms and data in our everyday lives and in our society. The tension created by algorithmic power arises primarily from its interface with society: What is of interest to us is not the structure of algorithms, but the interaction with them or the problems created by their existence. It is not important how an algorithm is implemented, but how it acts—and above all, what the result of its existence is. However, since users usually have no knowledge at all about which parts of an algorithm come from a programmer and which parts of an

---

something that should be viewed critically—the criticism always refers to the actions themselves.

24   Cf. Bartoletti 2020, p. 123.

25   There are various ways in which this learning process takes place exactly, but that is not important in the context of this book.

26   Of course, large is relative and also depends on the complexity of the task. Simple image recognition—i.e. recognizing a cat in an image—an algorithm will probably be able to learn after a low four-digit number of good images.

27   Since different brains, i.e. different neural networks, are better or worse suited depending on the problem, the structure of the network also plays an important role. Since corresponding frameworks, for example Tensorflow (https://www.tensorflow.org), are now available, the human activity required here cannot be referred to as "programming" in the true sense—it is actually more like "configuring". This configuration influences the structure of the computer brain, but does not directly influence the action.

algorithm have been developed with the help of a neural network, this would only distort our focus, as that discussion is on the one hand too technical and on the other hand too biased towards the perspective of computer science. Since many of the currently available books on the topic already give a lot of space to the computer science perspective, we deliberately decided not to put this perspective at the center of our discourse. The following contributions thus show perspectives from very different disciplines[28]—and our desire for multi-perspectivity at this point outweighs the technical view of how algorithms work.[29]

The perception of such algorithms is always also characterized by the lack of transparency, because it is not always communicated when and why algorithms are used. It also usually impossible to work out how and why an algorithm makes a decision, which reinforces the aforementioned problem of responsibility and the general moral dimension. At the same time, it is interesting to note that there is a relatively high level of trust in algorithms[30]—which seems absurd in view of their opaque decision paths and the countless reports of algorithm failures. We perceive algorithms as cold, mechanical, logical, deterministic systems that provide the only correct answer after fully considering all possible options. In the end, the decisive thing is not how an algorithm arrives at its results: What is important is that algorithms are quite prone to error and sometimes simply want to make statements about the future based on bad data[31] from the past (which makes them sexist or racist, for example) and that humans—as Hannah Fry, among others, ex-

---

28 However, the limits of a complete mapping of this range are then revealed by our reflection on the "perspectives".

29 Thus, there are formulations in the book that deviate from our understanding of an algorithmic mode of operation, and perhaps can also be criticized in the strict sense of computer science. More important to us, however, seems to be the implications for the matter at hand. The tension between "disobey" and "obey" is not only about how algorithms act, but, if we follow the principles of human-computer interaction and interaction design, about how people perceive these algorithms; thus, different perceptions are explicitly part of the overall perspective.

30 For example, a recent poll had 51% of respondents answering that they "support reducing the number of national parliamentarians and giving those seats to an algorithm," no doubt in part because there is not much understanding of their low performance among the general population. See: https://docs.ie.edu/cgc/IE-CGC-European-Tech-Insights-2021-%28Part-II%29.pdf (June 15, 2021).

31 Bad is of course a complex word in this context: What is bad data? It can simply mean data that is not suitable for training an algorithm because it is incomplete or imprecise. Of course, the word bad also implies that the data does not reflect the

plains in detail—often do not question these results[32]. Indeed, the question of the function and precision of algorithmic decision-making leads to a very fundamental question: Why do we obey algorithms and computers at all?[33] Even filter bubbles generated by algorithms are now perceived by certain political movements to be more objective than content curated by journalists.[34]

In the early days of computer technology, when for example Alan Turing defined his abstract Turing machine, the computer behaved analogously to a human, but ideally infallible, mathematician. If the computer was wrong, it could be traced back to a programming error or to a technical defect. But under conditions characterized by uncertain and incomplete information as well as by scarce time resources, two factors are often decisive: On the one hand, a fast approximation to the correct solution is often more important than the time-consuming, exact calculation of a solution, and on the other hand, thinking in terms of correct and incorrect solutions is in itself inappropriate. In addition, there are no exact questions in communication with people or in the search for information, so that the computer cannot provide exact answers in the mathematical sense either. To conclude the brief discourse on algorithms, the lack of transparency still needs to be addressed, because this aspect is often perceived as a central deficit of algorithms generated by artificial intelligences. But here, too, our look at social implications, our shift from white box to black box, shows that this aspect applies to all algorithms. We do not know the code or the exact workings of the algorithms that dominate our everyday lives.[35]

    complexity of reality for various reasons, or that these data represent an unfair status quo.

32 Cf. Fry, Hannah: Hello World. Was Algorithmen können und wie sie unser Leben verändern, Bonn 2019, p. 184–201.

33 In fact, the interesting question is: When exactly does acceptance tip over? In which context do users accept obvious errors? From the world of literature, we know the powerful description of Winston Smith's horror in 1984 as he had to accept an obviously wrong result as the new truth: That 2 plus 2 equals 5. But is that so outlandish? Why do people drive their cars into rivers just because their navigation system says so?

34 Cf. for example: Zweig, Katharina; Deussen, Oliver; Krafft, Tobias D.: Algorithmen und Meinungsbildung. In: Informatik Spektrum 40, 2017, p. 318–326.

35 For example, the cheat devices uncovered during the so-called Dieselgate scandal in Germany clearly show: From the outside view of the driver, it is not apparent how the exhaust gas purification algorithm works in detail. But even the authorities responsible for testing have not noticed the exact way the algorithms work over a long time. The

This brings us to the last term in the subtitle: Data. A joke that circulated on Twitter a long time ago went like this: "What idiot called it 'machine learning' instead of 'bias automation'"[36]? Learning processes such as machine learning are based on data, from which specific behaviors are then extracted—the quality of the learning thus depends crucially on the quality of the data used. Biases in computer systems are a complex issue—and they are not only relevant in the context of AI. Batya Friedman and Helen Nissenbaum, for example, distinguished between different types of bias: First, there are preexisting biases, i.e. existing biases that are adopted consciously or unconsciously.[37] Friedman and Nissenbaum also refer to technical biases—biases that arise, for example, from technical constraints or technical considerations[38]—and emergent biases, which can arise as a "result of changing societal knowledge, population, or cultural values" over time.[39] Biases in AI are an important topic to keep focus on: Since the data with which the algorithm is trained is rarely neutral[40], its actions afterwards are not either—often they only recreate an unjust past[41] or a (discriminatory) status quo, thereby perpetuating inequalities[42]. Algorithmic biases are thus ultimately

question of the extent to which those responsible in the companies were familiar with how the algorithms worked has not yet been conclusively clarified.

36 Tracing authorship in such jokes is difficult. We refer to the tweet of the Twitter user @fasterthanlime from 2017. See: https://twitter.com/fasterthanlime/status/868840530813353985?s=20.

37 Here, we should also briefly refer to the programmers, whose role in the process should certainly be discussed. The reference to problematic data is not sufficient to clarify the responsibility for non-biased systems.

38 They use the example of a limited screen size that lets the algorithm make a selection.

39 Cf. Friedman, Batya; Nissenbaum, Helen: Bias in computer systems. ACM Trans. Inf. Syst. 14, 3 (July 1996). p. 330–347. DOI: https://doi.org/10.1145/230538.230561.

40 The exciting question is: Is there such a thing as neutral data? It is very likely that large amounts of data can at least be assumed not to represent a balanced picture of the world. Above all, however, algorithmic decisions should be based exclusively on aspects that are thematically relevant.

41 The reference to discriminatory "redlining" is certainly relevant here. Especially in the context of the city and algorithms, new forms of this practice can of course emerge here. Cf. for example: Safransky, Sara: Geographies of Algorithmic Violence: Redlining the Smart City. Int. J. Urban Reg. Res., 44, 2020. p. 200–218. DOI: https://doi.org/10.1111/1468-2427.12833.

42 When algorithms are trained with data, they naturally also adopt the status quo of this data. For example, if images, texts, or the like show primarily white men in certain

a data problem: Large amounts of data often reflect an unjust world by reproducing a white male heteronormativity (described in this book in Katja Dill's contribution).[43] This is another reason why algorithms, for example, can be quickly attributed to racist behavior, as Ruha Benjamin[44] and Safiya Umoja Noble[45], among others, have demonstrated impressively. In the context of machine learning/deep learning, the biggest problem is likely to be as outlined above: it is almost impossible to tell whether an algorithm is currently exhibiting discriminatory behavior, not only for users but increasingly also for creators.[46]

At the same time, however, data naturally also constitute their own (new) form of power structure: The control of large volumes of data, or the ability to evaluate complex and good data structures or to recognize patterns in them, change established power relationships and supplement (or partially replace) the means of production as the basis of power and the economy—here we can refer to Karl Marx.[47] In the sense of an intangible economy, companies are taking on an enormous role in the global economy on an intangible

positions of power, an algorithm can understand this as an unchanging status quo and try to reproduce it. Prominent examples of this kind are the much-discussed sexist recruiting AI of Amazon but also the sexism of Google Translate. Cf. Dastin, Jeffrey: Amazon scraps secret AI recruiting tool that showed bias against women. In: Reuters, 10. Oktober 2018, https://www.reuters.com/article/amazon-com-jobs-automation-idINKCN1MK0AH (Jun 3, 2021) and Prates, Marcelo O.R.; Avelar, Pedro H.; Lamb, Luís C.: Assessing gender bias in machine translation: a case study with Google Translate. In: Neural Comput & Applic 32, 2020. p. 6363–6381.

43 Of course, unjust data is not only a problem in algorithms: There are countless examples of how data reinforces existing privileges or disadvantages marginalized people. Cf. for example Cirado-Perez, Caroline: Invisible Women: Exposing Data Bias in a World Designed for Men, London 2019.

44 Vgl. Benjamin, Ruha: Race After Technology: Abolitionist Tools for the New Jim Code, Hoboken 2019.

45 Noble, Safiya Umoja: Algorithms of Oppression. How Search Engines Reinforce Racism. New York City 2018.

46 Depending on the context, checking the training data or controlling the algorithm can already be important steps. This can be explained with a simple example: If parameters in the usage of a system are changed (for example, the name, the place of residence or the gender) and the algorithm then changes its behavior, whether it should not do so, then problematic behavioral pattern could quickly be identified.

47 With regard to the significance of the social means of production and the power over them, one could of course refer directly to Das Kapital. Because this cross-reference would go beyond the dimensions of this introduction, we refer here to the text by Michael Seemann, who writes about digital capitalism and also refers to Karl Marx.

basis—and this is primarily due to the large quantities of analyzable data. This data generates insights into individual, societal and political behavior[48], it reveals invisible connections, makes accurate forecasts—and it can be used to persuade people, influencing behavior in a targeted and large-scale way. At the same time, we seem to be unwilling to acknowledge this. As Timothy Snyder points out, cognitive dissonance is an important issue here—by insisting on being the authors of our own actions, we provide alibis for digital creatures.[49]

The current situation is thus that algorithms have a major impact on individual and social life—and their ubiquitous dissemination means that they touch on various disciplines in scientific discourse. These different fields of consideration also open up the field of possible strategies of disobedience and allow for a wide-ranging discussion. If we speak of disobedience in this interdisciplinary field of tension, then the vagueness of the term in our context allows for quite different interpretations of the term. It includes the fact that disobedience also refers to the regulation of algorithms, i.e. by sparking a discourse on possible the legal consequences of an algorithmic power structure—also in order to make clear that this power is something that has to be negotiated socially and politically (which is discussed in this book, for example, in the contribution by Johanna Mellentin and Francesca Schmidt and also in Matthias Pfeffer's contribution). The legal approach to algorithmic power is especially a topic of immense importance, since it is necessary, among other things, to shed legal light on the black box of algorithms—not least in order to exclude the potential discriminatory treatment of human beings (in the book, this discussion can be found, for example, in the contributions from Fabian Lütz and Victoria Guijarro Santos). Disobedience also involves a general discussion about the use of algorithms, and of course also the individual strategy for evading algorithmic power, even if algorithms are also used at different scales as instruments of surveillance. The enormous possibilities

---

Cf. Seemann, Michael: Eine beunruhigende Frage an den digitalen Kapitalismus. In: APuZ. Aus Politik und Zeitgeschichte 69, 2919, p. 10–15.

48 At this point, it should of course be pointed out that data and the use of the same through machine learning turn the consideration of the complex relationship between humans and computers, since users of services simultaneously become data suppliers and thus—as Jaron Lanier puts it—data models. Cf: Lanier, Jaron: Who owns the future? New York City 2013.

49 Cf. Snyder, Timothy: Und wie elektrische Schafe träumen wir Humanität, Sexualität, Digitalität. Wien 2020, p. 41.

that arise, for example, for the surveillance of a society—with algorithms tracking people and their movement patterns in public space or in concrete urban spaces—must at least generate a debate about potential disobedience strategies. This means both that there should be discussion on a societal level about the use of such strategies (as in Lotte Houwing's contribution) and that people (as, for example, Fabian Weiss, Moritz Ahlert and Bernd Friedrich Schon suggest in their contributions) develop individual strategies for disobedience. Especially in political activism, disobedience to algorithms can be a necessary strategy that makes protests possible in the first place, both in an urban space (here we refer to Carolin Höfler's contribution) and in the digital space that serves mobilization and exchange. The importance of the concrete urban space for the formation and execution of a political protest has been explained many times, especially in the post-Tahrir years[50], which are characterized by the occupation of public squares. Countless protest groups, from Occupy to Movimiento 15M, have used this method, creating an exciting field of discussion. An algorithmic monitoring of the public space is thus also the potential control of spaces for demonstrations, which in a democratic society should at least provoke a critical discourse.

The contributions in this book oscillate between the poles of obedience and disobedience. Again and again, the aim is to show the manifold, complex dependencies between data and algorithms as part of the reality of life (in the context of work, for example, this is done in Christina Hecht's contribution), in order to then document strategies of disobedience that can be based on this (Harald Trapp and Robert Thum do this in their contributions, in which they lay out the dependencies between digital platforms and their data and urban space and the work commissioned there). The consideration of disobedience—we emphasize once again—is not meant to serve a general critique of algorithmic processes (whose comprehensive significance for the contemporary world we are of course aware of). Nor is it meant to be understood as a legitimatization of structures (the datafied world of work, for example, can

---

50 A detailed note here would go beyond the scope of this introduction, because here both the detailed reference to the general importance of public space and the reference to the concrete urban space, with reference to Georges-Eugène Haussmann etc., would be important. But Tahrir Square in particular can be highlighted here, as the political events there in 2011 have influenced many subsequent protest movements. Cf.: Mohamed, Abdelbaseer A.; van Nes, Akkelies; Salheen, Mohamed A.: Space and protest: A tale of two Egyptian squares. In: SSS10: Proceedings of the 10th International Space Syntax Symposium, London, UK, 13–17 July 2015, p. 110:1–110:18.

also be viewed critically, even if there are possibilities for "resistance"). Furthermore, our discussions are also not to be understood as a direct injunction to commit acts of disobedience (we would prefer if this were not necessary), even if we attach great importance to the strategies for this. Rather, it is intended to focus on very fundamental techno-ethical questions and to initiate a comprehensive discourse, at the end of which concrete strategies of disobedience may indeed be posited. In this sense, the book's contributions span both very concrete ideas and strategies and much more abstract considerations. The book begins on an epistemological level, where the implied problem of disobedience and obedience in the context of algorithms is laid out in various contexts, before that is discussed more empirically and analytically in the middle section of the book. From these considerations, the normative thoughts or the concrete descriptions of possible disobedience at the end of the book can then be well framed: Despite our academic context, we allow this book to end almost on an activist note. As will become apparent in the following pages, strategies for disobedience can be found on very different levels: In the individual act of resistance as well as in a broad political debate. It can concern very private areas, but equally important social issues. And it ranges from humorous interventions, which perhaps are rather meant to initiate a discussion, to strategies for ensuring survival or freedom in repressive regimes. What unites these different levels is that it is always about questioning and breaking the dominance of technologies. We hope to contribute to a discourse whose importance for a society in the process of digital transformation can hardly be overestimated.

Literature

Arendt, Hannah: Ziviler Ungehorsam. In: Id.: In der Gegenwart. Übungen zum politischen Denken II, Edited by Ursula Ludz, München 2000, p. 283–321.

Bartoletti, Ivana: An Artificial Revolution. On Power, Politics and AI, London 2020.

Benjamin, Ruha: Race After Technology: Abolitionist Tools for the New Jim Code, Hoboken 2019.

Braune, Andreas: Zur Einführung: Definitionen, Rechtfertigungen und Funktionen politischen Ungehorsams. In: Id. (Ed.): Ziviler Ungehorsam. Texte von Thoreau bis Occupy, Stuttgart 2017, p. 9–38.

Cirado-Perez, Caroline: Invisible Women: Exposing Data Bias in a World Designed for Men, London 2019.

Coeckelberg, Mark: AI Ethics, Cambridge/London 2020.

Dastin, Jeffrey: Amazon scraps secret AI recruiting tool that showed bias against women. In: Reuters, 10. Oktober 2018, https://www.reuters.com/article/amazon-com-jobs-automation-idINKCN1MK0AH (June 3, 2021).

Friedman, Batya; Nissenbaum, Helen: Bias in computer systems. In: ACM Trans. Inf. Syst. 14, 3, July 1996, p. 330–347. DOI: https://doi.org/10.1145/230538.230561

Fry, Hannah: Hello World. Was Algorithmen können und wie sie unser Leben verändern, Bonn 2019.

Graeber, David: The Democracy Project. A History. A Crisis. A Moment, London 2014.

Gros, Frédéric: Disobey. The Philosophy of Resistance. London/New York 2020.

Kleger, Heinz; Makswitat, Eric: Digitaler Ungehorsam. Wie das Netz den zivilen Ungehorsam verändert. In: FJ SB 4/2014, p. 8–17, http://forschungsjournal.de/node/2654 (July 1, 2021).

Lanier, Jaron: Who owns the future? New York City 2013.

Latour, Bruno: Reassembling the Social. An Introduction to Actor-Network-Theory, Oxford 2012.

Manovich, Lev: AI Aesthetics, Moscow 2018.

Matthias, Andreas: The responsibility gap: Ascribing responsibility for the actions of learning automata. In: Ethics and Information Technology 6, 2004, p. 175–183.

Merlot, Julia: Autonome Waffe könnte Menschen erstmals eigenständig angegriffen haben. In: Der Spiegel, 2.6.2021, https://www.spiegel.de/wissenschaft/technik/autonome-waffe-koennte-menschen-erstmals-eigenstaendig-angegriffen-haben-a-ad06b93d-191c-4a5f-b4ae-853e7a7a177d (June 2, 2021).

Mohamed, Abdelbaseer A.; van Nes, Akkelies; Salheen, Mohamed A.: Space and protest: A tale of two Egyptian squares. In: SSS10: Proceedings of the 10th International Space Syntax Symposium, London, UK, 13–17 July 2015, p. 110:1–110:18.

Noble, Safiya Umoja: Algorithms of Oppression. How Search Engines Reinforce Racism. New York City 2018.

Popitz, Heinrich: Phänomene der Macht, 2. Auflage, Tübingen 1992.

Powell, Brent: Henry David Thoreau, Martin Luther King Jr., and the American Tradition of Protest. In: OAH Magazine of History 9, no. 2, 1995, p. 26–29.

Pranz, Sebastian: Der Berliner Schlüssel. Bruno Latour und die Akteur-Netzwerk-Theorie. In: Döbler, Thomas; Rudeloff, Christian; Spiller, Ralf (Eds.), Schlüsselwerke der Kommunikationswissenschaft, Wiesbaden 2021, in press.

Prates, Marcelo O.R.; Avelar, Pedro H.; Lamb, Luís C.: Assessing gender bias in machine translation: a case study with Google Translate. In: Neural Comput & Applic 32, 2020, p. 6363–6381.

Rawls, John: A Theory of Justice, Cambridge 1999.

Reicherts, Jo: Von Menschen und Dingen. Wer handelt hier eigentlich? In: Poferl, Angelika; Schröer, Norbert (Eds.) Wer oder was handelt? Zum Subjektverständnis der hermeneutischen Wissenssoziologie, Wiesbaden 2014, p. 95–120.

Safransky, Sara: Geographies of Algorithmic Violence: Redlining the Smart City. Int. J. Urban Reg. Res., 44, 2020. p. 200–218. DOI: https://doi.org/10.1111/1468-2427.12833

Seemann, Michael: Eine beunruhigende Frage an den digitalen Kapitalismus. In: APuZ. Aus Politik und Zeitgeschichte 69, 2919, p. 10–15.

Sharp, Gene: From Dictatorship to Democracy, Boston 2010.

Snyder, Timothy: Und wie elektrische Schafe träumen wir Humanität, Sexualität, Digitalität, Wien 2020.

Thoreau, Henry David: Resistance to Civil Government. In: Myerson, Joel (Ed.): Transcendentalism. A Reader. Oxford 2000, p. 546–565.

Thumfart, Johannes: Der Demokrator. In: Die Zeit, Nr. 10/2011, https://www.zeit.de/2011/10/Gene-Sharp (April 11, 2021).

Zinn, Howard: The Zinn Reader: Writings on Disobedience and Democracy, New York City 2011.

Zweig, Katharina; Deussen, Oliver; Krafft, Tobias D.: Algorithmen und Meinungsbildung. In: Informatik Spektrum 40, 2017, p. 318–326.

Florian Arnold

The Dialectics of Dis-Obedience

Notes from the Crystal Palace

"To live in a glass house is a revolutionary virtue par excellence. It is also an ecstasy, a moral exhibitionism that we very much need."[1]

One of the central questions of modern democracies can be formulated as the paradox of how to serve freedom. Inherent in this paradox is a tension in which, depending on one's situation and disposition, one must always find anew the right balance between obedience and disobedience to the rules set by the sovereign. This tense question of freedom shows itself all too easily in the context of our quarantine routine, as we can simply look at those attempting to escape, committing misdemeanors or even breaking the law, who try to attract attention. Today, one cannot talk about the subject of (dis)obedience without coming across the global phenomenon of the so-called 'Querdenker', literally "those who think across (or laterally or transversally)". In the middle of the 19th century, the movement named "Freigeister" was still committed to a liberal-democratic agenda and saw itself supported by a broad consensus in the bourgeoisie, but already appears to Friedrich Nietzsche only as philistine folklore of old revolutionaries, to whom he opposed the immoral aestheticism of a future generation of "freie Geister", "free spirits". According to Nietzsche, this rare type of people is characterized by a pronounced individualism and a radical self-enlightenment which no longer bow to any idols, be they fellow human beings, the state, or even God himself. Against this background, the fact that today a wide variety of groups unite under the banner of 'Querdenker' may at first seem like another chapter in the successful modern history of individual self-assertion: For is it not basically still the state authority, which today again shows its ugly face, hidden behind care and welfare, only to rob its citizens of their most elementary rights, and some even of their livelihood? Is it not the first duty of citizens to resist and to serve their own freedom as well as the freedom of all by defending it against police restrictions in public? Are we not already living in a digital dictatorship by design, established by the controlling mania of the elites, who today use the new media of a barely visible algorithmization to make us slaves? In short: Is the modern state of today not merely the citizen-friendly side of a global biopolitics, whose profiteers remain themselves invisible—a conspiracy?

---

1   Benjamin, Walter: Der Sürrealismus. Die letzte Momentaufnahme der europäischen Intelligenz. In: id.: Gesammelte Schriften, vol. II, 1, ed. by Rolf Tiedemann and Hermann Schweppenhäuser, Frankfurt a. M. 1977, p. 295–310, here p. 298.

Florian Arnold

On the following pages I will take this basically paranoid view seriously, in order to illuminate its dark motives—behind it—as inevitable consequences of the modern dialectics of dis-obedience. What was described as a tension in the introduction has, with the development of our 'algorithmic culture', grown into an actual dialectic in which the role of design can no longer be underestimated. Design, however, means here a certain mindset, which functions as a motor of modernization, on whose material and idealistic effects both its proponents and its critics still draw from today.[2] In order to understand the nature of this mindset, I will start with the Great Exhibition of 1851 in London. Here we will highlight certain essential features of modern thinking, which would, however, remain unrecognized in its Janus-facedness, if we did not at the same time step into an equally famous 'underground' of St. Petersburg. Fyodor M. Dostoevsky's *Notes from the Underground* shows the dark side of a glorious rationalism and its creative optimism, as it were the underworld to this earthly paradise. Only this dialectical transition from light to shadow makes it possible to gauge the dangers modern citizens face when they obey the state laws of freedom or follow the wild call of liberty.

I. The Great Exhibitionism

It was not the first industrial and commercial exhibition on the island, but it was the first on a global scale that Queen Victoria and Prince Albert ceremoniously opened in London's Hyde Park on May 1, 1851. And in fact, the organizing committee had managed to set up an internationally attended and respected show of performance. Prince Albert himself had made it his task to bring the technical and artistic progress to England, to both represent the status quo as well as possible ways into the future. Thus he declared at a preparatory banquet: "Gentlemen,—the Exhibition of 1851 is to give us a true test and a living picture of the point of development at which the whole of mankind has arrived in this great task, and a new starting point from which all nations will be able to direct their further exertions."[3] A certain sense of mission that speaks from these words was hard to ignore even for contemporaries.

[2] For a detailed account of this mindset, see Florian Arnold: Logik des Entwerfens. Eine designphilosophische Grundlegung, Paderborn 2018.
[3] Martin, Theodore: The Life of His Royal Highness the Prince Consort, Volume 2, New York 1877, p. 201–8, esp. 205.

The fact that this project was realized in England may hardly come as a surprise regarding its pre-eminence as an industrial nation as well as a trading and colonial power. In this format of a Great Exhibition that still travels around the world today as "Expo," the British sporting spirit of performance, competition and spectacle made its appearance in another arena, albeit initially as a kind of home match for the hosts (with about half of the exhibition space reserved for representatives of the Commonwealth). But other nations and principalities also took up the challenge and provided the showcase of a globalized industrial capitalism with all kinds of goods from their own production. During the almost five months of the exhibition, the approximately 6 million spectators walked along ranges of Indian spices, American agricultural machinery, or French haute couture. Yet, the real event and the most dazzling symbol of the entire occasion remained the exhibition building itself: the Crystal Palace.

This building had already been celebrated by contemporaries as an architectural wonder of the century, and even after its successor building fell victim to a fire in 1936, it was none other than Le Corbusier who wrote an epitaph for this building or this type of building. The historical significance of the Crystal Palace lay not just in the building itself, but in the sophisticated design concept that was extremely variable in scale: Joseph Paxton, its architect and at the time of its construction already a wealthy railroad shareholder and entrepreneur, was an inventive and experimental gardener to William Cavendish, the 6th Duke of Devonshire. Paxton at this time was already known (not least to the royal couple) for designing impressive green houses. Accordingly, the architecture of the Crystal Palace looked like an oversized greenhouse that could not only be easily erected and dismantled again, moreover it impressively symbolized the prosperity of modern life in an artificial atmosphere specially designed of glass and cast iron: "That with the Crystal Palace a revolution had taken place in the field of architecture was immediately recognized by clear-sighted contemporaries. The purely functionalist aesthetics of the building, the lavish use of the materials glass and iron, which until then had been considered luxurious, and the facilitated dissolution of limited space that this made possible, the interweaving or interpenetration of interior and exterior, thus also became the paradigmatic form of modern building."[4]

---

[4] Quoted from Lange, Wolfgang: "Kristallpalast oder Kellerloch? Zur Modernität Dostojewskijs". In: Merkur 40 (1/1986), p. 14–29, here p. 17 (translation by the author).

Above all, the use of glass on such a massive scale turned into the expression of a modern mechanism of inclusion and exclusion. In the end, its effects could not hide the fact that the boundary between inside and outside continues to exist, even when an envious or pitying glance penetrates the façade. Even if one might believe in enlightenment and transparency,[5] the glas still just reflects one's own milieu. No other material like glass is able to make visible through its semi-permeability what Peter Handke once put into the formula of the inner world of the outer world of the inner world: that the asymmetry between one's own inside and the other's outside is never cancelled for the observer, but can only be determined from a higher vantage point.

If this still relates to the horizontal separation of spaces, insiders and outsiders, then a vertical isolation can also be studied at the Crystal Palace, which in turn relates to the biotope of humankind as such in contrast to our 'natural' environment. As Peter Sloterdijk once described it in the course of his literary inspection of the "world interior of capital," an entry into the interior of the Crystal Palace is at the same time accompanied by the promise to turn the inhospitable outside more and more into a homely self-enclosure: "With its erection, the principle of the interior crossed a critical threshold: from then on, it meant neither the bourgeois or aristocratic dwelling nor its projection into the sphere of urban shopping arcades, rather, it set out to transpose the outside world as a whole into a magical immanence transfigured by luxury and cosmopolitanism. Having been converted into a great greenhouse and an imperial museum of culture, it betrayed the contemporary tendency to turn nature and culture together into indoor affairs."[6]

Whereas Walter Benjamin, against whom the side blow "of urban shopping arcades" is aimed here, had only recognized a gigantic Parisian passage in the Crystal Palace, Sloterdijk, on the other hand, sees in it the concept of "kosmos" renewed. Even if transcendent assistance has failed us, the natural neediness and cleverness of humankind now puts into action what, as an

---

5 Cf. ibid., p. 19: "What the crystal palace with its transparent walls promised aesthetically corresponds to the utopia of the bourgeoisie, the dream of an outwardly universalistic and inwardly transparent society, a society in which the gloomy arcanum of the old world would be illuminated by the radiant light of the Enlightenment and neither the individual with his drives and desires nor society with its political and economic institutions would any longer have anything to hide."

6 Sloterdijk, Peter: Im Weltinnenraum des Kapitals. Für eine philosophische Theorie der Globalisierung, Frankfurt a. M. 2005, p. 266 (translation by the author).

extension of our own comfort zone, tends towards an infinite expansion. Admittedly, to speak with Benjamin: Even if "the world exhibitions are the pilgrimage to the commodity as fetish", a "people's festival" of capital, a transfiguration of "the exchange value of commodities",[7] all these descriptions still only highlight rather arbitrary features of that all-embracing development, which shapes the overall constitution of the modern life-world: "The world exhibitions [do not simply] build up the universe of commodities",[8] instead the crystal palace exhibits by itself the world itself—as a 'universal' commodity, as the one comprehensive, 'turned-into-one,' immanent good of human-creative self-transfiguration. What is fetishized here, not unlike in Marx, is at last man's labor and creative power itself—hence the "Great Exhibitionism".

The fact that it is possible to exchange at all, and not just to consume, is precisely one of the achievements of an inner-world expansion that relieves itself of the wear and tear of a hostile environment. It allows to take part in a general metabolism without losing shape, and it does so via an artificial membrane that enables reproduction of one's own system according to one's own rules, i.d. via autopoiesis.[9] If one wants to call it luxury, then one should call this the relative surplus of an absolute luxury of survival. To propagate, on the other hand, the standards of a mere use-value would mean to be blind for the tendency inherent in the use of things itself to build up into ever more complex artifacts that inevitably participate in a general exchange of resources and materials. Exchange as opposed to use or consumption instead means postponement, differentiation, mediation, and refinement. Basically, it organizes the luxurious life of a deficient human being, a being that cannot leave anything in its natural place, since it does not possess a natural place itself, but must first establish "its own nature".

---

7 Benjamin, Walter: Das Passagen-Werk. Erster Band, Frankfurt a. M. 1983, p. 50 (translation by the author).

8 Ibid., p. 51.

9 Cf. Fyodor M. Dostojewski's remarks on his own imprisonment at a Siberian labor camp: "Those convicts who knew no trade tried, nevertheless, to earn a few copecks occasionally in different ways. Some bought and sold things which nobody but a prisoner would ever have thought of selling or buying, or even of calling things. But the convicts were poor and very practical, and could turn even a filthy rag to some account." (Dostojewski.: Buried Alive or Ten Years of Penal Servitude in Siberia, London 1881, p. 25.)

You may call this either a luxury economy or an economy of scarcity, anyway, in the Crystal Palace exchange as the substitution of nature and culture is expressed in the purest degree, literally in the sense of crystallization: "For Plato, the crystal was the embodiment of the idea immersed in matter. Since the 19th century has chosen the crystal as the symbol of an order of reason arising naturally from history, not only a homogeneous world society spanning the entire globe is emerging, but also the horror of what Gehlen will then sarcastically call 'cultural crystallization'—the fear of a time without history."[10] No less paradoxically than a spiritualized nature or a naturalized spirit, in the crystalline structure of the Crystal Palace a structure of space-time comes to light, which already grasps the brilliance of the beginning of modern history in the perfect symmetry of a petrified, eternal duration. Thus, from now on, it seems only possible to repeat on a large scale what has already taken shape on a small scale, in the microcosmic dimensions of the World Exhibition: the optimistic, enlightened cosmopolitanism of a technical utopia.

II. Bourgeois Babel

"The immense town, for ever bustling by night and by day, as vast as an ocean, the screech and howl of machinery, the railways built above the houses (and soon to be built under them) the daring of enterprise, the apparent disorder, which in actual fact is the highest form of bourgeois order, the polluted Thames, the coal-saturated air, the magnificent squares and parks, the town's terrifying districts, such as Whitechapel with its half-naked, savage and hungry population, the City with its millions and worldwide trade, the Crystal Palace, the World Exhibition. [...] You look at those hundreds of thousands, at those millions of people obediently trooping into this place from all parts of the earth—people who have come with only one thought, quietly, stubbornly and silently milling round in this colossal palace; and you feel that something final has been accomplished here—accomplished and completed."[11]

Among the contemporary critics of the World Exhibition building, which had migrated from Hyde Park to Sydenham in the same year to be rebuilt there in 1854 on an even bigger scale, Fyodor M. Dostoevsky was at

10 Lange, Kristallpalast oder Kellerloch? p. 21.
11 Dostoevsky, Fyodor M.: Winter Notes on Summer Impressions, Richmond 2008, p. 48f.

once the most tartly and the most sharp-sighted. When Dostoyevsky set out on his first trip to Europe via Paris, London, Geneva and Italy in 1862, the disillusionment that set in was almost indistinguishable from the ardor that was to find literary expression a year later, after his second trip to Europe. The results were his *Winter Notes of Summer Impressions*. One can hardly call it a travel diary, rather a reckoning in retrospect, which Dostoevsky wrote under the impressions he had gained of Western Europe. Above all, London, even before Paris, had shown itself as the epitome of a new world of droning machines, starving people and dark powers, with the Crystal Palace in the center like a newly constructed tower of a bourgeois Babel, erected with diabolical skill—nota bene a completed tower: " It is a biblical sight, something to do with Babylon, some prophecy out of the Apocalypse being fulfilled before your very eyes. You feel that a rich and ancient tradition of denial and protest is needed in order not to yield, not to succumb to impression, not to bow down in worship of fact, and not to idolize Baal, that is, not to take the actual fact for the ideal...".[12]

One sees Dostoevsky wrestling with words imposed by this "grandeur of the idea"; provoking in him the anxious question, "Can this [...] in fact be the final accomplishment of an ideal state of things?"[13]—And yet, at the same time, these doubts express a missionary tone that pervades his Slavophilic utterances throughout the decades, even where, at the end of his life, in his celebrated Pushkin speech, he passes from condemnation to reconciliation.[14] However, for him there is no doubt about one thing: the Crystal Palace as a symbol of technical progress remains a cathedral of idolatry that gathers people under the sign of Baal.

---

12   Ibid., p. 50f.

13   Ibid., p. 50.

14   ...a reconciliation, of course, that goes beyond the internal rift of the pro-Western and the folk factions among the Russian intellectuals, aiming at a fraternization of a pan-European civilization. Thus, among other things, the speech states: "And in course of time I believe that we—not we, of course, but our children to come—will all without exception understand that to be a true Russian does indeed mean to aspire finally to reconcile the contradictions of Europe, to find resolution of European yearning in our pan-human and all-uniting Russian soul, to include within our soul by brotherly love all our brethren. At last it may be that Russia pronounces the final Word of the great general harmony, of the final brotherly communion of all nations in accordance with the law of the gospel of Christ!" (Cf. Fyodor M. Dostoevsky: Pushkin Speech, June 8, 1880 at the Meeting of the Society of Lovers of Russian Literature. Source and Translation: https://pages.uoregon.edu/kimball/DstF.Puw.lct.htm#DstF.Puw.lct (February 5, 2021).

It is easy today to take offense at this tone, which is itself demonic, and Dostoevsky himself does so in the following passage. But a reply that follows in turn tells us more clearly what fascinates and repels him at the same time: "All right, [...] let us admit I had been carried away by the decor; I may have been. But if you had seen how proud the mighty spirit is which created that colossal decor and how convinced it is of its victory and its triumph, you would have shuddered at its pride, its obstinacy, its blindness, and you would have shuddered, too, at the thought of those over whom that proud spirit hovers and reigns supreme."[15]

Dostoevsky is talking about "pride", "obstinacy", and "blindness"—but what precisely is meant by this? What is this "mighty spirit", apart from its demonization, which in Dostoevsky's eyes drives those governed by it into the delusion of a consummate sinfulness? The wider context of these records reveals it: When Dostoevsky lashes out in a sweeping blow aimed at Paris, Heidelberg, and London alike, uniting their contrasts and transitions on a spectrum between the "calmness in order" on the one hand and the "harshness" of contradictions on the other, he hits a sore spot of the Western mind. With Herbert Marcuse one might call it its "repressive tolerance"—a repressive tolerance of a social technology fine-tuned down to the individual souls: "And what regimentation! Don't misunderstand me: I don't mean, so much, external regimentation, which is insignificant (relatively, of course) but a colossal internal, spiritual regimentation, having its sources in the very depths of the soul."[16]—This is true of Paris and Heidelberg, but at the other extreme no less true of London, insofar as it is the same matter of creating "some sort of community and to settle down in the same ant hill; even turning into an ant hill seems desirable—anything to be able to settle down without having to devour each other—the alternative is to turn into cannibals."[17]

In other words: Dostoevsky sees the western principle of individualism already as having failed, where it knows to preserve its specimens only by a total, external and internal regimentation, in the 'stahlharten Gehäuse der Hörigkeit' (Max Weber), "the adamantine casing of obedience", so that they do not endanger themselves continuously. But what would an alternative to this look like? Is there a possibility to assert one's own individual will without doing violence to others or even to oneself?

15 Dostoevsky, Winter Notes, p. 51.
16 Ibid., p. 48.
17 Ibid., p. 49.

III. The Phantasmagoria of Reason

We approach an answer to this question by consulting another of Dostoevsky's texts, which refers to the Crystal Palace once again, although this time on a more fictional than biographical level. It is the *Notes from the Underground* published in 1864, and so in the same period of the *Winter Notes* and his first two European journeys. Consisting of two parts, the first (to which we limit ourselves) presents a literary confession. Its anonymous author bears traits of Dostoevsky himself, even if the later declares his disagreement with the character at the very beginning in a preamble named: "Under the floorboards". According to this preamble, Dostoevsky gives a psychological outline of a "representative of the recent past", of that the nihilistic generation to which Dostoevsky himself belonged before he found himself in front of a court of indictment for political activities, was pardoned shortly before his execution, and then spent several years as an inmate of a labor camp in Siberia. It is probably not completely wrong to assume that Dostoevsky's experiences had influenced what was on his in mind, when he wrote down his Notes from the Underground.

The decisive occasion nevertheless for this may have been his London impressions, which were further strengthened while he read the contemporary novel *What to Do?* by Nikolai G. Chernyshevsky from 1863. In this famous book Chernyshevsky took up the utopias of Fourier's early socialism and spun them into new literary visions of the future for a revolutionary Russia.18 Dostoevsky in turn designed his Notes as a half-concealed polemic against Chernyshevsky's enterprise, which, after his conversion, seemed to him like a dangerous import of Western European fashions and their underlying nihilism. The tone therefore is harsh, but in the context of the rather association-like ramblings of its fictitious author, it blends into a sometimes sarcastic, profound to abysmal, almost delusional flight of thought, whose

---

18 Cf. Lange, Kristallpalast oder Kellerloch? p. 19: "The utopian potential of the Crystal Palace was grasped and literally exploited in the Fourier-inspired circles of the Petersburg intelligentsia. Grouped around Nikolai G. Chernyshevsky, this circle of utopian socialists instinctively recognized that the contours of an ideal future society were beginning to appear on the glistening façade of the Crystal Palace. Since they knew from Fourier the importance of architecture in the construction of a society, it is not surprising that they believed that with this building, even better than with those sketched by the master himself, they could realize the idea of the phalanstère, the living, working and entertainment place for the envisaged social associations, the phalanges."

vanishing point is an unspecified "Crystal palace". Detached from its contemporary context, this building has already become a symbol. Even more: the Crystal Palace forms the sore point of the narrator, who is sick of the present, and incites him to sustained assaults of his imagination against this modern bulwark of utopian-utilitarian reason. It is significant that the narrator's Crystal Palace increasingly becomes a phantasmagoria emerging from his own dwelling cave, an obsessive conceit of modern reason, a surface reflection of his own subliminal projections. But of his projections alone?

"You believe in a crystal building, for ever indestructible—that is, one at which you can neither furtively stick out your tongue nor secretly cock a snook. But the reason perhaps that I'm afraid of this building is just because it is made of crystal, is for ever indestructible, and it would be impossible to stick one's tongue out at it, even furtively. [...] Let it even be that the crystal building is a figment which, according to the laws of nature, is not supposed to exist and that I have only invented out of my own stupidity and because of the archaic, irrational habits of our generation. But what do I care that it is not supposed to exist? What does it matter so long as it exists in my desires or, rather, exists while my desires exist?"[19]

What comes to light in this passage grants insight into an underlying connection.[20] A stronger contrast than that between a Crystal Palace flooded with light and a stuffy dwelling hole can hardly be imagined, and yet it is precisely through this that the actual ambivalence in the ideals and wishful thinking of the anonymous author's generation is revealed. In relation to the faith of his contemporaries, however, he expresses a certain apprehension that leads to the following: He seems to fear an ultimate transfer of his *idée fixe* into reality, an indestructible realization of utopia, before which his own wishes could then only admit defeat and retreat into the underground of his pitiful apartment. Because the victory would not belong to his fantasy or desires, but their opposite, a reason realizing itself in total through a more and more reasonable reality.

Yet what would be so bad about that? The anonymous author speaks of a "figment", of the fact that this "crystal building" is perhaps not intended by the "laws of nature" at all, and thereby resumes remarks earlier in the text which had stressed an irrefutable lawfulness of reason, a certain "de-

---

19 Dostoevsky, Fyodor M.: Notes from the Underground, Richmond 2011, p. 32f.
20 Cf. Lange, Kristallpalast oder Kellerloch? p. 29.

ductive logic"[21]. We will now see how he tries to keep apart total reason and subversive fantasy, and how in doing so, he makes sure that both unite again under ambivalence mentioned above. This ambivalence, however, ultimately concerns nothing other than the question of the relationship between freedom and necessity, arbitrariness and regulation, namely in the course of the dialectics of dis-obedience.

IV. Pandemonium

The first passage, in which the Crystal Palace appears by name, can still be seen in the context of an ironic demonstration of scientific-technical progress, through which irrationalism, according to the hopes imputed to the directly addressed reader, would evaporate in the new world to be created. In the unlikely event that "common sense and scholarship have entirely re-educated and directed human nature along normal lines", then "human beings will stop making mistakes *voluntarily* and, so to speak, naturally, will no longer want their free will to operate against their normal interests".[22] "And not only that; at that time, you say, acquired knowledge will itself teach human beings (though this is a luxury, in my view) that in fact they have neither will nor whim of their own and never have had, that they are something like a piano key or an organ stop; and that, over and above this, there are laws of nature in the world so that everything they do is done not at all because they will it, but spontaneously, in accordance with the laws of nature. Consequently, all that is necessary is to discover these laws of nature and human beings will no longer be answerable for their actions and it will be very easy for them to live. [...] And then—it's still you speaking—new economic relations will arise, all ready-made, also calculated with mathematical accuracy, so that all kinds of questions will vanish in an instant, simply because all kinds of answers will become available. Then they will build a crystal palace."[23]

If there was any doubt which spirit exactly Dostoevsky had in mind when he demonized it and identified it with Baal, it becomes clear in this passage that it is about the famous demon of Laplace, which—with the help of a perfect analysis of present causalities—would be able at to predict the future.

---

21 Dostoevsky: Notes from the Underground, p. 22.
22 Ibid., p. 23.
23 Ibid., p. 23f.

It is the spirit of the positivist science of the 19th century, but expanded into the sphere of social welfare, which then would also be based on natural laws and a "mathematical accuracy" in organizing human life. The historical consequences of this doctrine, for example in the form of dialectical materialism, are well-known and still seem to be at work today, mutatis mutandis, in the reflections of a so called "solutionism"[24] that now tackles the imponderables of life with probabilistic extrapolations and digitally optimized equipment. No less well-known today is the criticism leveled against it. What makes Dostoevsky's anonymous critic from the underground worth mentioning, however, is his understanding of resistance, a certain form of irrationalism that unites voluntarism and vitalism in an attack on common sense and scientific reason.

Thus, in the very paragraph, after deriding the crystal palace as wishful thinking, our author turns the table by emphasizing two things: the threat of boredom in the midst of a normalized world, standardized down to the last detail, and the stupidity and ingratitude of man: "I, for example, wouldn't be at all surprised if, in the midst of all this reasonableness that is to come, suddenly and quite unaccountably some gentleman with an ignoble, or rather a reactionary and mocking physiognomy were to appear and, arms akimbo, say to us all: 'Now, gentlemen, what about giving all this reasonableness a good kick with the sole purpose of sending all these logarithms to hell so we can live for a while in accordance with our own stupid will!'"[25]—That the author describes this behavior in advance as stupidity and ingratitude does not matter, since he understands himself as this "gentleman" from whom he differs only in the one respect that he considers himself too weak to tempt his equals, who are no less repugnant to him than the positivists of the opposite party, to this *acte gratuit*. The lack of this degree of philanthropy or misanthropy which is no longer confused by itself, should not, however, prevent his brothers in spirit precisely from sticking out their tongues, to put it mildly, at the Crystal Palace through political or artistic terror. Dostoevsky's *Demons* testify to the former, modern shock aesthetics from Charles Baudelaire's *Fleurs du Mal* up to the actions of the French Surrealists to the latter. What both have in common, however, is that they oppose a well-intentioned reasonableness with the malice of one's own will and thus drive a wedge into the idealistic harmony of intelligence and will that ultimately blows it apart.

24 Cf. Morozov, Evgeny: To Save Everything, Click here, New York 2013, Chap. 1.
25 Dostoevsky: Notes from the Underground, p. 24.

For, as the author suggests, it is by no means a lack but a surfeit of insight, in the impossible choice between a knowing will and a willing knowledge, which make us consciously choose the impossible itself—precisely to demonstrate the impossibility of choice. Thus, the choice as such is subverted and only the decision as such is willed; the will wants only itself and becomes decisionism.

What is to be thought of this, the author of these notes from the underground already expresses with the first sentence: "I am a sick man…a spiteful man".[26] And what is to be understood by this is revealed by a deliberately placed phrase, an inconspicuous invocation, which always appears exactly in those passages concerned with the absurdity and abysmalness of the will itself in opposition to reason: another demon is meant, the adversary par excellence, the "Devil". After mentioning the "gentleman" who casts a different shadow in this light, the author goes on to discuss this "silliest reason"[27] of the human creature:

"One's own free and unfettered desire, one's own and wildest whim, one's own fantasy, worked up sometimes to the point of madness—this is the very thing omitted, the most advantageous advantage which doesn't fit any classification, and against which all systems and theories are continually smashed to smithereens. Where do they get it from, all these wise men, that human beings need some sort of normal, some sort of benign desire? Why should they necessarily imagine that man necessarily needs some sort of reasonably advantageous desire? All that man needs is desire that is independent, whatever the cost of this independence and wherever it may lead. Well, and desire—the devil only knows what that is…"[28]

The chapter breaks off. But the attentive reader has understood at this point, just by this act of interruption, by the blowing up of the logic of the sentence, that only the devil knows what he wants, what we want, what wanting is supposed to want in the first place—even if the following chapter starts again with an interruption, the fictitious objection of the reader: "Ha, Ha, Ha! But, you know, there is if you like really no such thing as desire […]. Science has by now succeeded in analysing human beings into their constituent parts to such an extent that we now know that desire and so-called free will are nothing but…"[29]—At the latest with this diabolic joke, however, it becomes

---

26 Ibid., p. 7.
27 Ibid., p. 24.
28 Ibid., p. 25.
29 Ibid.

clear that the very belief in the devil itself is taken by the devil and that he is therefore still at work where we deny it. But what shall we do now with this willful confusion? The author himself starts again: "That's how I myself meant to begin. I admit that it frightened me, even. I was just about to shout out that desire depends on the devil knows what, and that we have to thank god for it under certain circumstances. Then I suddenly remembered about science and… shut up."[30]

This silence, however, is eloquent, insofar as it is about the beginning of the human will: what the author suffers from, what his malice is ignited by ("I am a sick man…a spiteful man."), is, as is hardly surprising for Dostoevsky, the biblical Fall. The fact that we have to "thank God for it under certain circumstances" gives the matter another interesting twist: what exactly should we have to thank God for? For the fact that through God we could come into temptation at all, into the diabolical temptation to possess a wicked, unfavorable will of our own after having eaten from the tree of knowledge?—That seems all too circumstantial, I suppose. Or rather for the fact that he had created us in the beginning as paradisiacal beings, which were expelled for some reasons, with the result that we are still longing for our lost paradise and now try to restore it by recreating it on earth… "Then I suddenly remembered about science and… shut up."

Would the Crystal Palace therefore be basically willed by God? Or is it nevertheless a testimony of a Baal cult, a Babylonian building and thus ultimately of the devil? Do we have to see in it the last consequence of the fall of man, as it were the original sin of human freedom? Or quite the opposite, the scientific-technical attempt to undo our fall and with it the 'stupid ingratitude' of freedom? How does the doubtful paradise of the Crystal Palace relate to its underworld impressively described by Dostoevsky? Do they really represent diametrical or merely dialectical opposites? Last but not least: Is it possible at all to persist in one's own viewpoint after the fall and resurrection, so to speak?

---

30 Ibid. The original translation by Kyril Zinovieff and Jenny Hughes wants to have it: "I was just about to shout out that desire depends on who knows what, and that this is probably just as well." But as it looks like, and as the German standard translation suggests ("Ich wollte gerade ausrufen, daß das Wollen weiß der Teufel wovon abhängt und daß wir dafür unter Umständen Gott danken müssen […].'"), Dostoevsky is playing with words here in the sense that it is good as it is. Remember Gen. 1, 10ff.: "and God saw that it was good."

V. Nihilist Confession

To venture deeper into this religious confusion would lead us too far. Instead, let us take another look at the Crystal Palace itself by remembering a phrase that Dostoevsky had already used in his *Winter Notes* and that comes to the fore again in the Notes from the Underground, the "anthill":[31] "These honourable ants started off with an anthill and will probably end up with an anthill, which is a great tribute to their constancy and positive attitude. But man is a creature both frivolous and myopic and, perhaps like a chess player, he likes only the actual process of achieving and not the goal itself. But who knows (there's no guarantee), it may be that the entire earthly goal which humanity is striving towards consists solely in maintaining without a break the process of achievement—in other words, in life itself and not, properly speaking, in the goal which, of course, must be nothing but twice two is four, that is, a formula; and twice two is four is no longer life, gentlemen, but the beginning of death."[32]

While the "anthill" in the *Winter Notes* still represented the mocked goal of human striving to escape the threatening violence of social cannibalism, here, on the other hand, it is encountered precisely in its unattainability for humankind, who utterly lacks the instinctive constancy and the unclouded sense of reality of an ant. If human striving were nevertheless to come to its end, for instance in the Crystal Palace as global structure, it would mean death rather than life—at least for our author. "At least, man has always somehow been afraid of this twice two is four, and I'm afraid of it now. But man does nothing but try to find this twice two is four. He crosses oceans, sacrifices his life in that search; but to find it, to really track it down, he is, honest to God, somehow afraid. For he feels that as soon as he does find it, he will have nothing left to search for."[33]

Thus we seem to have reached a dead spot—and not only regarding the underground or the Crystal Palace: Is the freedom of striving driven only by the fear of reaching some God-willed or God-damned goal; by the fear of seeing it finally fulfilled instead of eternally unfulfilled; therefore by the fear of finitude inherent in all life and striving? But what then is this striving good for, what does its fear testify to, if not to that rebellion which represents the

---

31 See the quote above.
32 Ibid., p. 31.
33 Ibid.

actual hubris against the course of things—or, to speak with Dostoevsky: to the deepest and hopeless sinfulness of wanting to uphold one's own life against its divine destiny? "How can you after all resist the temptation to congratulate him on the fact that all this has not yet come about and that desire still depends on the devil knows what..."[34]—But what can this will then want in the end, except itself, except a devilish self-will that would rather have a cushy number than do things by the book (especially the Book)?

"Now I ask you: what can you expect of a man who is a creature with such strange qualities? Cover him with all the good things of the world, [...]; give him such material riches that there'll be nothing left for him to do but sleep, eat cakes and busy himself with making sure that world history goes on for ever—and then, even then, out of sheer ingratitude and a desire to slander you, he will commit some nastiness. He'll put even the little cakes at risk and will deliberately express a desire for the most pernicious nonsense, for the most counter-productive absurdity, for the sole purpose of adulterating all this positive reasonableness with his own pernicious, fantastic element. In fact, it is precisely his fantastic dreams, his exceedingly vulgar stupidity, that he wants to preserve, just in order to confirm for himself (as if it mattered) that humans are still humans and not piano keys [...]. And that's not all: if he ever really turned out to be a piano key, and even if you could prove it to him mathematically and by natural science, even then he won't become reasonable, but on the contrary will deliberately do something purely out of sheer ingratitude, really just to have his own way. And should he turn out not to have sufficient means to do it, he will invent destruction and chaos, devise various torments and end up getting his own way."[35]

What speaks from this tirade is the unconditional will to will, the phantasm of freedom against every higher necessity and reason. The one who speaks is the underworldling, the undergrounder, the adversary, the grumbler before the lord. The lord, however, is easily confused with the readers, before whom this hellish theater takes place as both a fictional chaos of destruction and torment, and real self-destruction and self-torment. In other words: We attend the mental contrition of a profane sinner who is no longer able to believe in God, the devil or himself and for this very reason, out of the most wanton despair, does it nevertheless, by wringing this belief from himself out of pure malice against goodness and his own last vestige of reason. In

---

34 Ibid., p. 29.
35 Ibid., p. 28f.

a word: We encounter a nihilist—who holds on to the nullity of his own will in order to be able to want anything at all, except the sober nothingness of not wanting anything anymore. He confesses and we are supposed to absolve him—or are we supposed to absolve him at all? Who could still do it?... How much can you need a God?

VI. The Dialectics of Dis-Obedience

At this point, we leave our "caveman"[36] and instead ask ourselves: What does this tell us?—With regard to our question about the dialectics of dis-obedience, the relation of Crystal palace and its underground, and finally the phenomenon of the "Querdenker", well, quite enough.

With this fictional character Dostoevsky has created a special type of human being which is only partially congruent with his own convictions as he has made clear from the beginning: The Crystal Palace and its underground are both expressions of the same self-will, which, on the one hand, no longer knows what it wants, except that it wants (Underground) and which, on the other hand, only wants what it can no longer want in the end, but must want (Crystal Palace). In both cases, however, it is a will to will that, on the one hand, consumes itself in its own negativity without coming to an end and, on the other hand, cancels itself out by its own positivity because it has already come to an end.

In contrast, it is now easy to understand why both ultimately remain phantasms, as the opening quotation above has already suggested: the one is a phantasm of strict necessity and the other of an arbitrary freedom. From this perspective, the Crystal Palace and its underground do not only behave like action and reaction, but as a regular interaction, in which on the first level, that of the Crystal Palace, reason seems to have achieved full control over the whims of fantasy; whereas on the second level, the critique and negation of the first, fantasy conducts itself in an unruly manner that is averse to any reason. The more arbitrary the fantasy, however, the more thoroughgoing and comprehensive its control by reason, so that the whole relationship threatens to escalate further and further.

The phantasmatic nature of this relationship only becomes clear when it is compared in a more circumspect way with the reality of the crystal palace

---

36 Ibid., p. 29.

and its underground. For neither a total law of reason can be thought of, as it is imagined by our author in his delusion of a demonic determination à la Laplace, nor would it be possible to assert one's freedom in any sense—instead of in mere nonsense—by the cultivation of mere caprices, by an absolute, diabolical or divine arbitrariness or even by a nihilistic chaos. Only if there is a certain belief in the phantasm of total reason, in the natural lawfulness of scientifically founded social technologies, both by its advocates and its critics, only there the latter fall into a crypto-religious resentment of rule-obeying and become martyrs of arbitrariness, apostles of the arbitrary.

Against both exaggerations, however, it is worth noting that the actual domain of human action always shows both moments at the same time: It is characterized by an ambivalence of reason and fantasy, law and arbitrariness, in the sense that it is structured by path dependencies of contingent courses. It is true that reality could always be a different one, but only in looking back and forth to future and past possibilities. This possibility space can indeed widen or narrow depending on the situation (and this is exactly what design as a "transcendental practice"[37] works on); however, to want to transform it into the extremes of a Crystal Palace or a cave-like underground dwelling would probably amount to either letting it implode or explode, in any case to de-realizing it rather than realizing it.

Since there is neither a formula which is able to dissolve the whole world into an equation according to the pattern "two times two equals four" (for logical-mathematical reasons alone), nor a confession (even in the sense of a *credo quia absurdum*) that already suffices to testify freedom, the unflinching belief in the world as a Crystal Palace seems to be more an expression of an obsessive-compulsive disorder as the Underground is an expression of a paranoia, than an actual solution or redemption. Ultimately, it is and remains a belief, which at first would not be a problem, but can become a pathological one if this belief, in appealing to a higher lawfulness of reason or to the divine power of grace, considers itself instead to be infallible knowledge. In the one case, one confuses one's own tics with the ticking of the world, and in the other, one projects the self-centeredness of one's own phantasmagoria of violence and arbitrariness, control and oppression onto a hostile outside world that seems to persecute one all the more angrily for the less one is willing to follow its rules.

---

37 Cf. Arnold, Florian: Logik des Entwerfens, p. 341ff.

But how can one escape these pitfalls of a will mercilessly pursuing itself instead of becoming an automaton or anarchist? If we hold on to a concept of contingency qua forced freedom of decision-making, then finally also the nihilistic social technology of the Crystal Palace as much as the religion of freedom from the underground can teach us something about dealing with contingency: What the dogma has always been for the priests, the algorithm is for the social engineers of today. Both, unless they are confused with the necessity of mathematical laws or the freedom of divine chaos, guide a contingency-conscious practice and theory. They are characterized by the fact that, once they are set, they have validity within the framework thereby set and can claim a kind of inner consistency for themselves; beyond that, however, they remain adaptable, even revocable.

With regard to our introductory question, how one should serve freedom, the examination of Dostoevsky's foresighted double scenario Crystal Palace/Underground gives us a deeper insight into the dialectics of dis-obedience taking place under our own eyes. Admittedly, the circumstances are different, some would say tightened, others loosened: the disciplinary society in the sense of Michel Foucault has long since become a digital control society in the sense of Gilles Deleuze. Normally we live under conditions of a 'voluntary self-control'. We feel an inner force to freely determine ourselves and, conversely, feel free from being forced by others—at least in principle.

However, in the subsoil of this outdated glass structure, as it were, the state of exception already lays in wait for its rule. If we look at the current conditions, we find ourselves in a paradoxical situation, quasi in a regulated exception, in a quarantine, in which all inhabitants of the Crystal Palace are called upon to crawl into the cellar vault of this gigantic community building as if into their own crawl space. That thereby some "Querdenker" get oblique, stupid, and ungrateful thoughts lies, as we have seen, in the nature of things and stems from the fact that one prefers to persecute one's own paranoia in projections upon the others. To thereby confuse one's own readiness for violence with that of the state is just the normal result of a self-fulfilling prophecy. Whoever thinks of himself as a god, together with the associated privileges of freedom, knowledge and omnipotence, can of course only think of the others as poor devils—or as ones even richer than oneself... In contrast, serving freedom today means trusting the algorithms and dogmas of our society to a certain extent, in order not to become deranged or, in the worst case, fatally ill as a result of one's own willfulness.

VII. An Uplifting Speech at the End

If we return from here to the *Winter Notes*, Dostoevsky makes his own proposal how to escape the fatal extremes of this dialectics of dis-obedience. At first glance, it should not be surprising that his answer turns out to be all too missionary in terms of his Slavophile agenda, and yet there are aspects pointing towards the future even after the end of the Soviet Union of the 20th century and today's Russia. Dostoevsky evokes the ideals of the 18th-century French Revolution in order to accentuate the ideal of fraternity in addition to the ones of freedom and equality. In the *Notes from the Underground*, we witnessed what happens when one isolates the three values and, moreover, invokes one only to the harm of the others: a senseless insistence on the individual freedom of the will ultimately runs the risk of ending up in the underworld; but also the one-sided emphasis on the equality of all particular interests, which would have to place themselves unconditionally at the service of the construction of a collective crystal palace, does injustice not only to the individual, but in the end also to society. Dostoevsky, on the other hand, demands that these fatally isolated ideals of a free or equal will be formed into a whole by a supposedly instinctive brotherhood of the Russian people, a fraternity that does not even shy away from a voluntary self-sacrifice:

> "[N]ot only should one not lose one's individuality, but one should in fact, become an individual to a degree far higher than has occurred in the West. You must understand me: a voluntary, absolutely conscious and completely unforced sacrifice of oneself for the sake of all is, I consider, a sign of the highest development of individual personality, its highest power, highest self-possession and highest freedom of individual will. Voluntarily to lay down one's life for all, be crucified or burnt at the stake for the sake of all, is possible only at the point of the highest development of individual personality."[38]

And in the same context we find the following:

> "But how can there possibly be any brotherhood if it is preceded by a distribution of shares and by determining how much each person has earned and what each must do?"[39]

---

38   Dostojevsky: Winter Notes, p. 68.
39   Ibid., p. 71.

In the eyes of Dostoevsky, of course, there is no possibility that would lead to true brotherhood in the manner of a material socialism, except via a Russian socialism of souls, so to speak. Not already the will, but first of all the willful self-sacrifice of the will, not its rationalization and technical regimentation, but its martyrdom proves to be the true basis of community building—if one follows Dostoevsky transrational and transnational agenda.

As we have pointed out, Dostoevsky's answer has an unmistakably Christian touch, in that the fall of man is overcome only with the birth, death and resurrection of Christ in eternity and consequently at least in principle by the congregational life here on earth. Only in the sign of this brotherhood will freedom and equality unite to form the harmony of (a) family. But again, this might be slightly too much to ask: after all, every family celebration, above all Christmas, can become the hour of birth of the most renegade hate....

What can be learned from this, nevertheless, results from "a voluntary, absolutely conscious and completely unforced sacrifice of oneself for the sake of all", from the "highest self-possession" and "highest freedom of individual will". Whether it is important here to "become an individual" may be debatable; perhaps it simply expresses a becoming that opens up in the space of possibilities—why not also one to renounce strict individuality. What remains remarkable about these considerations is that they describe a self-regulating process of asceticism, at the end of which stands the willful sacrifice of that will to the will, which at the end can want nothing except itself, and that means having arrived at the bottom of itself: precisely a meager nothingness, tired of itself.

Perhaps the actual idea of asceticism consists in 'letting things be'—in an indissoluble double sense. To let things be: one's own will as well as that of the others, one's own reason as well as that of the others; the crystal palace as well as its underground. Maybe even to let it be well.—But thank God only the devil knows how...

Dostoevsky's *Notes from the Underground* from 1864 is not only one of the most famous and influential novels of Russian literature in Europe but is itself essentially shaped by experiences that Dostoevsky wrote down after his first trip to Western Europe in 1862. The first part in particular takes up a phenomenon that was of decisive importance for the history of design: Joseph Paxton's glass-and-iron construction, which was erected on the occasion of the first London World's Fair in 1851: the so-called Crystal Palace as an architectural symbol for an enlightened new type of man, dedicated to materialism and science. What Dostoevsky takes offense at here can most easily be summed up in the formula of optimistic regulatory thinking, which from then on was to be exemplary for the fate of modern governmentality. What he opposes to this is a pessimistic cultural critique, which for its part is interspersed with clear ambivalences, but which, not least because of this, raises the critique of progress to a new level of debate: Against the "two times two equals four" of a smooth rationalism, a voluntaristic irrationalism is brought into position, which exposes the abysses of the *condition moderne* and turns the epochal picture into a real panorama.

The question of algorithmization in the sense of a social technology, as it becomes thematic again today, is thus not only revealed in its historical path dependency, but also reveals itself at the same time as bound in an inescapable dialectic of obedience and disobedience: How far can the rationalization of society be advanced before, with Dostoyevsky, the shift towards a conscious irrationalism of the mere act of will, out of protest, of the fanatical anti-reflex, finally of the radical negation of every form of social regulation threatens? The question at the bottom of this modern problem is: Is there a resentment of following rules? Furthermore, what does freedom mean as autonomy in this context? Especially today, in the midst of our "algorithmic culture", this underlying dialectic of (dis)obedience seems more effective than ever.

Literature

Arnold, Florian: Logik des Entwerfens. Eine designphilosophische Grundlegung, Paderborn 2018.
Benjamin, Walter: Gesammelte Schriften, ed. by Rolf Tiedemann and Hermann Schweppenhäuser, Frankfurt a. M. 1977.
Benjamin, Walter: Das Passagen-Werk, Frankfurt a. M. 1983.
Dostoevsky, Fyodor M.: Pushkin Speech, June 8, 1880 at the Meeting of the Society of Lovers of Russian Literature, https://pages.uoregon.edu/kimball/DstF.Puw.lct.htm#DstF.Puw.lct. (February 5, 2021)
Dostoevskj, Fyodor M.: Buried Alive or Ten Years of Penal Servitude in Siberia, London 1881.
Dostoevsky, Fyodor M.: Winter Notes on Summer Impressions, Richmond 2008.
Dostoevsky, Fyodor M.: Notes from the Underground, Richmond 2011.

Lange, Wolfgang: "Kristallpalast oder Kellerloch? Zur Modernität Dostojewskijs," in: Merkur 40 (1/1986), p. 14–29.
Martin, Theodore: The Life of His Royal Highness the Prince Consort, Volume 2, New York 1877.
Morozov, Evgeny: To Save Everything, Click here, New York 2013.
Sloterdijk, Peter: Im Weltinnenraum des Kapitals. Für eine philosophische Theorie der Globalisierung, Frankfurt a. M. 2005.

Johanna Mellentin /
Francesca Schmidt

Surveillance, Artificial Intelligence and Power

Artificial intelligence (AI) creates new possibilities for the algorithmic use of data and its automated analysis; thus, the public discourse on AI automatically leads to a discourse on algorithms. Increased and accelerated linking of data sets offer new surveillance images—of individuals, (marginalized) populations, and even entire societies. These new quantitative and qualitative changes in technical surveillance systems not only bring old, never sufficiently resolved decisions to the surface, but also give rise to entirely new and highly urgent questions—of a legal, social, and ethical nature. They concern the private sphere (mutual surveillance) and the relationship between the state and its citizens.

Also, these questions bring with them a severity by breaching issues such as the many encroachments on (fundamental) rights, such as informational self-determination, and human dignity. As we are currently experiencing during the Corona pandemic, times of crisis reinforce this spiral due to newly grown insecurities and fears; sometimes, used deliberately as a pretext. This shows itself in the often-misused data protection as an excuse for ineffective or faulty Corona protection measures in the past few months.

The (populist) call for security, order, and control is continuously getting louder. All these intensified calls, which make use of a paralyzing fear spiral, ultimately make the world seem more insecure by the day. Consequently, the increasing endowment of state authorities with legal and technical competencies for surveillance is justified and thus increases the acceptance of senseless and ineffective measures of surveillance, which mostly miss or even counteract an actual increase in security.[1]

At the same time, our fundamental democratic freedoms and values are facing increasing pressure. Above all, the private sphere, protected by fundamental rights, is constantly experiencing further restrictions—at times rapidly and with enforced media coverage, at times successively and quietly.

The networking of different technologies and data sets also reinforces that new technologies are increasingly being used categorically rather than just purposefully. Data taps and stockpiles are growing immeasurably; using artificial intelligence, or algorithms, these can be sifted through, clustered,

---

[1] Neumann, Linus: Untersuchung: Vorratsdatenspeicherung ist ineffektiv. In: netzpolitik, January 27, 2011, https://netzpolitik.org/2011/untersuchung-vorratsdatenspeicherung-ist-ineffektiv/ (May 24, 2021).; henning: Trügerische Sicherheit: Der elektronische Personalausweis. In: Chaos Computer Club, September 15, 2013, https://www.ccc.de/de/updates/2013/epa-mit-virenschutzprogramm (May 24, 2021).

merged, and entire societal graphs can be created.² Today, entire contexts are often surveilled rather than targeted individuals. In the state-citizen relationship, this development particularly effects state measures. For example, countless video cameras are demanded in public places in Berlin to prevent crimes.³

When these technologies are connected with artificial intelligence, a panopticon emerges wherein its dimensions go far beyond those imagined by Foucault.⁴ One of the fundamental ideas of the panopticon is centrality. The panoptic prison is a circular building with a surveillance tower in its center, separating guards and prisoners into those who see and those who are to be seen. The guards can observe all prisoners from the surveillance tower without them seeing the guards. Because the prisoner cannot be sure who is watching him or her from the top of the tower, he or she lives in the idea that he or she is always being watched. Surveillance thus takes place permanently, regardless of whether the guards are present or not. Especially in the course of digitalization, this model has been criticized, as it does not allow to respond to the wealth of data and technological interconnections. Kevin Haggerty and Richard Ericson, both Canadian sociologists, consider the principle of assemblage to be more appropriate for digital surveillance.⁵ They understand assemblages, following Gilles Deleuze and Felix Guattari, as a multiplicity of heterogeneous objects whose connection arises solely from their functionality. Those assemblages make it possible to think surveillance in differently interlinked spheres (social, financial, labor, health, gender/body), even though they initially appear unconnected.

In the 21st century, unprovoked mass surveillance is becoming more of a reality than ever before due to the use and development algorithms. A reality that is becoming more and more intense, and more and more expansive every day. More noticeable to some, and less noticeable to others. Visible? To

---

2 See also boyd, danah; Crawford, Kate: CRITICAL QUESTIONS FOR BIG DATA: Provocations for a cultural, technological, and scholarly phenomenon, Information, Communication & Society, xv/5 2012, pp. 662–679.

3 Biselli, Anna: Berlin: Keine rationalen Argumente für Videoüberwachung an S-Bahnhof. In: netzpolitik, March 1, 2019, https://netzpolitik.org/2019/berlin-keine-rationalen-argumente-fuer-videoueberwachung-an-s-bahnhof/ (May 24, 2021).

4 Foucault, Michel: Überwachen und Strafen: Die Geburt des Gefängnisses, Frankfurt am Main 1977.

5 Haggerty, Kevin D. and Ericson, Richard V.: The surveillant assemblage, The British Journal of Sociology, li/4 2000, pp. 605–622.

whom? To what extent, exactly? At what point in time? What information is stored, for how long, and for what purpose? This often remains non-transparent and invisible.

Necessary Change of Perspective

Although we are all affected by surveillance, it has different consequences for those who deviate from the culturally and historically implanted masculine white norm in its different forms. To change this, we need to address many aspects, but it takes two things above all: awareness/knowledge (of the difference in consequences) and will (to dissolve existing power structures). This includes the feminist, especially intersectional, view of the complexity of surveillance, even beyond the question of privacy.

Looking back, we can see that the surveillance of all of those who do not appeal to the patriarchally shaped male heteronormative norm, has a long tradition. Simone Browne, Professor of African and African Diaspora Studies at the University of Austin, Texas, emphasized that surveillance and its technologies are racialized and serve to restore the white norm and re-enforce who belongs and who does not. Many practices of surveillance used in the transatlantic slave trade, both discursive and real, continue to operate today.[6] This is the case, for example, with practices of bodily measurement used primarily to determine the age of young refugees. The biometric collection of fingerprints also follows this pattern.

From that very patriarchal surveillance, historically, women's bodies have also been shaped—to this day, dramatic forms of surveillance of the female or trans* body exist, which can take on different dimensions depending on the cultural and political context.

It becomes clear: Surveillance does not result in the same regulatory (fundamental rights) interventions for all people, and there are complex and severe differences, especially in the area of justification and, in particular, proportionality. Surveillance thus does not affect everyone equally. Within the white patriarchal norm, the freedom of some means the surveillance of others, i.e., of all those who are denied belonging or who choose not to be part of this norm.

---

6   Browne, Simone: Dark matters: on the surveillance of blackness, Durham 2015.

Nevertheless, We are All Surveilled...

The prominent sentence "I have nothing to hide"—expressing not having a problem with mass or unprovoked surveillance—falls short, as shown by the explanations above.

On the one hand, it reflects the opposite of self-determined, autonomous decision making; on the other hand, it is dangerous not to be aware of prospective risks and, above all, refusing to be knowledgeable about them. The awareness of what should be "hidden" is missing at this very point. What will be done with and extracted from the surveillance data and its results? Which data will be used for or against us in the future? We do not know at the time of this statement. Nor do we know how they will be linked and re-evaluated.

Nevertheless, quite fundamentally, as a society, we should fight back against a form of surveillance that is increasingly automated by algorithms. After all, maintaining privacy does not necessarily mean keeping secrets. Instead, such a sentence, which can only be in relation to a counterpart, suggests that surveillance seems to be well-founded in the case of this other. The others (beyond the norm), therefore, have something to hide.

Privacy: For Whom?

Surveillance is very often discussed in terms of privacy. However, in a first evaluation, we should distinguish here who invades privacy: the state, private companies, or other people (often again with the help of private companies, like Facebook & Co).

When we talk about state intrusions into privacy, we see that the intensity of these intrusions increases with the degree of dependence on the state. For example, people who receive state social benefits, people with disabilities, refugees, or asylum seekers have to reckon with much more numerous and more profound interventions than people who do not belong to any of these or other marginalized, stigmatized groups. Transparency becomes an essential requirement for social government services. Practices such as home visits, monitoring of activities on social networks[7], and disclosure of bank account

---

[7] Wermter, Benedict: Schnüffeln auf Facebook. In: Correctiv. Recherche für die Gesellschaft, June 22, 2015, https://correctiv.org/aktuelles/auskunftsrechte/2015/06/22/schnueffeln-auf-facebook/ (July 26, 2019).

transactions are used to surveil and spy on people who belong to low-income or less prosperous groups, ostensibly in the public interest.

People, however, exposed to the right education, technical knowledge, time, and money, can protect their data from the state or private companies to a greater extent, and, if such a possibility arises, can make their data available in a self-determined manner, protecting their privacy to a greater extent. A de facto privilege, as legally, it is equally available to all.

When we discuss surveillance under the dictum of privacy, it becomes clear that we have to think about societal structures of power and domination because the freedom that a few receive through the protection of privacy is at the same time the lack of freedom for others. Parallel to this, there are many forms of surveillance from which a few gain additional value, for example, financially or in the form of knowledge and superiority, whereas others face disadvantages without any additional value. In this respect, discussions around privacy versus security are once again deceptive because they distract from the more essential questions of privacy versus control and the central power structures that accompany and permeate these questions.

Big Data, Algorithms, and AI for Social Compartmentalization

The enormous amount of data that we as a society accumulate and store daily is the basis for increased surveillance, including state surveillance. At the very least, these data collections, which are also constantly improving in "quality," make it possible to establish (new) correlations and relationships of facts. In some countries this is already taking effect by being used for predictive policing.

The data collected at different points in time and from different locations, as well as by different systems are brought into new correlations by automated processes. To put it simply; these are algorithms that calculate probabilities based on an analysis of case data and make statements about who, when and where a possible crime might be committed. This technology is used to control the deployment of police forces, now also by some police authorities in German states. However, in the USA, it is already part of everyday life that potential offenders receive a visit from the police, as a result of an indication and warning for possible future criminal offenses.[8] A procedure that neither fits into our legal system nor should fit into our social value system and yet is increasingly applied.

Apart from the indiscriminate blanket suspicion and its severe (e.g., psychological, social, or financial) consequences, which emanate from such messages (and possibly making them public)[9] we should ask ourselves: What happens if the people concerned are only turned into potential offenders by new data correlations produced by algorithms? They are assigned to a risk cluster based on personal habits, past acquaintances, relatives, or their birthplace. From the outset, judgments are made that often reinforce existing discrimination. It is difficult for those affected to defend themselves against this bias. This is because they have to defend themselves against a suspicion that has only arisen based on a data correlation or what Algorithms has made of it.[10] The situation is further complicated because technology is often ascribed to objectivity and neutrality and is frequently said to be free of errors. Nevertheless, feminist research established years ago that technology is not neutral.[11] With all their discriminatory structures, ideas of society flow into and materialize in the developments of new technologies. Consequently, we must ensure that technologies, especially automatic decision-making systems, are developed according to transparent criteria and remain verifiable. As for now, it is the case that the police rarely know how the probabilities of possible future crimes are calculated. However, how are we supposed to trust these systems if we do not even know how they work?[12] Especially when they are accompanied by opacity and lack of verifiability? How does a person

---

[8] Gorner, Jeremy: Chicago Police Use Heat List as Strategy to Prevent Violence. In: Chicago Tribune, 2013, http://articles.chicagotribune.com/2013-08-21/news/ct-met-heat-list-20130821_1_chicago-police-commander-andrew-papachristos-heat-list (November 1, 2021); Merz, Christina: Predictive Policing—Polizeiliche Strafverfolgung in Zeiten von Big Data, Karlsruher Institut für Technologie (KIT), 2016, https://publikationen.bibliothek.kit.edu/1000054372 (November 1, 2021).

[9] Steinschaden, Jakob: Der "Chilling Effect": Massenüberwachung zeigt soziale Folgen—Netzpiloten.de. In: Netzpiloten Magazin, April 7, 2014, https://www.netzpiloten.de/der-chilling-effect-massenueberwachung-zeigt-soziale-folgen/ (May 24, 2021).

[10] Gless, Sabine: Predictive policing und operative Verbrechensbekämpfung. In: Herzog, Felix and Schlothauer, Reinhold and Wohlers, Wolfgang (eds), Rechtsstaatlicher Strafprozess und Bürgerrechte, Gedächtnisschrift für Edda Weßlau, Berlin 2016.

[11] See, for example Wajcman, Judy: TechnoFeminism, Cambridge UK 2004.

[12] Fry, Hannah: Hello World: How to be Human in the Age of the Machine, London New York Toronto Sidney Auckland 2018.

defend himself/herself against the accusation of a crime if there is no open and comprehensible decision-making process, and how can one even argue against a "future" crime that has not been completed, let alone prepared or planned? Isn't the surveillance, evaluation or assessment already criminal itself? Is the algorithmically calculated probability of crime already an accusatory situation made in the Blackbox? For good reason and with German history in sight the German constitutional state, despite all of its transparency, once decided against a too broad advance of criminal liability and thus against the Gesinnungsstrafrecht[13]. However, this decision seems to be continuously mellowed throughout the discourse and within law making. This can be seen in implementations such as the conceptualization of a "dangerous person" into criminal law—with the aid of verbal turns of phrase embedded in novel discourses on criminal law by individual instances of power[14]. These being more in favor of surveillance itself than of the (de facto hardly existing) alleged successes and advantages.

Thus, we are divided into potential perpetrators and victims; other clusters are also formed with the help of the data. This, in turn, determines our creditworthiness, the number of insurance premiums, job offers, or, in case of doubt, the cost of our health insurance (which is fortunately not yet the case in Germany). The specialist literature uses the term social sorting[15] for this clustering, i.e., the sorting into certain social classes and thus their location in the prevailing power structure.

This power structure (e.g., Europe) also becomes evident, by the process of it sealing itself off from the outside world with the help of artificial intelligence. Border controls are being automated and the electronic passport is supposed to save time but poses a challenge to people or places who cannot provide this document, or in case of any doubt can never receive it in the first place, elevating those who do have it to even more transparency. Furthermore, what happens to the existing state surveillance systems and hoarded

---

13   A term that basically means a kind of criminal law oriented primordially to punish attitudes or belief systems of offenders instead of the act itself, respectively, the traditional elements of mens rea.

14   See Böhm, María Laura: Der Gefährder und das Gefährdungsrecht: eine rechtssoziologische Analyse am Beispiel der Urteile des Bundesverfassungsgerichts über die nachträgliche Sicherungsverwahrung und die akustische Wohnraumüberwachung, Göttingen 2011.

15   Lyon, David: Surveillance as Social Sorting: Privacy, Risk and Automated Discrimination, London 2003.

data volumes beyond these factors if the current political system ever changes? A look at countries with other government structures, such as China, India, or Russia, gives insight on this.

The deadly point of compartmentalization is geofencing, when artificial intelligence is used to arm "digital fences". Video surveillance, motion sensors, and thermal imaging are used to track down border crossers daily, as practiced along the Turkish-Syrian border for example. With the help of integrated automated self-firing systems, such surveillance zones can kill people without manual labour. The debate over armed drone operations or computer game deliriums seems to have been resolved. The use of technology for surveillance is being expanded to the point where, ultimately, even the "dirty work" almost no longer requires direct human interaction. The accompanying questions of responsibility are becoming less and less tangible, moving away from the counterpart as a legal subject and thus also giving new meaning to the decisions to be made about social guidelines and responsibilities. Whereas usually, the core of surveillance is often secrecy, here surveillance and consequences seem shrill, neon flashing, and impossible to miss, almost like a statement. The use of surveillance is as complex and diverse as the expression of power behind it. The result of surveillance, in this case, is unmistakably, an expression of power over freedom of movement and even human life. Yet people choose to look the other way. In fact, technology is used precisely for this purpose: to be able to observe others more efficiently. In those cases unsolved ethical questions, or unfound answers, related to society as a whole, are easier to ignore than to solve. As a result many answers were often decided due to the implementation of a few and without the acquiescence of many.

Even if we, as a Western European society, oppose the use of lethal AI, the moral boundaries seem permeable: A conflation of migration policy, economic policy, and the arms industry lead to the conclusion that "digital fences" are provided by Germany and Europe as well, such as the one in Morocco. The fence delivered to Saudi Arabia in 2009, that was co-financed by EADS (now Airbus), was also, among others, enabled by the German Gesellschaft für Internationale Zusammenarbeit.[16]

---

[16] Grieger, Fabian and Schlindwein, Simone: Migrationspolitik und Rüstungsindustrie: Das Geschäft mit Hightech-Grenzen. In: taz.de, die tageszeitung 2016.

Critical Review Versus Perpetuation of Existing Discrimination?

That algorithms perpetuate discrimination because they produce discriminatory results in many cases is well known and widely documented.[17] Automated facial recognition designed not only to match people to "official" identities but in some cases even to look for possible affects and emotions such as anger, aggression, and propensity for violence, in order to preempt possible terrorist attacks, is considered highly error-prone. Concerning affective computing[18], we know from previous research that on the one hand emotions and affects are coded differently in various cultures. On the other hand, however, emotions continue to be stereotyped and gendered in a binary understanding: Herein anger, for example, is often classified as something masculine and hysteria as rather feminine trait.

How does this impact facial recognition? Often, programs fail to identify faces correctly, or even fail in recognizing them as human[19], especially concerning Black people. Joy Buolamwini of the MIT Media Lab found that facial recognition only works well for white men. Black women and Black men often fail to be recognized entirely. In the case of Black women, nearly one-third of all matches are simply wrong[20]. In 2018 The American Civil Liberties Union (ACLU), found that Amazon's facial recognition system incorrectly matched 28 members of the US Congress to mugshots. These false matches disproportionately involved people of color. These included six members of the Congressional Black Caucus, an association of African-American members of Congress. The recently deceased Congressman and icon of the Black

---

17 Benjamin, Ruha: Race after technology: abolitionist tools for the new Jim code, Medford, MA 2019; Buolamwini, Joy and Gebru, Timnit: Gender Shades: Intersectional Accuracy Disparities in Commercial Gender Classification, Proceedings of Machine Learning Research. In: Proceedings of Machine Learning Research, 2018, lxxxi 2018, pp. 77–91; Eubanks, Virginia: Automating inequality: how high-tech tools profile, police, and punish the poor, New York, NY 2017; Noble, Safiya Umoja: Algorithms of Oppression: How Search Engines Reinforce Racism, New York 2018; O'Neil, Cathy: Weapons of math destruction: how big data increases inequality and threatens democracy, New York 2016.

18 Picard, Rosalind W.: Affective computing, Cambridge, Mass 2000.

19 Barr, Alistair: Google Mistakenly Tags Black People as "Gorillas," Showing Limits of Algorithms. In: The Wall Street Journal, July 1,2015, http://blogs.wsj.com/digits/2015/07/01/google-mistakenly-tags-black-people-as-gorillas-showing-limits-of-algorithms/ (November 1, 2021).

20 Buolamwini; Gebru 2018.

American Civil Rights Movement, John Lewis, was also misattributed.[21] All of these members of Congress are public figures, represented broadly with a variety of imagery within various databases. Nevertheless, facial recognition failed in their correct identification. Used as a tool for (governmental) surveillance, it thus promotes discrimination, in that, police measures tend to be predominantly directed against Black people, as they are repeatedly associated with crime in this way. If state security authorities use such faulty systems, this has particularly severe consequences. Due to the power relationships at hand, and the state's duty to protect—discrepancies become evident in the disparity between the aim of security for all, that effectively cannot be applied to each individual due to the biases explained above.

Powerful algorithms, such as those used in facial recognition and speech recognition technologies, work with learning systems instead of simple rule-based conditional chains. This means that the database with which the system is fed directly impacts the system's subsequent decision making. If the unadjusted baseline databases already contain imbalances or discrimination, the algorithm will perpetuate it, leading to and further reinforcing inequality. To continue within the congressional example: If the database contains a majority of imagery linking Black people to criminal offences, the algorithm will automatically assign the images of Black people accordingly. This discrimination does not have to be intentional. However, it clearly shows a lack of intersectional problem awareness regarding power and hierarchical structures, and it also shows how institutionalized forms of discrimination such as racism and sexism are perpetuated in our society.

Flexible or Clear Boundaries?

Now we could—as is often done—ultimately state that it is simply a matter of cleaning up the technology's data set and its (training) data set, in order to make it socially and legally acceptable, i.e., to put an end to discrimination.

The use of technology and software could lead to diminishing existing patterns of discrimination and counteracting its perpetuation. Although in

---

21   Snow, Jacob: Amazon's Face Recognition Falsely Matched 28 Members of Congress With Mugshots. In: American Civil Liberties Union, July 26, 2018, https://www.aclu.org/blog/privacy-technology/surveillance-technologies/amazons-face-recognition-falsely-matched-28 (August 11, 2019).

the case of Algorithms, this is highly complex and never fully guaranteed, we as a society should be paying attention to and proactively driving such a development forward. There are many inspiring and progressive ideas and models for this that need to be discussed elsewhere. However, even if, in some cases, it is possible to minimize existing discrimination through the use of Algorithms and to present this in an open and factual manner, the real struggle remains within the acknowledgement that neutral technology will never be the product of neutral people, as these simply do not exist.

Thus, critical awareness leads us to question: How much and what kind of discrimination and/or surveillance should be "allowed"? To what extent must the assessment be different when the state acts with surveillance measures? The Basic Law provides the guidelines for this answer. Nevertheless, if legal measures were to be equated, there would probably be no mentioning of problems, as well as no need for any of the executive and judicial branches.

One thing becomes clear: Surveillance often results in a large number of encroachments and violations to our fundamental rights. It affects our fundamental democratic freedoms and values, such as our privacy protected by these fundamental rights, the right to sexual and reproductive self-determination, freedom of assembly and movement, and freedom from discrimination. Last but not least, it is also about human dignity, Article 1 of the German Basic Law. Concerning artificial intelligence, which increases the severity of the interference many times over, entirely new questions arise. The old questions, to which the answers are still lacking, not only remain topical, but they also partly arise anew with unprecedented urgency. With the amount of data collected and stored, it is possible to search for suspicious patterns and correlations on a microscopic scale. By linking data sets, it is even possible—especially with the help of metadata—to create entire population profiles. Even if artificial intelligence is still less relevant in German surveillance measures, a look at the Chinese social scoring program shows us where this journey can lead. Mass and profound surveillance powers and data retention not only harms democracy in many ways.

The relationship between citizens and the state is always linked to accompanying questions of power distribution, including the tension between duty and protection. In recent years, the latter has often been used to justify an increasing number of measures that are supposed to implement security. However, these can at times not only lead to opposing results, but also, because of their effects, show a substantial imbalance in the proportionality of their assessment. A long chain of shrill flashing warning lights becomes unavoidable. A warning expressed in the publications of Edward Snowden about the global surveillance system.

For example, a German parliamentary Committee of Inquiry have shed light, and its impact has been documented in scientific reports. Who surveils the overseers when the warning lights are not perceived equally by everyone, and the internet is not infrequently declared a lawless space?

For a long time, the expansion of state surveillance measures, which is growing into an almost unwieldy, opaque patchwork of authorization bases, was hardly considered in its entirety from a legal point of view. In Germany it has now been flanked by a clear edge on the part of the judiciary. In addition to the need to specify the differentiation of intrusion powers according to the weight of the intrusion in the decision of the German Federal Constitutional Court on inventory data disclosure II,[22] a lawsuit filed by civil society organizations recently led the judges in Karlsruhe to examine the right to intelligence services concerning the permissibility of warrantless surveillance of global internet traffic by the Federal Intelligence Service. The result of which should not be surprising: The human rights illegality and incompatibility of warrantless mass surveillance with the German constitution was established.[23] The actual novelty was associated with the former: a clarification regarding the previous unequal treatment of citizens and "foreigners abroad".

However, in addition to this milestone for the legal protection of millions of people, the question remains as to whether the constitutional corrective also leads to the setting of limits or the preservation of rights. Instead of addressing the issue of independent monitoring as a whole, which was already required by constitutional law in 2010[24] (to the question of how the existing surveillance practice of German security authorities is structured as a whole and what consequences current surveillance entails) we look at a continuous development of surveillance systems in terms of the constant expansion of measures—despite countless clear decisions by the highest courts on data retention, preventive telecommunications surveillance and online searches.

Not long ago, in Germany a "successful" attempt was made to finally defer expiring surveillance measures,[25] which were initially limited in time in the so-called Schily-catalogs and subject to the obligation of constant in-

---

22   BVerfG, 27.05.2020, 1 BvR 1873/13, 1 BvR 2618/13.
23   BVerfG, 19.05.2020, 1 BvR 2835/17.
24   BVerfG, 02.03.2010, 1 BvR 256/08.
25   BT-Drs 19/23706, https://www.bundestag.de/dokumente/textarchiv/2020/w45-de-terrorismusbekaempfung-802464 (May 24, 2021).

dependent evaluations, after numerous interim deferrals. Independent full evaluations are nonexistent up to date. The legislative package contains legal bases for surveillance measures that the Constitutional Court has long since overturned. Thus, to date, there is no overall account of surveillance, not even a list of criteria for an urgently needed scientific evaluation of all surveillance laws.[26] There is simply too little known about the technologies used by security authorities and the suitability or necessity of the far-reaching encroachments on fundamental rights that accompany them. Moreover, without technology assessment, the effects on individuals and society remain in the dark.

The argument that is always put forward in opposition to these concerns is security. However, without wanting to use this misleading security-liberty dichotomy: There is no security without freedom, without equality.

This is why, as early as 1983, the Constitutional Court, in its still highly topical decision on the census ruling, urged that the effects of surveillance on individuals and society as a whole ought to be reviewed: "Those who are uncertain whether deviant behavior will be noted at any time and permanently stored, used, or passed on as information will try not to be conspicuous by such behavior. Anyone who expects that, for example, participation in a meeting or a citizens' initiative will be recorded by the authorities and that risks may arise for him as a result will possibly refrain from exercising his corresponding fundamental rights (Articles 8, 9 of the Basic Law)."[27]

In its way of pointing out and admonishing uncertainties, a theoretical rationale focuses on the (subconsciously) action-changing component of surveillance measures (chilling effects). From a legal perspective, the chilling effect describes the deterrent effect of an intervention in fundamental rights. Surveillance can lead to citizens no longer exercising their fundamental rights due to this intervention.[28]

This also restricts the opportunity for self-determined individual development. Due to the power relations of the surveillance measures and exist-

---

26 Dolderer, Dr. Winfried: Deutscher Bundestag—Bedenken gegen Entfristung von Vorschriften zur Terrorismusbekämpfung. In: Bundestag, November 2, 2020, https://www.bundestag.de/dokumente/textarchiv/2020/kw45-pa-innen-antiterrorgesetze-799842 (November 8, 2020).

27 BVerfG, 15.12.1983, 1 BvR 209/83: 146.

28 See also Assion, Simon: Chilling Effects und Überwachung. In: Telemedicus: Recht der Infomationsgesellschaft, November 26, 2014, https://www.telemedicus.info/article/2866-Chilling-Effects-und-UEberwachung.html (March 19, 2018).

ing discrimination, the impairment is less intense for some and more intense for others. The social effects on our free democratic social structure are noticeable when action and participation are restricted. If the restrictions are of different kinds and affect us differently as a society, this fundamentally changes us, affecting the understanding of us as a diverse and varied society and ultimately altering democratic processes such as political opinion-forming. Such so-called chilling effects are difficult to present in court in individual cases, and a legal review faces numerous obstacles.[29] It is, therefore, also of fundamental value to question how we can approach the solution of this associated social task. How do we want to shape the way we live together and upon which measures to be base this? Under which and whose order and control do we want this to happen? Who is the "we," and who decides these questions? For a long time, not taking these questions into account, seemed to be an option. But it has proven to not be a good one. The use of Algorithms forces us to address these pressing questions, to deal with them and take action.

Without fulfilling the state's duty to accompany this decision-making process openly and transparently, without conducting and deciding in respect of interdisciplinary perspectives rather than isolated and elitist mannerisms, we will never be able to close the gap between the demands of society as a whole and our existing Basic Law. We will never be able to implement the factual situation of likewise existing violations of fundamental rights due to surveillance, and in any case, never be able to uncover them in the first place.

The logic problem inherent in any surveillance measures is the lack of transparency anchored within them. While a small part of society accumulates more and more information and thus power, most of the population simply knows too little about these processes. This is exacerbated by the use of computer technologies, if those are built with lack of transparency, filled with unchecked data, deployed, and ultimately unevaluated results.

So, in conclusion is digital self-defense the only option left as a last resort for self-protection? A situation that would certainly not contribute to equal participation.

This is cynical, mainly because of the power relationship between citizens and the state, as even the state has not yet clarified its relationship to

---

29   Sass, Ineke: Wie Überwachung die Meinungsfreiheit gefährdet. In: Amnesty International, May 9, 2016, https://www.amnesty.de/informieren/blog/deutschland-wie-ueberwachung-die-meinungsfreiheit-gefaehrdet (May 24, 2021).
Staben, Julian: Der Abschreckungseffekt auf die Grundrechtsausübung, Tübingen 2016.

encryption. It is increasingly taking or giving itself the right to state intervention, for example, with the help of state Trojans. While civil society organizations, in turn, have to demand a stop to surveillance through judicial clarification30, the attempt at expansion is being continued by the state, even going so far as to oblige companies to support surveillance by distributing malware and thus hacking their customers.[31]

Human or Algorithms—Who or What Needs to be Surveilled?

Furthermore, who should be given the responsibility to answer these questions? When it comes to warrantless mass surveillance, fundamental decisions can probably only be made by society as a whole. What kind of world do we want to live in, in what proportion, how should power be distributed, who belongs to society and who is left outside? In mass surveillance, we cannot decipher who is affected by the surveillance and to what extent. Or do we? As for now, we simply surveil everyone by general suspicion in order to define the individual object of surveillance afterwards. It is easy to say "no" to this in principle, but it is probably impossible to draw the boundaries in practice.

In the case of individual surveillance, surveillance in the private sphere or commercial enterprises, the question of which forms of surveillance we want and which we do not want seems easier to answer. Not only legally but also factually. However, already, the proactive approach shows its faultiness.

Is it not a matter of feeling? Or is it? To do justice to the responsibility of using technology, we need to move away from the perhaps unconscious decision that it is sufficient to use feelings to legitimize social decisions up to and including legal bases. Neither concerning the decision for more robust and extensive surveillance measures to cover feelings of fear nor concerning an unreflective trust in technology. This is especially true for the increasing use of artificial intelligence, which can often lead to wrong decisions and increase discrimination, as we have shown. Black boxes, i.e., non-transparent,

---

30　Mattes, Anna Livia: Pressemitteilung: Verfassungsbeschwerde gegen Staatstrojaner eingelegt—GFF—Gesellschaft für Freiheitsrechte e.V.. In: Gesellschaft für Freiheitsrechte, August 24, 2018, https://freiheitsrechte.org/pm-vb-trojaner/ (November 8, 2020).

31　Meister, Andre and Biselli, Anna: Wir veröffentlichen den Gesetzentwurf—Seehofer will Staatstrojaner für den VerfassungsschutzIn: netzpolitik, March 28, 2019, https://netzpolitik.org/2019/wir-veroeffentlichen-den-gesetzentwurf-seehofer-will-staatstrojaner-fuer-den-verfassungsschutz/ (November 8, 2020).

self-contained systems whose structure and inner workings can only be inferred—if at all—from reactions to input signals, used in surveillance pose a double threat.

That Means we Have to Surveil the Right One: Algorithms

To ensure that existing discrimination and systemic biases are minimized rather than exacerbated by AI systems, there needs to be fundamental transparency in their design. Starting with the open labeling of such systems, they must be developed and designed to be as comprehensible and verifiable as possible. Explainable AI is the keyword here.

A documentation and logging obligation seems unavoidable in order to be able to detect and correct errors and wrong decisions. When using AI, not only must unintended conclusions about individual persons be prevented, but counterfactual explanations such as claims for information for affected persons about which factors led to an unfavorable decision are also imperative.

The higher the potential for harm, the higher the requirements to be applied to the criteria of AI systems. Nevertheless, what is the point of open standards, data quality, robustness, or data protection rules if an AI system is used for surreptitious surveillance? What is the point of data subjects having rights with respect to automated algorithmic decisions if they cannot enforce them due to lack of knowledge on surveillance? Does this mean that when surveillance is used, the use of AI systems should be banned altogether? It seems clear that in the case of facial recognition technology in public spaces, for example, we must speak of an unacceptable risk of harm. In view of the sensitivity of most of the areas affected, the intensity of the intervention, the number of people affected, or the irreversibility of decisions, will be affirmative for many areas. At this point, it must be said that there are certain areas of applied surveillance, for example, in the medical field, where the balance expresses itself differently.

However, who takes responsibility for deciding what technology should or should not accompany us in the future, what data it should work with, and to what extent it must be verifiable? Who decides which switches are the right ones and where they should lead, and who is ultimately responsible for them? Who develops, certifies, or standardizes them? Furthermore, what are the social and private implications of these answers? This requires a fundamental decision—personally and for society as a whole, in Germany, Europe, and worldwide. Surveillance concerns us all. Opting out of the discourse has implications, usually on a larger scale for all those who are particularly affected by surveillance bias and its restrictions. We need to frame and conduct this debate in an intersectional feminist way, i.e., including power and domination structures, to view the different forms of discrimination and their effects. Otherwise, we cannot justly answer the questions on surveillance measures with or without AI systems—to how and with which result and to which extent concerning our future.

Literature

Assion, Simon: Chilling Effects und Überwachung. In: Telemedicus: Recht der Infomationsgesellschaft, November 26, 2014, https://www.telemedicus.info/article/2866-Chilling-Effects-und-UEberwachung.html (March 19, 2018).

Barr, Alistair: Google Mistakenly Tags Black People as "Gorillas," Showing Limits of Algorithms. In: The Wall Street Journal, July 1, 2015, http://blogs.wsj.com/digits/2015/07/01/google-mistakenly-tags-black-people-as-gorillas-showing-limits-of-algorithms/ (November 1, 2021).

Benjamin, Ruha: Race after technology: abolitionist tools for the new Jim code, Medford, MA 2019.

Biselli, Anna: Berlin: Keine rationalen Argumente für Videoüberwachung an S-Bahnhof. In: netzpolitik, March 1,2019, https://netzpolitik.org/2019/berlin-keine-rationalen-argumente-fuer-videoueberwachung-an-s-bahnhof/ (May 24, 2021).

Böhm, María Laura: Der Gefährder und das Gefährdungsrecht: eine rechtssoziologische Analyse am Beispiel der Urteile des Bundesverfassungsgerichts über die nachträgliche Sicherungsverwahrung und die akustische Wohnraumüberwachung, Göttingen 2011.

boyd, danah; Crawford, Kate: CRITICAL QUESTIONS FOR BIG DATA: Provocations for a cultural, technological, and scholarly phenomenon. Information, Communication & Society, xv/5 2012, pp. 662–679.

Browne, Simone: Dark matters: on the surveillance of blackness, Durham 2015.
Buolamwini, Joy; Gebru, Timnit: Gender Shades: Intersectional Accuracy Disparities in Commercial Gender Classification. Proceedings of Machine Learning Research, (Proceedings of Machine Learning Research, 2018), lxxxi 2018, pp. 77–91.
Dolderer, Dr. Winfried: Deutscher Bundestag—Bedenken gegen Entfristung von Vorschriften zur Terrorismusbekämpfung. In: Bundestag, November 2, 2020, https://www.bundestag.de/dokumente/textarchiv/2020/kw45-pa-innen-antiterrorgesetze-799842 (November 8, 2020).
Eubanks, Virginia: Automating inequality: how high-tech tools profile, police, and punish the poor, New York, NY 2017.
Foucault, Michel: Überwachen und Strafen: Die Geburt des Gefängnisses, Frankfurt am Main 1977.
Fry, Hannah: Hello World: How to be Human in the Age of the Machine, London, New York, Toronto, Sidney, Auckland 2018.
Gless, Sabine: Predictive policing und operative Verbrechensbekämpfung. In: Felix Herzog, Reinhold Schlothauer, and Wolfgang Wohlers (eds), Rechtsstaatlicher Strafprozess und Bürgerrechte, Gedächtnisschrift für Edda Weßlau, Berlin 2016.
Gorner, Jeremy: Chicago Police Use Heat List as Strategy to Prevent Violence. In: Chicago Tribune, 2013, http://articles.chicagotribune.com/2013-08-21/news/ct-met-heat-list-20130821_1_chicago-police-commander-andrew-papachristos-heat-list (November 1, 2021).
Grieger, Fabian; Schlindwein, Simone: Migrationspolitik und Rüstungsindustrie: Das Geschäft mit Hightech-Grenzen. In: taz.de, die tageszeitung 2016.
Haggerty, Kevin D.; Ericson, Richard V.: The surveillant assemblage. In: The British Journal of Sociology, li/4 2000, pp. 605–622.
henning: Trügerische Sicherheit: Der elektronische Personalausweis. In: Chaos Computer Club, September 15, 2013, https://www.ccc.de/de/updates/2013/epa-mit-virenschutzprogramm (May 24, 2021).
Lyon, David (Ed.): Surveillance as Social Sorting: Privacy, Risk and Automated Discrimination, London 2003.

Mattes, Anna Livia: Pressemitteilung: Verfassungsbeschwerde gegen Staatstrojaner eingelegt—GFF—Gesellschaft für Freiheitsrechte e.V. In: Gesellschaft für Freiheitsrechte, August 24, 2018, https://freiheitsrechte.org/pm-vb-trojaner/ (November 8, 2020).

Meister, Andre; Biselli, Anna: Wir veröffentlichen den Gesetzentwurf—Seehofer will Staatstrojaner für den Verfassungsschutz. In: netzpolitik, March 28, 2019, https://netzpolitik.org/2019/wir-veroeffentlichen-den-gesetzentwurf-seehofer-will-staatstrojaner-fuer-den-verfassungsschutz/ (November 8, 2020).

Merz, Christina: Predictive Policing—Polizeiliche Strafverfolgung in Zeiten von Big Data, Karlsruher Institut für Technologie (KIT), 2016, https://publikationen.bibliothek.kit.edu/1000054372 (November 1, 2021).

Neumann, Linus: Untersuchung: Vorratsdatenspeicherung ist ineffektiv. In: netzpolitik, January 27, 2011, https://netzpolitik.org/2011/untersuchung-vorratsdatenspeicherung-ist-ineffektiv/ (May 24, 2021).

Noble, Safiya Umoja: Algorithms of Oppression: How Search Engines Reinforce Racism, New York 2018.

O'Neil, Cathy: Weapons of math destruction: how big data increases inequality and threatens democracy, New York 2016.

Picard, Rosalind W.: Affective computing, Cambridge, Mass 2000.

Sass, Ineke: Wie Überwachung die Meinungsfreiheit gefährdet. In: Amnesty International, May 9, 2016, https://www.amnesty.de/informieren/blog/deutschland-wie-ueberwachung-die-meinungsfreiheit-gefaehrdet (May 24, 2021).

Snow, Jacob: Amazon's Face Recognition Falsely Matched 28 Members of Congress With Mugshots. In: American Civil Liberties Union, July 26, 2018, https://www.aclu.org/blog/privacy-technology/surveillance-technologies/amazons-face-recognition-falsely-matched-28 (August 11, 2019).

Staben, Julian: Der Abschreckungseffekt auf die Grundrechtsausübung, Tübingen 2016.

Steinschaden, Jakob: Der "Chilling Effect": Massenüberwachung zeigt soziale Folgen—Netzpiloten.de. In: Netzpiloten Magazin, April 7, 2014, https://www.netzpiloten.de/der-chilling-effect-massenueberwachung-zeigt-soziale-folgen/ (May 24, 2021).

Wajcman, Judy: TechnoFeminism, Cambridge UK 2004.

Wermter, Benedict: Schnüffeln auf Facebook. In: Correctiv. Recherche für die Gesellschaft, June 22, 2015, https://correctiv.org/aktuelles/auskunftsrechte/2015/06/22/schnueffeln-auf-facebook/ (July 26, 2019).

Fabian Weiss

Embodied Algorithmic Optimization

How Our Bodies are Becoming a Product of Code

Evolution itself is and has been a constant battle to create a better onset for each and every organism on this planet—from the earliest multicellular organisms to modern forms of intellectual life. Cells have found ways to solve problems of growth with strategies of maximizing cellular diffusion for energy consumption[1] and animals have developed patterns to prolong life and escape predators by blending in with nature or other defense mechanisms developed through natural selection. Biological evolution of individual species has been driven by reproduction and survival, instilling goals and yearnings to procreate and grow. That system continually evolves to regulate growth, increase diversity and complexity, and enhance its own resilience, adaptability, and sustainability.[2] Humans themselves have come a long way from their early beginnings. Naturalists and biologists like Darwin (mistakenly[3]) claimed that we are are driven by what he called the survival of the most adaptable. This is disputed and for example Dutch author and historian Rutger Bregman proclaims in his recent novel 'Humankind: A Hopeful History'[4] that it is rather the most kind and decent beings. If we listen today to the media buzz of companies like 'GOOP', 'FitBit', 'People Unlimited Inc.', and other ventures that deal with physical health and prolonging of life, the goal of evolution seems to be focused on those individuals living the longest, healthiest, and most optimized life, a definition that currently seems to take the lead in Western techno-capitalistic societies. And it fits the general belief system: Maximization is engrained in the core of everything and mainstream measures of progress are mostly based on technical developments and the endless increase in productivity. Everything seems possible and solvable by technology and financial leverage. So why stop at our own bodies especially when the rapid developments of technology and algorithms promise to hold the key to the long awaited desire to transform our bodies and make them eternal?

---

1   Kurzgesagt: In a Nutshell: How Large Can a Bacteria get? Life & Size 3, Youtube 2020.
2   Nowak, Martin: Evolutionary Dynamics—Exploring the Equations of Life, Cambridge 2006.
3   Darwin Correspondence Project: The evolution of a misquotation, https://www.darwin-project.ac.uk/evolution-misquotation (January 20, 2021).
4   Bregman, Rutger: Humankind—a hopeful history, London 2020.

Fabian Weiss

Transhumanism or the Longing to Transform Our Bodies

The quest for immortality and longevity is neither new nor exotic: Throughout the history, people have searched for the elixir of life and retained a fascination in designing, shaping and optimizing their bodies through various means of potions or other science.[5] Today we are not looking for a single elixir of life anymore, but try to reverse or even stop aging through a multitude of different approaches. We are living in a decisive time where technology, medical science, and interconnected knowledge allows us to modify our bodies in dimensions never known before and push the human body to unchartered territories. "All the techniques of the artificial body that were once advanced medical experiments have steadily normalized. Even the doubling of the average life expectancy over the last century (with the greatest increases occurring in the poorest parts of the world, like Africa) is evidence of a whole new body. The human is simply not what it used to be."[6] These days there are tons of options available promising to prolong life and

---

[5] The idea of creating living beings from inanimate materials can be found already in creation stories in Sumerian, Chinese, Jewish, Christian, and Muslim traditions. In Ancient Egypt for example it was common to use "various techniques such as masquerading, tattooing and mummifying as ways to fashion bodies and to preserve them from inevitable decay". (Velsinger, Antje: On Bodies and the Need to Appropriate Them. In: Hildebrandt, Paula; Evert, Kerstin; Peters, Sibylle; Schaub, Mirjam; Wildner, Kathrin; Ziemer, Gesa (Eds): Performing Citizenship. Performance Philosophy. Cham 2019, p. 77–89, here p. 77) During the Roman empire, techniques of care of the self were practices to aid one's ability to face any challenge and the goal of invulnerability has been ever-present. The ancient Greeks already had the idea of creating artificial humans, and in the famous myth of Pygmalion it eerily resembles a modern narrative for artificial companions: "[A] sculptor falls in love with the ivory statue of a woman he's made. He wishes that she would come to life, and the goddess Aphrodite grants his wish: her lips become warm and her body soft." (Voegeli, Fabian: Techniques of the Self in View of Potentiality, Belgrade 2015, p. 217) In our more recent history, practices of eugenics emerged through racially motivated ideology disguised as genealogy with the idea of improving the human species genetically, while singling out who can be optimized. Forms of eugenic practice have varied widely and the recently emerged vision of an evantropic body (Misseri, Lucas E.: Evantropia and Dysantropia. In A Possible New Stage in the History of Utopias. In: Olkusz, Ksenia (Ed.): More After More: Essays Commemorating the Five-Hundredth Anniversary of Thomas More's Utopia, Krakow 2016, p. 26–43, here p. 38) highlights the ultimate goal of immortality followed by eternal youth and the maximum use of our capacities.

[6] Colomina, Beatriz; Wigley, Mark: are we human? notes on an archaeology of design, Zurich 2021, p. 224.

good health: Anti-aging therapies, health and fitness-tracking devices, technological implants or even cryonics, the process of freezing a human corpse or severed head at ultra-low temperatures with the speculative hope that resurrection may be possible in the future. In line with those developments the term 'Transhumanism' has been coined not too long ago with similar ideas in mind—to describe a state where humans overcome the limitations of their own body and eternity. With the help of technology and artificial intelligence (AI), our bodies could become smarter, less vulnerable to diseases, live longer, and potentially even become a transcendence machine that promises immortality. Belgian philosopher Mark Coeckelbergh for example describes transhumanist and posthumanist ideas concerning the body as a constant need of upgrades or humans risk remaining the slow and increasingly inefficient part of AI:

> Whereas transhumanists think we should move on to a new type of human being that is enhanced by means of science and technology, humanists defend the human as it is and stress the value and dignity of the human, which is said to be threatened by transhumanist science and philosophy. [...] Posthumanists such as Donna Haraway offer a vision in which living together with machines, and even merging with machines, is seen no longer as a threat or a nightmare, as in humanism, or as a transhumanist dream come true, but as a way in which ontological and political borders between humans and nonhumans can and should be crossed.[7]

Extremists and some tech personalities such as the American engineer Elon Musk or the inventor Ray Kurzweil even go as far as predicting AI Singularity: an algorithm that will supersede humans with its exponential growth rendering everything we have done until now and are currently doing insignificant.[8] Israeli historian Yuval Noah Harari writes in his book 'Homo Deus' about a world, in which humans no longer dominate but worship data and trust algorithms to make their decisions "going where no human has gone before—and where no human can follow".[9] Some even fear that machines with emergent intelligence have discernibly different goals and as we

---

7   Coeckelbergh, Mark: AI Ethics, Cambridge 2020, p. 47f.
8   Ito, Joichi: Resisting Reduction: A Manifesto, https://doi.org/10.21428/8f7503e4 (January 22, 2018).
9   Harari, Yuval Noah: Homo Deus: A Brief History of Tomorrow, London 2015, p. 393.

introduce machines into the system, they will not only augment individual humans but complex systems as a whole. On the contrary, there is plenty of potential to be optimistic about: While threatening human autonomy and agency, artificial intelligence and smart algorithms will amplify human effectiveness and positively contribute to broad public-health programs built around big amounts of data. They already do and will increase capabilities in tasks such as complex reasoning and learning, sophisticated analytics, visual acuity, speech recognition and language translation, augmenting human capacities and disrupting eons-old human activities.

Dataquakes & the Cult of Dataism

While we might not be aware of every use case, algorithms are more and more structuring our world and they are at the forefront of shaping and enhancing our current and future bodies. As we are becoming increasingly optimizable in surface and depth, modern self-tracking systems can not only measure our bodies and movements but can also mine data concerning our habits and whereabouts. Given the exponential growth of computer power and the availability of big data due to billions of smartphones, algorithms are at the core of producing, managing, analyzing and interpreting massive data sets—and interpreting us. We are generating an innumerable amount of data each and every day, and some researchers already speak of 'dataquakes.'[10]

As we are using services and devices that are increasingly generating private data—like blood pressure, sleep cycles, reproductive health status, and exact locations, to name a few—we are becoming more and more a transparent user who in return is being greeted by an algorithmically designed life. Our bodies inform the functioning of the systems we use and vice versa. And with all cameras in public places recognizing and labeling people as well as the rise of so-called smart city projects around the world, the AI NOW Report of 2019 notes that we are "consolidating power over civic life in the hands of for-profit technology companies, putting them in charge of managing critical resources and information."[11] With the sheer amount of data being collected paired with modern algorithms the real-life effects on our bodies in return become quite tangible: Identifying the perfect employee, correctly classify-

---

10   Alpaydin, Ethem: Machine Learning. The New AI, Cambridge 2016, p. 16.
11   Crawford, Kate et al.: AI Now 2019 Report, New York: AI Now Institute 2019, p. 11.

ing feelings of customers, or tracking student attentiveness in class[12] are just the beginning. While these development are mind-blowing on a technical level, they are also packed with a lot of social implications as Coeckelbergh puts it quite trenchantly:

> Darwin and Freud dethroned our beliefs of exceptionalism, our feelings of superiority, and our fantasies of control; today, artificial intelligence seems to deal yet another blow to humanity's self-image. If a machine can do this, what is left for us? What are we? Are we just machines? Are we inferior machines, with too many bugs?[13]

Tracking regimes that we would once have thought bizarre are slowly becoming normal,[14] challenging us to re-evaluate what normal means. And challenging us to adapt a new form of wariness towards the technology and algorithms we use. Even if we can assume that modern AI programs like the word-generating AI GPT-3[15] are today not only pretending a real understanding of a conversation like the 1964 computer program ELIZA[16] by the late German American computer scientist Joseph Weizenbaum did, the data the algorithm relies on is still prone to manipulation, racism and often sourced with dubious tactics. Corporations and state agencies often use communication networks and digital surveillance to collect huge amounts of information on the activities of everyone using digital services. Calculative devices transform the nature of human subjectivity, pushing at the limits of what can be read, analyzed and thought about[17] and with new forms of data aggregation come also more advanced forms of profiling human behavior, fueling the emergence of often poorly regulated business models and new forms of 'dataveillance'.

Because right now, data aggregation is often hidden in plain sight and just mentioned vaguely within the fine-print. Or did you know that you al-

---

12   Ibid., p. 50.
13   Coeckelbergh 2020, p. 13.
14   Wolf, Gary: The Data-Driven Life, https://www.nytimes.com/2010/05/02/magazine/02self-measurement-t.html (December 12, 2020).
15   Maldonado, Adran; Pistunovich, Natalie: GPT-3 Powers the Next Generation of Apps, https://openai.com/blog/gpt-3-apps/ (March 27, 2021).
16   See Wikipedia: ELIZA, https://en.wikipedia.org/wiki/ELIZA (March 05, 2021).
17   Amoore, Louise; Piotukh, Volha: Algorithmic Life, Oxford 2015, p. 37.

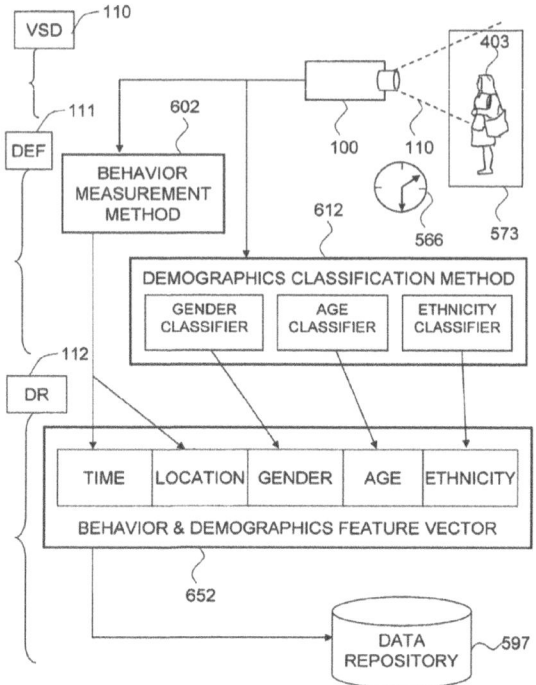

Figure 1—'Automatic detection and aggregation of demographics and behavior of people', a patent for a system that includes Automated Gender Recognition. Available at: Google Patents, https://patents.google.com/patent/US8351647B2/

lowed FitBit to collect and share even your female health with third parties,[18] that your outdoor activity gets uploaded into a global map where everyone can see exactly where people go actually running, swimming, or cycling,[19] or that racial and ethnic origins will be shared with others by the app Tinder?[20] A lot of companies and even governments seem to grab as much data as they can like in a modern age gold rush before legislation or citizen protests can actually catch up and make the act of doing so illegal. Sometimes it is mind-boggling how much data is collected and merged about a single person as French journalist Judith Duportail had to witness firsthand when she turned to Tinder asking what information has been collected about herself:[21] What she got was a collection of 800 pages of all of her activities using the app—including Facebook likes and friends, links to where her Instagram photos where taken, her education, the age-rank of men she was interested in, when and where every online conversation with every single one of her matches happened, and many other very private details.[22] In many cases, this information doesn't stay only with the company collecting it, but is being packaged neatly to sell it to whoever is interested in, mostly through middle men like data-brokers.

One of such data-broker companies was brought to light in 2017 by artist Joana Moll and the Tactical Tech collective, as they obtained one million online profiles from USDate, a U.S.-based company that trades dating profiles from all over the globe—for only 136 Euros! The batch of purchased profiles included "pictures (almost 5 million of them), usernames, e-mail addresses, nationality, gender, age and detailed personal information about all of the people who had created the profiles, such as their sexual orientation, interests, profession, thorough physical characteristics and personality

---

18 See FitBit: FitBit Privacy Policy, https://www.fitbit.com/global/us/legal/privacy-policy (November 18, 2020).

19 See for example Suunto 'Movescount' (https://www.movescount.com/map) or Strava 'Global Heatmap' (https://www.strava.com/heatmap).

20 See Tinder: Privacy Policy, https://policies.tinder.com/privacy/intl/en/ (January 17, 2021).

21 Duportail, Judith: I asked Tinder for my data., https://www.theguardian.com/technology/2017/sep/26/tinder-personal-data-dating-app-messages-hacked-sold (September 26, 2017).

22 Ibid.

traits."[23] If unlucky, such data is being used to feed systems like the in Figure 1 (**page 76**) depicted patent for 'Automated Gender Recognition' or other questionable undertakings like it happened with the purchase of Ancestry.com last year: The private equity firm Blackstone now owns the DNA data of 18 million people and is currently ramping up efforts to monetize the data amassed among the companies it owns.[24] But these two examples are not alone: Microsoft, IBM, Apple, Amazon, and Facebook, as well as a wide range of healthcare start-ups have all made data partnership agreements with healthcare organizations to gain access to health data for the training and development of AI-driven systems.[25]

The Code that Dictates Our Bodies

We are increasingly intertwined with algorithmic calculative devices as we consume information, inhabit space and relate to others and to the world around us. People we see and communicate with through our screens and networks are being altered and optimized, shifting our perception of how we see other humans—sometimes even shifting how we perceive ourselves. Norms and standards are being influenced by algorithmic alterations and even leading to change in our physical world as teenagers increasingly turn to plastic surgery in order to look like their alter egos online, just to mention one example. Louise Amoore, Professor of Political Geography at Durham University, and author Volha Piotukh sum up this current state of intertwined connection: "Just as being human may also be closely enmeshed with being algorithmic, these calculative devices also alter perception, filtering what one can see of big data landscapes, how one makes sense of what can be perceived."[26]

Like a horrifying prediction of the Black Mirror episode 'Nosedive'[27] turned into reality, Google's Sidewalk Labs[28] project even promoted the cre-

23 Moll, Joana: The Dating Brokers – An autopsy of online love, https://datadating.tacticaltech.org/viz (November 14, 2020).
24 Ponsford, Matthew: IS YOUR DNA DATA SAFE IN BLACKSTONE'S HANDS? https://neo.life/2021/01/is-your-dna-data-safe-in-blackstones-hands/ (January 28, 2021).
25 Crawford et al. 2019, p. 53.
26 Amoore; Piotukh 2015, p. 24.
27 See Nosedive, https://www.imdb.com/title/tt5497778/ (August 26, 2020).
28 See Sidewalk Labs, https://www.sidewalklabs.com/ (January 13, 2021).

ation of a Google-managed citizen credit score. Our bodies nearly cannot escape some sort of measurement, identification, and data generation driven by algorithms anymore and American journalist Rob Horning sums up this impossibility to hide: "Short of a total renunciation of the now routine conveniences of contemporary life and voluntary exile from the spaces where almost all social belonging and recognition takes place, you cannot escape."[29]

Officials in China have even gone a step further by not only using AI surveillance on the Uighur minority alone anymore, but slowly rolling it out for the entire population. With the help of a new 'health-code' they now even restrict access to certain areas if people are not living healthily. The code is implemented in most of the major Chinese transactional apps like AliPay (a payment platform) or WeChat (the number one app in China to do anything from blogging, instant messaging, ordering food, booking a flight, paying bills, etc.) and can only be obtained after the government has acquired your full name, ID and phone number. The code itself is then informed by a multitude of factors with most of them being produced by the app itself: The number of steps taken each day, the hours of sleep, or the proximity and time spent close to a Covid-19 positive person. It then adds the number of cigarettes smoked and the amount of alcohol consumed by scanning your shopping list when paying with the app[30] as well as the time spent playing video games through interconnected services.[31] Only with a green code you can then enter certain areas like public transport, public events, or even premises of bigger companies. Through that, personal data produced by our body in combination with algorithms is becoming a massive decentralized and panoramic power model informing the do's and don't of millions of people already today. The system not only investigates behavior—it steers it away from purchases and activities the government does not like, making people in a Foucauldian sense the object of information, not a subject of communication. The less obvious the mechanism, the more powerful the disciplinary function of surveillance.[32]

When we leave behind the notion of dystopian surveillance and focus on the benefits for human bodies, algorithms can achieve many long-sought

---

29   Horning, Rob: Hide and Seek—The Problem with Obfuscation, https://lareviewofbooks.org/article/hide-and-seek-the-problem-with-obfuscation/ (March 16, 2021).

30   Zhao, Yiran: [BigDataSur-COVID] When Health Code becomes Health Gradient: Safety or Social Control? https://data-activism.net/2020/10/bigdatasur-covid-when-health-code-becomes-health-gradient-safety-or-social-control-2/ (December 03, 2020).

31   Benjamin, Ruha: Race After Technology, New York 2019, p. 115.

32   Benjamin 2019, p. 181.

dreams concerning health and longevity. An AI developed by researchers at Houston Methodist Research Institute in Texas for example can already today diagnose a cancer risk 30 times faster than a human with 99 percent accuracy,[33] at the Beth Israel Deaconess Medical Center, an artificial intelligence is used to diagnose potentially deadly blood diseases at a very early stage,[34] the Framingham Heart Study used self-learning algorithms to predict future onset of Alzheimer's disease through automated linguistic analysis,[35] and AI is capable to predict schizophrenia or even diabetes years before it manifests in the body. Relating to recent events, a new study from Mount Sinai researchers even found out that wearable hardware can effectively predict a positive COVID-19 diagnosis up to a week before current PCR-based nasal swab tests.[36] Our bodies give away signals that can be read by algorithms and new technologies much better than humans have ever been able to. With bigger and better training sets, subtle nuances are already enough to give hints on ongoing problems in our body. Our breath changes with the level of stress, our iris changes with the activity of our brain, and our language changes with the status of our health. Advocates for AI like Poppy Crum, American neuroscientist at Dolby Laboratories, get very excited about these signs for a healthier future:

> I believe it is the era of the empath. And we are enabling the capabilities that true technological partners can bring to how we connect with each other and with our technology. If we recognize the power of becoming technological empaths we get this opportunity where technology can help us bridge the emotional and cognitive divide. [...] Imagine a high school counselor being able to realize, that an outwardly cheery student really was having a deeply hard time. [...] Or authorities

[33] Griffiths, Sarah: This AI software can tell if you're at risk from cancer before symptoms appear, https://www.wired.co.uk/article/cancer-risk-ai-mammograms (February 03, 2021).

[34] Daley, Sam: 32 Examples of AI in Healthcare That Will Make You Feel Better About the Future, https://builtin.com/artificial-intelligence/artificial-intelligence-healthcare (February 17, 2021).

[35] Eyigoz, Elif; Mathur, Sachin/Santamaria, Mar/Cecchi, Guillermo/Naylor, Melissa: Linguistic markers predict onset of Alzheimer's disease, https://doi.org/10.1016/j.eclinm.2020.100583 (March 20, 2021).

[36] Etherington, Darrell: Mount Sinai study finds Apple Watch can predict COVID-19 diagnosis up to a week before testing, https://techcrunch.com/2021/02/09/mount-sinai-study-finds-apple-watch-can-predict-covid-19-diagnosis-up-to-a-week-before-testing/ (February 10, 2021).

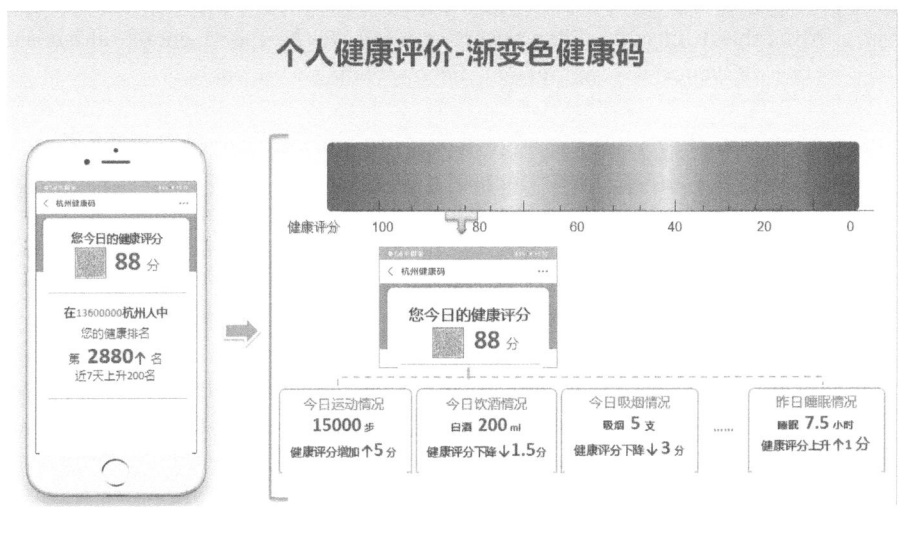

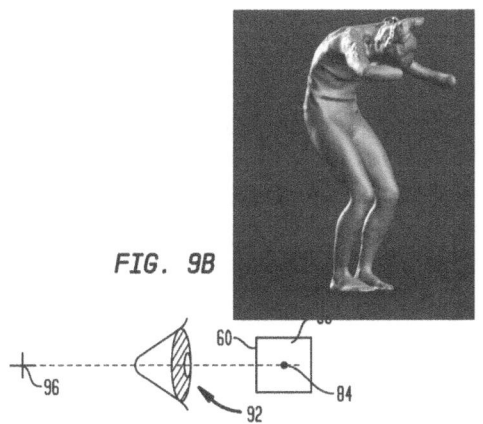

Figure 2—In this picture the individual health code value states a 88/100 grade corresponding to a green health code, calculated on a value resulting from the number of steps taken, the number of cigarettes smoked, the amount of alcohol assumed and the hours of sleep reached in one day by its owner. Available at: https://data-activism.net/2020/10/bigdatasur-covid-when-health-code-becomes-health-gradient-safety-or-social-control-2/

Figure 3—'Ideal Self #23—Naked Scanner', from the series 'Ideal Self' (2020) by Fabian Weiss.

being able to know the difference between someone having a mental health crisis and a different type of aggression, and responding accordingly.[37]

Also in our everyday life, algorithms are more and more deployed to improve our lives. Through smartphones or wearable activity trackers, we are having a lot of options at hand to measure vital functions in order to gain insights into our personal wellbeing. The image on the last page (**Figure 3**) shows for example a 3D model of a human body created with Naked Labs' body scanner called 'Naked Scanner', where not only weight and body fat is being collected over a period of time, but different areas of the body and their extent can be compared and analyzed as well. But options of analyzation give also way to modification: It is not only our digital alter ego anymore that can be altered by algorithms (imitating speech, recreating body movements, applying filters, or swapping our face in real time)[38], but our physical bodies as well. Algorithms are being inscribed into our physicality and have already far more control over our bodies than we might believe. Online dating platforms (and their matching algorithms) have fundamentally changed people's day-to-day practices of sex and love and screening algorithms are deciding already today over who gets a phone contract, a bank account, a loan, an employment or even which court sentence. Chance is being replaced by the technique of probability which is only as good as the data it is being trained on, resulting in outcomes that are determined in the worst case by historical notions of bias, racism, and sexism. As nearly every detail of our lives—financial transactions, online search terms, real-world movement, communication and many more—gets logged, digital technologies extend the reach of this structural surveillance, making it persistent for some and nearly invisible to those with enough power to escape its gaze.[39]

---

37 TED: Technology that knows what you're feeling | Poppy Crum, Available at: https://www.youtube.com/watch?v=HW2SSoYtels (March 14, 2021), 09:40.
38 See for example Ockenden, Sasha: Skin Deep: Deep Fakes and Misinformation, https://medium.com/digital-diplomacy/skin-deep-deep-fakes-and-misinformation-3c2f-9cc59045 (December 16, 2020).
39 Benjamin 2019, p. 251.

More Than Colorblind: Imitating and Reinforcing Inequalities

The given consequences mostly reinforce power structures, inequalities or biases that are already preexistent in society. American sociologist Ruha Benjamin argues in her book 'Race After Technology' that algorithms even speed up and deepen discrimination while appearing neutral or benevolent. As the input for most algorithmic systems stems from historical data, it also carries the burden of our society—for example racism or chauvinism. The system doesn't have to be built to intentionally prefer certain outcomes, but a lot of algorithms do not work fairly just because of unconscious biases. Let's take for example the COMPAS system, an algorithm that informs judges based on a 137-point questionnaire filled out by arrested people over their likelihood of becoming reoffenders. "Seven criminogenic needs, or risk factors, are identified. These include 'educational-vocational-financial deficits and achievement skills,' 'antisocial and procriminal associates,' and 'familial-marital-dysfunctional relationship.' All of these measures are outcomes of poverty. It's positively Kafkaesque"[40] argues the American data journalism professor Meredith Broussard in her book 'Artificial Unintelligence'. As a result, black defendants were 77 percent more likely to be flagged as a higher risk of committing a future violent crime as journalist Julia Angwin uncovered in a report for ProPublica.

Algorithms are erecting new digital caste systems structured by inequalities that are not just colorblind: "When these technical codes move beyond the bounds of the carceral system, beyond labeling people as 'high' and 'low' risk criminals, when automated systems from employment, education, healthcare, and housing come to make decisions about people's deservedness for all kinds of opportunities."[41] Due to the fact that both programmers and datasets[42] are still predominantly stemming from Western countries, the flaws in the algorithms have far-reaching consequences for non-white users. The result can be simply as annoying as it happened to Asian-American blogger Joz Wang: Her (ironically Japanese) Nikon camera had a feature built in for detecting a blink of a person as a gesture for capturing a selfie. When being tested by herself, it was triggering all the time when she was looking at the

---

40 Broussard, Meredith: Artificial Unintelligence: How Computers Misunderstand the World, Cambridge 2018, p. 347.
41 Benjamin 2019, p. 25.
42 Most facial recognition algorithms for example are being trained on the ImageNet dataset that has an overwhelming majority of white faces.

camera as the software had been trained on Caucasian faces and therefore often falsely detected a blink with more narrow eyes.[43] Going further, there have been incidents where the picture sorting app Google Photos misrecognized a Black man's face as a gorilla when labeling images within categories. Even until 2018 and presumably today, the solution was not to fix the algorithm, but to simply ban the label 'gorilla' altogether,[44] a workaround and not a real solution to the problem. Joy Buolamwini, an Ghanaian-American coder and activist working with facial analysis software, was even unable to use some software as it didn't detect her face at all[45] and she frequently uncovered other incidents concerning Black employees being "unable to use the elevators, doors, and water fountains or turn the lights on,"[46] as the systems would just not work with non-white faces.

But algorithmic bias doesn't stop at skin color, it also affects gender. In the beginning, voice recognition services like Apple's Siri, Google's Assistant or Microsoft's Cortona had problems understanding queries like 'I was raped'. This has been solved for most cases but even now, gender bias is still present: the default settings of audio assistants are nearly always set to female voices by default. American journalist Adrianne LeFrance explains this with the deep rooted prejudice as to first and foremost expect women, not men, to be in administrative roles[47]—either a willful neglect or a profit imperative that makes money from racism and sexism, arguably a key ingredient in the IT world of Silicon Valley.

43 Lum, Jessica: "Racist" Camera Phenomenon Explained—Almost, https://petapixel.com/2010/01/22/racist-camera-phenomenon-explained-almost/ (January 22, 2010).
44 See Simonite, Tom: When It Comes to Gorillas, Google Photos Remains Blind, https://www.wired.com/story/when-it-comes-to-gorillas-google-photos-remains-blind/ (November 17, 2020).
45 See Buolamwini, Joy: How I'm fighting bias in algorithms, https://www.ted.com/talks/joy_buolamwini_how_i_m_fighting_bias_in_algorithms (November 01, 2016).
46 Benjamin 2019, p. 163.
47 LaFrance, Adrienne: Why Do So Many Digital Assistants Have Feminine Names? Hey Cortana. Hey Siri. Hey girl., https://www.theatlantic.com/technology/archive/2016/03/why-do-so-many-digital-assistants-have-feminine-names/475884/ (April 02, 2021).

Becoming Mechanical Body Turks

Whereas modern data collection might have started as a byproduct to provide better services for each individual, now it often seems that services are being created in order to harness as much data as possible in order to distribute and sell it, using humans to achieve an overarching goal: Displaying relevant ads and increase income with the collected data. Our bodies are becoming modern slaves performing labour in exchange for services, hidden neatly in the fine-print of the Terms Of Service. We tag our friends on social media helping to create a massive database of people, upload tons of images that are frequently being used or misused to train algorithms in object recognition, let our phones track our movement for better traffic prediction, or just solve other little tasks (like solving CAPTCHAs[48]) that help companies to increase data and wealth, arguably making us modern Mechanical Body Turks, a term borrowed from a fake 18th-century chess-playing 'computer' that was actually driven by a small chess master hidden inside a case, utilizing the embodied chess playing skills of a human. In the industry, this kind of work is nothing new and a lot of development around artificial intelligence has actually been disguised as technical development. Micro-tasks have just been outsourced to cheap human labour, such as labelling a photo, transcribing a fragment of text or performing a small calculation. Amazon and its service 'Amazon Mechanical Turk (MTurk)' is in this realm the most notorious crowdsourcing marketplace to outsource processes and jobs to a remote workforce to perform these tasks virtually.[49]

What might sound promising to companies and startups at first should be treated very carefully and David M. Berry, Professor of Digital Humanities at the University of Sussex, already argued that "this notion of not only aggregating human beings through software, but also treating them as components or objects of a computational system is indicative of the kind of cybernetic thinking that is prevalent in computational society".[50] In that way you could see the warning of the American mathematician Norbert Wiener from over 60 years ago already as a prediction of how we are today turning into Mechanical Body Turks when being interweaved too closely with big corpo-

---

48 Kobie, Nicole: Google's reCAPTCHA test has been tricked by artificial intelligence, https://www.wired.co.uk/article/google-captcha-recaptcha (April 02, 2021).
49 For further information see https://www.mturk.com/
50 Berry, David M.: Against infrasomatization: towards a critical theory of algorithms, London 2019, p. 50.

rations and their tools: "When human atoms are knit into an organization in which they are used, not in their full right as responsible human beings, but as cogs and levers and rods, it matters little that their raw material is flesh and blood."[51] Through all the gadgets and tools we are using on a daily basis, we often forget that we do not only pay with our money for the services we receive, but with our data, too.

It has not only become an aggregation of humans knowingly working for machines, but essentially aggregating the 'work' of human bodies and their output without really informing people about the use of their data in full. Following American-German philosopher Herbert Marcuse's argumentation about the different forms of domination of the so-called free and non-totalitarian societies, "AI may lead to new forms of manipulation, surveillance, and totalitarianism, not necessarily in the form of authoritarian politics but in a more hidden and highly effective way: by changing the economy in a way that turns us all into smartphone cattle milked for our data."[52] These developments are slowly being addressed by researchers, developers and activists worldwide, but change is happening slowly. While many governments like the Communist Party of China even (secretly) promote data collection of Chinese companies,[53] awareness in other parts of the world like Europe and America is rising and some companies are slowly changing towards a more transparent and ethically sustainable approach towards data aggregation. Nevertheless, it needs the effort of artists and activists to touch unerringly on sore points of the de facto hidden collection and redistribution of bodily data.

Algorithmic Disobedience and Data Activism

It is often difficult to grasp the possible implications each and every step we take could have, as a lot of the actions taken by companies are illegal and unforeseen. A negative example is the 2020 case of the 'Clearview AI' scraping billions of images from social media sites and compiling them

---

51 Wiener, Norbert: The Human Use Of Human Beings, London 1989, p. 185.
52 Coeckelbergh 2020, p. 103.
53 Human Rights Watch: China—Big Data Program Targets Xinjiang's Muslims, https://www.hrw.org/news/2020/12/09/china-big-data-program-targets-xinjiangs-muslims (April 02, 2021).

into a facial recognition dataset in an unprecedented case of data theft.[54] Algorithms are being fed more and more data produced by us and our bodies, rendering our biometric data essentially what late German filmmaker Harun Farocki described as operational images—images that are being generated and used by machines only as part of an operation, "images without a social goal, not for edification, not for reflection."[55] We humans are increasingly excluded from the observation of code and the use of our own images feeding millions of databases, and mechanisms incorporated in algorithms and machine vision often remain opaque. If rendered visible, we are confronted with what the American sociologist Benjamin Bratton called "The Inverse Uncanny Valley"[56]: The feeling of unease we encounter when seeing ourselves through the eyes of an algorithm and being freaked out, because we don't recognize ourselves and how we are seen by the machine.[57]

The suppression of ethics and the management of everyday experience in favor of commercial logics based on politics of satisfaction and normalization of the average[58] has been discussed, but user agency is often neglected. As algorithms assume a dominant role in the mediation of power, it becomes increasingly important to consider to what extent and in what ways we can resist their power and become disobedient.[59] There are several ways to either question those mechanisms or actively respond to them, either by means of activism or art. Known examples of the later include the Italian artist-re-

[54] Hill, Kashmir: The Secretive Company That Might End Privacy as We Know It, https://www.nytimes.com/2020/01/18/technology/clearview-privacy-facial-recognition.html (February 11, 2021).

[55] Pantenburg, Volker: Working images: Harun Farocki and the operational image. In: Image Operations: Visual media and political conflict. Manchester 2017, 49–62, p. 49.

[56] Coined by the robotics professor Masahiro Mori in 1970, the Uncanny Valley Effect describes the hypothesized relationship between an object's resemblance to a human being and the emotional response. The concept claims that humanoid objects which imperfectly resemble real human beings provoke uncanny feelings of eeriness and revulsion in the observers.

[57] Fine Arts Museums of San Francisco: The Inverse Uncanny Valley—What We See When AI Sees Us | Benjamin Bratton, https://www.youtube.com/watch?v=2E3kQqrHwqo (February 14, 2021), 26:49.

[58] See Ananny, Mike: Toward an Ethics of Algorithms: Convening, Observation, Probability, and Timeliness. In: Science, Technology, & Human Values 41, no. 1 (January 2016), Newbury Park 2016, p. 93–117.

[59] Velkova, Julia; Kaun, Anne: Algorithmic resistance: media practices and the politics of repair. In: Information, Communication & Society, Volume 24, 2021 — Issue 4. Oxford 2021, p. 523–540, here p. 524.

searcher–activist Paolo Cirio, who illustrates the potential of art to construct new truths by producing digital instruments for an operational and participatory aesthetic.[60] His works address the 'black box' of algorithmic processes by either turning the view on the people in power itself or by making visible problems such as the erosion of digital subjects' privacy through algorithmically based surveillance systems. Another good example is the American artist Adam Harvey. His multi-year research project "MegaPixels" for example looks at the use of unconstrained and non-consensual data sources in AI systems.[61]

Whilst in the 1990s and 2000s scientists generally worked with volunteers to pose for operational images to train algorithmic systems,[62] in the last decade they started to harvest data that is available freely on the internet, beginning with the dataset 'Labeled Faces in the Wild'.[63] This practice is continuing with no or just little oversight until today like it was recently seen with the 'Yahoo Flickr Creative Commons 100 Million' dataset (YFCC100M),[64] and dozens of datasets with millions of images and identities feed into commercial facial recognition systems. Adam Harvey creates awareness by extracting modified data and making visible the extent of the privacy intrusion as seen above in the example of the Duke MTMC dataset. One recent sub-project includes the work 'Researchers Gone Wild' (**Figure 4**), where he investigated a dataset from researchers at Duke University in Durham, North Carolina, who released more than two million video frames of footage of students walking on the university campus.

Another example of art creating awareness is the author's body of work 'In the heat of the day' (2021) where he used geolocation-data generated by thousands of wearables illustrating the paths and whereabouts of the users of these services—shown on the following page in form of aggregated location data of people engaging in water-sports activities in Lake Müggelsee close to Berlin, Germany (**Figure 5**). With this work he wants to sound the alarm about

---

60   Manghani, Sunil: The art of Paolo Cirio. In: Theory, Culture & Society 34(7–8), Thousand Oaks 2017, p. 197–214, here p. 205.

61   See Harvey, Adam; LaPlace, Jules: MegaPixels: Origins and Endpoints of Datasets Created "In The Wild", https://megapixels.cc/megaface/ (December 14, 2020).

62   Van Noorden, Richard: The ethical questions that haunt facial-recognition research. In: Nature, November 2020, Issue 587, Basingstoke 2020, p. 354–358, here p. 355.

63   See 'Labeled Faces in the Wild', available at: http://vis-www.cs.umass.edu/lfw/

64   See 'Yahoo Flickr Creative Commons 100 Million (YFCC100m) dataset', available at: http://projects.dfki.uni-kl.de/yfcc100m/.

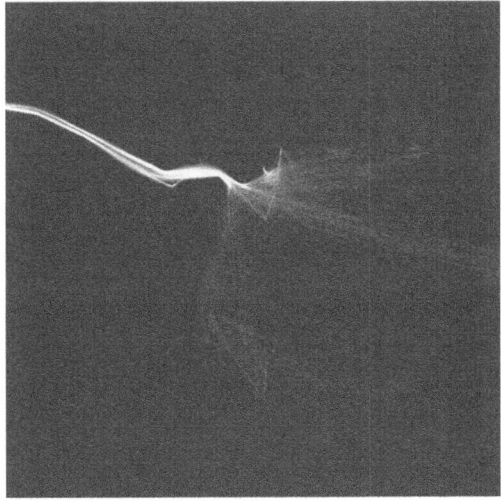

Figure 4—Adam Harvey, Datengeist. Visualization of camera 6 from the now revoked Duke MTMC dataset. Harvey, A. (2020) 'Face First: Researchers Gone Wild', Available at: https://ahprojects.com/researchers-gone-wild/.

Figure 5—'Müggelsee', from the series "In the heat of the day" (2021) by Fabian Weiss. Available at: https://phmuseum.com/fabianweiss/story/in-the-heat-of-the-day-4620f8a656.

possible unforeseen consequences such technology and the gadgets that we are using on a daily basis can have, as the data for example disclosed the locations of U.S. bases in the Middle East through uncensored data from soldiers' fitness watches.[65] Other artistic examples include the Austrian artist Margarete Jahrmann, whose installation 'The Artist is Measured'[66] combined face recognition, artistic interpretation and so-called breeding paintings to create awareness about the ongoing efforts of machine learning to recreate human bodies and faces.

The awareness created by artists and researchers does not necessarily lead to resistance and disobedience but has very much informed public discourse and even steered the course of political decisions in many instances. Positive examples can be observed for example with the work of the group Forensic Architecture, who is using artistic approaches and technical scrutiny to unveil security breaches, hidden observation and tracing, and government wrongdoings. Using methods of image recognition against state agents or companies themselves led in the case of a contact-tracing software in Israel even to a broad investigation into the case[67] and in other instances to the complete turnaround of a manufacturer against his own product amidst the use of tear gas grenades by police forces against Black Lives Matter activists across the U.S. in 2020.[68]

As algorithms are dependent on users for the queries that make them work, many activists and NGOs have started to recognize the role "they play in shaping the workings of algorithms, and they have begun to strategically intervene in political, commercial or playful ways in the algorithmic politics of attention".[69] What is being labelled as data activism explores how the vast amounts of data that is being generated not only results in new forms of con-

---

65 Scott-Railton, John: FitLeaking: When a FitBit blows your cover, https://www.johnscottrailton.com/fit-leaking/ (January 28, 2018).

66 Jahrmann, Margarethe: NEUROMATIC GAN PORTRAIT GAME—THE ARTIST IS MEASURED, https://neuromatic.uni-ak.ac.at/blog/eeg-stylegan-installation-at-parallel-vienna/ (February 15, 2021).

67 Whittaker, Zach: A passwordless server run by spyware maker NSO sparks contact-tracing privacy concerns, https://techcrunch.com/2020/05/07/nso-group-fleming-contact-tracing/ (May 07, 2020).

68 For details see: Forensic Architecture (2018) 'TRIPLE-CHASER', available at: https://forensic-architecture.org/investigation/triple-chaser

69 Velkova; Kaun 2019, p. 526.

trol, but also in new opportunities for citizenry.[70] Stefania Milán, Associate Professor of New Media and Digital Culture at the University of Amsterdam, and Miren Gutiérrez, director of the 'Data analysis, research and communication' program at the University of Deusto, understand data activism as a manifestation of citizen media, in which people and organizations give meaning to complex software central to civic actions aimed at social change, as well as reaction to new algorithmic control techniques that are challenging the very foundations of citizenship.[71] The umbrella term also embraces socio-technical practices that provide counter-hegemonic responses to the discrimination, social exclusion and privacy infringement that go hand in hand with big data. Data activism interrogates the politics of big data with an "action repertoire of data activists includes examining, manipulating, leveraging, and exploiting data, along with resisting and meddling in their creation and use"[72] involving individuals and organizations of civil society to promote social change and to broaden participation in decision-making.[73]

Take Hyphen-Labs for example, an U.S.-based afro-feminist group of women who work at the intersection of technology, art, and science. They have been experimenting with a wide array of subversive designs including "earrings for recording police altercations, and visors and other clothing that prevent facial recognition."[74] This field of clothing and gadgets used to prevent computer vision from detecting faces or other identifiable features—adversarial or camouflage fashion—is gaining a lot of traction. The same group also developed in cooperation with the aforementioned Adam Harvey the project HyperFace[75], a scarf that uses a scrambled pattern to obfuscate the data that cameras are receiving. Instead of the user's face, the algorithm sees 1200 faces that are printed on a scarf to camouflage the wearer (**Figure 6**). And a team of researchers from the Massachusetts Institute of Technology, the

70 Sastre Domínguez, Paz; Gordo López, Ángel: Data activism versus algorithmic control. New governance models, old asymmetries. In: IC—Revista Científica de Información y Comunicación 16, Sevilla 2019, p. 183–208, here p. 186.
71 Milan, Stefania/Gutierrez, Miren: Technopolitics in the Age of Big Data. In: Networks, Movements and Technopolitics in Latin America, London 2018, p. 95–109.
72 Milan, Stefania, Data Activism as the New Frontier of Media Activism. In: Yang, Goubin; Pickard, Viktor (Eds.): Media Activism in the Digital Age, Oxford 2017, p. 151–163, here p. 153.
73 Sastre Domínguez/Gordo López 2019, p. 191.
74 Benjamin 2019, p. 304f.
75 More details about the project is available at http://www.hyphen-labs.com/nsaf.html

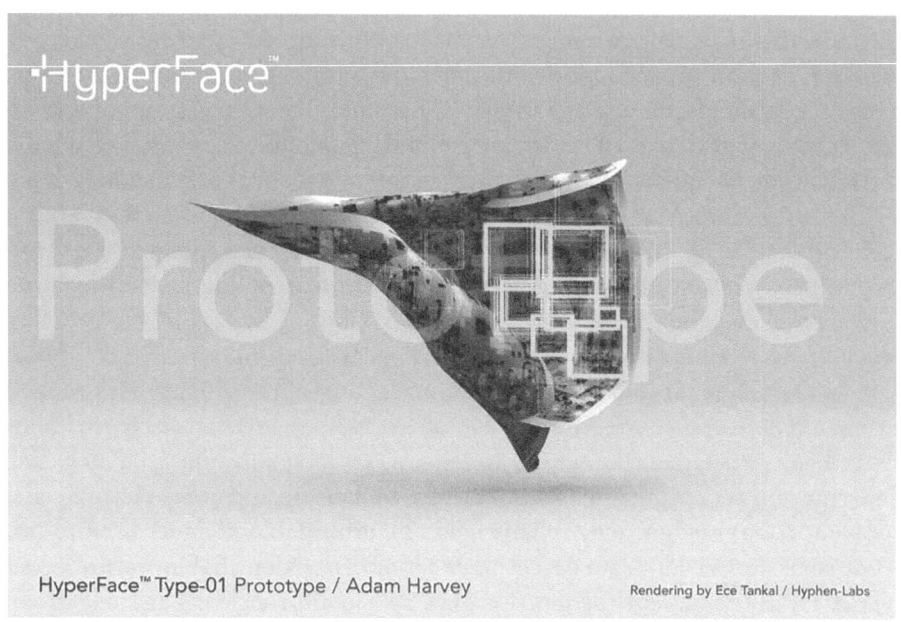

Figure 6—HyperFace prototype by Adam Harvey / ahprojects.com. Most of these pieces have been initially designed for the 'Viola-Jones' face detection algorithm and don't work as well on newer recognition software that use deep convolutional neural networks (DCNNs). Harvey, A. (2017) HyperFace False-Face Camouflage, Available at: https://ahprojects.com/hyperface/. Rendering by Ece Tankal / hyphen-labs.com.

Northeastern University, and IBM teamed up to create a T-shirt that fools AI software into not detecting and classifying the wearer as a person with a pattern on the shirt designed to manipulate just the right parts of a detection system's neural network to make it misidentify the wearer.[76]

But evasion from an algorithm can also be achieved differently: Camouflage fashion also combines makeup and hair styling, facial painting or other "aesthetic modifications, to create effective interference that renders the face unrecognizable or undetectable even to advanced computer [systems]".[77] In face recognition algorithms, contour information is one of the key factors and camouflages that interfere with the contour make feature extraction more difficult and often inaccurate. General rules for obfuscation include avoiding makeup that is amplifying key facial features but using one that contrasts the skin tone in unusual tones and directions, obscuring the region where nose, eyes, and forehead intersect, and partially obscuring the ocular regions as position and darkness of eyes and the nose is a key facial feature. Developing an asymmetrical look may also decrease the probability of being detected,[78] but evasion of facial recognition stays a cat-and-mouse game between detection and obfuscation.

Since a couple of years, there have also been numerous regulatory attempts to address surveillance concerns associated with biometrics—the measurement of unique biological characteristics, including data used in facial and affect recognition. In Europe, the Swedish government for example fined a school for its facial-recognition attendance registry as a violation of GDPR, and in France, the data protection authority declared it illegal to use facial recognition in schools based on privacy concerns.[79] Even Tim Cook, CEO of Apple Inc., recently jumped on the bandwagon decrying the emergence of what he called the data-industrial complex, describing "a vast and opaque industry that has arisen around the capture of massive amounts of personal data, often without the knowledge of users, which is then aggregat-

---

76　Quach Katyanna: Boffins don bad 1980s fashion to avoid being detected by object-recognizing AI cameras, https://www.theregister.com/2019/11/04/tshirt_ai_cameras (April 02, 2021).

77　Feng, Ranran; Prabhakaran, Balakrishnan: Facilitating fashion camouflage art. In: Proceedings of the 21st ACM international conference on Multimedia (MM '13). New York 2013, p. 793–802, here p. 793.

78　Harvey, Adam: Computer Vision Dazzle Camouflage, https://cvdazzle.com (January 29, 2021).

79　Crawford et al. 2019, p. 32.

ed and monetized and—at times—used for nefarious ends".[80] Where such self-regulation and lawmakers fail, community activism and creating public awareness through art is crucial to escape the fetishization of the upgrade culture in every parts of our lives.

While gadgets and wearable devices are becoming the new normal and optimization of our bodies in one way or the other a part of our everyday lives, it is important to find a good balance between both extremes of complete denial or reckless surrender—both personally and within the surrounding community. Algorithmic systems are here to stay and will continue to support, optimize and modify our bodies, opening up exciting opportunities for wellbeing, health and treatment of diseases. But as most systems are relatively new and developed in an unprecedented pace, ethical and global codes of conduct concerning algorithms are yet far from being perfect and hence a certain wariness towards data collection and training is a good advice. On a personal level, a good practice is to read at least the privacy statement of the fine print or trust external services such as 'Privacy Badger'[81] to gain an overview on how personal data is being handled by the company in question. Complete disobedience of all algorithmic services affecting our body seems on the one hand nearly impossible and is often painstakingly difficult, but gaining an overview of what people in exposed positions like journalists or representatives of minorities recommend is on the other hand a good way to implement some measures that can prevent excessive and maybe even unlawful collection of data. Looking at additional sources like the 'Digital Defense Playbook'[82]—a workbook that presents strategies individuals and organizations can use to evade detection and tracing—or the 'AI Incident Database'[83] can help to steer towards a healthy use of services of trust and shy away from others that are not handling privacy of user data well. Learning from previous incidents of algorithms may in general be the most powerful way to regulate the systems that track and dictate our bodies, as it is a living proof containing cases where algorithms have been harming groups or individuals. Current entries in listings like the 'AI Incident Database' or the project 'Where in the World is AI?'[84] range from Google offering arrest ads

[80] Baron, Zach: Tim Cook on Why It's Time to Fight the "Data-Industrial Complex", https://www.gq.com/story/apple-ceo-tim-cook-privacy-initiative (April 20, 2021).
[81] See 'Privacy Badger': https://privacybadger.org/
[82] See 'Our Data Bodies Tools', https://www.odbproject.org/tools/
[83] See 'Artificial Intelligence Incident Database', https://incidentdatabase.ai/
[84] See 'Where in the World is AI?', https://map.ai-global.org/

when searching for common names of Black people to Russia requesting Tinder to hand over data of the LGBTQ-community using the dating platform in Chechnya. With such activist projects, clear awareness of the possibilities and pitfalls of algorithmic control, and a healthy attitude towards algorithms, we can start to repress the great lie of individualist-consumerist culture to be able to improve our way to personal perfection and communal utopia, and contribute to consensual algorithmic data politics.[85] If we don't start now to think about the impact and possible consequences of the massively growing use of AI, our relationship with technology deployed for watching and analyzing us might stay a cat and mouse game, in which the ones deploying the code are always a step ahead. And if today's lawmakers don't protect the public against harmful AI, it will become increasingly difficult to catch up with such rapidly advancing technology as it can already be witnessed today in different parts of the world. Without a global consent and strategy about how we want to use and live with algorithmic control, we might face an increasingly tightened net of surveillance fed with data generated by our bodies day by day. In the wrong hands this could make our bodies soon become a product of code with people like Brad Smith, president at Microsoft, even warning that a "life as depicted in George Orwell's 1984 could come to pass in 2024".[86]

Literature

Alpaydin, Ethem: Machine Learning—The New AI. Cambridge 2016.

Amoore, Louise; Piotukh, Volha: Algorithmic Life. Calculative devices in the age of big data. Oxford 2015 (E-Book, Apple Books).

Ananny, Mike: Toward an Ethics of Algorithms: Convening, Observation, Probability, and Time-liness. In: Science, Technology, & Human Values 41, 2016, p. 93–117. DOI: https://doi.org/10.1177/0162243915606523

Baron, Zach: Tim Cook on Why It's Time to Fight the "Data-Industrial Complex". In: GQ, January 21, 2021, https://www.gq.com/story/apple-ceo-tim-cook-privacy-initiative (April 20, 2021).

---

85   Berry 2019, p. 48.
86   BBC News: Microsoft president—Orwell's 1984 could happen in 2024, https://www.bbc.com/news/technology-57122120 (June 01, 2021).

BBC News: Microsoft president: Orwell's 1984 could happen in 2024. In: BBC News, May 27, 2020, https://www.bbc.com/news/technology-57122120 (June 01, 2021).

Benjamin, Ruha: Race After Technology. New York 2019 (Apple Books E-Book Edition).

Berry, David M.: Against infrasomatization: towards a critical theory of algorithms. In: Bigo, Didier; Isin, Engin; Ruppert, Evelyn (Eds.): Data Politics: Worlds, Subjects, Rights, London 2019, p. 43–63. DOI: https://doi.org/10.1177/2053951717717749

Bregman, Rutger: Humankind: a hopeful history. New York 2020.

Broussard, Meredith: Artificial Unintelligence: How Computers Misunderstand the World. Cambridge 2018 (Apple Books E-Book Edition).

Brunton, Finn; Nissenbaum, Helen: Obfuscation: A User's Guide for Privacy and Protest. Cambridge 2015.

Buolamwini, Joy: How I'm fighting bias in algorithms. In: TED, November 2016, https://www.ted.com/talks/joy_buolamwini_how_i_m_fighting_bias_in_algorithms (January 22, 2021).

Coeckelbergh, Mark: AI Ethics. Cambridge 2020.

Colomina, Beatriz; Wigley, Mark: Are we human? notes on an archaeology of design. Zürich 2021.

Crawford, Kate et al.: AI Now 2019 Report. New York 2019, https://ainowinstitute.org/AI_Now_2019_Report.html (February 17, 2021).

Daley, Sam: 32 Examples of AI in Healthcare That Will Make You Feel Better About the Future. In: builtin, February 2021, https://builtin.com/artificial-intelligence/artificial-intelligence-healthcare (February 17, 2021).

Darwin Correspondence Project: The evolution of a misquotation. In: Darwin Correspondence Project, 2021, https://www.darwinproject.ac.uk/evolution-misquotation (January 20, 2021).

Duportail, Judith: I asked Tinder for my data. It sent me 800 pages of my deepest, darkest secrets. In: The Guardian, September 26, 2017, https://www.theguardian.com/technology/2017/sep/26/tinder-personal-data-dating-app-messages-hacked-sold (December 20, 2020).

ELIZA: Wikipedia, the free encyclopedia, https://en.wikipedia.org/wiki/ELIZA (March 05, 2021).

Etherington, Darrell: Mount Sinai study finds Apple Watch can predict COVID-19 diagnosis up to a week before testing. In: TechCrunch, February 09, 2021, https://techcrunch.com/2021/02/09/mount-sinai-study-finds-apple-watch-can-predict-covid-19-diagnosis-up-to-a-week-before-testing/ (February 10, 2021).

Eyigoz, Elif; Mathur, Sachin; Santamaria, Mar; Cecchi, Guillermo/Naylor, Melissa: Linguistic markers predict onset of Alzheimer's disease. In: EClinicalMedicine Volume 28, 100583, London 2020. DOI: https://doi.org/10.1016/j.eclinm.2020.100583

Feng, Ranran; Prabhakaran, Balakrishnan: Facilitating fashion camouflage art. In: Proceedings of the 21st ACM international conference on Multimedia (MM '13). New York 2013, p. 793–802. DOI: https://doi.org/10.1145/2502081.2502121

Fine Arts Museums of San Francisco: The Inverse Uncanny Valley: What We See When AI Sees Us | Benjamin Bratton. In: YouTube, February 11, 2021, https://www.youtube.com/watch?v=2E3kQqrHwqo (February 14, 2021).

FitBit: FitBit Privacy Policy. In: FitBit, https://www.fitbit.com/global/us/legal/privacy-policy (November 18, 2020).

Griffiths, Sarah: This AI software can tell if you're at risk from cancer before symptoms appear. In: WIRED, August 26, 2018, https://www.wired.co.uk/article/cancer-risk-ai-mammograms (February 03, 2021).

Harari, Yuval N.: Homo Deus—A Brief History of Tomorrow. London 2015.

Harvey, Adam; LaPlace, Jules: MegaPixels: Origins and Endpoints of Datasets Created "In The Wild". In: Exposing-AI, 2017–2020, https://megapixels.cc/megaface/ (December 14, 2020).

Harvey, Adam: Computer Vision Dazzle Camouflage. In: CVDazzle, June 2020, https://cvdazzle.com (January 29, 2021).

Hey Cortana. Hey Siri. Hey girl. In: The Atlantic, March 30, 2016, https://www.theatlantic.com/technology/archive/2016/03/why-do-so-many-digital-assistants-have-feminine-names/475884/ (April 02, 2021).

Hill, Kashmir: The Secretive Company That Might End Privacy as We Know It. In: The New York Times, January 18, 2020, https://www.nytimes.com/2020/01/18/technology/clearview-privacy-facial-recognition.html (February 11, 2021).

Horning, Rob: Hide and Seek: The Problem with Obfuscation. In: Los Angeles Review of Books, November 10, 2015, https://lareviewofbooks.org/article/hide-and-seek-the-problem-with-obfuscation/ (March 16, 2021).

Human Rights Watch: China: Big Data Program Targets Xinjiang's Muslims. In: HRW, December 12, 2020, https://www.hrw.org/news/2020/12/09/china-big-data-program-targets-xinjiangs-muslims (April 02, 2021).

Ito, Joichi: Resisting Reduction: A Manifesto. In: Journal of Design and Science, Cambridge 2017. DOI: https://doi.org/10.21428/8f7503e4.

Jahrmann, Margarethe. NEUROMATIC GAN PORTRAIT GAME: THE ARTIST IS MEASURED. In: Neuromatic Game Art, September 2020, https://neuromatic.uni-ak.ac.at/blog/eeg-stylegan-installation-at-parallel-vienna/ (February 15, 2021).

Kobie, Nicole: Google's reCAPTCHA test has been tricked by artificial intelligence. In: WIRED, March 25, 2019, https://www.wired.co.uk/article/google-captcha-recaptcha (April 02, 2021).

Kurzgesagt: In a Nutshell, How Large Can a Bacteria get? Life & Size 3. In: YouTube, November, 10, 2020, https://www.youtube.com/watch?v=E1KkQrFEl2I (January 22, 2021).

LaFrance, Adrienne: Why Do So Many Digital Assistants Have Feminine Names? Hey Cortana. Hey Siri. Hey girl., https://www.theatlantic.com/technology/archive/2016/03/why-do-so-many-digital-assistants-have-feminine-names/475884/ (April 02, 2021).

Lum, Jessica: "Racist" Camera Phenomenon Explained—Almost. In: PetaPixel, January 22, 2010, https://petapixel.com/2010/01/22/racist-camera-phenomenon-explained-almost/ (January 21, 2021).

Maldonado, Adran; Pistunovich, Natalie: GPT-3 Powers the Next Generation of Apps. In: Open AI, March 25, 2021, https://openai.com/blog/gpt-3-apps/ (March 27, 2021).

Manghani, Sunil: 'The art of Paolo Cirio'. In: Featherstone, Mike (Ed.): Theory, Culture & Society 34 (7–8), Thousand Oaks 2017, p. 197–214.

Milan, Stefania: Data Activism as the New Frontier of Media Activism. In: Yang, Goubin; Pickard, Victor (Eds.): Media Activism in the Digital Age, Oxford 2017, p. 151–163.

Milan, Stefania; Gutierrez, Miren: Technopolitics in the Age of Big Data. In: Caballero, F. Sierra; Gravante, Tommaso (Eds.): Networks, Movements and Technopolitics in Latin America, London 2018, p. 95–109.

Misseri, Lucas E.: Evantropia and Dysantropia: A Possible New Stage in the History of Utopias. In: Olkusz, Ksenia; Klosinski, Michal; Maj, Krzyztof M. (Eds.): More After More—Essays Commemorating the Five-Hundredth Anniversary of Thomas More's Utopia, Krakow 2016, p. 26–43.

Moll, Joana: The Dating Brokers: An autopsy of online love. In: Tactical Tech, 2018, https://datadating.tacticaltech.org/viz (November 14, 2020).

Nowak, Martin: Evolutionary Dynamics—Exploring the Equations of Life. Cambridge 2006.

Ockenden, Sasha: Skin Deep: Deep Fakes and Misinformation. In: DigitalDiplomacy—Medium, https://medium.com/digital-diplomacy/skin-deep-deep-fakes-and-misinformation-3c2f9cc59045. (December 16, 2020).

Pantenburg, Volker: Working images: Harun Farocki and the operational image. In: Eder, Jens; Klonk, Charlotte (Eds.): Image Operations: Visual media and political conflict, Manchester 2016, p. 49–62.

Ponsford, Matthew: IS YOUR DNA DATA SAFE IN BLACKSTONE'S HANDS? In: NEO.LIFE, January 28, 2021, https://neo.life/2021/01/is-your-dna-data-safe-in-blackstones-hands/ (January 28, 2021).

Quach, Katyanna: Boffins don bad 1980s fashion to avoid being detected by object-recognizing AI cameras. In: The Register, November 04, 2019, https://www.theregister.com/2019/11/04/tshirt_ai_cameras (April 02, 2021).

Sastre Domínguez, Paz; Gordo López, Ángel: Data activism versus algorithmic control. New governance models, old asymmetries. In: IC—Revista Científica de Información y Comunicación 16. Sevilla 2019, p. 183–208.

Scott-Railton, John: FitLeaking: When a FitBit blows your cover, https://www.johnscottrailton.com/fit-leaking/ (January 28, 2018).

Simonite, Tom: When It Comes to Gorillas, Google Photos Remains Blind. In: WIRED, November 01, 2018, https://www.wired.com/story/when-it-comes-to-gorillas-google-photos-remains-blind/ (November 17, 2020).

SR. RESEARCHER AT CITIZEN LAB: tracking threats against secure connectivity, January 28, 2018, https://www.johnscottrailton.com/fit-leaking/ (January 30, 2021).

Stefania, Milan: Data Activism as the New Frontier of Media Activism. In: Yang, Goubin; Pickard, Victor (Eds.): Media Activism in the Digital Age. Oxford 2016.

TED: Technology that knows what you're feeling | Poppy Crum. In: YouTube, July 10, 2018, https://www.youtube.com/watch?v=HW2SSoYteIs (March 14, 2021).

Van Noorden, Richard: The ethical questions that haunt facial-recognition research. In: Skipper, Magdalena; Maddox, John (Eds.): Nature, November 2020, Issue 587. Basingstoke 2020, p. 354–358. DOI: https://doi.org/10.1038/d41586-020-03187-3.

Velkova, Julia; Kaun, Anne: Algorithmic resistance: media practices and the politics of repair. In: Loader, Brian (Ed.): Information, Communication & Society, Volume 24, 2021—Issue 4, Oxford 2021, p. 523–540. DOI: https://doi.org/10.1080/1369118X.2019.1657162.

Velsinger, Antje: On Bodies and the Need to Appropriate Them. In: Hildebrandt, Paula et al. (Eds.): Performing Citizenship, London 2019, p. 77–90. DOI:10.1007/978-3-319-97502-3.

Voegeli, Fabian: Techniques of the Self in View of Potentiality. In: Zaharijevic, Adriana et al. (Eds.): Engaging Foucault, Belgrade 2015, p. 215–228.

Wachter-Boettcher, Sara: Technically Wrong. Sexist Apps, Biased Algorithms, and Other Threats of Toxic Tech. New York 2017.

Whittaker, Zach: A passwordless server run by spyware maker NSO sparks contact-tracing privacy concerns. In: TechCrunch, May 07, 2020, https://techcrunch.com/2020/05/07/nso-group-fleming-contact-tracing/ (March 12, 2021).

Wiener, Norbert: The Human Use Of Human Beings. London 1989.

Wolf, Gary: The Data-Driven Life. In: The New York Times Magazine, May 02, 2010, https://www.nytimes.com/2010/05/02/magazine/02self-measurement-t.html (December 12, 2020).

Zhao, Yiran: [BigDataSur-COVID] When Health Code becomes Health Gradient: Safety or Social Control? In: DATACTIVE—THE POLITICS OF DATA ACCORDING TO CIVIL SOCIETY, October 16, 2020, https://data-activism.net/2020/10/bigdatasur-covid-when-health-code-becomes-health-gradient-safety-or-social-control-2/ (December 03, 2020).

Carolin Höfler

The Lock Down City
and the Utopian Program
of Open Interfaces

Architectural Security Concepts

As a spatial-material and figurative configuration, architecture has always had major significance for aversion of hazards and the creation of security. Not only do buildings literally shield from external dangers, they impart experiences which can create feelings of security for the recipient. Architecture as a symbolic form of communication is traditionally marked by connotations which relate to stability and reliability. Looking at its conditions for production and creation, they are integrated in negotiation and decision processes in which security interests of individual social groups as well as of political and economic institutions are articulated.[1]

The present article takes this perspective and addresses current concepts and perceptions of urban security constituted and represented by specific types of architecture. The selected examples are significantly marked by the policy of internal and external security of the past two decades and they provide insight into what is regarded as a social threat. Here the issue will be explored as to whether and in which way they can be understood as being manifestations of a new security policy designated as "preemptive".[2] The policy of the preemptive presupposes that there are more and more existential, uncontrollable security threats which increasingly require security measures.[3] From this perspective almost all public spaces, urban infrastructures and buildings are declared security-critical zones and for this reason are to be planned and designed in such a way that they prevent the emergence of any potential risks, thereby eliminating the risk of damage from the start. Their materializations are regarded as speculation toward future risks of any kind.

Whereas façades and enclosures are being increasingly locked and fortified, new virtual barriers, whose marked effects remain invisible in many

---

[1] See Krause, Katharina: Sichtbar und sicher: Wohnhöfe des Adels in Münster in der ersten Hälfte des 18. Jahrhunderts, Politiken der Sicherheit 4, Baden-Baden 2018, p. 17–22 (Chapter "Die Fassade: Schnittstelle zwischen Wohngebäude und Straße").

[2] Albrecht, Hans-Jörg: Wandel der Sicherheit—Von präventiver zu präemptiver Sicherheit? Entwicklungen der Sicherheitspolitik in Systemen des öffentlichen Personentransports. In: Fischer, Susanne; Masala, Carlo (Eds.): Innere Sicherheit nach 9/11. Sicherheitsbedrohungen und (immer) neue Sicherheitsmaßnahmen? Wiesbaden 2016, p. 209–229, here p. 209.

[3] See Fischer, Susanne; Masala, Carlo: Die Politik der inneren Sicherheit nach 9/11. In: Eid. (Eds.): Innere Sicherheit nach 9/11. Sicherheitsbedrohungen und (immer) neue Sicherheitsmaßnahmen? Wiesbaden 2016, p. 1–9, here p. 5.

cases, are being created using GPS-controlled technologies. It is these extensions of building envelopes into multi-layer, overlapping systems out of structural and digital spatial barriers which shall be elucidated below. The architecture historian Dietrich Erben calls the façade a "means of social distancing"[4] which applies with greater account also to the hybrid limitation systems of current security architecture. Where the architectural envelope moreover becomes a support for digital monitoring images, distancing can reach the point of systematic intimidation. Image façades designed in this way then become means of social disciplining which are chiefly being re-discovered by authoritarian states.

In conclusion, the article elaborates an alternative interpretation which does not regard security and a sense of security as a condition or impression, but as an activity which is created through urban diversity, social encounters and human interaction in a public space. This interpretation of social-spatial security characterizes a series of contemporary architectural drafts which transform building envelopes into publicly walkable spaces. They take up concepts developed by the US urbanologist and architecture critic Jane Jacobs who blamed the disintegration of urban functions for an increasing degree of social insecurity and spatial dilapidation in the 1960s. Current Common-Spaces movements and Hybrid-Places projects indirectly resort to her controversial ideas and practices of informal social security. In this sense, the article discusses the relationship of *obedience* and *disobedience* in the conflict of physical-virtual control architecture on the one hand and intensively-used public urban spaces on the other hand. Requests for co-production of the city, for urban mixture of utilization and living neighborhoods are regarded as forms of criticism of post-democratic security obsessions. The article then concludes with the question as to what consequences the Jacobs' concept of an open, unpaved city has for the digitalization of the city: To what extent does it offer the opportunity of imagining a type of *smart city* which does not follow the interest of competitive and surveillance states and a few influential Internet companies but serves the common good, thereby creating security.

---

4   Erben, Dietrich: Zur Architektur der Frühen Neuzeit aus der Sicht der historischen Anthropologie. In: Schweizer, Stefan; Stabenow, Jörg (Eds.): Bauen als Kunst und historische Praxis. Architektur und Stadtraum zwischen Kunstgeschichte und Geschichtswissenschaft, vol. 2, Göttinger Gespräche zur Geschichtswissenschaft 26, Göttingen 2006, p. 461–492, here p. 472 (translated from German by the author).

Anticipation of Disaster

Whereas political enemies could be geographically pinpointed during the decades of the Cold War, current threats to industrial nations cannot be localized. Terrorism, organized crime and cyberattacks, but also risks such as financial crashes, climate change and pandemics lack any territorial definable profile, any nationality, they can emerge at any time and in any place. Although there was already mobilization against continuous, unforeseeable and undefined threats during the Cold War era, the vague fears were always aimed at external risks. A logical consequence of such threat scenarios was to move architecture below ground and to refrain from visible buildings as potential targets of attack.[5] The model *Nuke Proof Manhattan* (1969) by the architect and urban planner Oscar Newman showed the paradox which building as protection against external threats produced: An internal world submerged underground requires a fictional external world (Figure 1).[6] As protection against nuclear attacks on the densely populated big cities along the East Coast of the United States, Newman imagined a gigantic hollow sphere below Manhattan in which a modern city was built underneath an artificial sky dome. An idealized external world was part of the internal world and suggested the illusion of control over the environment and hence the mode of survival during the disaster. Even if the subterranean model of the world remained a utopia, it anticipated what Newman called "defensible space" in 1972.[7] In view of rising crime rates in the large-scale housing projects of the United States he developed the concept of the protective urban space with the hallmarks of territoriality, surveillance and control.

These concepts are also the basis for the safety narratives of contemporary urban development and architecture in Western societies.[8] National security institutions such as the United States Department of Homeland Security founded in 2002 or the Justice Department which invoke an exaggerated threat sensitivity by using ritual mantras such as "Don't be afraid,

---

[5] See Colomina, Beatriz: Domesticity at War, Cambridge, Mass. 2007, p. 279–283.
[6] See Newman, Oscar: Countdown for Small Towns. In: Esquire Magazine 73 (6), 1969, p. 180–187.
[7] See Newman, Oscar: Defensible Space: Crime Prevention Through Urban Design, New York 1972.
[8] See basically Graham, Stephen: Cities Under Siege: The New Military Urbanism, London and New York 2010.

be ready!"[9] or "The crisis [...] is right on our doorstep"[10] are ensuring their reemergence. Phenomena such as vagrant violence are included in the new global threats which can no longer be sufficiently contained by the control regimes in spite of preventive measures.[11] They have supplanted the figure of enemy nations and systems and thus the concept of clear enemy lines and identifiable enemies.[12] Accordingly, it is the risks coming from within society which are increasing and can emerge anywhere. Contemporary architecture intends to counter the alleged invisibility and non-locatable spatial presence of risk with the powerful image of fortress-like security buildings. As the threat to be averted becomes increasingly vaguer, architecture itself is becoming more and more a compact and well-visible object of defense. The need for security is vulnerable to authoritarian seduction.[13] First, all government architecture, in particular state departments, embassies or secret services, were built like citadels which in recourse to early modern fortress architecture not only constitute a functional, but a semantic armament.[14] At least since the 9-11 attacks many civilian buildings have also been transformed into armored protected buildings whose façades simultaneously operate as *tactical envelopes*, as the multi-layered, bulletproof and stab-proof protective vests for police and military are called.

9   Banner headline of a new U.S. Department of Homeland Security website unveiled as part of Tom Ridge's Get Ready program, 2003. See Brzezinski, Matthew: Fortress America: On the Front Lines of Homeland Security—An Inside Look at the Coming Surveillance State, New York 2004, p. 103.
10 Barr, William, quoted from: Oval Office: Remarks by President Trump on the National Security and Humanitarian Crisis on our Southern Border, March 15, 2019, https://trumpwhitehouse.archives.gov/briefings-statements/remarks-president-trump-national-security-humanitarian-crisis-southern-border-2/ (June 1, 2021).
11 See Heitmeyer, Wilhelm: Kontrollverluste. Zur Zukunft der Gewalt. In: Heitmeyer, Wilhelm; Soeffner, Hans-Georg (Eds.): Gewalt. Entwicklungen, Strukturen, Analyseprobleme, Frankfurt am Main 2004, p. 86–106.
12 See Albrecht 2016, p. 210.
13 See Heitmeyer, Wilhelm: Autoritäre Versuchungen. Signaturen der Bedrohung 1, Berlin 2018, p. 10–11.
14 See Moos, Stanislaus von: Turm und Bollwerk. Beiträge zu einer politischen Ikonographie der italienischen Renaissancearchitektur, Zurich and Freiburg i. Br. 1974.

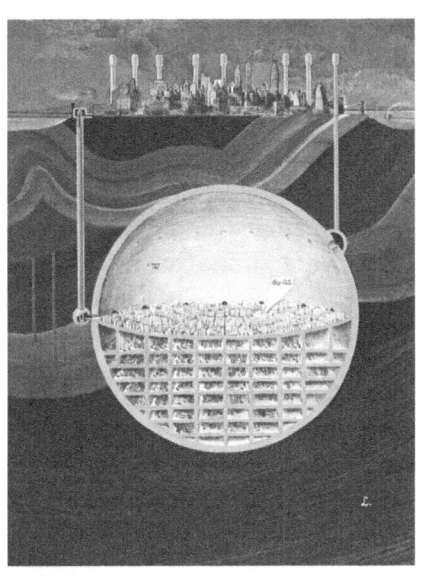

Figure 1—Oscar Newman, Nuke Proof Manhattan, 1969. Sectional perspective.
In: Esquire Magazine 73 (6), 1969, p. 187.

Figure 2—David Childs (SOM), One World Trade Center, New York, 2003–2014. Photo:
Luigi Novi, 2012, https://de.wikipedia.org/wiki/Datei:4.28.12FreedomTowerByLuigiNovi5.jpg
(June 1, 2021).

Carolin Höfler

Massive Distancing

The skyscraper of the *One World Trade Center* in New York proved to be a manifestation of the new security paradigms in the recent past. The most noticeable building protection precautions includes the almost sixty-meter high, windowless concrete base, whose steel-titanium mix is intended to withstand even the most powerful explosions (**Figure 2**). The glass cladding is unable to hide the bunker-like impression given by the building. The architecture critic of the New York Times, Nicolai Ouroussoff, presciently revealed the new landmark as a "barricaded fortress", which "speaks of paranoia"[15] — as architecture of trauma, embodiment of fear of attacks: "It announces to terrorists: Don't attack here—we're ready for you. Go next door."[16]

Since the globalization of threats and the corresponding loss of control, Western governments, institutions and companies have been advised by military experts, security companies and the police on the protection of their buildings.[17] Whereas in the 1980s and 1990s the technical security recommendations were initially limited to improvement of measures for prevention of crime such as steel grids in front of the windows, heavy gates and surveillance cameras, its impact has been increasing massively over the last 20 years. Its preventive measures aim less at retrofitting and more at the advance planning of buildings. They are implemented through a specific shaping and materialization of the architecture and its externally oriented surfaces instead of through visible defense facilities. When terrorists successfully drove a truck loaded with propane gas cans through the glass doors of Glasgow Airport in 2007, setting the terminal on fire, the UK government published guidelines for architects, planners and builders for securing new buildings with a high degree of symbolic content. They demanded that new government administration and bank buildings, commercial properties as well as public

---

15   Ouroussoff, Nicolai: A Tower That Sends a Message of Anxiety, Not Ambition. In: The New York Times, February 19, 2007, https://www.nytimes.com/2007/02/19/arts/design/19towe.html (June 1, 2021).

16   Ouroussoff, Nicolai: An Appraisal: A Tower of Impregnability, the Sort Politicians Love. In: The New York Times, June 30, 2005, https://www.nytimes.com/2005/06/30/nyregion/an-appraisal-a-tower-of-impregnability-the-sort-politicians-love.html (June 1, 2021).

17   See Pawley, Martin: Phantomsicherheit. In: Bruyn, Gerd de; Hundsdörfer, Daniel; Markov, Iassen et al. (Eds.): 5 Codes. Architektur, Paranoia und Risiko in Zeiten des Terrors, Basel, Boston, and Berlin 2006, p. 208–211, here p. 210.

institutions be moved back 50 meters from the street. In the case of more than two stories, brick-built façades were to be refrained from and windows were to be reduced to an maximum area of three square meters.[18] The new headquarters of the German Federal Bureau of Investigation in Berlin-Mitte is an impressive example of the conscious implementation of such architectural measures against transnational security threats (Figure 3).[19] In contrast to its predecessor in the Bavarian city of Pullach, which was shielded behind high walls and optically inconspicuous, the new building in Berlin with its cohesive base area and its monumental, rigidly structured concrete cube provides visible proof of its alleged impregnableness.

The adaptation of the architecture to potential threat scenarios is increasingly also determining every-day buildings without any symbolic power such as office and commercial buildings or residences. They are also given monolithic concrete or steel framing to withstand the force of an explosion. Terraces and other protruding parts which are accessible to uninvited guests are avoided. Inner courtyards and shafts instead of windows on the outer walls provide light. All niches, openings and stairwells on the outside vanish, as they could be used as hiding places for bombs. The number of potential access ways to the building is limited, making it easier to lock it up entirely at any time.

Non-Public Walls

Through such security measures a building becomes a freestanding, cohesive property without a façade. Its exterior is in no way a "public wall" pointing to the "city interior" and "expressing something that connects both sides," as the architectural theorist Fritz Neumeyer defines the façade based

---

18   See Wainwright, Oliver: Fortress London: The New US Embassy and the Rise of Counter-Terror Urbanism. In: Harvard Design Magazine 42, S/S 2016, http://www.harvarddesignmagazine.org/issues/42/fortress-london-the-new-us-embassy-and-the-rise-of-counter-terror-urbanism (June 1, 2021).

19   See Maak, Niklas: Architektur der BND-Zentrale. Kämpfen gegen das Unsichtbare. In: Frankfurter Allgemeine Zeitung, April 26, 2014, https://www.faz.net/aktuell/feuilleton/kaempfen-gegen-das-unsichtbare-die-architektur-der-neuen-bnd-zentrale-12911768.html (June 1, 2021).

Figure 3—Jan Kleihues, Headquarters of the Federal Intelligence Service, Berlin, 2005–2019. Photo: Soeren Stache, AFP via Getty Images, 2014.

Figure 4—Robert Konieczny/KWK Promes, Safe House, near Warsaw, 2004–2008. Photos, https://www.kwkpromes.pl/en/safe-house/2248, Fig. 12 and 16 (June 1, 2021).

The Lock Down City and the Utopian Program of Open Interfaces

on Albertis *frons aedis*.[20] Instead, the bare, not clearly structured exteriors of the new security architecture point to an open, unstructured urban space, provoking a sense of forlornness and insecurity. They create spaces which are meant for running through, passing through and leaving quickly, but not for lingering. Without collateral spatial surfaces edging the public space of the city a "sense of belonging, a collective experience, a sense of unity" is lost, which can produce a feeling of identity and security.[21] It could be said bluntly that the loss of the façade as a means of social integration is not only the consequence of a new security policy of *post-democracy*, but simultaneously also it cause.[22] The overwhelming feeling of insecurity caused by complex global threat scenarios is to be countered by a type of architecture which shuts itself off in defense from the outside world or even opposes it with animosity. Its exteriors are reduced to mere tactical surfaces of visual security communication. Separated from its spatial-functional body, the façade is equipped with the symbolism of isolation, which transforms the architecture into a security icon.

The absurd radicalization of this kind of security mentality is manifested in the single-family house with the descriptive title of *Safe House* built by the Polish architect Robert Konieczny near Warsaw (**Figure 4**).[23] Mobile exteriors controlled via electric engines can transform the two-storey low rise building into a bunker with the press of a button. But first impressions are deceptive: The over dimensional strong exteriors merely consist of a steel frame filled in with mineral fiber and are thus not bulletproof. In this sense, the *Safe*

---

20 Neumeyer, Fritz: Was ist eine Fassade? Lernen von Leon Battista Alberti. In: Mäckler, Christoph (Ed.): Stadtbaukunst: Die Fassade, catalog for Dortmund architecture days and exhibition, no. 12 (Dortmunder U—Center for Arts and Creativity, 2010), Dortmunder Architekturheft 23, Dortmund 2011, p. 86–102, here p. 89–90 and p. 97 (translated from German by the author).

21 Neumeyer 2011, p. 89 (translated from German by the author).

22 With the term "post-democracy" the British political scientist Colin Crouch popularized the ongoing discussion about a crisis of Western democracies in 2004. The loss of sovereignty of states in view of complex global challenges and the transfer of political decisions to superordinate organizations leads to a dismantling of democratic standards according to Crouch, invoking an extensive collective sense of insecurity. See Crouch, Colin: Post-Democracy, Themes for the 21st Century Series, Cambridge, UK 2004.

23 See Schmidt, Urte: "Safe House" bei Warschau. Wandelbare Festung. In: Baunetz Wissen. Sicherheitstechnik, http://www.baunetzwissen.de/objektartikel/Sicherheitstechnik-Safe-House-quot-bei-Warschau-PL_1060461.html (June 1, 2021).

House is less a protective building than a parody of a safety obsession which has disclosed the distance between the societal elites and the less privileged.

In different dimensions and scales the new types of security architecture embody a new "fortress culture," as already described by the art historian Otto Karl Werckmeister in the 1980s in his eponymous book.[24] He uses the fortress as a metaphor for a contemporary culture which expresses itself in a continuous crisis awareness. The fortress culture acknowledges social crisis, but does not contribute to its solution. Instead, it stabilizes and normalizes it. In this sense, precisely by stressing its absolute security architecture can exacerbate the feeling of insecurity. Moreover, the fortified steel concrete walls are a constant reminder of an attack on the one hand and on the other hand they let the surroundings fall into neglect to the extent that crime and in particular fear of crime increase. The structural build-up can even induce the anticipated threat scenario by garnering the attention of potential burglars and attackers in the first place. As anticipated by the architectural theorist Martin Pawlyey, preventive security measures terminate in "architecture without style," with a low degree of identifiability.[25] The lack of experience of the architecture consolidates the feeling of unease.

But it is precisely the seemingly styleless, functional buildings which are desired by military planners in order to be able to assess the threat scenario of urban operations more optimally. Buildings with simple structure exteriors are ideal for these operations, as they facilitate the assessment of the inner structure and function. In contrast, style collages of postmodern buildings manifesting a conscious conflict between the exterior and interior prove to be problematic.[26]

Unbroken Lines

In order to counter the inevitable neglect of architecture and urban space the US Embassy on the outskirts of London opened in 2018 seemed to usher in a paradigm shift of structural security design. Simultaneous with the start of planning the US Embassy in Baghdad was completed, which

---

24 See Werckmeister, Otto Karl: Zitadellenkultur. Über die schöne Kunst des Untergangs in den achtziger Jahren, München 1989.
25 Pawley 2006, p. 211 (translated from German by the author).
26 See Kripa, Ersela; Mueller, Stephen: Fronts: Military Urbanisms and the Developing World, New York 2020, p. 74–77.

followed the old type of fortress architecture in an even more intense form through an isolated facility the size of an urban district (**Figure 5**). The new embassy in London countered this sample of *standard embassy design*[27] of the Bush government, calling for openness and transparency as a glass cube (**Figure 6**).[28] But the new, allegedly airy glass building only operates with visual signals of transparency and accessibility. The glass walls enveloping the cube are 15-centimeters thick and consist of a complicated construction of laminated plates intended to withstand the most powerful explosives. Moreover, the glass envelope constitutes only one of several defense rings. Additional protective measures are concealed in the artificial landscape in which the building is embedded. Following the type of a Medieval tower hill castle the 60-meter-high building stands upon an elevation, removed 30 meters from the next street and surrounded by a ditch. Supporting walls and low walls as well as plant pots and yew hedges reinforced with steel and concrete bollards form additional rings are meant to stop driving trucks. Such barriers are transferred from the surfaces of the building to the surrounding zone, with the urban space increasingly becoming an association of monitored fortress islands.

On the basis of Alberti, Robert Venturi and Colin Rowe Neumeyer stresses the necessity of a multi-layer façade: Only through spatial layering and overlayering can the façade be opened and, in this way, generate an association with the surrounding space, he argues.[29] Through overlayering the façade becomes a medium of exchange with which inner structures of the building are brought to the exterior. This creates new types of intermediate zones which interact with the public space. However, in the case of contemporary types of architecture the layering principle has a contrary function. It acts as material optimization of risk aversion and symbolic representation of power and cohesion.

---

27 See Houseal, Ian: Contemporary Embassy Planning: Designing in an Age of Terror, Master's Project, University of North Carolina, Department of City and Regional Planning, Chapel Hill, 2007, p. 53, https://core.ac.uk/download/pdf/210605264.pdf (June 1, 2021); American Institute of Architects: Best Practices: Adapting Standard Embassy Design to Specific Sites, contributed by the U.S. Department of State and the U.S. General Services Administration, June 4, 2005 (revised May 2007); Bureau of Overseas Building Operations, United States Department of State: Standard Embassy Design.

28 See Wainwright 2016.

29 See Neumeyer 2010, p. 95 and p. 98–99.

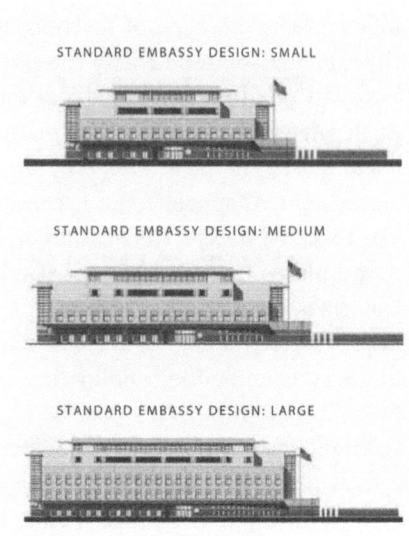

Figure 5—Bureau of Overseas Building Operations, United States Department of State, Standard Embassy Design (SED) prototypes, 2007. Renderings, https://core.ac.uk/download/pdf/210605264.pdf, p. 53, Fig. 3.10 (June 1, 2021).

Figure 6—Kieran Timberlake, US Embassy, London, 2010–2017. Photo: Justin Tallis, AFP via Getty Images, 2017.

The prototype of a modern, multi-layered security architecture type is the Pentagon, headquarters of the US Department of Defense (Figure 7). Each side of the pentagonal monumental building consists of five parallel building rows, the "rings," which indicate the hostility of the exterior space. The contemporary concept of a security façade also thinks along the lines of layers, even if the physical surface of a building is expanded through virtual and dynamic borders. As the targets of risk aversion are becoming increasingly mobile and vaguer, physical immobile façades and barriers seem to be of only limited usefulness now. Of course, buildings exhibited today are still protected by fortified exteriors. But it is becoming more and more frequent for moveable and reversible facilities to replace the former enclosures and protective walls. The programming of constantly shifting spatial limits and orders thus stands for another paradigm shift of the architectural security concept. What started as a visible line of reinforced building envelopes and their fortification ring of walls, bollards and strategic planting with *Rambo bushes*[30] has gradually dissolved into a nigh invisible borderline consisting of AI-capacity surveillance cameras, motor vehicle license plates recognition and facial recognition software, as well as virtual geographic boundaries. Such measures aim at the destabilization of spatial boundaries and the identification of invaders.

Virtual Enclosures

Geofencing is defined as a technology which uses the GPS coordinates or RFID signals to draw a virtual boundary in the space and on the basis of this boundary to automatically trigger specific actions. People as well as objects can be located within a geofence. Where this technology is used, the objective is not to fix an area permanently, but to create a possibility of changing the secured area at any time. The virtual security boundaries can be shifted constantly and flexibly adapted to the extent that depending on the threat scenario open and closed zones of a building or city can be separated from each other. The changes of the virtual spatial limitations need not take place covertly, their overt implementation constitutes an essential security component. Whether visible or invisible, the primary objective is to take away control over time and space from potential attackers, to take away their ori-

---

30 Young, Lauren: The Hidden Security Bugs in Architecture That You Never Noticed. In: Atlas Obscura, June 24, 2016, https://www.atlasobscura.com/articles/the-hidden-security-bugs-in-architecture-that-you-never-knew-about (June 1, 2021).

entation and to interrupt their routines. Constriction of the opponent's spatial scope of movement as well as the uninterrupted and direct localization of any suspicious target object is more important than the continuous threat aversion through physical, fortified surfaces. Instead of reacting to an external enemy with defensive architecture, each building and every location is now to be able to be transformed into a potential scenario for operations for maintenance of security and order.

The notion of elastic geofence sectors to which specific rules for intervention are attributed, can be traced back to the military-geographical concept of *kill box* developed in the early 1990s (**Figure 8**).[31] The *kill box* can be conceived of as a transparent cube of modulable size placed on an orthogonal grid field, adapted to a three-dimensional, global geodetic reference system. With this cube a battlefield is defined which can be demarcated flexibly with regard to time and space.[32] The direct purpose of a *kill box* is to authorize the air force to set up temporary battle zones and to carry out short-notice attacks against identified target objects, without having to coordinate further with the command level.[33] Every cube is declared an autonomous operation zone for those battle units in whose area of responsibility it falls. With the kill box the scene of armed conflict is re-defined as a global mobile location. In the perspective of this military concept civilian buildings and places also become dynamic surveillance and attack zones. With systems such as *geofencing*, the zones become concrete, as the virtual boundaries are not only for the purpose of flexible division of the city ground into spatial and organizational areas but act as real barriers within the physical space which trigger actions to limit movement where they are exceeded.

---

31   See Air Land Sea Application Center: Kill Box: Multi-Service Tactics, Techniques and Procedures for Kill Box Employment, Field Manual 3-09.34, August 2009, p. I-1, https://info.publicintelligence.net/fm3_09×34.pdf (June 1, 2021).

32   See MacGregor, James W.: Bringing the Box into Doctrine: Joint Doctrine and the Kill Box, School of Advanced Military Studies, United States Army Command and General Staff College Fort Leavenworth, Kansas, 2004, p. 43–44, https://apps.dtic.mil/sti/pdfs/ADA429320.pdf (June 1, 2021).

33   See Air Land Sea Application Center 2009, p. I-1.

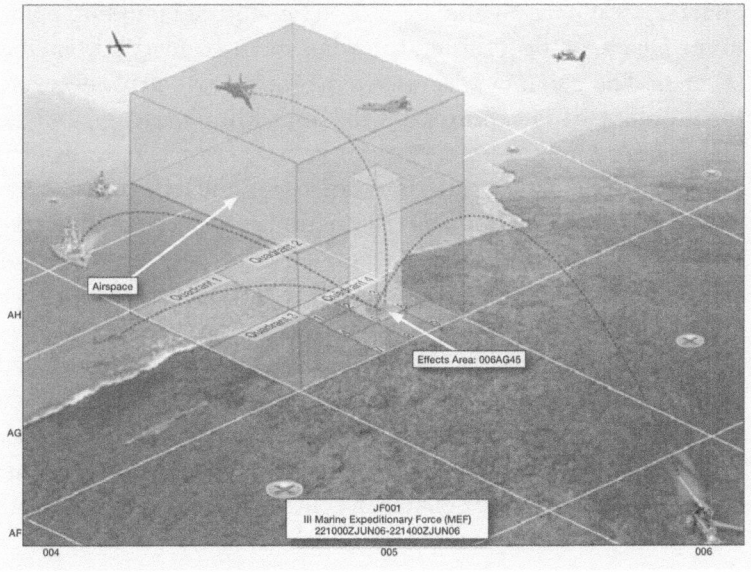

Figure 7—George Bergstrom and David J. Witmer, The Pentagon, headquarters of the United States Department of Defense, Arlington, VA, 1941–1943. Photo: Digital Vision, Getty Images.

Figure 8—Three-dimensional representation of the U.S. Air Force Kill Box system, 2008. Rendering. In: Fires Bulletin, March-April 2008, p. 39.

Predictive Architecture

When threats can emerge at anytime and anywhere security planning faces the question of how buildings and public spaces can be monitored so as to prevent incidents of damage before they occur. The answer to this is provided by *remote guarding*, a security system that combines AI-based video cameras, real time functions such as personal and vehicle recognition, facial recognition and people counting with alarm systems, surveillance centers and security services. Using this intelligent remote surveillance, suspicious incidents, characteristics or behavioral patterns are to be determined and prevented via live contact with the perpetrator. If someone lounges about for too long at the entrance of a building the system sends an alarm to the surveillance headquarters which replies with a customized loudspeaker warning such as, "You in the blue shirt, please leave,"[34] explains Ken Young of the US company Edgeworth Security. Where an unidentified person exceeds a virtual limit, AI-capacity security systems send an alarm to the police headquarters.[35] Where an employee of the monitored building uploads an image of the façade to the Internet, the Edgeworth-security system marks it within seconds, and the image is removed. Every movement, every activity in the monitored area is captured by the algorithm-based systems and analyzed and assessed in real-time. The pre-defined criteria on which the algorithms are based are mostly guided by stereotypes and external features such as ethnicity, religion or national origin, making the monitored spatial boundaries into means of racial discrimination.

Sound recognition systems ultimately perfect the total remote surveillance. A network of microphones is fixed to the façades or in the surveillance cameras. *ShotSpotter* of the eponymous Californian company is capable of identifying shooting sounds, locating these, specifying the most probable type of weapon used and of automatically sending all this information to the relevant police departments.[36] *FlexZone,* a fence-mounted sensor system by the Canadian company Senstar in contrast detects any attempt to cut, climb

---

34 Sullivan, Paul: Can Artificial Intelligence Keep Your Home Secure? In: The New York Times, June 29, 2018, https://www.nytimes.com/2018/06/29/your-money/artificial-intelligence-home-security.html (June 1, 2021).
35 See Sullivan 2018.
36 See ShotSpotter, https://www.shotspotter.com/ (June 1, 2021).

The Lock Down City and the Utopian Program of Open Interfaces

over or otherwise get around a fence.[37] Potentially, the environments can be filtered and evaluated by such systems also with regard to other sounds, snatches of conversations or keywords, with the consequence that the surveillance mechanisms can be expanded to previously uncontrolled areas.

In combination with virtual enclosures, this extensive form of surveillance aims at increasing the potential for threat aversion of exterior walls and enclosures. At the same time the technology can be used independent of physical building façades or property boundaries in order to define and control flexible virtual activity zones with limited accessibility. This is perhaps their most important objective, viz. to divide up the city into an "endless series of securitized passage points (either visible or invisible)".[38]

Ultimately, the aim of the new security architecture types is to "come before the event" using the technology, i.e., to be one step ahead of attackers and invaders to a certain extent. The connection and assessment of diverse data as recorded by police departments, private security providers and biotechnology companies are playing an increasing role in this context. Just recently, such a connection of different data sources and applications was able to be disclosed in the case of the US start-up Clearview AI. The company produces facial recognition software with which it has already stored over three billion images of human faces and their profile data from freely accessible websites and platforms such as Facebook, YouTube or Instagram. Numerous US departments and security services have already used this technology for identification and prosecution of suspects.[39] Connected with the AI-controlled surveillance systems in buildings and in the public space, possible whereabouts and other suspicious acts by these suspects can be identified.

The objective of a similar algorithmic panopticon is also the connection of intelligent surveillance systems by private security companies with procedures of *predictive policing*, a data analytical forecast technology for supporting police preventive work which has been widespread primarily in

---

37 See Senstar: FlexZone: Locating Fence-Mounted Intrusion Detection Sensor, 2020, https://senstar.com/products/fence-sensors/flexzone/ (June 1, 2021).

38 Graham, Stephen, quoted from: Lobe, Adrian: Bedrohte Stadt. In: Neue Zürcher Zeitung, November 24, 2015, https://www.nzz.ch/feuilleton/kunst_architektur/bedrohte-stadt-1.18651386 (June 1, 2021) (translated from German by the author).

39 See Hill, Kashmir: The Secretive Company That Might End Privacy as We Know It. In: The New York Times, January 18, 2020, https://www.nytimes.com/2020/01/18/technology/clearview-privacy-facial-recognition.html (June 1, 2021).

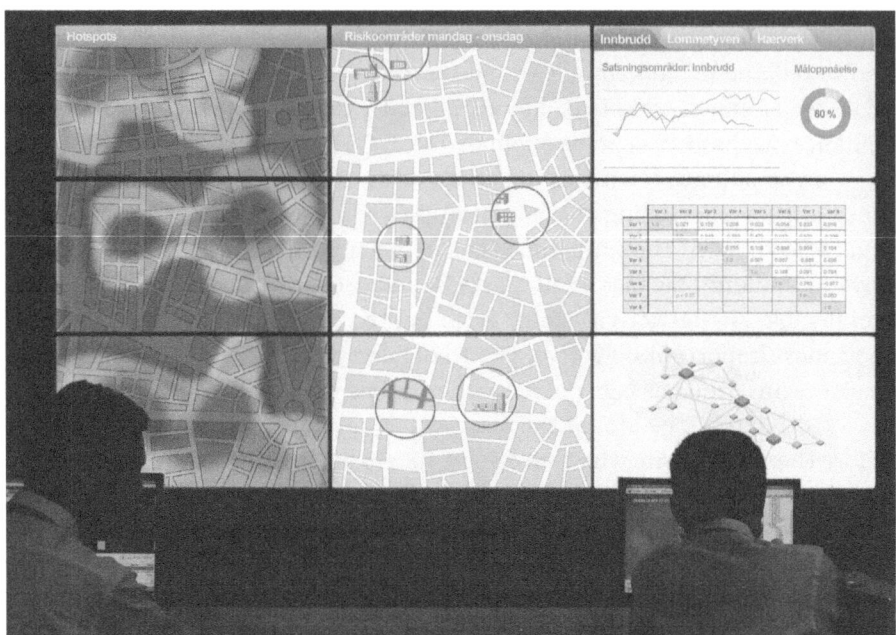

Figure 9—Predictive policing systems identifying hotspots where crime risk is the highest, Norway. Illustration: Birgitte Blandhoel, 2013, http://volta.pacitaproject.eu/big-data/ (June 1, 2021).

Figure 10—Blacklisted debtor displayed on a LED screen, Taishan city, Guangdong, China. Photo: Taishan Government via WeChat, 2018, https://theconversation.com/chinas-social-credit-system-puts-its-people-under-pressure-to-be-model-citizens-89963 (June 1, 2021).

the US since the early 2010s (**Figure 9**).⁴⁰ Within the scope of preventive police work probabilities for the incidence of a crime at specific locations at specific times are calculated, in order to respond with the corresponding police measures. But not only in police work, but also in the private security industry predictive analytics tools are used. They provide legitimacy to use of even more limitation and monitoring systems in areas with a high risk for victimization of places and people which take advantage of all possibilities of data collection and information processing. In this way, the protective function of architecture is ultimately outsourced to major security companies.

Gradually, AI-capacity systems decouple themselves from the sensory perception of concrete material spaces and impact the use and experience of buildings and urban spaces with a high degree of intensity. The American sociologist and design theorist Benjamin H. Bratton accurately described this phenomenon with the model of a stack: In his book *The Stack* from 2016, he explores a new governing architecture in the form of a globally comprising stack of digital systems linked to each other seamlessly penetrating all areas of social life, a coherent, constantly changing megastructure whose engine is the digital economy.⁴¹ Physical-material or territorial boundaries have become useless in this megastack.

Visual Pillories

In such a space in which the architecture is increasingly de-architecturalized, the façade is being re-discovered as the tactical surface of visual deterrence communication. Thus, for example, in authoritarian states such as China it is becoming a flat image screen which turns the building into a type of modern pillory and the city into an open-air movie theater for public sanctioning. With the Chinese social credit system, a totalitarian, omni-surveillance system regulating behavior is being pushed entirely over social life and organizes the public space in the form of visual mega-symbols. People who break the rules are shamed by having high-resolution portraits projected on giant LED screens on façades together with their surname and part of

---

40   See Knobloch, Tobias: Vor die Lage kommen: Predictive Policing in Deutschland, Gütersloh 2018, p. 9–10, https://www.bertelsmann-stiftung.de/fileadmin/files/BSt/Publikationen/GrauePublikationen/predictive.policing.pdf (June 1, 2021).

41   See Bratton, Benjamin H.: The Stack: On Software and Sovereignty, Cambridge, Mass. 2016, p. 52–55.

Figure 11—Images of jaywalkers displayed on a screen at a crossroad equipped with cameras and facial recognition technology, Xiangyang, China. Photo: Gilles Sabrié, 2018, https://www.nytimes.com/2018/07/24/business/dealbook/china-facial-recognition.html (June 1, 2021).

Figure 12—MvRdV, Expo 2000 Netherlands Pavilion, Hannover, 2000. Photo, https://architizer.com/projects/expo-2000-netherlands-pavilion/ (June 1, 2021).

their personal ID number (Figure 10). This type of programmed media façades acts both as sanctioning and prevention systems aimed at protection against internal enemies of the state. The nightmarish scenarios are embedded in a collection of advertising signs and blips, which cover the principal fronts of commercial buildings in the megacities of China. Thus, the public parading of delinquents on electronic screens is part of the urban entertainment of the consumer and leisure society.

In a cynical way, the Chinese *walls of shame* invert the idea of the façade as public wall. They are tools of public sanctioning and simultaneously function as supporters of advertising messages, whereby they reach a new climax in the militarization of the urban.[42] Instead of signaling accessibility and referring to a common space, the façade equipped with surveillance technology can be regarded as a means of government power through which every action can be recorded, assessed, rewarded or punished. This applies both to freestanding fortifications as well as to freely hanging screens in the space. In both cases the façade is reduced to a tactical, defensive or disciplining envelope.

Security-promising contemporary architecture spans itself equally between two poles. One pole is architecture that has the goal of making itself invisible. It blends itself with the surroundings in the form of glass or mirror façades, low walls or hedges or is even completely virtual and nigh immaterial. The other pole is occupied by such architecture which captivates the eye and intends to defeat the threat in this way. They suggest strength with traditional symbols of stability or triumph over the breach of rules with theatrical symbols. In both cases the architecture becomes an effective medium of appeasement rhetoric in culture of insecurity marked by authoritarianism which mutes as well as stokes fears.

Eyes on the Street

Given the collective security obsession in authoritarian and neoliberal systems the question of counter-concepts creating a sense of security other than through isolation, surveillance and public sanctioning must be posed. A look back at unconventional ideas of crime prevention in the 1960s can be

---

42   The entanglement of consumption and pillory can be seen in the screens placed at the crossings in Xiangyang on which pedestrians are shown jaywalking (Figure 11). Such roadside screens are customarily used for digital outdoor advertising.

helpful in this context.⁴³ In her book *Death and Life of Great American Cities* from 1961, the American architecture critic Jane Jacobs pointed to the concept of informal, voluntary social control, which is activated by the invigoration of public spaces. With her vision of urban society as an institution of informal social control she counters the argument that criminal acts and fear of crime can be reduced by greater police presence. Instead, with her mantra "eyes on the street"⁴⁴ Jacobs propagated a coherent security concept for the social space according to which co-determination and autonomy of the urban society are to be encouraged in order to reduce surveillance of urban areas by police departments. The prerequisite for this is urban diversity which causes an intensive use of public spaces. Appropriation and social production of urban spaces in turn guarantee a high degree of social control and contribute to the security of streets and places. According to Jacobs, functional socially mixed urban areas are also safer because they encourage contacts, thus strengthening the identification of the urban users with their surroundings. These ideas are currently being re-discovered within the context of debates on *smart cities:* To bring back human presence in urban spaces offering numerous automated services and products, is regarded as one of the most significant security measures in future digital cities.⁴⁵

Walkable Façades

Looking at contemporary experimental architecture and its façades, it can be observed that it indirectly resorts to Jacobs' idea of informal social control by integrating public uses in spacious and walkable building envelopes. At first glance, the new buildings look as if they had rid themselves of the protective, closed façade. Whereas hitherto fortified façades had separated exterior and interior like a cut, and the private from the public, in the

---

43   See Schubert, Dirk: "Open City"—From "Eyes on the Street" to "Zero Tolerance". Jane Jacobs' Visionen einer sichereren Stadt. In: Häfele, Joachim; Sack, Fritz; Eick, Volker et al. (Eds.): Sicherheit und Kriminalprävention in urbanen Räumen. Aktuelle Tendenzen und Entwicklungen, Wiesbaden 2016, p. 47–68, here p. 48.

44   Jacobs, Jane: The Death and Life of Great American Cities, New York 1961, p. 54.

45   See Johnston, Elizabeth: Wir haben Jane Jacobs' Grundkonzept vergessen. Im Gespräch mit Brigitte Schultz. In: Bauwelt 6, 2017, StadtBauwelt 213, p. 18–23, here p. 23.

new buildings they seem to dissolve in favor of open, accessible labyrinths.[46] The façade as a cut in space is declared obsolete. Instead, it becomes a material interface, a transition medium between interior and exterior. Private and public space are no longer separated by walls and doors but by an open structure with a number of uses and simultaneously connected to each other. The building then starts with a deep room in which guest and host, service provider and customer, stranger and resident meet and interact.[47] The question as to how far one can enter the building is not decided with space-separating walls but is re-negotiated every time.

A prototype precursor of such open buildings was the Netherlands Pavilion by the Rotterdam architecture firm MvRdV at the World Expo in Hanover from 2000 (**Figure 12**).[48] Winy Maas, Jacob van Rijs and Nathalie de Vries stacked Dutch symbol landscapes on top of each other in an eight-storey building without external walls and organized the levels as volume with diverse height scales and fluid spatial connections. Their architecture paved the way for the idea of verticalization of the public space which twenty years later was picked up again by the architectural office querkraft in Vienna: In their current design for an Ikea building the architects suggest a simple building box surrounded by a spatial frame with public uses and which closes on top with a souk-like roof garden (**Figure 13**).

Even more radically, the Iranian architect Farshad Mehdizadeh pursues the idea of the publicly useable building envelope: In Tehran he re-builds an unsuccessful nine-storey shopping center by enveloping it with an open structure out of common and access areas (**Figure 14**).[49] Streets extend into the architecture: pedestrian crossings, squares, parks unfold into a public space; the former protective façade consisting of a separating wall becomes its own space which is equally as big and deep as the core structure. This type of structure actually forces the visitors to deal with their surroundings and

---

46   See Maak, Niklas: Zutritt erbeten. In: Frankfurter Allgemeine Zeitung, February 12, 2020, https://www.faz.net/aktuell/feuilleton/wie-architekten-aus-fassaden-einen-eigenen-raum-machen-16624258.html (June 1, 2021).

47   See Maak, Niklas: "Ein neues Verständnis von Nähe". Im Gespräch mit Gregor Becker. In: Ping! Für mehr Sinn und Verstand in der Redaktionellen Gesellschaft. Der Newsletter der Looping Group, October 19, 2020, https://looping.group/en/ping/artikel/harvard-professor-niklas-maak-ein-neues-verstandnis-von-nahe-5269581 (June 1, 2021).

48   See MVRDV, Expo 2000, https://www.mvrdv.nl/projects/158/expo-2000 (June 1, 2021).

49   See Farshad MehdiZadeh Design, Tehran Eye, https://fmzd.co/projects/detail?id=5 (June 1, 2021); further examples: Nicolas Laisné Architectes, https://nicolaslaisne.com/en/projects/ (June 1, 2021).

Figure 13—querkraft, Ikea City Center, Wien, 2020. Rendering, https://www.querkraft.at/projekte/ikea-city-center#&gid=lightbox-group-756&pid=5 (June 1, 2021).

Figure 14—Farshad MehdiZadeh Design, Tehran Eye, Tehran, 2019. Rendering, https://www.archdaily.com/931944/fmzd-transforms-an-existing-concrete-structure-in-tehran-into-a-contextual-shopping-mall (June 1, 2021).

to exert incidental social control, as it constantly guides their views between the interior and exterior.

Whether the new façade-less buildings will keep their security promises remains to be seen. Initially, they only provide images of increased accessibility and keep the ideal of an open city alive. Both the new Ikea building and the Tehran shopping center are financed privately, and that is why it is dubious whether their open façades will be accessible to the public at any time. However, the question as to whether profit-oriented building projects which open the façades for common use are not already products of cultural capitalism and hence ineffective as criticism of the neoliberal city and its dominant security discourses is even more quintessential. Especially in the case of consumer buildings for globally producing enterprises or shopping malls in authoritarian systems it can be suspected that the walkable façade is merely a simulation of city and public with the aim of better marketing of goods. This would level the antagonistic, political potential of the public space.

City of Disobedience

In conclusion, in view of simulated urbanity under the diktat of economics, the question must be posed as to which concepts of citizens' security would apply outside of authoritarian and neoliberal control techniques. What forms and strategies of urban and algorithmic disobedience can be developed which do not risk being taken over by esthetic economics, thereby losing their effect? In order to deal with this question openly, the contrasting concepts of a secure city will be compared with the topics of *obey* and *disobey* in a more concentrated manner and discussed.

The physical-digital security constructs presented here can be interpreted as a new architecture of obedience which will fundamentally transform the organization of future cities. Buildings and public spaces will be shaped and materialized in such a way that they are able to be registered, monitored and where necessary, locked by police authorities, private security services and autonomously acting digital systems without any trouble. The city of obedience consists of isolated architectural objects with fortified surfaces and an extensive vacant, but intensely controlled surrounding space which accelerates the urban fragmentation. With the progressive militarization of the city, all urban spaces lacking specific purposes of use and predetermined significance will gradually vanish. They are the counter-spaces of urban order in which unique, strange, cryptic and boundary-pushing actions can occur unobserved. Instead of opening up such potential-laden spaces to creative appropriation and utopian occupation, the city of obedience disintegrates into individual security passages with a scaled degree of publicness.

Through the expansion of border and control systems the urban social space becomes increasingly homogenized and regulated, whereas in contrast the practices for the restriction of access and participation become increasingly diverse. The visible protective walls and architectural forts are expanded through invisible boundaries of AI-capacity monitoring systems, audio visual detection sensors and virtual fences. The algorithms embed themselves subtly and with little transparency in the public space, impacting social interactions and individual modes of behavior there. They can be programmed to take racist decisions on the basis of which government and private security staff operate. Through algorithms, urban areas can be designated risk areas legitimizing increased police intervention. In this way, the city is transformed into a closed space for disciplining, discrimination and sanctioning. Not only is the protective function of architecture outsourced to security technology and Internet companies through digital surveillance, but legislative and legal implementation authority of the government is transferred to globally operating companies.

Given this advancing production of hyper-determined urban spaces ruled by security and efficiency empires, the question of counter-concepts of the city must be posed. What strategies of disobedience aimed at an open city can be developed? A potential form of disobedience being proposed here is a concept of urban security based on a critical-emancipatory practice of urban development whose prerequisite is social cooperation. This kind of socially-driven idea of urban resilience against crises and risks was formulated by Jane Jacobs in the 1960s, when she propagated urban mixed-use development and living neighborhoods for the creation of a positive type of social control of public space. Her call for the opening of urban spaces and cooperation in the city and society act as fundamental criticism of post-democratic security obsessions from contemporary commons movements. Resistance against urban and algorithmic surveillance can, however, only be kindled if the concept of the open city can be extrapolated to the digital city. For example, there is a strategy for disobedience in the demand for all city users to have free access to any digital data being collected which relates to their identity, abode or movements within the urban space. This means that these data are no longer stored centrally and able to be used by profit-oriented platforms or authoritarian regimes.⁵⁰

Since 2016, information on peak visitor frequency times at a public space or store has been shown on online maps by the US company Google LLC, which are calculated using the aggregated data of local users. The objective of this is for the residents and visitors to be better informed about their environment. However, this information does not serve the purpose of invigorating an urban place in the spirit of Jane Jacobs and thus of guaranteeing its security, but on the contrary leads to the avoidance of interpersonal meetings. This application is a classical neoliberal control technology which regards unplanned social contacts as obstacles for individual efficiency aspirations.⁵¹

It is thus not enough to open up architecture and urban spaces to diverse urban uses or to make data freely accessible, but it is necessary to reflect critically and change the values of its clients, developers and users. This too, would be a strategy for potential disobedience. The objective of resistance programming would have to be to develop new areas of cooperation and collective action in the urban-digital space which are democratically legitimized and decommercialized. Only then will architecture and digital tools be able to develop their potential for the informal social securing of the city.

Literature

Air Land Sea Application Center: Kill Box: Multi-Service Tactics, Techniques and Procedures for Kill Box Employment, Field Manual 3-09.34, August 2009, https://info.publicintelligence.net/fm3_09×34.pdf (June 1, 2021).

50 See Bria, Francesca. In: Brandlhuber, Arno; Grawert, Olaf; Hirsch, Nikolaus et al.: 2038—The New Serenity, German Pavilion at the 17th International Architecture Exhibition—La Biennale di Venezia, May 22, 2021 – November 21, 2021, https://2038.xyz (June 1, 2021).

51 See Stalder, Felix: Algorithmen, die wir brauchen. Überlegungen zu neuen technopolitischen Bedingungen der Kooperation und des Kollektiven. In: Standpunkte 1, 2017, p. 1–4, https://www.rosalux.de/fileadmin/rls_uploads/pdfs/Standpunkte/Standpunkte_1-2017.pdf (June 1, 2021).

Albrecht, Hans-Jörg: Wandel der Sicherheit—Von präventiver zu präemptiver Sicherheit? Entwicklungen der Sicherheitspolitik in Systemen des öffentlichen Personentransports. In: Fischer, Susanne; Masala, Carlo (Eds.): Innere Sicherheit nach 9/11. Sicherheitsbedrohungen und (immer) neue Sicherheitsmaßnahmen? Wiesbaden 2016, p. 209–229.

American Institute of Architects: Best Practices: Adapting Standard Embassy Design to Specific Sites, contributed by the U.S. Department of State and the U.S. General Services Administration, June 4, 2005 (revised May 2007).

Brandlhuber, Arno; Grawert, Olaf; Hirsch, Nikolaus et al.: 2038—The New Serenity, German Pavilion at the 17th International Architecture Exhibition—La Biennale di Venezia, May 22, 2021 – November 21, 2021, https://2038.xyz (June 1, 2021).

Bratton, Benjamin H.: The Stack: On Software and Sovereignty, Cambridge, Mass. 2016.

Brzezinski, Matthew: Fortress America: On the Front Lines of Homeland Security—An Inside Look at the Coming Surveillance State, New York 2004.

Bureau of Overseas Building Operations, United States Department of State: Standard Embassy Design.

Colomina, Beatriz: Domesticity at War, Cambridge, Mass. 2007.

Condliffe, Jamie: Big Investors Are Placing Bets on China's Facial Recognition Start-Ups. In: The New York Times, July 26, 2018, https://www.nytimes.com/2018/07/24/business/dealbook/china-facial-recognition.html (June 1, 2021).

Crouch, Colin: Post-Democracy, Themes for the 21st Century Series, Cambridge, UK 2004.

Erben, Dietrich: Zur Architektur der Frühen Neuzeit aus der Sicht der historischen Anthropologie. In: Schweizer, Stefan; Stabenow, Jörg (Eds.): Bauen als Kunst und historische Praxis. Architektur und Stadtraum zwischen Kunstgeschichte und Geschichtswissenschaft, vol. 2, Göttinger Gespräche zur Geschichtswissenschaft 26, Göttingen 2006, p. 461–492.

Farshad MehdiZadeh Design, Tehran Eye, https://fmzd.co/projects/detail?id=5 (June 1, 2021).

Fischer, Susanne; Masala, Carlo (Eds.): Innere Sicherheit nach 9/11. Sicherheitsbedrohungen und (immer) neue Sicherheitsmaßnahmen? Wiesbaden 2016.

Fischer, Susanne; Masala, Carlo: Die Politik der inneren Sicherheit nach 9/11. In: Ead. (Eds.): Innere Sicherheit nach 9/11. Sicherheitsbedrohungen und (immer) neue Sicherheitsmaßnahmen? Wiesbaden 2016, p. 1–9.

Graham, Stephen: Cities Under Siege: The New Military Urbanism, London and New York 2010.

Heitmeyer, Wilhelm: Kontrollverluste. Zur Zukunft der Gewalt. In: Heitmeyer, Wilhelm; Soeffner, Hans-Georg (Eds.): Gewalt. Entwicklungen, Strukturen, Analyseprobleme, Frankfurt am Main 2004, p. 86–106.

Heitmeyer, Wilhelm: Autoritäre Versuchungen. Signaturen der Bedrohung 1, Berlin 2018.

Hill, Kashmir: The Secretive Company That Might End Privacy as We Know It. In: The New York Times, January 18, 2020, https://www.nytimes.com/2020/01/18/technology/clearview-privacy-facial-recognition.html (June 1, 2021).

Houseal, Ian: Contemporary Embassy Planning: Designing in an Age of Terror, Master's Project, University of North Carolina, Department of City and Regional Planning, Chapel Hill, 2007, https://core.ac.uk/download/pdf/210605264.pdf (June 1, 2021).

Jacobs, Jane: The Death and Life of Great American Cities, New York 1961.

Jing Zeng, Meg: China's Social Credit System Puts Its People Under Pressure to Be Model Citizens. In: The Conversation. Academic Rigour, Journalistic Flair, January 23, 2018, https://theconversation.com/chinas-social-credit-system-puts-its-people-under-pressure-to-be-model-citizens-89963 (June 1, 2021).

Johnston, Elizabeth: Wir haben Jane Jacobs' Grundkonzept vergessen. Im Gespräch mit Brigitte Schultz. In: Bauwelt 6, 2017, StadtBauwelt 213, p. 18–23.

Knobloch, Tobias: Vor die Lage kommen: Predictive Policing in Deutschland, Gütersloh 2018, https://www.bertelsmann-stiftung.de/fileadmin/files/BSt/Publikationen/GrauePublikationen/predictive.policing.pdf (June 1, 2021).

Krause, Katharina: Sichtbar und sicher: Wohnhöfe des Adels in Münster in der ersten Hälfte des 18. Jahrhunderts, Politiken der Sicherheit 4, Baden-Baden 2018.

Kripa, Ersela; Mueller, Stephen: Fronts: Military Urbanisms and the Developing World, New York 2020.

Lobe, Adrian: Bedrohte Stadt. In: Neue Zürcher Zeitung, November 24, 2015, https://www.nzz.ch/feuilleton/kunst_architektur/bedrohte-stadt-1.18651386 (June 1, 2021).

Maak, Niklas: Architektur der BND-Zentrale. Kämpfen gegen das Unsichtbare. In: Frankfurter Allgemeine Zeitung, April 26, 2014, http://www.faz.net/aktuell/feuilleton/kaempfen-gegen-das-unsichtbare-die-architektur-der-neuen-bnd-zentrale-12911768.html (June 1, 2021).

Maak, Niklas: Zutritt erbeten. In: Frankfurter Allgemeine Zeitung, February 12, 2020, https://www.faz.net/aktuell/feuilleton/wie-architekten-aus-fassaden-einen-eigenen-raum-machen-16624258.html (June 1, 2021).

Maak, Niklas: "Ein neues Verständnis von Nähe". Im Gespräch mit Gregor Becker. In: Ping! Für mehr Sinn und Verstand in der Redaktionellen Gesellschaft. Der Newsletter der Looping Group, October 19, 2020, https://looping.group/en/ping/artikel/harvard-professor-niklas-maak-ein-neues-verstandnis-von-nahe-5269581 (June 1, 2021).

MacGregor, James W.: Bringing the Box into Doctrine: Joint Doctrine and the Kill Box, School of Advanced Military Studies, United States Army Command and General Staff College Fort Leavenworth, Kansas, 2004, https://apps.dtic.mil/sti/pdfs/ADA429320.pdf (June 1, 2021).

Moos, Stanislaus von: Turm und Bollwerk. Beiträge zu einer politischen Ikonographie der italienischen Renaissancearchitektur, Zurich and Freiburg i. Br. 1974.

MVRDV, Expo 2000, https://www.mvrdv.nl/projects/158/expo-2000 (June 1, 2021).

Neumeyer, Fritz: Was ist eine Fassade? Lernen von Leon Battista Alberti. In: Mäckler, Christoph (Ed.): Stadtbaukunst: Die Fassade, catalog for Dortmund architecture days and exhibition, no. 12 (Dortmunder U—Center for Arts and Creativity, 2010), Dortmunder Architekturheft 23, Dortmund 2011, p. 86–102.

Newman, Oscar: Countdown for Small Towns. In: Esquire Magazine 73 (6), 1969, p. 180–187.

Newman, Oscar: Defensible Space: Crime Prevention Through Urban Design, New York 1972.

Ouroussoff, Nicolai: A Tower That Sends a Message of Anxiety, Not Ambition. In: The New York Times, February 19, 2007, https://www.nytimes.com/2007/02/19/arts/design/19towe.html (June 1, 2021).

Ouroussoff, Nicolai: An Appraisal: A Tower of Impregnability, the Sort Politicians Love. In: The New York Times, June 30, 2005, http://www.nytimes.com/2005/06/30/arts/30appraisal.html?_r=0 (June 1, 2021).

Oval Office: Remarks by President Trump on the National Security and Humanitarian Crisis on our Southern Border, March 15, 2019, https://trumpwhitehouse.archives.gov/briefings-statements/remarks-president-trump-national-security-humanitarian-crisis-southern-border-2/ (June 1, 2021).

Pawley, Martin: Phantomsicherheit. In: Bruyn, Gerd de; Hundsdörfer, Daniel; Markov, lassen et al. (Eds.): 5 Codes. Architektur, Paranoia und Risiko in Zeiten des Terrors, Basel, Boston, and Berlin 2006, p. 208–211.

Schmidt, Urte: "Safe House" bei Warschau. Wandelbare Festung. In: Baunetz Wissen. Sicherheitstechnik, http://www.baunetzwissen.de/objektartikel/Sicherheitstechnik-Safe-House-quot-bei-Warschau-PL_1060461.html (June 1, 2021).

Schubert, Dirk: "Open City"—From "Eyes on the Street" to "Zero Tolerance". Jane Jacobs' Visionen einer sichereren Stadt. In: Häfele, Joachim; Sack, Fritz; Eick, Volker et al. (Eds.): Sicherheit und Kriminalprävention in urbanen Räumen. Aktuelle Tendenzen und Entwicklungen, Wiesbaden 2016, p. 47–68.

Senstar: FlexZone: Locating Fence-Mounted Intrusion Detection Sensor, 2020, https://senstar.com/products/fence-sensors/flexzone/ (June 1, 2021).

ShotSpotter, https://www.shotspotter.com/ (June 1, 2021).

Stalder, Felix: Algorithmen, die wir brauchen. Überlegungen zu neuen technopolitischen Bedingungen der Kooperation und des Kollektiven. In: Standpunkte 1, 2017, p. 1–4, https://www.rosalux.de/fileadmin/rls_uploads/pdfs/Standpunkte/Standpunkte_1-2017.pdf (June 1, 2021).

Sullivan, Paul: Can Artificial Intelligence Keep Your Home Secure? In: The New York Times, June 29, 2018, https://www.nytimes.com/2018/06/29/your-money/artificial-intelligence-home-security.html (June 1, 2021).

Wainwright, Oliver: Fortress London: The New US Embassy and the Rise of Counter-Terror Urbanism. In: Harvard Design Magazine 42, S/S 2016, http://www.harvarddesignmagazine.org/issues/42/fortress-london-the-new-us-embassy-and-the-rise-of-counter-terror-urbanism (June 1, 2021).

Werckmeister, Otto Karl: Zitadellenkultur. Über die schöne Kunst des Untergangs in den achtziger Jahren, München 1989.

Young, Lauren: The Hidden Security Bugs in Architecture That You Never Noticed. In: Atlas Obscura, June 24, 2016, https://www.atlasobscura.com/articles/the-hidden-security-bugs-in-architecture-that-you-never-knew-about (June 1, 2021).

Moritz Ahlert

Hacking Google Maps

"99 second-hand smartphones are transported in a handcart to generate virtual traffic jams in Google Maps. Through this activity, it is possible to turn a green street red which has an impact in the physical world by navigating cars on another route to avoid being stuck in traffic." #googlemapshacks[1]

Google Maps has, since its start in 2005, repeatedly been the target of activist or artistic interventions. In February 2020, on the occasion of the fifteenth anniversary of the map service, the Berlin-based artist, Simon Weckert, pulled a red handcart through the streets of Berlin, which contained 99 used Android smartphones—all switched on, with the Google Maps navigation app running. Weckert documented how his movements in the urban space changed the traffic forecast from the green of a clear road to a red traffic jam in a video he later uploaded to YouTube. The app reported a traffic jam that actually did not exist. His video went viral (up until today, over 3.3 Mio clicks). His performative disobedience received worldwide media coverage: a young artist who managed to manipulate the omnipotent and omnipresent algorithms of the tech giant Google, with very simple means.

This chapter is taking Weckert's intervention as a starting point to discuss the topic of hacking digital maps and to reflect on the means, the significance and the potential of 'civic disobedience' in todays—and tomorrows—smart cities dominated by the logic of 'platform urbanism'[2].

City as Code

The impact of algorithms in shaping the urban fabric is highly contested. The main promises of the 'smartness mandate',[3] how Orit Halpern puts it, is that cities become more efficient, productive, sustainable and resilient, as well as enhancing security, safety and quality of life. Cities worldwide are becoming increasingly data-driven, analyzing data about citizens and infra-

---

1 Weckert, Simon: "Google Maps Hacks, Performance & Installation, 2020," February 2020, http://simonweckert.com/googlemapshacks.html
2 Barns, Sarah: Platform Urbanism: Negotiating Platform Ecosystems in Connected Cities, Singapore 2020.
3 Halpern, Orit; Mitchell, Robert; Geoghegan, Bernard Dionysius: "The Smartness Mandate: Notes toward a Critique." In: Grey Room 68 (September 1, 2017), https://doi.org/10.1162/GREY_a_00221, p. 106–129.

Figure 1—Simon Weckert, 2020.

structure to create a more responsive urban ecosystem, like smart city promoter Carlo Ratti from MIT frames it in his book 'The city of tomorrow'.

A frequent critique is the reliance of so-called smart cities on 'big data' collected, monitored, and geo-localized or as Orit Halpern describes it, by a 'cocoon of ubiquitious computing'[4]. While collectable and marketable data is prioritized and algorithms becoming the most important urban actors, the actual realities of urban inhabitants are being ignored and compromised. Commercialized smart city approaches foster the fragmentation of urban fabrics instead of 'bringing the world closer together' like Mark Zuckerburg promised. Keller Easterling describes these technologies as 'Spatial software'[5], which are actively shaping urban transformation processes, but also functioning as new gateways for private corporations to enter the urban sphere.

Role of Digital Maps

Maps play a crucial role in the process of platformization of cities. To reflect its tension-filled relationship as instruments of power and counter-power and 'obeying' and 'disobey' it is worth to re-read the critical cartography discourse: Maps, digital or analogue, have always been instruments of power. They have always been a significant instrument of government and domination. The map is and was an instrument of disciplinary and sovereign power, as Foucault would have defined it. From the late 1980 onwards authors like John B. Harley, Denis Wood, and Jeremy Crampton have taken a critical look at the ways in which maps function, and have explored the current perception of maps.

A particularly interesting and tension-filled relationship between power and counter-power can be noted in the maps produced by the transnational corporation Google.

The advent of Google's Geo Tools began in 2005 with Maps and Earth, followed by Street View in 2007. They have since become enormously more technologically advanced. Google's virtual maps have little in common

---

[4] Halpern, Orit; LeCavalier, Jesse; Calvillo, Nerea; Pietsch, Wolfgang: "Test-Bed Urbanism." In: Public Culture 25, no. 2 70 (April 1, 2013), https://doi.org/10.1215/08992363-2020602, p. 272–306.

[5] Easterling, Keller: Extrastatecraft: The Power of Infrastructure Space. London and New York 2014.

with classical analogue maps. The most significant difference is that Google's maps are interactive—scrollable, searchable and zoomable. Google's map service has fundamentally changed our understanding of what a map is, how we interact with maps, their technological limitations, and how they look aesthetically. Thanks to Google, maps are more 'ubiquitous' today than ever before, and, with the widespread use of smartphones, are influencing users' patterns of behaviour. By using maps as a form of synaptic real-time networking, smart digital devices are creating a novel form of hyperlocality, a situation in which things and users are interconnected and can be localized, and in which the physical world fuses with the virtual world. Google's Geo Tools have become the nerve center and logbook of this world order.

In his 2010 book 'Mapping: A Critical Introduction to Cartography and GIS' the geographer Jeremy Crampton writes, "that Paul Rademacher may be the most influential cartographer of the twenty-first century, but you have probably never heard of him. He is not famous."[6] Even though Rademacher is not a cartographer, he created the first map mash-up. To make his own search for an apartment easier, he reverse-engineered Google Maps so that the housing listings would appear georeferenced on the online map, instead of having just an list.

His reverse-engineering was not only received as the first Map Mash-Up but also the first Google Maps Hack.

As a response of Rademacher's hack Google soon put in place official programming interfaces called APIs which allowed the programmers of other web tools to combine their data with Google Maps and to geo-reference it, known as map-mash-ups. It was the opportunity produced by the mash-ups that first made possible the emergence of new economic models, such as large parts of the digital shared or gig Economies. In this fashion, Google Maps makes virtual changes to the real city. Applications such as 'Airbnb' and 'Carsharing' have an immense impact on cities: on their housing market and mobility culture, for instance. There is also a major impact on how we find a romantic partner, thanks to dating platforms such as 'Tinder', and on our self-quantifying behaviour, thanks to the 'nike' jogging app. Or map-based food delivery-app like 'deliveroo' or 'foodora'. All of these apps function via interfaces with Google Maps and create new forms of digital capitalism and commodification. Without these maps, car sharing systems, new

---

6   Crampton, Jeremy W. Mapping: A Critical Introduction to Cartography and GIS. Blackwell Companions to the Ancient World, Malden 2010, p. 27

Figure 2, 3—Simon Weckert, 2020.

taxi apps, bike rental systems and online transport agency services such as 'Uber' would be unthinkable. An additional mapping market is provided by self-driving cars; again, Google has already established a position for itself.

As a further step in the algorithmization and urbanization, Sidewalk Labs, a Google/Alphabet owned company announced in 2017 that it would develop its own smart neighbourhood, called Quayside at the waterfront of Toronto and turn it into a testbed for the fusion of technology and urbanism. Surprisingly, the end of the project was announced almost one year ago, justified with the financial uncertainties caused by the Covid-pandemic.

But what we can learn from their 2017 proposal[7] is that Sidewalk Lab planned an active digital layer to manage their neighborhood, consisting of a central map platform which synthesizes all location-based information on infrastructure, buildings, and public space in a centralized manner. A 3D-map as a virtual live-model of the city. The map was supposed to measure urban data in real time in order to better understand the users of the district and their needs. The maps records everything in real time, from static objects such as buildings, streets and park benches to autonomous vehicles, delivery robots or drones. It enables a better understanding of user patterns in parks, on streets and other resources and thus form the base for a continuously self-optimizing planning unit.

With its Geo Tools, Google has created a platform that allows users and businesses to interact with maps in a novel way. But what is the relationship between the art of enabling and techniques of supervision, control and regulation in Google's maps? Do these maps function as dispositive nets that determine the behaviour, opinions and images of living beings, exercising power and controlling knowledge?

Before the advent of Google Maps, in the beginning of the nineties, Deleuze writes in his 'Postscript on the Societies of Control': "In the societies of control, it is no longer either a signature or a number that is important, but a code: the code is a password." Individuals have become "dividuals". He cites Guattari's vision in which a dividual card becomes the control material:

> "Felix Guattari has imagined a city where one would be able to leave one's apartment, one's street, one's neighbourhood, thanks to one's 'dividual' electronic card that raises a given barrier; but the card could just as easily be rejected on a given day or between certain hours; what counts is not the barrier but the com-

---

7   See: Sidewalk Labs, "Vision Sections of RFP Submission," October 27, 2017.

puter that tracks each person's position—licit or illicit—and effects a universal modulation."[8]

The dividual card described by Deleuze in 1992 could be read as the algoritmic Google Maps of today. The digital map of today is an instrument of the surveillance and control dispositive described by Deleuze and Guattari. Every click on the net, every step in space is recorded and registered. Everything that moves around—goods, information, communication, capital, and consumers—is tracked.

Certainly Quayside is not Google's last attempt to penetrate urban space with its services. In future projects, it will continue to privatize urban space under the guise of resource-efficiency and promises of digital real-life utopias. As a circuit diagram, the digital map will be an important key technology for Google's ambitious plans to conquer the urban sphere.

As showed with the examples from above, Google Maps has led to novel displacements and overlapping of physical and virtual spaces. In this context, simulation techniques are used not only to generate virtual worlds, but to form realities and to intervene in physical spaces.

Rademacher and his early Google Maps Mash-up, allowed Google to expand its mapping service to become a central platform that allows users and business to interact with maps in a novel way.

This means that questions relating to power in the discourse of cartography and urban planning have to be reformulated. Maps, which themselves are the product of a combination of states of knowledge and states of power, have an inscribed power dispositive, which have a major impact on urban space. Google's simulation-based map and world models determine the actuality and perception of physical urban spaces and the development of urban action models.

To echo the words of Agamben: "today, it seems that there is not a single instant in the life of an individual that cannot be formed, contaminated, ordered or controlled by dispositives—in the form of maps"[9].

---

[8] Deleuze, Gilles: "Postscript on the Societies of Control." In: October 59 (1992), p. 3–7, here p. 6.

[9] Agamben, Giorgio. Was ist ein Dispositiv? 1. Aufl. TransPositionen. Zürich 2008, p. 29.

Hacking Alternative Platform Futures

Due to technical development digital maps are not only a representation of space, but actively shape the urban fabric. The meaning of 'map hacking' has changed, as the city itself became a platform. Hacking became an urban practice. The potential of hacking maps in a city dominated by cooperate platforms is not only to hack the map itself, like Rademacher in 2005, but to hack the operating algorithms itself.

Today's urban hacking has little in common with the idea of gaining access to computers or networks by overcoming security measures or stealing personal data or identity, or to reverse-engineer data. But the fundamental tenet of the hacker ethic has remained the same: information should be free and that technology is supposed to be open source. Also as described in the text by Mark Graham: 'An Informational Right to the City? Code, Content, Control, and the Urbanization of Information'.[10]

The dutch researchers Martijn de Waal and Michiel de Lange outline their concept of a hackable city as a model to create new alternative imaginaries:

"Whereas the smart city often takes a solutionist and depoliticized approach, introducing technologies as a means to 'neutrally' solve urban problems, the hackable city departs from the city as a political site. It highlights a vision of the city as a site of both collaboration as well as struggle and conflicts of interests. In this account, new media technologies enable citizens to organize, mobilize, innovate and collaborate towards commonly defined goals. Yet the hackable city also recognizes the messiness of such a process, the conflicts of interest at play and the continuous struggle between the alignment of private goals, collective hacks and public interests."[11]

Mapping and location-based technology are important entry points to hack urban infrastructure. 'Civic hackers'[12], like Simon Weckert, exploit todays loopholes of the digital city and execute hacks to discover vulnerabili-

---

[10] See: Shaw, Joe; Graham, Mark: "An Informational Right to the City? Code, Content, Control, and the Urbanization of Information: An Informational Right to the City?" In: Antipode 49, no. 4 (September 2017), https://doi.org/10.1111/anti.12312, p. 907–927.

[11] Waal, Martijn de; Lange, Michiel de: "Introduction—The Hacker, the City and Their Institutions: From Grassroots Urbanism to Systemic Change." In: Ead. (Eds.):The Hackable City, Singapore 2019, https://doi.org/10.1007/978-981-13-2694-3_1, p. 1–22, here p. 6.

[12] Townsend, Anthony M.: Smart Cities: Big Data, Civic Hackers, and the Quest for a New Utopia. First edition. New York 2013.

ties. He used 99 smartphones in order to manipulate the corporate urban infrastructure, to simply make the invisible infrastructures of the algorithmic city visible. His hack creates awareness of this ubiquitous computing used by people on daily basis, but without reflecting on how it actually works, how it is maintained. Urban hackers like him working towards creating open systems and disassembling and revers-engineering closed ones. Urban hackers see the creative reuse and repurposing of technology as a hands-on way of learning about the city.

To challenge the omnipotent platform urbanism of big cooperation's there needs certainly to be more then artistic hacks like the one by Simon Weckert. But they can be important starting points to rethink alternative pathways, especially because they can create awareness and a discourse outside the academic discipline.

In an imaginary hackable city, artists, urban designers, institutions and citizens work together to create alternative urban algorithmic futures, in participatory and inclusive ways.

Literature

Agamben, Giorgio. Was ist ein Dispositiv? 1. Aufl. TransPositionen. Zürich 2008.
Barns, Sarah. Platform Urbanism: Negotiating Platform Ecosystems in Connected Cities. Singapore: Springer Singapore, 2020. https://doi.org/10.1007/978-981-32-9725-8.
Crampton, Jeremy W. Mapping: A Critical Introduction to Cartography and GIS. Blackwell Companions to the Ancient World. Malden 2010.
Deleuze, Gilles: "Postscript on the Societies of Control." In: October 59 (1992), p. 3–7.
Easterling, Keller: Extrastatecraft: The Power of Infrastructure Space. London and New York 2014.
Halpern, Orit; LeCavalier, Jesse; Calvillo, Nerea; Pietsch, Wolfgang: "Test-Bed Urbanism." In: Public Culture 25, no. 2 70 (April 1, 2013), https://doi.org/10.1215/08992363-2020602, p. 272–306.
Halpern, Orit; Mitchell, Robert; Geoghegan, Bernard Dionysius: "The Smartness Mandate: Notes toward a Critique." In: Grey Room 68 (September 1, 2017), https://doi.org/10.1162/GREY_a_00221, p. 106–129.

Shaw, Joe; Graham, Mark: "An Informational Right to the City? Code, Content, Control, and the Urbanization of Information: An Informational Right to the City?" In: Antipode 49, no. 4 (September 2017), https://doi.org/10.1111/anti.12312, p. 907–927.

Sidewalk Labs: "Vision Sections of RFP Submission," October 27, 2017. https://sidewalktoronto.ca/wp-content/uploads/2017/10/Sidewalk-Labs-Vision-Sections-of-RFP-Submission.pdf

Townsend, Anthony M.: Smart Cities: Big Data, Civic Hackers, and the Quest for a New Utopia. First edition. New York 2013.

Waal, Martijn de; Lange, Michiel de: "Introduction—The Hacker, the City and Their Institutions: From Grassroots Urbanism to Systemic Change." In: Ead. (Eds.): The Hackable City, Singapore 2019, DOI: https://doi.org/10.1007/978-981-13-2694-3_1, p. 1–22.

Weckert, Simon. "Google Maps Hacks, Performance & Installation, 2020," February 2020, http://simonweckert.com/googlemapshacks.html

Harald Trapp / Robert Thum

The Algorithmic Construction of Space

Epistemologically experiencing space is not a purely sensual act. Rather perception is an act of construction. As Kant demonstrated in his "Critique of Pure Reason", the mind is not a purely receptive vessel conditioned by the world, but has an active role in structuring and organizing it, providing at least some of the conditions needed to make our experience possible. Digitalisation increasingly substitutes human spatial perception through algorithmic models, thus replacing the individual and social construction of space, which works through the active appropriation of the physical world. But experimental evidence has shown that the development of spatial perception is preconditioned on the active bodily exploration of the environment.[1]

In Bertolt Brecht's play "The Caucasian Chalk Circle", obedience is connected to space. Two women are fighting for the same child. To determine who the real mother is, the judge places the child at the centre of a chalked circle and asks the women to remove the child from the circle. She who succeeds in taking the child is the real mother. Grusha, who refuses to pull the child out of the ring for fear of hurting it, wins the case. Disobedience against the judge's demand proves the true love of a mother. A rational rule, could be learned from this example, does not necessarily cover the complexity of human behaviour. Obedience (literally "listen to," from ob "to" (see ob-) and audire "listen, hear") in human behaviour is often directly linked to space, to boundaries and borders. Disobedience, on the other side, in all societies is meant to be prohibited by spatial measures, i.e. incarceration or surveillance.

Algorithms per se demand obedience, as they are instructions. Due to their nature, this obedience is twofold: towards the instruction itself and towards the reality, on which the instruction is based. As space is increasingly captured through digital methods, the resulting data have to be processed by algorithms. These therefore not only reorganize, but define and produce space and new forms of boundaries. Obedience also has a relationship to human intelligence, as a large part of learning is coupled to following and repeating instructions or staying within certain boundaries. But specific parts of creative thinking are equally bound to challenging rules and instructions or the transgression of borders.

---

[1] Held, Richard; Hein, Allan: Movement-Produced Stimulation in the Development of Visually Guided Behavior. In: The Journal of Comparative and Physiological Psychology, 1963, p. 872–876.

Harald Trapp / Robert Thum

Construction and Reconstruction

In expansion of Lefebvre's dictum, space is no longer only produced, but constructed, through the replacement of human perception as well as through an algorithmic cartography based on a multi-stage process of recording and filtering.[2] The algorithmic construction of space is developing along two lines. On one side as a digital re-construction of the analogue world (e.g. Google-Earth), which, in stark contrast to traditional cartography, uses information gathered from outside our planet. The global positioning and continuous surveying of the surface of the earth is conducted by a network of satellites, circling at a distance of 40.000 kilometres in orbit. But digital reconstruction also leads to the zoning of a city into equidistant areas for services of the platform economy. It is followed by an algorithmic construction of space, if these zones can be switched on and off to block the reception of digital information and thus services, a technique known as "geofencing".

In space algorithms demand obedience through acceptance of the constructed reality they provide (e.g. Google-Maps) and in the instructions (e.g. wayfinding) derived from this construction. "Because the thought turns into the solution of assigned tasks, the unassigned is also treated according to the scheme of the task."[3] Human disobedience takes this into account. Visual representation, for example, is based on pixilation, which is a harsh geometrical abstraction. Hence resolution is a critical issue and can become a source of rebellion against image-recognition. Artistic interventions like Hito Steyer's "How Not to Be Seen: A Fucking Didactic Educational. MOV File 2013" propose ways in which individuals can resist being captured visually by digital technology.[4] Her video projection plays with the notion, that, "resolution determines visibility; whatever is not captured by resolution is invisible", as the voice-over announces. Steyerl juxtaposes analogue aerial surveillance through the cameras of spy planes with the techniques of contemporary digital technology to identify objects and people. In one sequence, three individuals try to camouflage themselves by wearing pixel-like boxes in an attempt to become smaller than a pixel.

2   See: Lefebvre, Henri: The Production of Space, Blackwell Publishing, Oxford 1991 (1974)
3   Adorno, Theodor W.: Minima Moralia, Frankfurt a.M. 2001 (1951), own translation p. 374.
4   Steyerl, Hito: How Not to Be Seen: A Fucking Didactic Educational .MOV File, 2013, www.tate.org.uk/art/artworks/steyerl-how-not-to-be-seen-a-fucking-didactic-educational-mov-file-t14506 (September 28, 2020).

Map

Originally maps were static material objects made of parchment or paper, with a tangible scale and edges that intuitively defined the limits of the terrain. The word 'map' encapsulates these qualities. It originates from the Latin mappa mundi, literally "sheet of the world". Maps provide an overview and a grasp of the territory's totality. From the map reader they demand skill, expertise and the ability to actively construct space by relating abstraction and real-world experience. Navigating with physical maps enhances the reader's understanding of the environment and spatial proficiencies. With digital technology, satellite imaging, GPS and GIS, the 'sheet of the world' has become the world itself. The Indoor Positioning Systems extends this survey to smaller and smaller scale, invading homes, multi-story buildings, alleys, parking garages and underground locations. Not by extra-terrestrial machinery but by seemingly benign and often personal devices already deployed indoors: smartphones, WIFI routers and Bluetooth antennas, smart speakers and digital cameras with a projected overall accuracy of two centimetres.

But the world as a whole is only known by the digital system which concentrates on relaying routes between points to its user. In the name of comfort, which has become a major motivator in late modern societies, obedience to the directions of navigational systems replaces individual orientation. It is a change from finding or even constructing a route, making errors and learning from detours and deviations, to the blind surrender to navigational orders. The system often does not even hide its authority, using penetrant voices and signals.

In digital maps the sense of scale is lost, a meaningful overview impossible. This superimposition of world and map has forced an important consequence: a perspectival shift from the whole to the personal. "'You are here' no longer needs to be said. We are by default the centre of the world. Our surroundings emanate from us, from a little blue dot that sits on the screen. It's perhaps the single most important change in how we view the city. Around this blue dot stem not only cafes and banks but our own experiences, our pictures and tweets."[5] The map is no longer abstract but immediate and immersive. It itself has become the territory as anticipated by Lewis Carroll in his

---

5   McMullan, Thomas: How digital maps are changing the way we understand our world. In: The Guardian, 02.12.2014, www.theguardian.com/technology/2014/dec/02/how-digital-maps-changing-the-way-we-understand-world (October 28, 2020).

novel 'Sylvie and Bruno concluded' : "'What do you consider the largest useful map?' I asked. 'Well, we got to six yards to the mile. Then we tried a hundred yards to the mile. And then came the best idea of all! We actually made a map of the country, on the scale of a mile to the mile! ' exclaimed Mein Herr. 'Have you used it?' I enquired. 'It has never been spread out' said Mein Herr."[6] Today, as reality is gradually replaced by its model, its users increasingly depend on it. Spatial awareness withers and as a malleable projection it is open to manipulation and external control. The denizens of this constructed space obediently follow its algorithmic logic when navigating through the city. The urban surroundings are reduced to a narrow corridor, zoomed in on the user tracing from position A to position B while the world outside the line of direction drops off the edge of the phone's screen.

Position

In the early stages of algorithmic space an abstract replication of the existing and the instructions based on this reconstruction leads to a reversal of agency: the environment dictates on how to deal with it. Resistance, creativity, innovation are no longer initiated by individuals, but depend on algorithmic interventions. The functionality of algorithmic space "[...] highly depends on adapting the behaviour to the environment data, not the other way around [...]"[7] On a global scale this can lead to absurd phenomena. The global positioning system GPS, like so many technological innovations, is a product of the arms race after the Second World War. Launched in 1973 by the U.S. Department of Defense, it was originally limited to military operation. Since an executive order by Ronald Reagan in 1983, the System was opened for civilian use. Although accuracy at that time was only in the range of a few meters, since the 1990s the United States have used their authority over the system to downgrade its quality through a program called "Selective Availability". This seems to be an adequate summary for many algorithmic activities, which increasingly depend on positioning systems. In the beginning, digital cartography of the world lay in the hands of one political and

---

[6] Carroll, Lewis: Sylvie and Bruno concluded. In: Green, Roger Lancelyn (Ed.): The Works of Lewis Carroll, London 1965.

[7] Borries, Christian von: The Disappearance of Architecture and Society in the Algorithm, Conversation with Olaf Grawert and Arno Brandlhuber. In: Arch+ The Property Issue, Politics of Space and Data, 2020, p. 12.

military power, which held a decisive advantage over all other states. During that time, the government of the United States could not only downgrade its Global Positioning System, but also deny whole regions access. Such an early case of large scale "geo-fencing" happened to India in 1999 during the Kargil war. This initiated the first act of disobedience of a whole state in that context, as the Indian government in response started the production and installation of its own satellites.[8]

The precision of a position lies in the power of the operator of such a system. In the year 2000, when the "Selective Availability"-program was ended, the accuracy of GPS lay within a five-meter range. Nowadays this has been brought down to within thirty centimetres. Noone knows if this development is depending on technological progress, or if algorithmic distortion to impede potential enemies continues to be effective. Today China not only disenables the use of most Western digital services (Google, Facebook, Instagram etc.), but in a mixture of refusal and secrecy, uses algorithms to systematically distort geographical data produced by GPS. This case of state disobedience against the monopoly of a positioning system is called the China "GPS shift problem". The latter is based on a coordinate system called WGS-84. Due to national law, all maps of China must use the alternative GCJ-02 coordinate system, which additionally produces an obfuscation effect on GPS-data. There is speculation, that a special algorithm creates the offset towards the WGS-84 coordinates, leading to applications like Google maps mismatching satellite photographs and Chinese maps. The offset cannot easily be corrected, as it is random in any direction and seems to vary between 50 and 500 meters. Any independent mapping done in China, trying to overcome this obfuscation, is persecuted. The case of students from Imperial College London being questioned and fined is proof for this policy.[9]

Until the twentieth century cartography could only map the movement of people, resources, weather etc. a posteriori. Today algorithms can process all physical movement in real-time and the complexity of flows (and thus life) is reduced to patterns and regularities. Digital space is increasingly based on an autopoietic cartography, a circular, independent self-production of a mul-

---

8   Srivastava, Ishan: How Kargil spurred India to design own GPS. In: The Times of India, 05.04.2014, https://timesofindia.indiatimes.com/home/science/How-Kargil-spurred-India-to-design-own-GPS/articleshow/33254691.cms (October 15, 2020).

9   Spencer, Richard: British students fined for 'illegal map-making' in China. In: The Telegraph, 05.01.2009, www.telegraph.co.uk/news/worldnews/asia/china/4125477/British-students-fined-for-illegal-map-making-in-China.html (October 15, 2020).

tiplicity of worlds, based on recording and interpreting positional data. Reality as a whole is turned into virtuality even before any simulation begins. The physical infrastructure of the algorithmic space is predominantly disguised or invisible, constructing the illusion of immateriality and ephemerality. The satellites of the positioning systems are not only out of view, but also far beyond comprehension. Data centres are hiding in faceless boxes. The superimposition of the digital and the old analogue city, as we know it, therefore can be seamless. Mobile phone antennas are everywhere, but are not identified as the centres of cellular territories, handing mobile phone users from one to the next. The constant surveillance is presented to the operators of smart phones only as the benefit of identifying their position. Whereas in reality, it is used in many cases as a permanent tracking and monitoring of all movements. One of the first (and probably irreversible) steps of government control during the Covid-crisis was to pass legislation that assured unlimited access to the data of movement of their citizens.[10] The only escape from this new mapping of the world is to not use smart-phones. Criminals like drug dealers are either using encryptive methods or old mobile phones that cannot be tracked.

Platform

Digital platforms are in themselves emblematic of what algorithmic space is about: the spatial term "platform" is used to camouflage a virtual, hybrid market-place organised by algorithms, which has neither location, nor architecture and—officially—no workers. But the operations of the platform, which attempts to repaint dependent work into self-employment, have increasing repercussions with the real world. Besides being operated from new building typologies like server farms and data centres, the platform economy extensively uses public space for its services. Their "independent contractors" or workers with their bikes, scooters, cars and vans are already taking up a large amount of inner-city traffic. This supports one of the few options for disobedience, as strike actions of delivery workers cannot only be easily organised by switching off apps, but achieve high public visibility, as their

---

10   Al-Youssef, Muzayen; Anders, Theo; Schmid, Fabian; Weiss, Stefan: Die neuen Gesetze zur Bekämpfung der Corona-Pandemie. In: Der Standard, 20.03.2020, www.derstandard.de/story/2000115935419/die-neuen-gesetze-zur-bekaempfung-der-corona-pandemie (April 20, 2020).

workplace is the street. In this way, the system can be turned against itself, as the strikes by food delivery workers in Great Britain in 2016 showed. Uber Eats drivers not only logged out in a coordinated manner via WhatsApp, but also ordered food using a promotion that promised five pounds for each new customer. In this way, they not only had almost free food delivered to the picket lines, but also managed to convince other riders to join the strike.[11]

In China Alibaba, the equivalent to Amazon, has transformed "Singles Day" on 11.11. into an online shopping event, exemplary for the production of consumption created by the digital industry. "Singles Day" is constantly growing and produces a surge in demand for services around the delivery of parcels. This peak workload causes backlogs in the delivery-chain and late deliveries. Due to the logic of platform-contracts, any delays have to be compensated by the delivery drivers or riders. Around "Singles Day" last year, unrest accelerated. Many of the small intermediate companies could not handle the sudden increase in traffic, which led to chaotic scenes: "Workers in Hunan Province went on strike last month for more than $45,000 in back wages, leaving orders of hairy crab to rot in their boxes. In Shenyang, a city in the northeast, abandoned packages were dumped in an empty field last week. Internet users have joked that their packages are going on vacation, posting screenshots of tracking details that show their orders meandering across the country as they are redirected to functioning courier stations."[12]

On September 8th, 2020 Renwu[13] one of China's most widely read magazines, published a research into the working conditions of delivery workers under the title "Delivery Riders, Trapped in the System"[14]. One of the key findings of the Renwu report is the fact that riders in China using the two main platforms Meituan-Dianping and Ele.me register what they call "the disappearance of time"[15]. Rides that had been calculated by the platform's algorithm for 50 minutes where in some cases over the years reduced down

---

11 See: Shenker, Jack: Strike 2.0: how gig economy workers are using tech to fight back. In: The Guardian, 31.08.2019, www.theguardian.com/books/2019/aug/31/the-new-resistance-how-gig-economy-workers-are-fighting-back (November 12, 2020).

12 Wang, Vivian: On Singles' Day in China, Couriers Clamor for More. In: New York Times, 11.11.2020, www.nytimes.com/2020/11/11/business/alibaba-singles-day-couriers.html (November 15, 2020).

13 人物, "People".

14 Chuang: Delivery Workers, Trapped in the System, 12.11.2020, https://chuangcn.org/2020/11/delivery-renwu-translation/ (November 12, 2020).

15 Ibid.

to 35 minutes within which the driver had to arrive at his or her destination. This is partly due to policies of the platform owners, who are handing "speed up" notifications to their stations, which pass them on to the riders. But Renwo indicates, that it also might be a result of machine-learning, which takes the shortest instances of deliveries over a certain distance as a measure for its learning. "For the system's creators, this is a praiseworthy advancement, a real-world embodiment of the deep-learning capacity of AI."[16]

Meituan's slogan is "Send anything fast", aiming at an average delivery time of 28 minutes. The machine learning of its algorithm seems to continuously consume delivery time, which, according to the logic of service and consumption, is considered the most important metric in the system. As the contracts between platform and its alleged entrepreneurs accumulate all responsibilities connected to the quality of the service on the delivery riders, these are left with only one option: to increase their speed. This application of machine-learning forces drivers and riders to violate traffic laws, e.g. to run lights and ride against oncoming traffic. In respect to the way the delivery times are calculated, Sun Ping, assistant researcher at the Chinese Academy of Social Sciences describes the delivery riders' disobedience of traffic rules as a direct reflection of the dispatch logic: "Riders who have long been under the control and management of the algorithm have no choice but to use this labour practice. The direct result of this 'inverse algorithm' is a sharp rise in the number of traffic accidents involving delivery riders."[17] To use the term "inverse" in this context accentuates the built-in obedience of algorithms. In reality, the disobedient behavior triggered by machine learning and algorithmic management could be interpreted as a sign of a power shift from social and legal rules to those incorporated in digital codes. Obedience to the delivery-algorithm makes disobedience towards existing rules mandatory. This leads to the question of legitimization—whereas traffic rules are part of a legal structure that is the result of a democratic process of law-making, algorithmic rules are the clandestine product of private interests. Nick Seaver's anthropological interpretation of algorithms seems to fail in the case of the delivery system: "There is no such thing as an algorithmic decision; there are only ways of seeing decisions as algorithmic. In other words, algorithms are not autonomous technical objects, but complex sociotechnical systems. As I

---

16   Ibid.

17   Chuang: Delivery Workers, Trapped in the System, 12.11.2020, https://chuangcn.org/2020/11/delivery-renwu-translation/ (November 14, 2020).

have argued elsewhere, this change in framing reverses many of algorithms' supposedly essential qualities: if the idealized algorithm is supposed to be generic, stable, and rigid, the actual algorithmic system is particular, unstable, and malleable (Seaver 2013)."[18]

Following Seaver's argumentation, algorithmic practices are principally social practices. In the case of delivery platforms, the relevant practice is the exploitation of human labour. But the algorithms do not merely reflect or translate social practices, but transform them. Their actual implementation, e.g. as a dispatch system, is not intended to operate under human influence. They have to follow the limitations of coding and its execution through application. The effect might be compared to that of mechanization and the change from craft to industrial production in the 18th century. Machines, although invented, produced and maintained by humans, through their repetitious manipulations caused alienation among the workers. This could only happen through their agency as an objective mechanical device. The shift today is from the mechanical and material to the digital and immaterial—and it is only possible through a radical abstraction of culture into mathematical algorithms and the replacement of human by algorithmic management.

Adversarial Algorithms

Five years ago, the Chinese delivery service Meituan reorganised their delivery management algorithm around machine learning. "Super Brain" is an artificial neural network system performing in-depth sensing and problem analysis to manage complex real-world situations, quickly making decisions, and generate accurate predictions. Artificial neural network algorithms are open malleable structures with the ability to learn, but no functionality initially embedded in the code itself. Only after supervised training with large quantities of semantically labelled datasets, the algorithms learn to perform specific tasks. The same algorithm can be applied to a diverse variety of assignments such as optimising delivery routes, attempting to achieving high customer ratings in relation to rider time efficiency. Empirical data for real-world rides, traces left behind by rider or other motorists, costumers' ratings and traffic patterns are used as training sets. In the environment of Big

[18] Seaver, Nick: What should an Anthropology of Algorithms do? In: Cultural Anthropology, Vol. 33, Issue 3, 2018, p. 385.

Data, the rise of machine learning is inevitable. Not only is this technology best equipped to process enormous quantities of data, recognising and making sense of patterns and autonomously triggering actions. But at the same time the learning algorithm consumes the data to improve its own functionality, becoming, at least in a very narrow sense, more intelligent.

In image-recognition, the algorithm takes large quantities of pixels with all the information such as RGB value, and creates a multidimensional space which is called 'latent space'. "Typically, it is a 100-dimensional hypersphere with each variable drawn from a Gaussian distribution with a mean of zero and a standard deviation of one."[19] In the process of learning classifiable features that, for example, belong to road signs and differ from other features belonging to car, people or buildings are shifted within the latent space to particular positions in such a way that a definitive multi-dimensional boundary can be created between areas occupied by traffic sign features and all other recognised features. Activists and artists searching for ways of subverting machine learning for surveillance systems, have developed two tactics: poison attacks and adversarial attacks.

In so called poison attacks the aim is to intentionally contaminate the deep learning algorithm's memory with erroneous inputs. Machine learning is only as good as its training sets are and when fake information enters their database, reliability will be compromised. The American fashion label adversarial fashion for example uses textiles with license plate patterns to subvert the A.L.P.R. (Automatic license plate recognition), a mass surveillance system that intrusively collects thousands of plates, tracing the vehicles locations and movement patterns. The label's website states: "The patterns on the goods in this shop are designed to trigger Automated License Plate Readers, injecting junk data in to the systems used by the State and its contractors to monitor and track civilians and their locations."[20] Wearers of these t-shirts become identified as motorcycles or cars from specific states, even indicating vehicle-colour and other information. To be effective this method requires large numbers of adopters wearing adversarial patterns to trigger multiple automatic detection sequences. This could, at least in theory, render the whole system useless, which controls vehicular movement in public space.

---

19   Brownlee, Jason; How to Explore the GAN Latent Space When Generating Faces. In: Generative Adversarial Networks, 03.07.2019, https://machinelearningmastery.com/how-to-interpolate-and-perform-vector-arithmetic-with-faces-using-a-generative-adversarial-network/ (November 22, 2020).

20   See: Adversarial Fashion, website, https://adversarialfashion.com (November 22, 2020).

Other tactics work on single instances. In adversarial attacks so-called adversarial images are placed on real-world objects to confuse the deep learning algorithm. Faces and object such as road signs can become invisible or are mistaken for something else. As Tom Goldstein of the University of Maryland portrays machine-learning algorithms: "They have weaknesses that occur in the interactions between feature maps and artificial neurons. There are strange and exploitable pathways in these neural networks that probably shouldn't be there."[21] It is not easy to find adversarial images, but they appear to work with most other recognition algorithms as well. "This 'transferability' enables attackers to fool systems in what are known as 'black-box attacks', where they don't have access to the model's architecture, parameters or even the training data used to train the network."[22] Activists, like the Berlin based artist Adam Harvey have developed various types of adversarial tools, T-shirt, stickers, glasses or patches that can be worn or applied on objects making people disappear from the algorithm's view, or turn stop signs into speed limit signs. Software engineers are working to repair their networks by training them with adversarial images, so far with limited success.

Machine-learning algorithms are opaque, black boxes, and although the mechanics are clear, their inner workings, like that of the brain, are little understood. They are difficult to manipulate; their structure can only be altered in limited ways and the resulting behaviour is not easily predictable. The algorithm's functionally can be subverted with greater effect at the level of input and output as the process of training is neither objective, nor impartial. On the contrary, it is open to deliberate manipulation or unintentional bias. The type of training data will stir the algorithm towards certain results. In the example of the "inverse algorithm", if for the improvement of efficiency data sets on delivery routes are used and the highest ranked routes are achieved only by traffic code violations, then this becomes part of the system's normative knowledge. It will reinforce unlawful behaviour of the recipients of the algorithm's instructions, because the training parameters exclude traffic code as an explicit set of rules. They are only inscribed implicitly in the collected data. Once the algorithm is trained sufficiently it can autonomously

---

21 Seabrook, John, Dressing for the Surveillance Age. In: The New Yorker, 09.03.2020, www.newyorker.com/magazine/2020/03/16/dressing-for-the-surveillance-age (November 22, 2020).

22 Jain, Anant: Breaking neural networks with adversarial attacks. In: towards data science, 09.02.2019, https://towardsdatascience.com/breaking-neural-networks-with-adversarial-attacks-f4290a9a45aa (November 22, 2020).

manage responsively large numbers of requests in the management of deliveries. For example, as soon as a customer places an order, the system begins to locate the closest riders with the shortest route between his or her own location, restaurant and customer location. For maximum efficiency the system will start to match further orders before assigning them to a rider. The rider always has to perform two tasks per order: picking up and delivering. The machine learning algorithm has to resolve what is known as the "Traveling Salesman Problem". From a path of 10 points, it will calculate, generate and compare around 11,000 possibilities before selecting the optimal route for delivery.[23]

Situational parameters like the weather are not yet part of "Super Brain's" calculations. Although heavy rain immediately increases consumer demand because people prefer to stay at home, the conditions for drivers are getting worse. The same route takes considerably longer. Late delivery is immediately penalised by the dispatch programme. This for the riders leads to extreme stress, accumulating a considerable number of extra hours on an unusual high number of orders, with the total salary being less than on a normal day due to penalties. The performance of riders, stations and their managers are measured against the number of orders, the rate of late orders, the amount of bad reviews and complaints. As complaints mainly result from delayed deliveries, the speed at which the riders fulfil their orders is crucial. If certain benchmarks are not reached, first the salaries are cut for both rider and manager and finally a station is closed. Delivery workers are driven into depression by the consequences of the algorithmic organisation of their work and it is only the shared disobedience not to the algorithm, but to the law, that offers relief: "He said that when he and his fellow riders are all going the wrong way at once, he is even able to feel at ease."[24]

As the machine learning in the delivery dispatch system seems to be based on a restricted number of parameters (the most important overall being the meta-algorithm of profit maximisation) manual overruling has to take place in special situations. During extreme weather or on important holidays, dispatch managers take over from the machine. This is due to the fact that an accumulation of irregularities cannot yet be compensated by the programmes. But human interference is not meant to alleviate work for the riders, rather simply to replace its algorithmic management by the human

[23] See: https://chuangcn.org/2020/11/delivery-renwu-translation/ (November 12, 2020).
[24] Ibid.

capacity to cover complex situations.[25] The final option is the manager becoming a worker himself again and delivering orders he cannot assign to riders.

Human Behaviour

Many problems result from a deficiency in refined navigation. The systems used at the moment, whether on purpose or out of a lack of advanced technology, advise riders to drive against traffic or often indicate wrong distances. As rider Xiao Dao told the researchers of Renwu: "'There are some places where there is no shoulder or sidewalk where I can drive against traffic. If there is an overpass, the navigation system will direct me to go over the overpass, even if it is an overpass that does not allow electric scooters. If there is a wall, it will tell you to go directly through the wall.'"[26] Often walking directions are used for motorised vehicles like the delivery-scooters, as they do not have to distinguish direction or type of traffic. In addition to time as an equivalent of money replacing space, walking is used not as the slow way of movement that it is, but because digital orientation can thus cancel traffic restrictions in its calculations. The resulting distance is considerably shorter and applying the speed of a vehicle a earlier delivery time is set. Of course, it is the capitalist who owns the platform who sets the framework for its programmes and thus the algorithms. But the inflexibility of rules that are non-negotiable in daily interactions adds new rigidity to the organisation of work.

> "At the end of 2017, in an article introducing optimizations and upgrades to the platform's intelligent delivery system, Meituan's technology team also mentioned cost. The article explains that algorithm optimization reduces the platform's capacity loss by 19 percent: Delivery volumes that previously needed five riders can now use only four."[27]

Algorithmic space does not only reconstruct a city's network of streets, roads, pathways and public transport lines, but captures even small infra-

25   See: ibid.
26   Ibid.
27   Ibid.

structures like elevators. "In an interview with tech media platform 36Kr, Meituan's delivery algorithm team lead He Renqing emphasized elevators' role in delivery time: Meituan's delivery algorithm specifically accounts for the time riders take to arrive at a certain floor, even to the point of investigating the speeds at which riders can go up and down elevators in tall buildings."[28] Many office-buildings in China do not allow delivery riders to use staff elevators and often there is only one service-elevator. Human routines and irregularities mean delivery is depending on too many parameters to make any reliable calculation for its duration. As a response, delivery riders under stress press the "delivered"-button before they actually deliver. This disobedient behaviour is countered by the platform through an escalation of surveillance, a seamless automatic monitoring of the position of recipient and rider through GPS. Any violation automatically triggers a hefty deduction of wage.[29]

Although the system aspires to become increasingly more intelligent through learning, especially preparation time for the meals is depending on too many factors to predict. "The system continually improves itself in the name of 'intelligence', repeatedly shrinking the time allotted for food pickups—but shopkeepers' slow pace in getting food out the door has always been an issue. In a public article, Meituan's senior algorithm expert Wang Shengyao explains that even after analysing the history of completed orders it is still very difficult to accurately predict how long it will take a shop to prepare an order. As long as the predicted preparation time is not correct, the food delivery ecosystem will continue to contain a random variable."[30] As the Renwu report found out in its interviews, the problem of slow preparation and delays are countered by the riders through a variety of measures. They try to develop personal relations to shop-keepers and restaurant staff, some of their activities bordering on bribery. Quite often the stress drivers are permanently exposed to through digital management leads to verbal or physical abuse and violence, escalating even into fights with lethal outcome.

28   Ibid.
29   Li ,Tangzhe: Feeding the Chinese City, 12.10.2020, https://progressive.international/wire/2020-10-12-feeding-the-chinese-city/en (November 23, 2020).
30   Chuang: Delivery Workers, Trapped in the System, 12.11.2020, https://chuangcn.org/2020/11/delivery-renwu-translation/ (November 12, 2020).

Algorithmic Apparatus

In the end, the platform economy depends on one device: the smart phone. The whole process of orders, navigation and communication with customers or station runs through the algorithmic apparatus, the embodiment of digitalisation. This little handheld machine dictates the life and the relationship of service-worker and customer. The influence of the time-based programmes that structure everybody's daily life is increasingly all-encompassing. Aiming at just-in-time, the inability to tolerate any waiting time or unquantifiable moments in life does not only rule the work of the delivery rider, but also that of his or her client. Nervously counting down the minutes, the hungry recipient of a fast food meal is unable to focus on anything else whilst waiting. The growing influence of consumers in the service industries leads, as the Renwu report indicates, to the use of algorithms to construct a power hierarchy between worker and customer.[31] As demand is pushing for ever shorter delivery times, the dispatch programmes begin to spread divergent schedules between rider and customer. To please the latter, the arrival-time of his or her order is set earlier than the delivery time for the rider. But what is meant to appease customers, is on the contrary increasing tension, as the rider will inevitably arrive late given that he can hardly keep the steadily shrinking delivery times.

Algorithmic space today is based on a disavowal of the human body as a located conscious organism, as it coincides with a technical device, mainly the smartphone. If obedience is connected to maintaining a defined position, then this primitive identification of body and device is simple to undermine. Examples of disobedience could be seen during the Covid pandemic in South Korea, where mobile phones were left at home to simulate the presence of the quarantined individual to escape the rigid digital tracing system. The necessary consequence for algorithmic space is the fusion of device and body, through ankle-monitors, implanted microchips or improved body-recognition. Until the latter is reliable, there will be variations of the disobedient operation of the "phonebody", as the Berlin artist Simon Weckert has demonstrated, who used a local, mobile concentration of phones to simulate traffic congestions on public streets. By placing a number of switched-on phones in a handcart and pulling it along Berlin's main roads, Google maps interpret-

---

31 See ibid.

ed this information as a concentration of vehicles which led to warnings for heavy traffic being fed into their navigation-system.[32]

As the smartphone merges with the body and its position in space, in the United States correctional system ankle-bracelets are now replaced by apps which demand regular interactions with parole officers, as reported by the British newspaper "The Guardian": "Once a month, Keck would open up the Shadowtrack app and speak his answers to a series of questions so that a voice-recognition algorithm could confirm it was really him. He would then type out answers to several more questions—such as whether he had taken drugs—and the app would send his responses and location to his parole officer."[33] What seems like a simple change from one mode of digital surveillance to another, has wide-ranging consequences due to the use of intelligent software. The control is so pervasive and the panoptical feeling of being permanently watched so penetrating, that some offenders would prefer incarceration to the psychological stress caused through the app. "'It was cool to not have to report to a probation officer, it was cool to not have to take drug tests any more, Keck says. 'But that peace of mind, of not having somebody track your every move … it was like being locked up again.'"[34]

But the "Shadowtrack"-system does not only seamlessly monitor every movement of its user. It increasingly implements behavioural predictions through algorithms and machine learning in what the companies call "experimental predictive analytics", which could lead to wrong arrests for violation of probation laws.[35] Shadowtrack's voice-recognition algorithm claims to be able to detect the use of drugs or alcohol by a person, combining slurs of speech with other parameters. Another system, called "SmartLink" follows movement-patterns of the smartphone user to predict his or her likelihood of absconding or any approach to what the system qualifies as "risk locations".[36]

---

32   See: Hern, Alex, Berlin artist uses 99 phones to trick Google into traffic jam alert. In: The Guardian, 03.02.2020, www.theguardian.com/technology/2020/feb/03/berlin-artist-uses-99-phones-trick-google-maps-traffic-jam-alert (April 20, 2020).

33   Feathers, Todd: 'They track every move': how US parole apps created digital prisoners. In: The Guardian, 04.03.2021, www.theguardian.com/global-development/2021/mar/04/they-track-every-move-how-us-parole-apps-created-digital-prisoners (April 20, 2020).

34   Ibid.

35   Ibid.

36   See: ibid.

All the companies behind these applications are private, most of them connected to the correctional industry of the USA. By using smartphones, which are increasingly the equivalent of a person's identity, their business potentials seem without limits. "The next generation of monitoring technology promises to go even further. Researchers at Purdue University in Indiana, funded by a federal grant, are combining tracking apps with devices that monitor the user's cortisol levels and heart rate as markers for stress. That biometric data, along with location histories and other information collected through apps, will be fed into algorithms to determine whether a person is engaging in risky behaviour that could lead to reoffending, potentially sending an automatic alert to a parole officer."[37] All this is happening in what could be called "digital capitalism", and the revenue for companies thus even extends to pulling vast amounts of biometric data from people being convicted by the state to use these apps. As minorities and people of colour are overrepresented in the incarceration system, the bodies of black individuals and their space are turned into commodities.[38] Where two hundred years ago, with the change from physical punishment to workhouses the manual labour of the prisoner was exploited, now his body dissolves into data and this information is not only used against him, but also marketed by private companies.

Proximity equals time and saving time is one of the highest preferences in a capitalist service-economy. The recent example of delivery-drivers hanging smart-phones in trees next to shops in the USA shows their despair to satisfy the algorithm.[39] This applies not only to the delivery-times, but also the response-time of riders working in delivery trying to get jobs. Therefore, the dispatch-algorithm has a preference for drivers as close to the pick-up point of the delivery as possible. The closer a driver is, the higher the probability to be the first to receive the order. But due to the logic of the identification of an individual with its smartphone, the simple logic of the delivery dispatch algorithms can be tricked by the use of multiple devices per person. As the phones are among the most expensive possessions of many of the riders, locations difficult to reach are used to expose their multiplied identities. Hanging high up they are waiting to be detected by the delivery-app, equivalent to a small queue of identical people. "Someone places several devices in a tree located

37 Ibid.
38 See: ibid.
39 Soper, Spencer, Amazon Drivers Are Hanging Smartphones in Trees to Get More Work. In: Bloomberg Quint, 01.09.2020, www.bloombergquint.com/business/amazon-drivers-are-hanging-smartphones-in-trees-to-get-more-work (November 12, 2020).

close to the station where deliveries originate. Drivers in on the plot then sync their own phones with the ones in the tree and wait nearby for an order pickup. The reason for the odd placement [...] is to take advantage of the handsets' proximity to the station, combined with software that constantly monitors Amazon's dispatch network, to get a split-second jump on competing drivers."[40] The delivery system of Amazon can locate smartphones in a radius of four meters, which creates a pattern for the distribution of proxy-phones around the origin of orders, e.g. a supermarket of the company's Whole Foods chain. What used to be the queue of casual workers lining up outside a factory waiting for jobs, is now replaced by the phones in the hands and pockets of self-employed entrepreneurs. This rather traditional disobedience on the borderline between the physical and the virtual world is accompanied by attempts to directly tap into the technology and the code running the system. In their zeal to accumulate orders and with that income, drivers are surveilling each other by taking pictures and filming to speculate via social media, which technologies are used to receive orders faster than competitors. This also leads to informing on colleagues and reporting them to Amazon for alleged rigging of the company's delivery dispatch system.[41]

Offline

To escape the regime of algorithmic management and the space it constructs, there are attempts to bring workers together, although the platforms do not allow such organisation. The disobedience in this case is as old as it is simple: empathy, friendship and care, as the example of a rider in Shanghai shows: "Yongqiang's style is to build a face-to-face community, letting brothers and sisters participate in more activities and have more heart-to-heart conversations and social interactions. In so doing, they can strengthen their ties of friendship and de-stress. 'I hope to be able to organize offline activities within this community, such as making a community flag, organizing offline dinners where we would all split the bill, and so on. To let everyone, interact to the full and have support.'"[42] To go offline or to discard your phone seems

40   Ibid.
41   See: ibid.
42   Li, Tangzhe: Feeding the Chinese City, 12.10.2020, https://progressive.international/wire/2020-10-12-feeding-the-chinese-city/en (Dezember 10, 2020).

the ultimate disobedience to a system that dehumanises work. So parallel and in contrast to the inescapable and fake "community" of the platform, a complete retreat into the world of real communication is offering not only logistical, but also emotional solidarity and relief.

Another way is using digital means for the development of delivery driver mass channels, which are expanding rapidly in China. They even spread self-made maps, as reliable systems of numbering houses are still missing or incomplete in many Chinese cities. "Jiang Yilong is precisely the designer of the Hangzhou area 'delivery driver building number sorting map'. He rendered the residential neighbourhoods within a 5–10-kilometre radius into a two-dimensional map and then labelled it with building numbers. This has made things much easier for newly inducted delivery drivers."[43] So new maps are unfolding, parallel to algorithmic space but at the moment only filling the gaps of the system. The delivery driver media do not stop there, but offer support with providing information about "cheaper battery-powered bike rentals, lithium battery rentals, emergency bike repair, battery charging and other services."[44] Their services meanwhile also include information on affordable flats and even "delivery driver meals"[45] of healthy food at a low price. Thus, a new commons arises, if only at the level of reproduction and in reaction to existing grievances. But there is also a growing number of platform cooperatives evolving, trying to use digital methods of work-organisation to increase the welfare both of workers and customers.

Where algorithms are used in liberal market capitalism to enforce individualisation or even atomisation of the work-force and a winner-takes-it-all mentality, the workers under their regime organise to counteract against the antagonising conditions the underlying ideology produces. These new communities are based on mutual aid, communication and practical help. They are oscillating between counteracting against the regime of the platforms and mollifying the destructive effects of their business principles. "If there is anyone in the community who has come into special circumstances and cannot deliver an order on time, or if there is any need for help in life or in work, community members will encourage each other to help out."[46]

43 Ibid.
44 Ibid.
45 Ibid.
46 Ibid.

Algorithms tend to contract space, leading to paradoxical situations like navigating unlawful routes and trespassing regulations. They tend to ignore human behaviour, obstacles, weather conditions or any other aspects that are not reducible to the minimum distance between points. Algorithmic space at the moment is a flatland without places, if places are locations loaded with qualities beyond geometrical or topographical information. Digital abstraction reduces space to the geometrical distribution of positions. The complexity of what culturally, socially and architecturally is perceived as a "place" is therefore reduced to points on surfaces in a coordinate system. Place is reduced to locations between movements, to calculable positions. "This is not just a matter of nostalgia. An active desire for the particularity of place—for what is truly 'local' or 'regional'—is aroused by such increasingly common experiences. Place brings with it the very elements sheared off in the planiformity of site: identity, character, nuance, history."[47]

Obedience is no longer a conscious act, voluntarily following rules or instructions, but immanent to this construction and reconstruction of space. Disobedience can only either altogether ignore it, beat it with its own weapons, or try to critically balance it through sufficient manipulatory and social exchange with the real world. Because, as the psychologist George Herbert Mead said: "The reality of what we see is what we can handle—it is this which is congruous, it is this which is contemporaneous, it is this which may be conceived of as existing at an instant for the purposes of exact measurement, it is this which may in imagination be indefinitely subdivided without reaching a contradiction, it is this which existing at a distance has the same character as at hand [...]."[48]

Literature

Adorno, Theodor W.: Minima Moralia, Suhrkamp, Frankfurt a.M., 2001 (1951), own translation.
Adversarial Fashion, website, https://adversarialfashion.com (November 22, 2020).

[47] Casey, Edward S.: The Fate of Place, Los Angeles, London 1998 (1997), p. xiii.
[48] Mead, George Herbert: Perspective Theory of Perception, Essay 7. In: Morris, Charles W.; Brewster, John M.; Dunham, Albert M.; Miller, David (Eds.): The Philosophy of the Act, Chicago 1938, p. 104.

Al-Youssef, Muzayen; Anders, Theo; Schmid, Fabian; Weiss, Stefan: Die neuen Gesetze zur Bekämpfung der Corona-Pandemie. In: Der Standard, 20.03.2020, www.derstandard.de/story/2000115935419/die-neuen-gesetze-zur-bekaempfung-der-corona-pandemie (April 20, 2020).

Borries, Christian von: The Disappearance of Architecture and Society in the Algorithm, Conversation with Olaf Grawert and Arno Brandlhuber. In: Arch+ The Property Issue, Politics of Space and Data, 2020, p. 12.

Brownlee, Jason: How to Explore the GAN Latent Space When Generating Faces, 03.07.2019. In: Generative Adversarial Networks, https://machinelearningmastery.com/how-to-interpolate-and-perform-vector-arithmetic-with-faces-using-a-generative-adversarial-network/ (November 22, 2020).

Carroll, Lewis: Sylvie and Bruno concluded. In: Green, Roger Lancelyn (Ed.): The Works of Lewis Carroll, London 1965.

Casey, Edward S.: The Fate of Place, University of California Press Berkeley, Los Angeles, London 1998 (1997).

Chuang: Delivery Workers, Trapped in the System, 12.11.2020, https://chuangcn.org/2020/11/delivery-renwu-translation/ (November 14, 2020).

Feathers, Todd: 'They track every move': how US parole apps created digital prisoners. In: The Guardian, 04.03.2021, www.theguardian.com/global-development/2021/mar/04/they-track-every-move-how-us-parole-apps-created-digital-prisoners (April 20, 2020).

Held, Richard; Hein, Allan: Movement-Produced Stimulation in the Development of Visually Guided Behavior. In: The Journal of Comparative and Physiological Psychology, 1963, p. 872–876.

Hern, Alex: Berlin artist uses 99 phones to trick Google into traffic jam alert. In: The Guardian, 03.02.2020, www.theguardian.com/technology/2020/feb/03/berlin-artist-uses-99-phones-trick-google-maps-traffic-jam-alert (April 20, 2020).

Jain, Anant: Breaking neural networks with adversarial attacks. In towards data science, 09.02.2019, https://towardsdatascience.com/breaking-neural-networks-with-adversarial-attacks-f4290a9a45aa (November 22, 2020).

Lefebvre, Henri: The Production of Space, Blackwell Publishing, Oxford 1991 (1974).

Li, Tangzhe: Feeding the Chinese City, 12.10.2020, https://progressive.
international/wire/2020-10-12-feeding-the-chinese-city/en (December 10, 2020)

McMullan, Thomas: How digital maps are changing the way we understand our world. In: The Guardian, 02.12.2014, www.theguardian.com/technology/2014/dec/02/how-digital-maps-changing-the-way-we-understand-world (October 28, 2020).

Mead, George Herbert: Perspective Theory of Perception, Essay 7. In: Morris, Charles W.; Brewster, John M.; Dunham, Albert M.; Miller, David (Eds.): The Philosophy of the Act, University of Chicago 1938, p. 103–124.

Seabrook, John: Dressing for the Surveillance Age. In: The New Yorker, 09.03.2020, www.newyorker.com/magazine/2020/03/16/dressing-for-the-surveillance-age (November 22, 2020).

Seaver, Nick: What should an Anthropology of Algorithms do? In: Cultural Anthropology, Vol. 33, Issue 3, (2018), p. 375–385.

Shenker, Jack: Strike 2.0: how gig economy workers are using tech to fight back. In: The Guardian, 31.08.2019, www.theguardian.com/books/2019/aug/31/the-new-resistance-how-gig-economy-workers-are-fighting-back (November 12, 2020).

Soper, Spencer: Amazon Drivers Are Hanging Smartphones in Trees to Get More Work. In: Bloomberg Quint, 01.09.2020, www.bloombergquint.com/business/amazon-drivers-are-hanging-smartphones-in-trees-to-get-more-work (October 15, 2020).

Spencer, Richard: British students fined for 'illegal map-making' in China. In: The Telegraph, 05.01.2009, www.telegraph.co.uk/news/worldnews/asia/china/4125477/British-students-fined-for-illegal-map-making-in-China.html (October 15, 2020).

Srivastava, Ishan: How Kargil spurred India to design own GPS. In: The Times of India, 05.04.2014, https://timesofindia.indiatimes.com/home/science/How-Kargil-spurred-India-to-design-own-GPS/articleshow/33254691.cms (October 15, 2020).

Steyerl, Hito: How Not to Be Seen: A Fucking Didactic Educational .MOV File, 2013, www.tate.org.uk/art/artworks/steyerl-how-not-to-be-seen-a-fucking-didactic-educational-mov-file-t14506 (September 28, 2020).

Wang, Vivian: On Singles' Day in China, Couriers Clamor for More. In: New York Times, 11.11.2020, www.nytimes.com/2020/11/11/business/alibaba-singles-day-couriers.html (November 15, 2020).

Christina Hecht

Torn Between Autonomy and Algorithmic Management

(Dis)Obedience of Solo Self-Employed Working via Digital Platforms

The transformation problem is a classical concept in the sociological analysis of power dynamics in employment relations, which describes an incompleteness of contracts between employers and employees. The basis of the problem is that the capacity to work is always tied to a subject. Therefore, when transforming this capacity into actually performed work, a "minimum degree of 'voluntary' willingness to perform"[1] by the subject is required. The contract may cover the "right to use [workers, CH] work capability for a certain period of time".[2] It cannot, however, specify how much effort a person spends on the labor process. Additionally, employers and employees are characterized by divergent interests: the former seek to maximize productivity and profit, while the latter aim for an optimal wage-effort-balance and want to preserve their labor capacity.[3] This constellation generates the employers' need to control their workforce, or, put differently: to maximize obedience. But workers, being reflexive subjects, are capable of disobedience in various forms.[4]

There are two ways employers can handle this transformation problem, which differ in the extent of obedience they are allowed to demand from the respective worker: dependent employment and self-employment. In the former case, obedience is controlled by employers, but employees enjoy the benefits of workers' rights and security through permanent employment. Self-employed workers do not have this security, but in exchange enjoy more autonomy in their work. In the following, I will explain how digital platform companies use strategies of algorithmic management to monitor, track and influence solo self-employed workers in order to enforce obedience from them. In doing so they undermine the differentiation between dependent employment and self-employment. From the employers' perspective, this strategy brings about the best of both worlds: being able to control the workers' labor process while not being obligated to guarantee them the benefits and rights dependent employees are entitled to. It allows platform companies to

---

1 Marrs, Kiara: Herrschaft und Kontrolle bei der Arbeit. In: Böhle, Fritz et al. (Eds.): Handbuch Arbeitssoziologie, Wiesbaden 2010, p. 331–356, here p. 331, own translation.
2 Ibid.
3 Ibid., p. 332.
4 Of course, the specific form of this relationship varies in different work contexts. For example, direct external control may be replaced by a market-centered mode of control that gives employees extensive freedom of action in their work as long as it is profitable in the end (ibid., p. 343 f., translation by the author).

maximize obedience while simultaneously narrowing the workers space for disobedience.

I develop my argument in four steps. First, the organizational principles of digital platform companies are described. Subsequently, I differentiate between dependent and self-employment based on ideal types. Third, in a literature review on algorithmic management and workers' strategies of disobedience, I show that there is an inscribed imbalance of negotiation power in platform mediated labor relations—privileging the platform over the self-employed worker. In the fourth, empirical part of this study, I further illustrate the tension between obedience and disobedience emerging in this context by presenting a case study on cleaning workers mediated by the platform company Helpling. The paper ends with a conclusion.

The Platform as an Organizational Principle of Digital Markets

Companies with digitally based business models can be described as platforms. Linking supply and demand of certain products or services is their fundamental feature: "At the most general level, platforms are digital infrastructures that enable two or more groups to interact."[5] For instance, if some friends want to order dinner on a Friday night, they will probably resort to the german platform service of Lieferando, which offers an overview of multiple restaurants, handles the purchasing process as well as the payment.

In capitalist economies, connecting supply and demand is the most central task of a free market, characterized by competition of multiple companies. The key feature about digital platforms is, that they constitute a market themselves. Single companies seize the market-mechanism and the relevant infrastructure in a given economic field.[6] Building on this economic power, they not only control the access to a respective market, but further unfold the ability to "dominate and shape"[7] it. Consider the example of mobile application software. In order to sell their product, developers have no choice but to use the Apple App- or the Google PlayStore. There is no way around those

---

[5] Srnicek, Nick: Platform Capitalism, Cambridge 2017, p. 43.
[6] Staab, Philipp: Digitaler Kapitalismus. Markt und Herrschaft in der Ökonomie der Unknappheit, Berlin 2019, p. 30.
[7] Staab, Philipp; Nachtwey, Oliver: Das Produktionsmodell des digitalen Kapitalismus. In: Soziale Welt Sonderband—"Soziologie des Digitalen" (2017), p. 6 (translation by the author).

gates. If an app does not exist in the stores, it's like it doesn't exist at all. Exploiting their gatekeeping positions, platforms rely on a commission model: Apple and Google, respectively, demand a fifteen or thirty percent share of all turnovers mediated by their platform.[8]

To gain this kind of dominance, a platform has to become a product specific monopoly[9] by maximizing the number of its users. Two features of digital goods and services foster platform companies' tendency towards monopolization. First, the marginal reproductions costs[10] approximate zero. A mobile phone application can be copied with one click, and the registration of another customer on, e.g., AirBnb does not create any costs for the company, whatsoever. Thus, platform companies can take advantage of economies of scale.[11] The production of industrial goods, in contrast, illustrates this point. Even if the marginal costs for building an automobile drop because of rationalization, it is still necessary to purchase materials and the needed workforce to assemble a car. Second, digital goods and services are characterized by network effects.[12] This term describes the fact that a platform becomes increasingly attractive to new customers (and to profitable advertising customers), the more people are already on board.[13] You can ask yourself: Why use a niche social network, when all your friends and colleagues are on Facebook? Network effects constantly self-reinforce the process of monopolization. Since platform companies collect and analyze their users' data to optimize their services, more users lead to more data, which in turn consolidates their local monopoly.

In summary, the developments in the commercial part of the internet are characterized by processes of concentration, control and power.[14] This diagnosis stands in sharp contrast to the self-representation of platform com-

---

8   Staab 2019, p. 221. Also demanding thirty percent before, in November 2020 Apple announced to half that commission for companies with yearly turnovers lower than a million. But the key point concerns the power of a single company to set that rate.
9   In a more detailed theoretical differentiation, a distinction can be made between product and metaplatforms, see: Dolata, Ulrich: Volatile Monopole. Konzentration, Konkurrenz und Innovationsstrategien der Internetkonzerne. In: Berliner Journal for Soziologie 24 (2015), p. 505–529, here p. 511.
10 The costs that arise with the production of an additional unit of the product.
11 Staab; Nachtwey 2017, p. 6.
12 Srnicek 2017, p. 45.
13 Dolata 2015, p. 511.
14 Ibid., p. 523.

panies. Their description is marked by the narrative that they only provide infrastructure, positioning themselves as neutral actors. Indeed, the market power these companies accumulate does not adversely affect customers, as it is the case with classic monopolies.[15] In fact, customers benefit from cheap and efficient services. One example of the above mentioned data based product or service optimizations are recommendations based on algorithms. In addition, platforms apply a multitude of strategies to increase trust and confidence in commercial transactions on the internet. This is especially important given that the internet can only show digital representations of products. Customers can not inspect products in detail, which generally leads to lower levels of trust. To counteract this, platforms offer extensive informations and customer ratings.[16] Ratings are also used to reduce uncertainty regarding vendors, which find themselves exposed to intra-platform competition, while customers enjoy market transparency.[17] It is essential to note, that the power that platforms can exercise over service providers is the real source of conflict. Platform companies have argued that they do not permanently nor directly control service providers.[18] The crucial point, however, is that these are dependent on the infrastructure offered by the platforms to distribute their products and services. As was said: platforms control access to a market.

Differentiating between Self- and Dependent-Employment

In this section, I seek to develop an ideal type of self-employment and define its characteristic features by distinguishing it from dependent employment. While the former is characterized by autonomy and the ability of workers to organize everyday work independently, control and dependency are features of the latter.[19] An ideal type is a construction that will inevita-

---

15 Staab 2019, p. 226 f.
16 Kirchner, Stefan; Beyer, Jürgen: Die Plattformlogik als digitale Marktordnung. In: Zeitschrift für Soziologie 45 (2016), issue 5, p. 324–339, here p. 330.
17 Ibid., p. 330 f.
18 Cunningham-Parmeter, Keith: From Amazon to Uber: defining employment in the modern economy. In: Boston University Law Review 96 (2016), p. 1673–1728, here p. 1677.
19 Which is related to, as mentioned earlier, the way an employer deals with the transformation problem.

bly fail to grasp all of social reality.[20] Besides, the self-employed workforce is quite heterogenous in itself.[21] Yet, two reasons support the application of ideal types when researching digitally mediated labor. First, they do not aim to level out existing differences but they provide a tool to describe the empirical world in a specific context, "by measuring the distance between the ideal type and the empirical cases".[22] Second, this ideal-typical view of self-employment is precisely the starting point for the social and labor law consequences associated with this occupational status. And these consequences are not heterogenous. The real heterogeneity refers to whether and to what extend these circumstances lead to secure or precarious working and living conditions.

Self-employment is defined in demarcation to dependent employment. "The self-employed person must be free to organize his or her activities and be able to determine the working hours and place of work freely. Self-employed persons are not bound by instructions."[23] The work of the self-employed is marked by the absence of a superior requesting and controlling obedience. Rather, it is characterized by autonomy in a twofold way—autonomy regarding the work itself as well as the general working conditions. Following Frey, this can be expressed in terms of autonomy of conduct and autonomy of negotiation.[24] Autonomy of conduct describes freedom of decision-making in the actual work process,[25] while autonomy of negotiations captures the ability to influence and shape the conditions of work.[26] In addition, self-employed

20   Vester, Heinz-Günter: Kompendium der Soziologie II: Die Klassiker, Wiesbaden 2009, p. 119.
21   Bögenhold, Dieter/Fachinger, Uwe: Berufliche Selbstständigkeit. Theoretische und empirische Vermessungen, Wiesbaden 2016, p. vii.
22   Vester 2009, p. 119 (translation by the author).
23   Obermeier, Tim/Schultheis, Kathrin: Selbstständigkeit. In: Bundeszentrale für politische Bildung—Dossier Arbeitsmarktpolitik 2014 (translation by the author).
24   Frey, Michael: Autonomie und Aneignung in der Arbeit. Eine soziologische Untersuchung zur Vermarktlichung und Subjektivierung von Arbeit, München 2009, p. 39. Also: Moldaschl, Manfred: Herrschaft durch Autonomie—Dezentralisierung und widersprüchliche Anforderungen. In: Lutz, Burkhart (Ed.): Entwicklungsperspektiven von Arbeit: Ergebnisse aus dem Sonderforschungsbereich 333 der Universität München, Berlin 2001, p. 132–164, here p. 136. Both authors apply these concepts to capture potentials of autonomy in dependent employment. Transferring them to self-employment seems unproblematic, since they should be even more pronounced in this case.
25   E.g. when and how to do each task.
26   E.g. the decision about business partners (whom to work for) or the salary.

persons work for several clients. Therefore, they have more room for negotiations and self-organization in their job. By contrast, an indication for dependent employment according to the Social Security Law is "an activity in accordance with directives and an integration into the work organization of the employer".[27] Employees are dependent insofar as they only work for one employer. They are required to obey instructions in their work processes and undergo varying degrees of control.

Since the days of mass production in fordism, employees' obedience is compensated by company integration which implicates stable and secure working conditions. Certainly, these have been challenged in light of deregulation of employment since the 1990s.[28] However: in Germany, being part of a company as a permanent employee is still linked to the integration into social security systems, labor law as well as entitlement to corporate codetermination and collective representation of interests.[29] In sharp contrast, self-employed workers are not formally part of a company, which is why safety standards and legal protection regarding working hours or salary do not apply to them.[30] They have to cover insurances themselves. In return, as stated earlier, they typically enjoy more autonomy at work and are able to organize hours and tasks independently.

Self-employed workers have professional competence, they dispose of "trade-specific knowledge accompanied by a particular degree of uniqueness".[31] The ideal type of the self-employed individual is an expert in her or his field. This expert knowledge can be gained in formal education or practical experience at work[32] and is accompanied by business administration skills.[33]

Compared to employees, self-employed persons hold a much more powerful position vis-à-vis the companies they provide services for. Moreover, they are on the same level as those companies: they run their own business.

---

27 Sozialgesetzbuch: SGB IV Beschäftigung, https://www.sozialgesetzbuch-sgb.de/sgbiv/7.html (January 15, 2021).
28 Nachtwey, Oliver; Staab, Philipp: Die Avantgarde des digitalen Kapitalismus. In: Mittelweg 36 6 (2015), p. 59–84, here p. 78.
29 Ibid.
30 Obermeier; Schultheis 2014.
31 Müller, Günter F.: Berufliche Selbstständigkeit. In: Moser, Klaus (Ed.): Wirtschaftspsychologie, Heidelberg 2007, p. 379–398, here p. 385 (translation by the author).
32 Fritsch, Michael: Entrepreneurship. Theorie, Empirie, Politik, Wiesbaden 2019, p. 53.
33 Müller 2007, p. 394.

This balance of power results from the characteristics of self-employment. Because self-employed workers provide services for several companies, they are not dependent on one employer, but their professional activity is characterized by self-organization of work relations. At the same time, their professional knowledge and skills are a valuable asset to clients because they lack these qualifications in their own company. Self-employed persons acquire business administration skills that are also beneficial to them in negotiations with potential clients. This allows, for example, to make an informed decision when weighing the profitability of an offer. In conclusion, the ideal typical self-employed person should have greater negotiating power than employees when it comes to negotiating contractual conditions with their clients.

On the Relevance of the Research Topic

The Increased Risk of Precarity

The descriptions above cover what can be called 'normal entrepreneur': professionally experienced, gainfully working men without migration background, with adequate economic resources, who restlessly run their business and earn a safe income that way.[34] It has been object to criticism because it increasingly fails to describe the empirical situation.[35] More and more companies are founded by solo self-employed people without additional staff.[36] Those individuals are more frequently subject to precarious levels of income and high working hours,[37] since they are directly confronted with market volatility and competition. As described above, these market imponderability is not mitigated by integration into a company.[38]

---

34   Bührmann, Andrea D.: Unternehmertum jenseits des Normalunternehmers: Für eine praxistheoretisch inspirierte Erforschung unternehmerischer Aktivitäten. In: Berliner Journal für Soziologie 22 (2012), p. 129–156, here p. 132.

35   An increasing amount of business foundations have been advanced by women or people with migration background, see ibid., p. 136.

36   Bundeszentrale für politische Bildung: Datenreport 2018. Ein Sozialbericht für die Bundesrepublik Deutschland, Bonn 2018, p. 159.

37   Bögenhold; Fachinger 2016, p. 18.

38   Pongratz, Hans J.; Simon, Stefanie: Prekaritätsrisiken unternehmerischen Handelns. In: Bührmann, Andrea D.; Pongratz, Hans J. (Eds.): Prekäres Unternehmertum. Ungewissheiten von selbstständiger Erwerbsarbeit und Unternehmensgründung, Wiesbaden 2010, p. 25–60, here p. 31.

An increased risk for precarious living conditions can be shown in increased existential uncertainty: "Criteria for this include a relatively low income and lack of sufficient protection against social risks such as retirement, illness, invalidity or unemployment."[39] Survey data suggest that around 17% of all solo self-employed in Germany experience precarious job situations. On average, this group has financial reserves that cover living expenses less than one month without any jobs. Moreover, additional savings for retirement are much rarer existent compared to other groups. Another 44% of the sample experience inadequate backup in one of the two dimensions.[40]

Solo self-employed people find themselves confronted with increased exigencies on their conduct of life and work. There are no organizational structures to arrange working hours, as well as the extent and place of work. They are also on their own when it comes to giving meaning to their work and finding daily motivation. A qualitative study concludes, that "the private life in form of personal or family time is at risk of being subsumed and transformed in its entirety by the external demands of self-employment [...]. For all persons there is an external pressure to rationalize their way of life".[41] Regarding potential autonomy in solo self-employment, another study arrives at a sobering conclusion. The working reality of the people interviewed was marked by "permanent self responsibility, high financial pressure and precarious living conditions".[42] The characterization of their work as lacking "autonomy and room to maneuver"[43] provides a preview of the empirical strategies platform companies apply when digitally mediating labor.

Taken together, the review of empirical research summarized above clearly shows that solo self-employed individuals face higher risks of precarious working and living conditions. That is why the question whether these

---

39 Schulze Buschoff, Karin; Conen, Wieteke; Schippers, Joop: Solo-Selbstständigkeit— eine prekäre Beschäftigungsform? In: WSI Mitteilungen 1 (2017) p. 54–61, here, p. 57 (translation by the author).
40 Ibid.
41 Egbringhoff, Julia: Ständig selbst: eine Untersuchung der alltäglichen Lebensführung von Ein-Personen-Selbstständigen, München 2007, p. 286 (translation by the author).
42 Lorig, Phillip: Soloselbstständige Internet-Dienstleister im Niedriglohnbereich: Prekäres Unternehmertum auf Handwerksportalen im Spannungsfeld zwischen Autonomie und radikaler Marktabhängigkeit. In: Arbeits- und Industriesoziologische Studien 8 (2015), issue 1, p. 55–75, here p. 72 (translation by the author).
43 Ibid., p. 72.

risks are accompanied by the advantages of self-employment—autonomy and self-organization—is even more pressing.

Algorithmic Management and Worker's Reflexivity

Moore and Joyce summarized strategies platforms employ to shift the balance of power between themselves and independent contractors. They conclude: "Far from being neutral 'market' facilitators, platforms exhibit highly active agency and control."[44] Still, they emphasize the social, two-way nature of labor relationships. There are no one-way control mechanisms, as workers are capable of reflexive and resistant action. Every introduction of a new management system is accompanied by the promise to solve this problem of control. "Yet in each case, the problem of worker resistance returned."[45] On these grounds, the following discussion of attempts to enforce obedience based on algorithmic management also focuses on workers' strategies of disobedience and resistance.

Platforms seek to control service providers via algorithmic management,[46] which is based on information asymmetries. The companies own the digital infrastructure, so they are able to appropriate the data on all transactions they mediate. This provides them with information control,[47] meaning that platform companies possess more relevant information on the business transactions compared to the other parties (customer, service providers) involved.

Algorithmic management can be realized by means of interface, tracking, and scoring.[48] The interface is the visual area of a website or an app where tasks are offered to service providers. The assignment is done automatically by algorithms,[49] while the parameters underlying this process remain hidden from service providers. In addition, crucial questions regarding the task

---

44   Moore, Phoebe V.; Joyce, Simon: Black box or hidden abode? The expansion and exposure of platform work managerialism. In: Review of International Political Economy 27 (2020), issue 4, p. 926–948, here p. 931.
45   Ibid.
46   Shapiro, Aaron: Between autonomy and control: Strategies of arbitrage in the "on-demand" economy. In: new media & society 20 (2018), issue 8, p. 2954–2971, here p. 2956.
47   Staab 2019, p. 229.
48   Ibid.
49   Moore; Joyce 2019, p. 930.

or customer are usually left unanswered. For instance, Uber drivers have got fifteen seconds to decide whether or not to accept a job, with no information about the customer's destination.[50] Another example are crowd workers on Amazon Mechanical Turk (AMT)[51], which often do not have information on the actual subject or scope of assignments being offered to them.[52] To stick to this example: AMT could make it a requirement that requesters provide information about their company and the job that is to be done. But they do not. Tracking is used to exert algorithmic management by monitoring service providers during their work. This is particularly relevant for courier drivers, who are permanently located by GPS. But also in the context of online crowdsourcing processes, clients may check the progress of freelance workers via screenshots.[53] In this way, it is possible to control work and break time in a ostensibly precise way, in order to minimize the remuneration to be paid over it. Thus, clients expand their company's system of control to workers outside the company without integrating them. In industrial labor, there are gloves that send vibrational feedback straight to the skin, when there is an alleged wrong movement in the workflow.[54] The most common technique of algorithmic management is scoring: customers (or even coworkers) are encouraged to review service providers (colleagues) after each completed order. These ratings of different dimensions are subsequently summarized into an index that is supposed to describe the quality of work, usually ranging from one to five. These scores have far-reaching consequences, for instance, the account of Uber drivers is blocked in case their rating drops below 4.6 of 5.[55] At the same time, the score serves as a figurehead for potential new customers of the

---

50 Rosenblat, Alex; Stark, Luke: Algorithmic Labor and Information Asymmetries: A Case Study of Uber's Divers. In: International Journal of Communication 10 (2016), p. 3758–3784, here p. 3762.

51 On AMT, companies can offer micro tasks to freelance crowd workers all over the world. The so called human intelligence tasks are easily solved by humans, but cannot be automated, e.g. the categorization of pictures.

52 McInnis et al.: Taking a HIT: Designing around Rejection, Mistrust, Risk, and Workers' Experiences in Amazon Mechanical Turk. Proceedings of CHI Conference 2016, San Jose 2016, p. 2271–2282, here p. 2273.

53 Staab; Nachtwey 2017, p. 9.

54 Raffetseder, Eva-Maria/Schaupp, Simon/Staab, Philipp: Kybernetik und Kontrolle. Algorithmische Arbeitssteuerung und betriebliche Herrschaft. In: PROKLA 47 (2017), issue 2, p. 229–247, here p. 240.

55 Rosenblat et al.: Discriminating Tastes: Uber's Customer Ratings as Vehicles for Workplace Discrimination. In: Policy and Internet 9 (2017), issue 3, p. 256–279, here p. 260 ff.

self-employed. For them, it signals the reputation they have accumulated and thus serves as a proxy for establishing trust in digital markets.[56] After analyzing interviews with craftsmen, Lorig summarizes: "Contractors cannot escape the disciplinary effect of ratings, as they are the decisive principle of contracting in the sense of a virtual business card. [...] Autonomy of self-employed work and order acquisition turns into its opposite, a radical market and customer dependence."[57]

As indicated earlier, where there are attempts to control, there is resistance. To counteract algorithmic management via the interface, some AMT workers developed the browser extension 'turkopticon', which enables workers to anonymously rate requesters based on different categories (e.g., generosity of payment or fairness).[58] Using this tool, the workers are able to counteract information asymmetries and make more informed decisions about whether to accept an offer or not. In the context of food delivery or the cab business, some drivers use multiple smartphones to find the most lucrative offer.[59] Another example of circumventing control via interfaces can be found in how workers handle digital documents. These forms often contain fields that must be filled to proceed to the next page, e.g., in customer support. While managers try to gather as much information about customers as possible, workers can make conversations easier by writing meaningless entries into the fields.[60] Regarding scoring, some research has shown that Uber drivers actively engage in conversations with their customers to educate them on the relevance of ratings.[61] In the context of dependent employment, solidarity and collective action among colleagues play a major role in resisting algorithmic management. For example, the company Zalando used the management tool Zonar, where workers must rate the performance of colleagues. In a case study, a number of interviewees reported that they emphasize positive and downplay negative evaluations.[62] Taken together, these

---

[56] Kirchner; Beyer 2016, p. 331.
[57] Lorig 2015, p. 61.
[58] Ettinger, Nancy: The governance of crowdsourcing: Rationalities of the new exploitation. In: Environment and Planning A 48 (2016), issue 11, p. 2162–2180, here p. 2174.
[59] Moore; Joyce 2019, p. 10.
[60] Raffetseder; Schaupp; Staab 2017, p. 239.
[61] Rosenblat; Stark 2016, p. 3775.
[62] Staab, Philipp; Geschke, Sascha-Christopher: Ratings als arbeitspolitisches Konfliktfeld. Das Beispiel Zalando. Hans Böckler Stiftung—Study 429 (2019), p. 40.

examples illustrate that workers employ a variety of strategies to disobey algorithmic management.

As expected, algorithmic management strategies cannot impede reflexive and disobedient strategies of workers. But control is more extensively integrated into the organization of work and work itself, and thus independent of management personnel monitoring it. Remember, the reason why platforms classify their workers as independent contractors in the first place, is because there is no direct instance that controls them. The described asymmetries of information lead to a structurally imbalanced distribution of power between platform companies, customers and service providers, disfavoring the latter group. Following Staab and Nachtwey, service providers mediated by digital platforms can be classified as "contingency workforce".[63] Due to formal independency, this workforce is confronted with contingency in a twofold sense. On the one hand, they are dependent on the coincidence of demand and supply—their labor disposition on required conditions. On the other hand, they have no effective influence on the price or conditions of their own labor, given that there is a potential army of reserve waiting to fill their spot. The expansion of competition as well as digital strategies of control enforce the obedience of the self-employed.[64] The comparison of the ideal type and the reality of platform-mediated self-employment reveals a blatant mismatch. Autonomy and independence are expected to accompany that kind of work, but are limited by various mechanisms. It seems like the service providers are left with the worst of both worlds: external control and radical dependency on the market.

Case Study: Solo Self-Employed Cleaners Working via Helpling

Description of the Case and Methodological Approach

The company Helpling was founded in 2014 and offers a platform for mediating household related services in 10 countries. According to its founders, Helpling is not a cleaning, but a software business.[65] Helpling corresponds to

63   Nachtwey; Staab 2015, p. 81 (translation by the author).
64   Ibid.
65   Schlenk, Caspar T.: Streitgespräch. Das passiert, wenn man Helpling und Verdi an einen Tisch setzt. In: Gründerszene, 10.02.2016, https://www.gruenderszene.de/allgemein/streitgespraech-verdi-helpling (February 25, 2020).

what Srnicek calls a "lean platform".[66] Building on venture capital[67], these are based on a "hyper-outsourced model"[68], which means that Helpling does not own any mops or equipment, but only the digital infrastructure and algorithms steering and analyzing actions on the platform. Cleaners create an account on the platform and are, as one of the founders puts it: "[…] our customers, to whom we provide a technological platform and selected services such as invoicing and payment processing. […] The cleaners are free to decide whether to accept or reject each and every task, there is no authority to issue directions whatsoever."[69] The narrative of platform companies describing themselves as neutral mediator between supply and demand is evident in the case of Helpling. Service providers can set their own prices in their profile. Being self-employed, they have to take care about insurances and tax declarations themselves. In contrast, customers use the website by issuing requests for services on a certain date. They are shown a selection of service providers that could do the job. Upon booking, Helpling receives a commission from the cleaners ranging between 20–32 percent of the total payment.

Given the digital mediation and organization of work, Helpling could be characterized as a typical case[70] reflecting the relationship of obedience and disobedience in digital work. This would imply that the features accompanying digitally mediated work summarized earlier, should be expected to reoccur in the present case. While, in most other cases, the control of service providers is mainly based on tracking, the activity of cleaning itself can neither be digitally mediated nor monitored via the service provider's smartphone. Solo self-employment mediated via Helpling could therefore also be characterized as a divergent case[71] due to the specific nature of household-related services. Because control by tracking is absent, this case offers the chance to carve out possible other modes of control and disobedience.

---

66   Srnicek 2017, p. 75 ff.
67   Alvares de Souza Soares, Philipp: Warum Putz-Start-ups es schwer haben. In: manager magazin, 30.08.2018, https://www.manager-magazin.de/unternehmen/artikel/helpling-book-a-tiger-putz-start-ups-haben-es-schwer-a-1225697.html (February 25, 2020).
68   Srnicek 2017, p. 76, 87.
69   Schlenk 2016.
70   Seawright, Jason; Gerring, John: Case Selection Techniques in Case Study Research. A Menu of Qualitative and Quantitative Options. In: Political Research Quarterly 61 (2008), issue 2, p. 294–308, here p. 297.
71   Flyvberg, Bent: Five Misunderstandings About Case-Study Research. In: Qualitative Inquiry 12 (2006), issue 2, p. 219–245, here p. 229.

Semi-structured interviews with three persons working via Helpling were carried out to assess this topic. I derived relevant dimensions from the state of research, which served as sections of the interview guideline. Each started with an open question that was intended to encourage the interviewees to tell their story. Follow-up questions were designed in order to bring up aspects that were relevant to the research question but had not yet been addressed by the interviewee. Overall, the interview can be classified as dialogic and theme-centered. The interviewees were recruited by means of volunteer sampling.[72] Their experiences were assessed using qualitative content analysis and combining deductive and inductive categories.[73] The age of the interviewees is estimated to range from late twenties to late thirties. A common feature of the interviewees is that they all have an academic background. At the time of the interview, the participants did no longer work at all, or only very rarely via Helpling. The narratives have to be classified as retrospective for the most part and may therefore be outdated in some aspects. However, they were self-employed, and that remains a central feature of work via Helpling until today. As this brief summary indicates, the volunteer sampling did not reach people who were permanently earning their primary income as cleaners via Helpling. The interviewees' experiences were largely made in the context of bridging between life stages. Consequently, this potential distortion has to be kept in mind when reading the following results of the analysis.

Obedience and Disobedience in the Case of Helpling

Formally, there are several aspects of the work routine that can be organized by workers themselves. They have the flexibility to decide how intensively they want to use the platform and how many jobs they want to accept. The workload can thus be adjusted according to their current (financial) situation. While the interviewees tried to select their customers in a targeted manner, in order to avoid long travel times between work locations, the existent information asymmetries restricted this autonomy. Indeed, all interviewees faced ambiguity when selecting offers in the Helpling interface. They described the given information as "vague" or "minimal". For example, sometimes there was incomplete information about the location of the house-

---

[72] Blatter, Joachim K.; Langer, Phil C./Wagemann, Claudius: Qualitative Methoden der Politikwissenschaft. Eine Einführung, Wiesbaden 2018, p. 59.

[73] Kuckartz, Udo: Qualitative Inhaltsanalyse. Methoden, Praxis, Computerunterstützung, Weinheim 2018, p. 97–120.

hold, making it impossible to assess the travel time between clients. Often, making an informed decision about whether to take an offer or not was not possible. Well aware of the reserve army of other cleaners, the interviewees felt pressured to accept offers as quickly as possible. Another problem were insecurities about the amount of the commission the platform would charge. The exact amount was not communicated transparently and varied from order to order. As one interviewee pointedly summarized: "So when they apply which commission rates, that's not really clear to me either." Another aspect are the ratings that customers assign to the performance of the cleaners. The interviewees can only speculate about the criteria according to which customers can rate them via the platform. Only through the information of a customer, the first interviewee learned that the customers have three criteria, which are not only related to cleaning, but also to reliability and friendliness. This is a well-known aspect from research on evaluations of platform-mediated work: It is not (only) the work performance that is quantified, but the person as such. Thus, the evaluations reflect arbitrary and, in the worst case, systematically discriminatory subjective assessments.[74]

Due to their inherent information asymmetries, ratings and scores represent an instrument of algorithmic management. Scores help customers to decide about which cleaner to book. Apparently, scores also determine how much and how lucrative offers the cleaners receive. "You have to get reviews. And the more reviews you get, it's better for your job offers", one interviewee reports. Because there is no clear communication of Helpling regarding this relation, cleaners tend to speculate about the relevance of scores. For example, one interviewee was offered significantly fewer jobs after a poor evaluation. The lack of information about the reasons puzzled her: "Well, after that there were not so many orders. And of course I can't say at all whether that was the reason now, but I thought, yes, that's stupid."

Another dimension of algorithmic management concerns the payment cleaners charge for their services. In contrast to other case studies, the present study did not identify a race to the bottom process. Rather the opposite, the comparison with fees charged by other service providers was described as a tool of empowerment. One interviewee described how she always tried to set her wage in the upper end of the range. As we can see, comparison on and formal independence from the platform opened up space for disobedient behavior, challenging the threatening scenario of being substituted by a re-

74   Rosenblat et al. 2017.

serve army, which platforms usually thrive on to mediate services as cheap as possible. However, the platform applies several strategies to undermine this wage autonomy. On the one hand, the platform provided suggestions on how high the wage should be in a given region. The proposed amount, in turn, is based on the supposedly neutral pooling of data and may, in fact, significantly influence a cleaner's decision to set a wage. On the other hand, one interviewee reported being shown statistics in the profile section that forecast how much money could be earned if one continued to work at the current level. He described this as "toxic manipulation". Similar to surge pricing[75] known from Uber, these statistics are probably intended to keep workers in line and to meet the demands of customers in the long term.

A key feature of the work discussed here allows cleaners to disobey the algorithmically imposed rules: Their actual work is not (yet) digitally mediated or controlled. While there are formal cleaning guidelines, and service providers are encouraged to watch a video explaining those, when they register, these are hardly realistic or practical when it comes to actual work situations: "Well, I always did this, so to speak, what was obligatory, I also kept to the structure, only, in retrospect, it was so that it was never like that, never, thats not possible." Even whether the work clothes supplied by Helpling are worn cannot be checked by the company: "They sent it and suggested, so to speak, that you could wear it at work … but I didn't want to wear that". This autonomy of conduct even goes so far that cleaners and customers jointly outsmart the platform. For example, appointments can be moved to other days of the week in consultation with customers. This scenario is described by one interviewee, who along with her customer "simply cheated by mutual agreement, and said it was Wednesday, but it was Thursday. So the main thing is that this invoice is somehow correct". Why didn't they just bypass the platform altogether? Customers could hire cleaners directly as domestic help. According to interviewees, the reason for this is that customers do not want to miss out on the convenience of the platform. Another aspect concerns the additional services that customers can book. One interviewee mentioned that he had advised his customers not to book any of these additional services. He did the work on the side in order to gain time for other work: "This way, I have been avoiding some tasks, because I was also under time pressure, and then I sort of relieved them [the customers, CH] of having to pay another 5, 6 euros." This strategies of circumvention have allowed the cleaners to partial-

---

75   A dynamic pricing strategy: the payment of drivers is based on current demand.

ly disobey the interests Helpling seeks to impose on their work—a consistent brand identity in terms of the appearance and working practices of the cleaning staff, strict scheduling and maximizing profits by trying to get customers to book additional services. Despite these opportunities to circumvent algorithmic management strategies: all interviewees emphasized their perception, that they are being controlled like an employee, even though they were formally self-employed.

Two conclusions can be derived from the discussion on the relation between obedience and disobedience in the Helpling case. First, obedience and disobedience occur in different realms. As Lessig puts it: "Code is Law."[76] Helpling owns the platform and exerts infrastructural power. They systematically limit the autonomy of cleaners negotiating with customers by enforcing obedience to the digital systems in place (e.g. ratings and incomplete information about offers). It's simply impossible for cleaners to disobey these information asymmetries. As the AMT browser extension 'turkopticon' illustrates, there are attempts to challenge this imbalance of power in the digital realm. Further research could shed light on how similar organizational processes operate among service providers who are not digitally connected. Second, the analogous character of the work opens up space for disobedience in the organization and the actual process of work, which corresponds to autonomy of conduct. This leads to the crucial importance of the relationship between service provider and customer. Unlike courier drivers, cleaners must maintain a lasting and harmonic relationship with their customers. If this is the case, it may be possible to postpone appointments or skip some cleaning activities. This unbalanced constellation is reinforced by the fact that customers submit a rating after the cleaning and thus play a crucial role in determining the service provider's future chances of winning (lucrative) contracts. So in addition to handling algorithmic management, cleaners have to perform emotional labor. Several questions remain unanswered at present: How is that double burden perceived? Does it lead to a further dissolution of boundaries between work and other dimensions of life?

---

76 Lessig, Lawrence: Four puzzles from Cyberspace. In: id. (Ed.): Code Version 2.0, New York 2006, chapter 1.

Conclusion

This paper addressed the distinguishing features of digitally mediated work and the influence of algorithmic management on solo self-employed service workers. First, I defined the characteristics of platform companies, which provide fertile ground for monopolization. I emphasized that the relation between platforms and service providers, not customers, is likely to be conflictual. Following the ideal type of self-employment, service providers are not exposed to an employer who enforces their obedience through mechanisms of control—as it is the case in dependent employment. Dependent- and self-employment are two different ways of employers handling the transformation problem which was defined in the introduction. They shape the relationship between autonomy and security differently: while dependent employees have to obey instructions from the employer to a higher degree than self-employed workers, they also benefit from integration into the company in various ways. Based on a literature review and a condensed report of an empirical study investigating cleaners who work mediated by the platform company Helpling, I have argued that algorithmic management undermines the distinction between dependent and self-employment. Based on information asymmetries and by means of interface, tracking and scoring, the platform companies can impose their structures of relevance without direct control of the service providers. Because of the infrastructural character of platforms, strategies of disobedience are mostly limited to the realm of the actual conduct of work. Thus algorithmic management structurally undermines the negotiation autonomy of the self-employed. Yet specifically this shared experience may be a source of collective organization and the repolitization of algorithms.[77]

Literature

Alvares de Souza Soares, Philipp: Warum Putz-Start-ups es schwer haben. In: manager magazin, 30.08.2018, https://www.manager-magazin.de/unternehmen/artikel/helpling-book-a-tiger-putz-start-ups-haben-es-schwer-A-1225697.html (February 25, 2021).

---

[77] Ulbricht, Lena: Algorithmen und Politisierung. In: Leviathan 48 (2020), p. 225–278.

Blatter, Joachim K.; Langer, Phil C.; Wagemann, Claudius: Qualitative Methoden der Politikwissenschaft. Eine Einführung. Wiesbaden 2018.

Bögenhold, Dieter; Fachinger, Uwe: Berufliche Selbstständigkeit. Theoretische und empirische Vermessungen. Wiesbaden 2016.

Bundeszentrale für politische Bildung: Datenreport 2018. Ein Sozialbericht für die Bundesrepublik Deutschland. Bonn 2018.

Bührmann, Andrea D.: Unternehmertum jenseits des Normalunternehmertums: Für eine praxistheoretisch inspirierte Erforschung unternehmerischer Aktivitäten. In: Berliner Journal für Soziologie 22 (2012), p. 129–156.

Cunningham-Parmeter, Keith: From Amazon to Uber: defining employment in the modern economy. In: Boston University Law Review 96 (2016), p. 1673–1728.

Dolata, Ulrich: Volatile Monopole. Konzentration, Konkurrenz und Innovationsstrategien der Internetkonzerne. In: Berliner Journal für Soziologie 24 (2015), p. 505–529.

Egbringhoff, Julia: Ständig selbst: eine Untersuchung der alltäglichen Lebensführung von Ein-Personen-Selbstständigen. München 2007.

Ettinger, Nancy: The governance of crowdsourcing: Rationalities of the new exploitation. In: Environment and Planning A 48 (2016), issue 11, p. 2162–2180.

Flyvberg, Bent: Five Misunderstandings About Case-Study Research. In: Qualitative Inquiry 12 (2006), issue 2, p. 219–245.

Frey, Michael: Autonomie und Aneignung in der Arbeit. Eine soziologische Untersuchung zur Vermarktlichung und Subjektivierung von Arbeit. München 2009.

Fritsch, Michael: Entrepreneurship. Theorie, Empirie, Politik. Wiesbaden 2019.

Kirchner, Stefan; Beyer, Jürgen: Die Plattformlogik als digitale Marktordnung. In: Zeitschrift für Soziologie, 45 (2016), issue 5, p. 324–339.

Kuckartz, Udo: Qualitative Inhaltsanalyse. Methoden, Praxis, Computerunterstützung. Weinheim, Basel 2018.

Lessig, Lawrence: Four puzzles from Cyberspace. Code Version 2.0. New York 2006.

Lorig, Philip: Soloselbstständige Internet-Dienstleister im Niedriglohnbereich: Prekäres Unternehmertum auf Handwerksportalen im Spannungsfeld zwischen Autonomie und radikaler Marktabhängigkeit. In: Arbeits- und Industriesoziologische Studien, 8 (2015), issue 1, p. 55–75.

Marrs, Kiara: Herrschaft und Kontrolle bei der Arbeit. In: Böhle, Fritz; Voß, Günter G.; Wachtler, Günther (Eds.): Handbuch Arbeitssoziologie. Wiesbaden 2010, p. 331–356.

McInnis, Brian; Cosley, Dan; Nam, Chaebong; Leshed, Gilly: Taking a HIT: Designing around Rejection, Mistrust, Risk, and Workers' Experiences in Amazon Mechanical Turk. Proceedings of the CHI Conference 2016, San Jose 2016, p. 2271–2282.

Moldaschl, Manfred: Herrschaft durch Autonomie—Dezentralisierung und widersprüchliche Arbeitsanforderungen. In: Lutz, Burkhart (Ed.): Entwicklungsperspektiven von Arbeit: Ergebnisse aus dem Sonderforschungsbereich 333 der Universität München. Berlin 2001, p. 132–164.

Moore, Phoebe V.; Joyce, Simon: Black box or hidden abode? The expansion and exposure of platform work managerialism. In: Review of International Political Economy 27 (2020), issue 4, p. 926–948.

Müller, Günter F.: Berufliche Selbstständigkeit. In: Moser, Kurt (Ed.): Wirtschaftspsychologie. Heidelberg 2007, p. 379–398.

Nachtwey, Oliver; Staab, Philipp: Die Avantgarde des digitalen Kapitalismus. In: Mittelweg 36 6 (2015), p. 59–84.

Obermeier, Tim; Schultheis, Kathrin: Selbstständigkeit. In: Bundeszentrale für politische Bildung—Dossier Arbeitsmarktpolitik 2014.

Pongratz, Hans J.; Simon, Stefanie: Prekaritätsrisiken unternehmerischen Handelns. In: Bührmann, Andrea D./Pongratz, Hans J. (Eds.): Prekäres Unternehmertum. Ungewissheiten von selbstständiger Erwerbsarbeit und Unternehmensgründung. Wiesbaden 2010, p. 25–60.

Raffetseder, Eva-Maria; Schaupp, Simon; Staab, Philipp: Kybernetik und Kontrolle. Algorithmische Arbeitssteuerung und betriebliche Herrschaft. In: PROKLA 47 (2017), issue 2, p. 229–247.

Rosenblat, Alex; Levy, Karen E. C.; Barocas, Solon; Hwang, Tim: Discriminating Tastes: Uber's Customer Ratings as Vehicles for Workplace Discrimination. In: Policy and Internet 9 (2017), issue 3, p. 256–279.

Rosenblat, Alex; Stark, Luke: Algorithmic Labor and Information Asymmetries: A Case Study of Uber's Drivers. In: International Journal of Communication 10 (2016), p. 3758–3784.

Schlenk, Caspar T.: Streitgespräch. Das passiert, wenn man Helpling und Verdi an einen Tisch setzt. In: Gründerszene, 10.02.2016, https://www.gruenderszene.de/allgemein/streitgespraech-verdi-helpling (February 25, 2021).

Schulze Buschoff, Karin; Conen, Wieteke; Schippers, Joop: Solo-Selbstständigkeit—eine prekäre Beschäftigungsform? In: WSI Mitteilungen 1 (2017), p. 54–61.

Seawright, Jason; Gerring, John: Case Selection Techniques in Case Study Research. A Menu of Qualitative and Quantitative Options. In: Political Research Quarterly 61 (2016), issue 2, p. 294–308.

Shapiro, Aaron: Between autonomy and control: Strategies of arbitrage in the "on-demand" economy. In: new media & society 20 (2018), issue 8, p. 2954–2971.

Sozialgesetzbuch: SGB IV Beschäftigung, https://www.sozialgesetzbuch-sgb.de/sgbiv/7.html (January 09, 2021).

Srnicek, Nick: Platform Capitalism. Cambridge, Malden 2017.

Staab, Philipp: Digitaler Kapitalismus. Markt und Herrschaft in der Ökonomie der Unknappheit. Berlin 2019.

Staab, Philipp; Geschke, Sascha-Christopher: Ratings als arbeitspolitisches Konfliktfeld. Das Beispiel Zalando. In: Hans Böckler Stiftung—Study, 429 (2019).

Staab, Philipp; Nachtwey, Oliver: Das Produktionsmodell des digitalen Kapitalismus. In: Soziale Welt, Sonderband—"Soziologie des Digitalen" (2017), http://philippstaab.de/wp-content/uploads/2020/01/Nachtwey_Staab-DasProduktionsmodell-des-digitalen-Kapitalismus.pdf (February 12, 2021).

Ulbricht, Lena: Algorithmen und Politisierung. In: Leviathan, 48 (2020), Sonderband 35/2020, p. 255–278.

Vester, Heinz.-Günter: Kompendium der Soziologie II: Die Klassiker. Wiesbaden 2009.

Victoria Guijarro Santos

A Crack in the Algorithm's Facade

A Fundamental Rights Perspective on "Efficiency" and "Neutrality" Narratives of Algorithms[1]

---

[1] First ideas of this work were published in Guijarro Santos, 'Effiziente Ungleichheit', netzforma* e.V. (Ed.) Wenn KI—Dann feministisch (2020), p. 47; I would like to thank Eva Maria Bredler, Phillip Lücking, Fabian Endemann and Nazli Aghazadeh-Wegener for their time and comments as well as Johanna Schlingmann and André Bartsch for their editorial fine tuning.

Member States of the European Union (EU) increasingly implement Artificial Intelligence (AI) systems to assist or replace human decision-makers in more and more sensitive areas of life. AI systems are used to predict school grades, job prospects, or even crime.[1]

In Austria, for example, an AI system has been used since 2018 in a pilot phase to predict the prospects of job seekers to reintegrate into the Austrian job market. It calculates a "reintegration value" based on the data input of a job seeking person. Job seekers are classified into different groups according to the calculated reintegration value. The group defines the eligibility for support measures.[2] Unlike other AI systems deployed by welfare States, the methods paper of this so-called "AMS-algorithm"[3] is publicly available and debated widely in Austrian media and academia. The focus of concern is a table in the methods paper revealing that the AMS-algorithm categorical-

---

[1] E.g. Algorithms in UK's schools: Katwala, Amit: An Algorithm Determined UK Students' Grades. Chaos Ensued, https://www.wired.com/story/an-algorithm-determined-uk-students-grades-chaos-ensued/ (October 12, 2021); prediction of job probabilities and the allocation of welfare in Austria: Wimmer, Barbara: Computer sagt nein: Algorithmus gibt Frauen weniger Chancen beim AMS, https://futurezone.at/netzpolitik/computer-sagt-nein-algorithmus-gibt-frauen-weniger-chancen-beim-ams/400345297 (October 12, 2021); for the welfare State in general: Alston, Philip: Report of the Special rapporteur on extreme poverty and human rights. UN Doc. A/74/48037, 2019; Prediction of crime in Germany: Singelnstein, Tobias: Hessen sucht mit Palantir-Software nach Gefährdern, https://netzpolitik.org/2019/big-data-bei-der-polizei-hessen-sucht-mit-palantir-software-nach-gefaehrdern/ (October 12, 2021), against which a constitutional complaint is pending: Mattes, Anna Livia: Polizeigesetz und Verfassungsschutzgesetz Hessen, https://freiheitsrechte.org/polizeigesetz-hessen/ (October 12, 2021); for further examples see Chiusi, Fabio et al.: Automating Society Report 2020, Algorithm Watch; for the intention to automate even more processes see representative for many: European Commission: White Paper On Artificial Intelligence. COM(2020) 65 final, 2020, p. 1: "Artificial intelligence [...] will change our lives by improving healthcare [...] increasing the security of Europeans, and in many other ways that we can only begin to imagine."

[2] Holl, Jürgen et al.: Das AMS-Arbeitsmarktchancen-Modell. Dokumentation zur Methode, Wien 2018, p. 14; substantive socio-technical analyses by Lopez, Paola: Reinforcing Intersectional Inequality via the AMS Algorithm in Austria. In: Proceedings of the STS Conference Graz 2019, p. 289; Allhutter, Doris et al.: Der AMS-Algorithmus. Eine Soziotechnische Analyse des Arbeitsmarktchancen-Assistenz-Systems (AMAS). Institut für Technikfolgen-Abschätzung, Vienna 2020.

[3] "AMS-algorithm" is the most common name, see for other circulating names Berner, Heiko/Schüll, Elmar: Bildung nach Maß. Die Auswirkungen des AMS-Algorithmus auf Chancengerechtigkeit, Bildungszugang und Weiterbildungsförderung. In: Magazin erwachsenenbildung.at (2020), p. 3.

ly attributes negative coefficients to job seekers which meet the data points "female gender", "over 50 years old", or "health impairment".[4] In contrast, a "male gender", "under 30 years old", or "able-bodied" is neither assigned a positive nor a negative coefficient. These coefficients are crucial for the calculation of the reintegration value: the more negative the coefficient, the lower the reintegration value and the higher the probability to be classified as a group "C"[5]-job seeker. Job seekers of this group "C" will be separated from the regular job center system and assigned to another institution where, amongst others, psychosocial counseling is offered.[6] Job seekers with a mediocre reintegration value are classified into group "B" and will receive the most expensive support. Researchers called the AMS-algorithm a "prime example for discrimination",[7] whereas the director of the Austrian job centers argued that the AMS-algorithm merely reflected reality. According to him, access to the Austrian job market is simply more difficult for women. The AMS-algorithm just represented this harsh reality for women on the Austrian job market and thus by no means discriminated.[8] Moreover, he indicated that expensive support measures were not profitable for group "C"-job seekers— hence the distribution of support measures by the AMS-algorithm was just efficient.[9]

The AMS algorithm vividly illustrates important aspects of the current debate about AI systems in decision making. On the one hand, researchers, civil society, and media keep referring to the discrimination risks inherent

---

4   Holl et al. 2018, p. 11.
5   Actually, the groups are named "H", "M", "N": Holl et al. 2018, p. 14. For simplicity the paper replicates the name used in media.
6   Berner; Schüll 2020, p. 4.
7   Wimmer, Barbara: Der AMS-Algorithmus ist ein "Paradebeispiel für Diskriminierung", https://futurezone.at/netzpolitik/der-ams-algorithmus-ist-ein-paradebeispiel-fuer-diskriminierung/400147421 (October 12, 2021).
8   Cf. Kopf, Johannes: Wie Ansicht zur Einsicht werden könnte, https://www.johanneskopf.at/2018/11/14/wie-ansicht-zur-einsicht-werden-koennte/ (October 12, 2021).
9   Szigetvari, András: AMS-Vorstand Kopf: "Was die EDV gar nicht abbilden kann, ist die Motivation", https://www.derstandard.at/consent/tcf/story/2000089096795/ams-vorstand-kopf-menschliche-komponente-wird-entscheidend-bleiben (October 12, 2021); Kopf, Johannes: Der Beipackzettel zum AMS-Algorithmus, https://futurezone.at/meinung/der-beipackzettel-zum-ams-algorithmus/400641347 (October 12, 2021).

in AI systems.[10] On the other hand, others (like the director of the Austrian job centers) justify its use by pointing to the statistical accuracy of a specific AI system—that is to the alleged neutrality of the system's epistemic foundation—and to a gain in efficiency.[11] Thereby it seems that on efficiency a facade of algorithmic neutrality and statistical unambiguousness is built behind which concerns about algorithmic discrimination are relegated. However, I argue in this paper that embedded in a fundamental and human rights framework, this facade cracks.

After specifying the technological terminology used in the following (I), I will situate the narrative of "efficient" and "neutral" AI systems within a fundamental and human rights framework and analyze the epistemic foundation of the AMS-algorithm through the lens of fundamental rights and science and technology studies (STS). Thereby I demonstrate that an increase in efficiency cannot serve as a catch-all-justification (II), and that even a statistically accurate result—indeed reflecting the "harsh reality" for a specific social group—breaches fundamental rights guaranteeing autonomy, equality, and non-discrimination (III). This shall not be a glass bead game but instead is meant to respond to the problem of regulating discrimination risks through AI systems.[12] For the sake of a responsive regulation it is pivotal how academia, civil society and policy imagine the potentials as well as the limits of AI systems and what they define as the harm in algorithmic discrimination.[13] Therefore, it is crucial that they look through the crack, that is, behind the narratives of "efficient" and "neutral" AI, instead of blindly obeying them.

---

10   Cf. Alston 2019; Achiume, E. Tendayi: Racial discrimination and emerging digital technologies. A human rights analysis. UN Doc. A/HCR/44/57, 2020; Barocas, Solon/Selbst, Andrew: Big Data's Disparate Impact. In: California Law Review 104(3) (2016), p. 671–732.

11   Kopf 2018; Kopf 2019; see also Kischel, Uwe: Art. 3. In: Epping, Volker/Hillgruber, Christian (Eds.): BeckOK Grundgesetz, München 2021, at § 218d 1.

12   As aspired inter alia by German Data Ethics Commission: Opinion of the Data Ethics Commission, 2020; German Parliament/Bundestag: Unterrichtung der Enquete-Kommission Künstliche Intelligenz. BT-Drs. 19/23700, 2020; European Commission: Proposal for a Regulation of the European Parliament and of the Council Laying Down Harmonised Rules on Artificial Intelligence (Artificial Intelligence Act) And Amending Certain Union Legislative Acts. COM(2021)206 final, 2021.

13   Cave, Stephen et al.: Introduction. In: ibid: AI Narratives. A History of Imaginative Thinking about Intelligent Machines, Oxford 2020, p. 1–19; Seyfert, Robert: Algorithms as regulatory objects. In: Information, Communication & Society (2021), p. 1–17.

I. AI? What AI?

I called the AMS-algorithm an AI system because according to the proposed Artificial Intelligence Act of the EU Commission (that is not yet hard law) the AMS-algorithm would be classified as such.[14] However, the same AMS-algorithm could also be named otherwise as in the interdisciplinary discourse about AI many labels exist for the same system.

Terminology is important because it influences our imagination about technology, its potentials, and risks.[15] But terminology is not everything. More important than a label is what a specific system does, what for, and for whom. This is part of my argument which aims at acknowledging the potentials and limits of a specific system and deploying it accordingly.

The systems I am referring to in this paper evaluate training data, recognize patterns in this training data, generalize and apply these patterns to new data *(what)*. Its developers validate the results according to mathematical state of the art standards.[16] In this method "all is about data".[17] To better catch this I prefer to use the term data-based algorithmic system instead of AI system.[18] Furthermore, the data-based algorithmic systems referred to in this paper are deployed in (semi-)automated decision-making and shall predict human behavior and not the weather or energy consumption (what for). Their users are State actors and not private actors like companies (by whom). For all these systems, I use the AMS-algorithm as a representative example.

---

14   Article 3 (1) AIA in conjunction with Annex I: "'artificial intelligence system' (AI system) means software that is developed with one or more of the techniques and approaches listed in Annex I and can, for a given set of human-defined objectives, generate outputs such as content, predictions, recommendations, or decisions influencing the environments they interact with", Annex I lit. c compromises "statistical approaches".

15   Sommerer, Lucia M.: Personenbezogenes Predictive Policing, Baden-Baden 2020, p. 193 f.; especially in law according to Crooto, Rebecca: "Tech cases quickly turn into battles of analogies" cited in Thomson-DeVeaux, Amelia: The Supreme Court Is Stubbornly Analog. By Design, https://fivethirtyeight.com/features/the-supreme-court-is-stubbornly-analog-by-design/ (October 12, 2021).

16   For a summary cf. Bishop, Christopher M.: Pattern Recognition and Machine learning, New York 2006.

17   Ng, Annalyn; Soo, Kenneth: Numsense! Data Science for the Layman. No Math Added. 2017, p. 2.

18   Suggestion by Lopez, Paola: Artifical Intelligence und die normative Kraft des Faktischen. In: Merkur 75 (863) (2021), p. 45.

II. "Efficient" Algorithms

According to a report of the EU's Agency for Fundamental Rights (FRA), across the public sector "[t]he single most important reason for using AI is increased efficiency".[19] However, efficiency is just another unprecise term. As such it merely describes the relation between the aim and the means. For example, wood is chopped faster (aim) if a power saw is used instead of a nail file (means). But what exactly is making a specific data-based algorithmic system more efficient? What for and for whom?

The economically profitable distribution of State resources is an important reason for the State to implement algorithmic systems.[20] Research suggests that the economization of society affects government policies, as they "are frequently assessed against conceptions of efficiency based on financial cost-benefit analysis".[21] In this liberal paradigm it is fitting that, for example, predictive policing tools are "generally sold as a more efficient way to distribute police personnel and resources"[22] and that according to the FRA report respondents of the public sector placed "greater speed" and "cost reduction" as a motivation for deploying data-based algorithmic systems.[23]

Nonetheless, this narrative of cost-reducing and efficient algorithms is already questionable for economic reasons alone. This equation often neglects the financial, personal, and time resources spent on the development of data-based algorithmic systems.[24] This negligence might be because—as

---

19 European Union Agency for Fundamental Rights: Getting the Future Rights. Artificial Intelligence and Fundamental Rights. Vienna 2020, p. 29; see also Benjamin, Ruha: Race After Technology, Medford 2019, p. 7, 31, 72: "'efficiency' and 'progress' as lingua franca of innovation"; German Federal Government/Die Bundesregierung: Stellungnahme der Bundesregierung der Bundesrepublik Deutschland zum Weißbuch zur Künstlichen Intelligenz, 2020: "the deployment of AI will contribute to [...] a more efficient and citizen friendly public administration" (translation by the author); European Commission 2020, p. 30: "AI offers important efficiency and productivity gains".

20 Allhutter et al. 2020, p. 48

21 Birch, Kean: Techno-economic Assumptions. In: Science as Culture 26(4) (2017), p. 434; cf. Sommerer 2020, p. 289.

22 Katz, Yarden: Artificial Whiteness. Politics and Ideology in Artificial Intelligence, New York 2020, p. 138.

23 European Union Agency for Fundamental Rights 2020, p.29.

24 Likewise, climate change costs are often neglected cf. Hao, Karen: Training a Single AI model can emit as much carbon as five cars in their lifetimes,

Kean Birch put it—"capital-intensive technologies are frequently normalized as innovation".[25] The "innovation" AMS-algorithm cost 1,8 Million €.[26]

Further, within a fundamental and human rights framework "efficiency" is not a desirable value as such. It is not a maxim superior to fundamental and human rights. On the contrary: by opting for a fundamental and human rights framework, the State rejects a framework in which efficiency—more abstractly understood as the highest possible (economic or other) benefit for a majority[27]—determines if a person is protected by fundamental rights or not.[28] Fundamental and human rights are attributed to humans for being humans,[29] not because efficiency says so. The deployment of an algorithmic system in decision-making processes about humans must comply with fundamental and human rights law—always and regardless of any smartness, opacity, or economic efficiency of a system.[30]

That does not mean that fundamental and human rights are untouchable. They can be interfered with, but the interferences must be justified.[31]

       https://www.technologyreview.com/2019/06/06/239031/training-a-single-ai-model-can-emit-as-much-carbon-as-five-cars-in-their-lifetimes/ (October 12, 2021).

25   Birch 2017, p. 434.

26   Wimmer, Barbara: Der AMS-Algorithmus sollte ganz abgedreht werden', https://futurezone.at/netzpolitik/ams-algorithmus-sollte-ganz-abgedreht-werden/401009924 (October 12, 2021).

27   Cf. Bentham, Jeremy: A Fragment on Government, New York 1988, p. 3.

28   Cf. Eidenmüller, Horst: Effizienz als Rechtsprinzip, Tübingen 2015, p. 480 f.; Mathis, Klaus: Effizienz statt Gerechtigkeit? Auf der Suche nach den philosophischen Grundlagen der Ökonomischen Analyse des Rechts, Berlin 2019, p. 158 f.; similiar and illustrative Dworkin, Robert: Law's Empire, Cambridge/Massachusetts/London/England 1986, p. 290 f.; Posner, Richard A.: Wealth Maximization Revisted. In: Notre Dame Journal of Law, Ethics & Policy 2(1) (1985), p. 105.

29   Cf. Holzleithner, Elisabeth: Gerechtigkeit, Wien 2009, p. 92; Stern, Klaus: Idee der Menschenrechte und Positivität der Grundrechte. In: Isensee, Josef; Kirchhof, Paul (Eds.): Handbuch des Staatsrechts IX, München 2011, p. 5 f.

30   Cf. McGregor, Lorna et al.: International Human Rights Law as a Framework for Algorithmic Accountability. In: International and Comparative Law Quarterly 68(2) (2019), p. 341; District Court of the Hague, NJCM vs. De Staat der Nederlanden, ECLI:NL:RBDHA:2020:865; R (Bridges) vs. CC South Wales & ors, [2020] EWCA Civ 1958, Case № C1/2019/2670; German Federal Constitutional Court, 'Ausland-Ausland-Fernmeldeaufklärung' (May 19, 2020) BVerfGE 154, p. 152, at p. 260 § 192: algorithms must be reviewable.

31   Hillgruber, Christian: Schutzbereich, Ausgestaltung und Eingriff. In: Isensee/Kirchhof (Eds.): Handbuch des Staatsrechts IX, München 2011, p. 985 f., § 10 f.; Klatt, Matthias: Proportionality and Justification. In: Herlin-Karnell, Ester/Klatt, Matthias (Eds.): Constitu-

Fundamental and human rights law does not forbid to exert State power; it limits State power. The abstract standards of justification follow from different legal sources and wordings but are roughly the same: in principle, any fundamental and human rights breach must have a legal basis to ensure that the State exercises democratically legitimized power. Additionally, the intervention must be appropriate, necessary, and reasonable in pursuit of a specified and legitimate aim. In a nutshell, the intervention must be proportionate.[32] In this concept of justification, efficiency as such disaggregates. Since the State must specify the aim followed, efficiency decomposes into an aim like "cost reduction" and must be supported by explanations describing how the deployment of a data-based algorithmic system is necessary and appropriate to achieve this aim and whether its deployment is reasonable in view of the fundamental and human rights breach. This cannot be answered in the abstract but only on a case-by-case basis. It is, thus, evident that within a fundamental and human rights framework efficiency cannot serve as a catch-all justification argument.

And neither can the epistemic foundation of a data-based algorithmic system.

III. "Neutral" Algorithms

Since algorithmic systems are not led by their own subjective judgments, they are often portrayed as being neutral[33] and surrounded by an "aura of truth, objectivity, and accuracy".[34]

Yet, technology is a normative artifact formed by the values of its developers and the political system within which the technological artifact is de-

---

tionalism Justified, Oxford/New York 2020, p. 169: judicial review "as the institutionalization of a right to justification" referring to Rainer Forst.

32 Cf. e.g. Article 52(1) ECFR.
33 Cf. e.g. Smith, Mitch: In Wisconsin, a Backlash Against Using Data to Foretell Defendants' Futures, https://www.nytimes.com/2016/06/23/us/backlash-in-wisconsin-against-using-data-to-foretell-defendants-futures.html (October 12, 2021).
34 boyd, danah; Crawford, Kate: Critical Question For Big Data. In: Information, Communication and Society 15(5) (2012), p. 663.

veloped and deployed.[35] Algorithms do not just appear from the ether:[36] It is persons who decide to automate decision-making and to develop a data-based algorithmic system in the first place. It is persons who decide which output the algorithmic system shall generate. It is persons who choose the training data, who label it (regularly under bad working conditions)[37], who set the calculation parameters, who evaluate and verify the results. This whole process is not a straightforward one, but one of trial and error:[38] was the training data good enough? What does "good enough" mean to the developers? Must the parameters be adapted? In which way? The development of a data-based algorithmic system can be imagined as a dance with data,[39] and the data does not dance alone.

In this dance many steps can go wrong. Every (wrong) step impacts the knowledge the algorithmic system produces. In STS literature it is agreed that different "biases" can arise within technology.[40] In the context of data-based algorithmic systems, "biases" can be understood as a discrepancy between what the epistemic foundation of a data-based algorithmic system is supposed to represent and what it actually does represent.[41] For instance, it is likely that a data-based algorithmic result is biased because of errors like a data-entry error or because some parts of the training data were labeled falsely.[42] Then the training data is supposed to represent, for example, persons living in zip code "A", but the training data set contains persons actually living in zip code "C" falsely labeled as "A". Other biases can occur when a data-based algorithmic system is supposed to make a statement about "everyone", but the training data simply does not include "everyone". The AMS-al-

35 Cf. Winner, Langdon: Do Artifacts Have Politics? In: Daedalus 109(1) 1980, p. 121–136.
36 Lehr, David; Ohm, Paul: Playing with the Data: What Legal Scholars Should learn About Machine Learning. In: U.C. Davis Law Review 51(2) (2017), p. 667.
37 Hao, Karen: The AI gig economy is coming for you, https://www.technologyreview.com/2019/05/31/103015/the-ai-gig-economy-is-coming-for-you/ (October 12, 2021).
38 Ng/Soo 2017, p. 5.
39 Lehr; Ohm 2017, p. 655: "most machine learning dances back and forth".
40 Cf. Friedman, Batya; Nissenbaum, Helen: Bias in Computer Systems. In: ACM Transactions on Information Systems 14(3) (1996), p. 330–347; Suresh, Harini/Guttag, John V.: A Framework for Understanding Unintended Consequences of Machine Learning. In: arXiv:1901.1000 2020, p. 1–11.
41 Cf. Barocas, Solon et al.: Fairness and machine learning. Limitations and Opportunities, fairmlbook.org 2019 (work in progress), introduction.
42 Brodley, Carla E.; Friedl, Mark A.: Identifying Mislabeled Training Data. In: Journal of Artificial Intelligence Research 11 (1999), p. 131–167.

gorithm, for example, is deployed on all job seekers. However, "gender" was coded binarily (men/women) although non-binary persons are equally clients to the job centers.[43] This can lead to less accurate—biased—algorithmic results for non-binary persons.[44] Both kinds of biases are supposed to be technologically rectifiable, e.g. by correcting the false labels or integrating data about non-/underrepresented groups in the training data.[45]

The tech industry has been criticized for ignoring these technological shortcomings and instead promoting algorithmic systems as neutral and objective.[46] Amongst others, Evgeny Morozov stated: "Its founders prefer to treat technology as an autonomous and fully objective force rather than spending sleepless nights worrying about inherent biases in how their systems [...] operate".[47] Today, however, a growing international and interdisciplinary community of researchers is indeed worried and is actually trying to find technological solutions to fix the kind of biases just mentioned.[48]

Nonetheless, this research branch adds a new dimension to the neutrality narrative. Namely that once fixed, the algorithmic result could represent an objective truth on which decisions could be based without concern.[49] This is the direction in which such a statement like the one of the director of the Austrian job centers is heading: because the algorithmic result is statistically accurate regarding a specific social group like women—or in other words: because there is nothing to be technically rectified regarding this specific algorithmic result—the deployment of the algorithmic system is legiti-

---

43 Wagner, Ben et al.: Der AMS-Algorithmus. Transparenz, Verantwortung, Diskriminierung im Kontext von digitalem staatlichem Handeln. In: juridikum (2)2020, p. 195.
44 "Representation bias" Suresh/Guttag 2020, p. 5 ff.
45 Calders, Bart; Žliobaitė, Indre: Why Unbiased Computational Processes Can Lead to Discriminative Decision Procedures. In: Custers, Bart et al. (Eds.): Discrimination and Privacy in the Information Society, Berlin/Heidelberg 2013, p. 55 f.
46 E.g. Balkin, Jack M.: 2016 Sidley Austin Distinguished Lecture on Big Data Law and Policy. The Three Laws of Robotics in the Age of Big Data. In: Ohio State Law Journal 78(5) (2017), 1217–1241; Katz, Yarden: Manufacturing an Artificial Intelligence Revolution, https://ssrn.com/abstract=3078224 (October 13, 2021).
47 Morozov, Evgeny: Don't Be Evil, https://hci.stanford.edu/courses/cs047n/readings/morozov-google-evil.pdf (October 13, 2021).
48 Žliobaitė, Indre: Measuring discrimination in algorithmic decision making. In: Data Mining and Knowledge Discovery 31(4) (2017), p. 1060–1089; institutionalized e.g.. In: https://www.fatml.org/.
49 Cf. Prietl, Bianca: Das Versprechen von Big Data im Spiegel feministischer Rationalitätskritik. In: GENDER (3) 2019, p. 13.

mized. The numbers "speak for themselves" as Chris Anderson, the former editor-in-chief of the technology magazine Wired, once wrote.

I respond, however, that the deployment of statistically accurate algorithms in decision-making is not neutral in terms of fundamental and human rights and hence must be justified, that is, entails State accountability. More concretely, its deployment interferes with fundamental and human rights guaranteeing autonomy (1) and equality (2)—and can even amount to a legally prohibited discrimination (3). This is due to the inherent epistemic limitations of data-based algorithmic systems which I coin as the generalization effect and the effect of stabilizing social biases.

I will unfold this argument by using German fundamental rights as an example. Since I am more interested in the "idea behind these rights" than in its idiosyncrasies, the following analysis can be useful for fundamental and human rights of other jurisdictions, especially within the European multilevel fundamental and human rights framework.[50]

1. Do You See Me? Autonomy and the Generalization Effect

Fundamental and human rights protecting the personality, autonomy, and identity of a person are often subsumed under privacy rights[51] and inter alia enshrined in Articles 7 and 8 of the European Charter of Fundamen-

---

[50] There are fundamental rights of EU member States, of the European Union itself and European human rights enshrined in the European Convention on Human Rights. They influence each other. For instance, EU's fundamental rights arose of the ECHR rights and are still guiding for interpretation (Article 53 ECFR). On the (contested) relation of German fundamental rights and EU fundamental rights see ECJ, Judgment of 23.2.2013, 'Melloni', C-399/11, EU:C:2013:107, § 60; German Federal Constitutional Court, 'Recht auf Vergessen I' (November 6, 2019) BVerfGE 152, p. 152, at p. 173 § 53 as translated by the German Federal Constitutional Court, Order of the First Senate of 6 November 2019, 'Right to be forgotten I', 1 BvR 16/13; German Federal Constitutional Court, 'Recht auf Vergessen II' (November 6, 2019) BVerfGE 152, p. 216, at p. 246 § 77 f. as translated by the German Federal Constitutional Court, Order of the First Senate of 6 November 2019, 'Right to be forgotten II', 1 BvR 276/17. Regarding the organization of the EU member States' social systems national fundamental rights are guiding—at least in principle and until the member States do not decide differently, cf. Art. 4(2) lit. b, Art. 152 f. TFEU.

[51] Hildebrandt, Mirelle: Law for Computer Scientists and Other Folk, Oxford 2020, p. 99 f.

tal Rights (ECFR)[52] and in Article 8 of the European Convention on Human Rights.[53] In Germany, according to Article 2 (1) of the Basic Law "[e]very person shall have the right to the free development of his personality".[54]

The general right of personality (Allgemeines Persönlichkeitsrecht) contained therein does not protect against every possible influence or impairment of the autonomous evolvement of personality and identity.[55] Rather, external factors need to surpass a certain threshold. Indeed, identity develops only in interaction and communication with others.[56] It is evolved in a game[57] of private and public, of constructing and de-constructing one's own identity, of sending self- and receiving external images about oneself.[58] The right to self-presentation (Recht auf Selbstdarstellung), deduced from the general right to personality, guarantees that we can participate in this game.[59] It does not confer a right to be represented only in the way in which we want to, and even less so to be seen only in such a way.[60] The right to self-presentation merely guarantees that individuals are co-deciders, not the

---

52 On the relation of both Hildebrandt 2020, p. 130 f.; Gonzáles-Fuster, Gloria: The Emergence of Personal Data Protection as a Fundamental Right of the EU, Cham/Heidelberg/New York/Dordrecht/London 2014, p. 253 f.

53 ECtHR, 2.8.1984, App. Nº 8691/79, Malone vs. UK, Concurring opinion of Judge Pettiti; ECtHR, 16.12.1992, App. Nº 13710/88, Niemitz vs. Germany, § 42; ECtHR, 16.2.2000, App. Nº 27798/95, Amann vs. Switzerland, § 65 f.

54 Basic Law for the Federal Republic of Germany, Federal Law Gazette I, Nº 1, p. 1, as last amended by Article 2 of the Act of 29 September 2020 (Federal Law Gazette I, Nº 44, p. 2048), English translation according to Tomuschat et al.

55 German Federal Constitutional Court, 'Isolierte Vaterschaftsfeststellung' (April 19, 2016) BVerfGE 141, p. 186, at p. 202 § 32; German Federal Constitutional Court, 'Geschlechtsidentität' (October 10, 2017) BVerfGE 147, p. 1, at p. 19 § 38.

56 Ibid; cf. Altmann, Irwin: The Environment and Social Behavior. Privacy, personal space, territory, crowding, Monterey, California 1975, p. 23.

57 Similar figure by Cohen, Julie E.: Configuring the Networked Self, New Haven 2012, p. 127: "play of subjectivity".

58 Cf. Fried, Charles: An Anatomy of Values, Cambridge Massachusetts 1970, p. 143; Hildebrandt, Mireille: Smart Technologies and the End(s) of Law, Celtenham 2016, p. 80 f.; Rössler, Beate: Der Wert des Privaten, Berlin 2001, p. 260 f.; Rössler, Beate: Autonomie, Berlin 2019, p. 293.

59 Britz, Gabriele: Freie Entfaltung durch Selbstdarstellung, Tübingen 2007, p. 35.

60 German Federal Constitutional Court, 'Caroline von Monaco I' (January 14, 1998) BVerfGE 97, p. 125 at p. 149 § 86; Britz 2007, p. 47.

sole deciders, when the public creates an image of them.[61] From this right, the right to informational self-determination (Recht auf informationelle Selbstbestimmung) is deduced[62] which guarantees conditions for an autonomous evolvement of identity in a digitized context.[63]

This autonomous evolvement and one's own participation in the process of identity building is called into question when powerful external images of an individual prevent self-images to evolve and to arrive.[64] This is the case when data-based algorithmic systems are deployed in decision-making.[65] To better grasp this argument, we need to immerse into the algorithm's epistemic foundation, its limits, and—what I named—the effect of generalization.

Data-based algorithmic systems are designed to generalize.[66] By evaluating historical data and taking up patterns, they produce knowledge about a mass of people in the past and apply it to the individual case in the present.[67] To be more specific: The AMS-algorithm assigns a negative coefficient to women. This coefficient stands for a pattern found in the historical training data—it stands for the generic experience of women on the Austrian job market. The coefficient is negative because it reflects the negative deviation from the "ground truth" which was chosen by the developers to be young, male, and able-bodied Austrian job seekers without care duties.[68] It shows that women in general achieved the defined output, that is finding a job in a specific time frame less often than men. This generic knowledge about job

61 Britz, Gabriele: Verfassungsrechtlicher Schutz der freien Persönlichkeitsentfaltung. In: Bumke, Christian; Röthel, Anne (Eds.): Autonomie im Recht, Tübingen 2017, p. 357.

62 German Federal Constitutional Court, 'Volkszählung' (December 15, 1983) BVerfGE 65, p. 1, at p. 43 § 154 f.; English summary: Abstract of the German Federal Constitutional Court's Judgment of 15 December 1983, 1 BvR 209, 269, 362, 420, 440, 484/83 [CODICES].

63 German Federal Constitutional Court, 'Recht auf Vergessen I' (November 6, 2019) BVerfGE 152, p. 152, at p. 192 § 90 as translated by the German Federal Constitutional Court, Order of the First Senate of 6 November 2019, 'Right to be forgotten I', 1 BvR 16/13; Britz 2007, p. 52 f.; Kunig, Philip; Kämmerer, Jörn-Axel: Art. 2. In: Kämmerer, J.; Kotzur, M. (Eds.): v. Münch/Kunig Grundgesetz Kommentar, München 2021, at § 77.

64 Britz 2017, p. 360.

65 Cf. for credit-scoring Britz, Gabriele: Einzelfallgerechtigkeit versus Generalisierung, Tübingen 2008, p. 185.

66 Cf. Ng; Soo 2017, p. 12 f.; how generalization and "targeting" (which cannot be treated here) relate see Lopez 2021, p. 46.

67 Lopez 2021, p. 46.

68 Holl et al. 2018, p. 11.

seeking women in the past is applied to an individual job seeking woman in the present. Thus, the images that decide about her job prospects were fixed beforehand without her or her personal data being involved in this process. Even before she knew that she would be in search for a job, it had been designed, calculated, and determined how her female gender was going to be evaluated. Namely negatively. End. Naturally, generalizations are commonplace. But in contrast to an analogue, communicative process in which the person concerned has at least a chance to oppose generic assumptions about her person, the decision of a data-based algorithmic system is fixed. It no longer matters whether and how the woman concerned presents herself. Regardless of the individual capacities of a particular woman, the AMS-algorithm will assign each and every woman a negative coefficient. This generic assumption is simply imposed. What is more, this "error" in the individual case is a feature. Data-based algorithmic systems do not predict truths, but probabilities. The accuracy rate of the AMS-algorithm even varies across social groups: for some it lies at 95%, for others at 69%.[69]

Since the idea behind the right to informational self-determination and privacy rights is to guarantee the evolvement of identity in a digitalized world,[70] it is interfered with when predetermined, powerful digital profiles are imposed without the person concerned being able to effectively influence or control this process.[71]

But again, interferences with fundamental and human rights can be justified. They must be based on a legal basis and be proportionate (see II). Many requirements for a proportionate interference with the right to informational self-determination are by now specified in statutory data protection laws, especially in the Federal Data Protection Act (Bundesdatenschutzgesetz, BDSG), which refers broadly to the General Data Protection Regulation (GDPR) applicable in all EU member States.[72] These legal acts

---

69   Allhutter et al. 2020, p. 50.
70   See for the entanglement of data protection rights and identity protection: District Court of the Hague, 'NJCM vs. De Staat der Nederlanden', ECLI:NL:RBDHA:2020:865, § 6.24; Cohen 2012; Goldenfein, Jake: Monitoring Laws. Profiling and Identity in the World State, Cambridge 2020, p. 78 f.
71   Similar recently German Federal Constitutional Court, 'Recht auf Vergessen I' (November 6, 2019) BVerfGE 152, p. 152, at p. 192 § 90 as translated by the German Federal Constitutional Court, Order of the First Senate of 6 November 2019, 'Right to be forgotten I', 1 BvR 16/13.
72   Cf. requirements Eifert, Martin: Das Allgemeine Persönlichkeitsrecht des Art. 2 Abs. 1 GG. In: Juristische Ausbildung 37(11) (2015), p. 1186.

merely regulate fully automated decision-making (Article 39 BDSG; Article 22 GDPR) and not supported automated decision-making as is the case with the AMS-algorithm.

And indeed, if the decision-making process is only supported, the case workers could theoretically decide against the classification suggestion of the algorithmic system. But since the narrative of neutral and efficient algorithm is held high[73] and/or a case worker is not adequately trained to understand the algorithm's limit[74] and/or the case worker does not have much time per client (in some Austrian job centers the time per client is circa ten minutes),[75] it is unlikely that she decides against the algorithm. This psychological effect has been evidenced by research and is called automation bias.[76] Humans, in general, trust machines. In Polish job centers, for example, using a similar algorithmic system as in Austria, it was revealed that case workers decided only in 0,58% against the algorithmic result.[77] Thus, the threats for autonomy are similar in semi- as well as fully automated decision-making processes.[78] It remains open to discussion if the data protection rights at hand are sufficient to justify and cope with this threat for autonomy rights.[79]

---

73 Lopez 2019, p. 304.

74 E.g., Caseworker at the German Federal Office for Migration and Refugees, who use a speech recognition tool to verify the indicated origin of asylum seekers, are not sufficiently trained to do so: Keiner, Alexandra: Algorithmen als Rationalitätskontrolle. In: Leineweber, Christian/de Witt, Claudia (Eds.): Algorithmisierung und Autonomie im Diskurs, Hagen 2020, p. 47, 57 f.; Biselli, Anna: Eine Software des BAMF bringt Menschen in Gefahr, https://www.vice.com/de/article/a3q8wj/fluechtlinge-bamf-sprachanalyse-software-entscheidet-asyl (October 12, 2021).

75 Allhutter et al. 2020, p. 78.

76 Cf. Skitika, Linda J. et al.: Does automation bias decision-making? In: International Journal of Human-Computer Studies 51(5) (1999), p. 991–1006.

77 Allhutter et al. 2020, p. 90.

78 Fröhlich, Wiebke; Spiecker gen. Döhmann, Indra: Können Algorithmen diskriminieren? https://verfassungsblog.de/koennen-algorithmen-diskriminieren/ (October 12, 2021). The Austrian Data Protection Authority actually interpreted Article 22 GDPR to compromise also the AMS-algorithm as supported decision-making systems, Zavadil, Andreas: Datenschutzrechtliche Zulässigkeit des "AMS-Algorithmus". In: DSB Newsletter (4) (2020), p. 3–4.

79 Cf. Fröhlich; Spiecker 2021 / Wachter, Sandra; Mittelstadt, Brent: A Right to Reasonable Inferences. In: Columbia Business Law Review (2) (2019), p. 1–130; Martini, Mario: Fundamentals of a regulatory system for algorithmic-based processes, Verbraucherzentrale Bundesverband, Speyer 2019, p. 15 responding to Wachter/Mittelstadt 2019.

In any event, the reliance on the algorithmic result hides that already the mere automation of the decision-making process calls autonomy rights into question.

2. Are Calculated Likes Alike? The Right to Equal Treatment and the Generalization Effect

The generalization effect, moreover, is problematic from the standpoint of equality. Imagine a woman and a man register as unemployed with the job center. They are evaluated by the AMS-algorithm according to their data input. The woman is classified into the group with low reintegration chances, group "C", which will possibly be separated from the regular job center services to another institution. In comparison, the man is categorized into group "B". Just by assigning the woman and the man to different groups of social aid, they are treated unequally.

According to Article 3 (1) Basic Law and Article 20 ECFR all people are equal before the law. However, that does not mean that all persons shall be treated identically; the State is allowed to differentiate.[80] And in fact, differentiating is what the legislature and the executive do all the time: is matter A to be regulated, but not matter B? Should the police intervene in situation A, but not in situation B? Instead of an identical treatment, likes shall be treated alike, and unequals unequally. If the State deviates from this rule, it must justify this deviation.[81]

Hence, it must be analyzed if the generic rule on which the AMS-algorithm bases its classification decision can justify the unequal treatment. In this regard it must be acknowledged that the AMS-algorithm does not base its decision on any criteria but explicitly on social markers like gender which is a category protected under the non-discrimination clause. Thus, the epistemic foundation of the AMS-algorithm and the general rule deduced must be measured against the prohibition of discrimination, and not the right to equal treatment.

---

80 Gerhard, Ute: Gleichheit ohne Angleichung, München 1990.
81 German Federal Constitutional Court 'Erbschaftssteuer' (December 17, 2014) BVerfGE 138, p. 136, at p. 180 § 121; ECJ, Judgment of 16.9.2010, 'Chatzi', C-149/10, ECLI:EU:C:2010:534, § 64; ECtHR, 6.4.2000, App. Nº 34369/97, Thlimmenos vs. Greece, § 44 f.

3. The Effect of Stabilizing Social Biases and Non-Discrimination

The prohibition of discrimination is lex specialis to the right to equal treatment. It forbids a specific unequal treatment of persons on the grounds of legally enumerated categories.[82] Article 3 (3) Basic Law, for example, stipulates that no one shall be disadvantaged or privileged on the grounds of categories like gender or race. Similarly, Article 21 ECFR and Article 14 ECHR forbid discrimination on the grounds of the categories named therein.

What is "specific" about the "specific unequal treatment" depends crucially on the underlying understanding of equality and the view on society mediated by it.[83] A formal understanding of equality forbids the mere differentiation based on, for instance, (any) gender. Such an understanding (just) forbids to write laws that explicitly link one of the "taboo" criteria to different legal effects. From the viewpoint of substantive equality, however, the prohibition of discrimination does not forbid mere differentiation but to deepen social inequalities through the individual disadvantage of persons attributed to listed, socially marginalized groups.[84] Regarding gender-based discrimination in the EU and in Germany, a substantive understanding of equality is applied.[85] Since this understanding already acknowledges that individual discrimination can be the result of discriminatory social structures, it is in

---

82 Cf. Mangold, A. Katharina: Demokratische Inklusion durch Recht. Antidiskriminierungsrecht als Ermöglichungsbedingungen der demokratischen Begegnung von Freien und Gleichen, Tübingen 2021, p. 5 f.

83 For an overview and critiques of a formal understanding see Fredman, Sandra: Discrimination Law, Oxford 2011, p. 8 f.; for German Constitutional Law: Röhner, Cara: Ungleichheit und Verfassung. Vorschlag für eine relationale Rechtsanalyse, Weilerswist 2019, p. 169 f.

84 MacKinnon, Catharine: Toward a Feminist Understanding of the State, Cambridge Massachusetts 1991, p. 215 f.; MacKinnon, Catharine: Substantive Equality. A Perspective. In: Minnesota Law Review 96(1) 2011, p. 1, 12 f.; for German Constitutional Law: Baer, Susanne: Würde oder Gleichheit? Zur angemessenen Konzeption von Recht gegen Diskriminierung am Beispiel sexueller Belästigung am Arbeitsplatz in der Bundesrepublik Deutschland und den USA, Baden-Baden 1995, p. 235 f.

85 In German constitutional law, however, it is contested if a substantive understanding of equality applies also to other non-discrimination categories, cf. infra Fn. 92; in EU law, while applying to all non-discrimination categories, the nuances and details in legal doctrine are not yet fully elaborated cf., Wachter, Sandra et al.: Bias Preservation in Machine Learning. In: West Virginia Law Review 2021 (forthcoming), p. 17 f.

general better equipped to deal with the effect of stabilizing social biases as will be demonstrated in the following.[86]

a) What's Gender Got to Do With It?

In our example, the woman does not get the more expensive State aid which is reserved for persons categorized into group "B". Instead, she will be transferred from the regular job center system to an alternative institution. Thereby, she is treated unequally in comparison to persons in group "B" and individually disadvantaged. Is this on the grounds of gender? The classification into group "C" and the potential outsourcing from the job center service is directly based on the reintegration value, the calculation of which is based on a number of data points, not only on female gender. However, the German Federal Constitutional Court ruled that a disadvantaging decision is already discriminatory if it takes, amongst others, also gender negatively into account.[87] A female gender is always attributed a negative coefficient, while a male gender is neutral to the algorithm. The AMS-Algorithm, thus, takes a female gender negatively into account. However, some might argue that the unequal treatment is not gender-based because other women are indeed classified into group "B" and some men also classified into group "C". This argument is flawed because the negative assessment of a female gender in contrast to a male gender persists. If a female gender was not assigned a negative coefficient, probably even less women would be assigned to group "C".

Besides, the AMS-algorithm illustrates vividly that axes of inequality position persons differently in society. For example, a woman may be privileged compared to another woman because she is not burdened with care work (negative coefficient of -0,15) and/or is particularly young (neither a negative nor a positive coefficient). Kimberlé Crenshaw coined the term "intersectionality" to describe this complexity according to which not all axes of inequality always have the same effect on each person, but rather it is necessary to carefully examine which power relations intertwine and how.[88] Ac-

---

86 See also Xenidis, Raphaele: Tuning EU equality law to algorithmic discrimination. Three pathways to resilience. In: Maastricht Journal of European and Comparative Law 27(4) (2020), p. 736–758.
87 German Federal Constitutional Court, '§ 611a BGB' (November 16, 1993) BVerfGE 89, p. 276 at p. 289 § 50.
88 Crenshaw, Kimberlé: Demarginalizing the Intersection of Race and Sex. In: The University of Chicago Legal Forum (1) 1989, p. 139, 151 f.

cordingly, the AMS algorithm functions as an intersectional slide rule. The corresponding legal figure of intersectional discrimination is rarely acknowledged by Courts.[89] Nonetheless, legal scholars are polishing the doctrinal lenses to make intersectional discrimination visible to judges as well.[90] This is not decisive for our hypothetical and simplified example, but important for other cases of discrimination by the AMS-algorithm or any other data-based algorithmic system.[91]

Likewise, in this context it is important to be aware that with the legal concept of "indirect discrimination" EU and German[92] non-discrimination law can also handle masked forms of discrimination. Accordingly, by suppressing "taboo criteria" and using formally neutral criteria instead, the prohibition of non-discrimination cannot be circumvented, in case this criterion has a disadvantaging effect on a social group protected under non-discrimination law.[93] Legal discrimination does not need to be intentional; no bad faith must be proved.[94] Here again, the AMS-algorithm offers an example: The AMS-algorithm does not differentiate expressly because of the category of race. However, a study revealed that persons with fragmented data are twice as often classified into group "C" than those with no fragmented da-

89   ECJ, Judgment of 24.11.2016, 'Parris', C-443/15, ECLI:EU:C:2016:897; German Federal Constitutional Court, 'Kopftuch I' (September 24, 2003) BVerfGE 108, p. 281; but see ECJ, Judgment of 20.10.2011, 'Brachner', C-123/10, ECLI:EU:C:2011:675; German Federal Constitutional Court, 'Kopftuch II' (January 27, 2015) BVerfGE 138, p. 296.
90   Cf. Atrey, Shreya: Intersectional Discrimination, Oxford UK 2019; Mangold, A. Katharina: Mehrdimensionale Diskriminierung. In: Rechtsphilosophie 2(2) (2016), p. 152–168.
91   Cf. Xenidis 2020, p. 739 f.
92   In German Constitutional law as regards gender-discrimination it is agreed that indirect discrimination is covered by Article 3(3) Basic Law: Sacksofsky, Ute: Art. 3 (2–3). In: Umbach, Dieter C.; Clemens, Thomas (Eds.): Mitarbeiterkommentar und Handbuch 1, Karlsruhe 2002, at § 331 f.; for other categories confirming Baer, Susanne; Markard, Nora: Art. 3(2–3). In: Huber, Peter M.; Voßkuhle, Andreas (Eds.), v. Mangoldt/Klein/Starck Grundgesetz Kommentar, München 2018, at § 429; Nußberger, Angelika: Art. 3. In: Sachs, Michael (Ed.): Grundgesetz, München 2018, at § 255; dissenting Langenfeld, Christine: Art. 3(2–3). In: Herdegen, Matthias et al. (Eds.): Maunz/Dürig Grundgesetz-Kommentar, München 2020, at § 38; Kischel 2020, at § 215. In EU non-discrimination law indirect discrimination is deeply rooted in EU's legal doctrine regarding all forms of discrimination cf. ECJ, Judgment of 13.5.1986, 'Bilka Kaufhaus', C-170/84, ECLI:EU:C:1986:204.
93   Cf. Art. 2(2) lit. b, Council Directive 2000/43/EC, 29.6.2000.
94   Baer; Markard 2017, § 428.

ta.⁹⁵ Job seeking persons with fragmented data are inter alia persons with a third-country nationality or persons with an immigrated parent.⁹⁶ Thus, the formally neutral criterion of fragmented data is likely to have a disadvantaging effect on the protected group of racialized persons.

Compared to this case, our example is admittedly a rather obvious case of discrimination: a woman is individually disadvantaged because of expressly taking her gender negatively into account. More interestingly in that case is whether the discrimination can be justified.

b) Looking for Justification

The standard of justification for discrimination is higher than that of an "ordinary" unequal treatment.⁹⁷ Gender-based discrimination can only be justified in exceptional cases.⁹⁸ Because of the algorithm's epistemic limitation, that I name the effect of stabilizing social biases, this is not the case here.

A data-based algorithmic system merely reflects one possible relation between the input and the output and only the "what was" instead of the "why it was".⁹⁹ This is why a statement like that of the head of the Austrian job centers, arguing the AMS-algorithm just reflected the "harsh reality" for women, is shortsighted. It accepts the algorithmic result, the "what was", as

---

95 Allhutter et al. 2020, p. 30, 44.
96 Allhutter et al. 2020, p. 31; for a high correlation between a "migrant background" and racism see Gummich, Judy: Migrationshintergrund und Beeinträchtigung. In: Jacob, Jutta et al. (Eds.): Gendering Disability, Bielefeld 2010, p. 131, 132 f.
97 German Federal Constitutional Court, 'Kindererziehungszeiten' (April 5, 2005) BVerfGE 113, p. 1, at p. 20 § 69.
98 Ibid; ECtHR, 28.5.1985, App. N° 9214/80, Abdulaziz et al. vs. UK, § 78.
99 Mayer-Schönberger, Viktor; Cukier, Kenneth: Big Data. A Revolution That Will transform How We Live, Work And Think, London 2013, p. 70 f.; Vigen, Tyler: Spurious correlations, https://tylervigen.com/spurious-correlations (October 12, 2021).

a definitive truth.[100] But algorithms do not exist in a neutral limbo.[101] The reasons for the algorithmic result, that is the "why", needs to be scrutinized. As Catherine D'Ignazio and Lauren F. Klein respond to Chris Anderson: "The numbers do not speak for themselves."[102]

Rather, only be embedding the negative coefficient into qualitative inequality research, it becomes clear that in the past women in Germany, Austria and other EU member States were assigned to the private sphere and excluded from the public job market by laws, court rulings, social conventions etc.[103] Today, these laws are mostly abolished, and the separation of private and public is more fluid. However, the exclusion persists in subtle ways in the shape of social structures and social biases;[104] patterns taken up by the algorithm and reflected in the negative coefficient.[105] Of course, social structures can change, and access to the job market is not always hampered for all women. However, in the world of the AMS-algorithm it is. It freezes social norms and biases. Thus, the AMS-algorithm does not base its decision on a random generic rule but on knowledge formed by sexist social structures. Its deployment stabilizes and even deepens these sexist structures by further disadvantaging women on its basis.

So, what then justifies the sexist discrimination through the AMS algorithm? Is the legitimate aim to avoid discrimination by deploying an allegedly "neutral" device? Then the AMS algorithm is evidently not appropriate for

---

[100] Cf. Berry, David M.: Against Infrasomatization. Towards a Critical Theory of Algorithms. In: Bigo, Didier et al.: Data Politics. Worlds, Subjects, Rights, London 2019, p. 43, 45: "The cult of data-ism is a turn away from the project of seeking to understand society and culture through the application of critical reason in human affairs towards a data-deterministic world."; Hu, Lily; Kohler-Hausmann, Issa: What's Sex Got To Do With Fair Machine Learning? In: Proceedings of the 2020 Conference on Fairness, Accountability and Transparency, p. 513–524.

[101] Cf. Wachter et al. 2021 (forthcoming), p. 31 f.

[102] D'Ignazio, Catherine; Klein, Lauren F.: Data Feminism, Massachusetts 2020, Chapter 6.

[103] E.g., in Germany according to § 1356 Civil Code in the version of 18.6.1957 wives were responsible for housekeeping. They were allowed to work for money if this was compatible with their care and housekeeping duties, Gesetz über die Gleichberechtigung von Mann und Frau auf dem Gebiete des bürgerlichen Rechts, 18.6.1957, Federal Law Gazette I, № 26, p. 609; seminal Fredman, Sandra: Women and the Law, Oxford 1997, p. 98 f.

[104] Fröhlich, Laura et al.: Gender at Work Across Nations. In: Folberg, Abigail M. (Ed.) Social Issues' Special Issue: Global Perspectives on Women and Work 76(3) (2020), p. 484–511.

[105] Lopez 2019, p. 302.

this purpose. Moreover, individual caseworkers certainly also discriminate. But they can consciously decide to act against a stereotype. Discriminatory social structures are powerful but not determinative. Algorithms, on the other hand, are exactly that. They take the same discriminatory decision again and again and again.[106]

Is the legitimate aim the profitable distribution of scarce State resources to spare the welfare State? The AMS-algorithm is not appropriate for that aim either. In what way is it profitable for the State to spend money on psychosocial counseling when the reason for the woman's poor reintegration value is not her individual need of psychosocial help but a sexist Austrian labor market? Mere sexist stereotypes cannot justify discrimination, as the German Federal Constitutional Court already ruled in 1992.[107] Moreover, the Basic Law stipulates that the State must promote actual equal rights for women and men by eliminating factually disadvantageous barriers (Article 3(2) Basic Law).[108] If—as with the AMS-algorithm—a discriminatory status quo is frozen and used as a justification for further disadvantages, this constitutional objective is missed.

In sum, the discrimination of the woman in the example cannot be justified and, thus, would be prohibited under German Constitutional law. This demonstrates that the accuracy of a data-based algorithmic system does not shield against the State's accountability for legal discrimination. It demonstrates that embedded in a fundamental and human rights framework, the algorithm's facade of neutrality and statistical unambiguousness cracks.

IV. From Disobedience to Justice

If we look through this crack and behind the narratives this facade is made of, we see a mathematical function. The conditions of its deployment[109] in decision-making must be politically negotiated.

---

106 O'Neil, Cathy: Weapons of Math Destruction, New York 2015: "scale".
107 German Federal Constitutional Court, 'Nachtarbeitsverbot', (January 28, 1992) BVerfGE 85, p. 191 at p. 207 § 56 f.
108 Ibid. Recital 3.
109 And not only its development Hoffmann, Anna L.: Where Fairness Fails. Data, Algorithms, and the Limits of Antidiscrimination Discourse. In: Information, Communication & Society 22(7) (2019), p. 910.

This paper is not about banning all data-based algorithmic systems. It rather adds another layer to the ongoing discussion about the regulation of algorithmic discrimination. Therefore, fundamental and human rights offer guidance. They inform us that a regulation of data-based algorithmic systems should not be driven by the narrative and liberal paradigm of economic efficiency but rather by the protection—or at least not the foreseeable violation—of fundamental and human rights. Moreover, they alert us to question the process of automation and the epistemic foundation of data-based algorithmic systems. They call for the informed identification of their potentials as well as their limits. If a data-based algorithmic system generates knowledge about a mass of people and the past, should it then be deployed to take a decision about the individual case in the present?

The response to this question must not lead to stalemate. Rather, a way out could be to use data-based algorithmic systems precisely for what they are good at: to identify past discriminatory structures. Instead of basing adverse individual decisions on data-based algorithmic systems, these systems could be used to identify discriminations and to justify affirmative action like diversity trainings for case workers or promotion programs for socially marginalized groups. In this way, past inequalities would be compensated instead of deepened.

Thus, if the narratives of efficient and neutral algorithms are not blindly obeyed, data-based algorithmic systems can lead us to a more just society.

Literature

Achiume, E. Tendayi: Racial discrimination and emerging digital technologies. A human rights analysis. UN Doc. A/HCR/44/57, 2020.

Allhutter, Doris; Mager, Astrid; Cech, Florian; Fischer, Fabian; Grill, Gabriel: Der AMS-Algorithmus. Eine Soziotechnische Analyse des Arbeitsmarktchancen-Assistenz-Systems (AMAS). Institut für Technikfolgen-Abschätzung, Vienna 2020.

Alston, Philip: Report of the Special rapporteur on extreme poverty and human rights. UN Doc. A/74/48037, 2019.

Altmann, Irwin: The Environment and Social Behavior. Privacy, personal space, territory, crowding, Monterey, California 1975.

Atrey, Shreya: Intersectional Discrimination, Oxford UK 2019.

Baer, Susanne: Würde oder Gleichheit? Zur angemessenen Konzeption von Recht gegen Diskriminierung am Beispiel sexueller Belästigung am Arbeitsplatz in der Bundesrepublik Deutschland und den USA, Baden-Baden 1995.

Baer, Susanne; Markard, Nora: Art. 3(2–3). In: Huber, Peter M./Voßkuhle, Andreas (Eds.), v. Mangoldt/Klein/Starck Grundgesetz Kommentar, München 2018.

Balkin, Jack M.: 2016 Sidley Austin Distinguished Lecture on Big Data Law and Policy. The Three Laws of Robotics in the Age of Big Data. In: Ohio State Law Journal 78(5) (2017), p. 1217–1241.

Barocas, Solon; Hardt, Moritz; Narayanan, Arvind: Fairness and machine learning—Limitations and Opportunities, 2019 (work in progress), fairmlbook.org.

Barocas, Solon; Selbst, Andrew: Big Data's Disparate Impact. In: California Law Review 104(3) (2016), p. 671–732.

Benjamin, Ruha: Race After Technology, New York 2019.

Bentham, Jeremy: A Fragment on Government, New York 1988.

Berner, Heiko; Schüll, Elmar: Bildung nach Maß. Die Auswirkungen des AMS-Algorithmus auf Chancengerechtigkeit, Bildungszugang und Weiterbildungsförderung. In: Magazin erwachsenenbildung.at (2020), p. 1–12.

Berry, David M.: Against Infrasomatization. Towards a Critical Theory of Algorithms. In: Bigo, Didier/ Isin, Engin/ Ruppert, Evelyn: Data Politics. Worlds, Subjects, Rights, London 2019, p. 43–63.

Biselli, Anna: Eine Software des BAMF bringt Menschen in Gefahr, https://www.vice.com/de/article/a3q8wj/fluechtlinge-bamf-sprachanalyse-software-entscheidet-asyl (October 12, 2021).

Bishop, Christopher M.: Pattern Recognition and Machine learning, New York 2006.

Birch, Kean: Techno-economic Assumptions. In: Science as Culture 26(4) (2017), p. 433–444.

boyd, danah; Crawford, Kate: Critical Question For Big Data. In: Information, Communication and Society 15(5) (2012), p. 662–679.

Britz, Gabriele: Freie Entfaltung durch Selbstdarstellung, Tübingen 2007.

Britz, Gabriele: Einzelfallgerechtigkeit versus Generalisierung, Tübingen 2008.

Britz, Gabriele: Verfassungsrechtlicher Schutz der freien Persönlichkeitsentfaltung. In: Bumke, Christian/Röthel, Anne (Eds.): Autonomie im Recht, Tübingen 2017, p. 353–363.

Brodley, Carla E.; Friedl, Mark A.: Identifying Mislabeled Training Data. In: Journal of Artificial Intelligence Research 11 (1999), p. 131–167.

Calders, Bart; Žliobaitė, Indre: Why Unbiased Computational Processes Can Lead to Discriminative Decision Procedures. In: Custers, Bart/Calders, Toon/Schermer, Bart/Zarsky, Tal: Discrimination and Privacy in the Information Society, Berlin/Heidelberg 2013, p. 43–56.

Cave Stephen; Dihal, Kanta; Dillon, Sarah : Introduction. In: ibid: AI Narratives. A History of Imaginative Thinking about Intelligent Machines, Oxford 2020, p. 1–19.

Chiusi, Fabio; Fischer, Sarah; Kayser-Brill, Nicolas; Spielkamp, Matthias: Automating Society Report 2020, Algorithm Watch.

Cohen, Julie E.: Configuring the Networked Self, New Haven 2012.

Crenshaw, Kimberlé: Demarginalizing the Intersection of Race and Sex. In: The University of Chicago Legal Forum 1 (1989), p. 139–169.

District Court of the Hague, 'NJCM vs. De Staat der Nederlanden', ECLI:NL:RBDHA:2020:865.

D'Ignazio, Catherine; Klein, Lauren F.: Data Feminism, Massachusetts 2020.

Dworkin, Robert: Law's Empire, Cambridge/Massachusetts/London/England 1986.

ECJ, Judgment of 13.5.1986, 'Bilka Kaufhaus', C-170/84, ECLI:EU:C:1986:204.

ECJ, Judgment of 16.9.2010, 'Chatzi', C-149/10, ECLI:EU:C:2010:534.

ECJ, Judgment of 20.10.2011, 'Brachner', C-123/10, ECLI:EU:C:2011:675.

ECJ, Judgment of 23.2.2013, 'Melloni', C-399/11, EU:C:2013:107.

ECJ, Judgment of 24.11.2016, 'Parris', C-443/15, ECLI:EU:C:2016:897.

ECtHR, 2.8.1984, App. Nº 8691/79, Malone vs. UK, Concurring opinion of Judge Pettiti.

ECtHR, 28.5.1985, App. Nº 9214/80, Abdulaziz et al. vs. UK. § 78.

ECtHR, 16.12.1992, App. Nº 13710/88, Niemitz vs. Germany.

ECtHR, 16.2.2000, App. Nº 27798/95, Amann vs. Switzerland.

ECtHR, 6.4.2000, App. Nº 34369/97, Thlimmenos vs. Greece.

Eidenmüller, Horst: Effizienz als Rechtsprinzip, Tübingen 2015.

Eifert, Martin: Das Allgemeine Persönlichkeitsrecht des Art. 2 Abs. 1 GG. In: Juristische Ausbildung 37(11) (2015), p. 1181–1191.

European Commission: White Paper On Artificial Intelligence. COM(2020) 65 final, 2020.

European Commission: Proposal for a Regulation of the European Parliament and of the Council Laying Down Harmonised Rules on Artificial Intelligence (Artificial Intelligence Act) And Amending Certain Union Legislative Acts. COM(2021)206 final, 2021.

European Union Agency for Fundamental Rights: Getting the Future Rights. Artificial Intelligence and Fundamental Rights,Vienna 2020.

Fredman, Sandra: Women and the Law, Oxford 1997.

Fredman, Sandra: Discrimination Law, Oxford 2011.

Fried, Charles: An Anatomy of Values, Cambridge Massachusetts 1970.

Friedman, Batya; Nissenbaum, Helen: Bias in Computer Systems. In: ACM Transactions on Information Systems 14(3) (1996), p. 330–347.

Fröhlich, Laura; Olsson, Maria I.T.; Dorrough, Angela R.; Martiny, Sarah E.: Gender at Work Across Nations. In: Folberg, Abigail M. (Ed.): Social Issues' Special Issue: Global Perspectives on Women and Work 76(3) (2020), p. 484–511.

Fröhlich, Wiebke; Spiecker gen. Döhmann, Indra: Können Algorithmen diskriminieren?. In: Verfassungsblog, December 26, 2018, https://verfassungsblog.de/koennen-algorithmen-diskriminieren/ (October 12, 2021).

Gerhard, Ute: Gleichheit ohne Angleichung, München 1990.

German Data Ethics Commission: Opinion of the Data Ethics Commission, 2020.

German Federal Constitutional Court, 'Volkzählung' (December 15, 1983) BVerfGE 65, p. 1.154 f.; English summary: Abstract of the German Federal Constitutional Court's Judgment of 15 December 1983, 1 BvR 209, 269, 362, 420, 440, 484/83 [CODICES].

German Federal Constitutional Court, 'Nachtarbeitsverbot', (January 28, 1992) BVerfGE 85, p. 191.

German Federal Constitutional Court, '§ 611a BGB' (November 16, 1993) BVerfGE 89, p. 276.

German Federal Constitutional Court, 'Caroline von Monacco I' (January 14, 1998) BVerfGE 97, p. 125.

German Federal Constitutional Court, 'Kopftuch I' (September 24, 2003) BVerfGE 108, p. 281.

German Federal Constitutional Court, 'Kindererziehungszeiten' (April 5, 2005) BVerfGE 113, p. 1.

German Federal Constitutional Court 'Erbschaftssteuer' (December 17, 2014) BVerfGE 138, p. 136.

German Federal Constitutional Court, 'Kopftuch II' (January 27, 2015) BVerfGE 138, p. 296.
German Federal Constitutional Court, 'Isolierte Vaterschaftsfeststellung' (April 19, 2016) BVerfGE 141, p. 186. German Federal Constitutional Court, 'Geschlechtsidentität' (October 10, 2017) BVerfGE 147, p. 1.
German Federal Constitutional Court, 'Recht auf Vergessen I' (November 6, 2019) BVerfGE 152, p. 152, at p. 192 § 90 as translated by the German Federal Constitutional Court, Order of the First Senate of 6 November 2019, 'Right to be forgotten I', 1 BvR 16/13.
German Federal Government/Die Bundesregierung: Stellungnahme der Bundesregierung der Bundesrepublik Deutschland zum Weißbuch zur Künstlichen Intelligenz, 2020.
German Parliament/Bundestag: Unterrichtung der Enquete-Kommission Künstliche Intelligenz. BT-Drs. 19/23700, 2020.
Goldenfein, Jake: Monitoring Laws. Profiling and Identity in the World State, Cambridge 2020.
Gonzáles-Fuster, Gloria: The Emergence of Personal Data Protection as a Fundamental Right of the EU, Cham/Heidelberg/New York/Dordrecht/London 2014.
Gummich, Judy: Migrationshintergrund und Beeinträchtigung. In: Jacob, Jutta/ Köbsell, Swantje/ Wollrad, Eske (Eds.): Gendering Disability, Bielefeld 2010, p. 131–151.
Hao, Karen: Training a Single AI model can emit as much carbon as five cars in their lifetimes. In: MIT Technology Review, June 06, 2019, https://www.technologyreview.com/2019/06/06/239031/training-a-single-ai-model-can-emit-as-much-carbon-as-five-cars-in-their-lifetimes/ (October 12, 2021).
Hao, Karen: The AI gig economy is coming for you. In: MIT Technology Review, May 31, 2019, https://www.technologyreview.com/2019/05/31/103015/the-ai-gig-economy-is-coming-for-you/ (October 12, 2021).
Hildebrandt, Mireille: Smart Technologies and the End(s) of Law, Celtenham 2016.
Hildebrandt, Mirelle: Law for Computer Scientists and Other Folk, Oxford 2020.
Hillgruber, Christian: Schutzbereich, Ausgestaltung und Eingriff. In: Isensee/ Kirchhof (Eds.): Handbuch des Staatsrechts IX, München 2011, p. 981–1031.

Hoffmann, Anna L.: Where Fairness Fails. Data, Algorithms, and the Limits of Antidiscrimination Discourse. In: Information, Communication & Society 22(7) (2019), p. 900–915.

Holl, Jürgen/Kernbeiß, Günther/Wagner-Pinter, Michael: Das AMS-Arbeitsmarktchancen-Modell. Dokumentation zur Methode, Wien 2018.

Holzleithner, Elisabeth: Gerechtigkeit, Wien 2009.

Hu, Lily; Kohler-Hausmann, Issa: 'What's Sex Got To Do With Fair Machine Learning?. In: Proceedings of the 2020 Conference on Fairness, Accountability and Transparency, p. 513–524.

Katwala, Amit: An Algorithm Determined UK Students' Grades. Chaos Ensued. In: WIRED, August 15, 2020, https://www.wired.com/story/an-algorithm-determined-uk-students-grades-chaos-ensued/ (October 12, 2021).

Katz, Yarden: Manufacturing an Artificial Intelligence Revolution, https://ssrn.com/abstract=3078224 (October 13, 2021).

Katz, Yarden: Artificial Whiteness. Politics and Ideology in Artificial Intelligence, New York 2020.

Kischel, Uwe: Art. 3. In: Epping, Volker/Hillgruber, Christian (Eds.): BeckOK Grundgesetz, München 2021.

Keiner, Alexandra: Algorithmen als Rationalitätskontrolle. In: Leineweber, Christian/de Witt, Claudia (Eds.): Algorithmisierung und Autonomie im Diskurs, Hagen 2020, p. 47–67.

Klatt, Matthias: Proportionality and Justification. In: Herlin-Karnell, Ester/Klatt, Matthias (Eds.): Constitutionalism Justified, Oxford/New York 2020, p. 159–196.

Kopf, Johannes 2018: Wie Ansicht zur Einsicht werden könnte. In: johanneskopf.at, November 14, 2018, https://www.johanneskopf.at/2018/11/14/wie-ansicht-zur-einsicht-werden-koennte/ (October 12, 2021).

Kopf, Johannes 2019: Der Beipackzettel zum AMS-Algorithmus. In: futurezone, October 9, 2019, https://futurezone.at/meinung/der-beipackzettel-zum-ams-algorithmus/400641347 (October 12, 2021).

Kunig, Philip; Kämmerer, Jörn-Axel: Art. 2. In: Kämmerer, J./Kotzur, M. (Eds.): v. Münch/Kunig Grundgesetz Kommentar, München 2021.

Langenfeld, Christine: Art. 3(2–3). In: Herdegen, Matthias/Scholz, Rupert/Klein, Hans H. (Eds.): Maunz/Dürig Grundgesetz-Kommentar, München 2020.

Lehr, David; Ohm, Paul: Playing with the Data: What Legal Scholars Should Learn About Machine Learning. In: U.C. Davis Law Review 51(2) (2017), p. 653–717.
Lopez, Paola: Reinforcing Intersectional Inequality via the AMS Algorithm in Austria. In: Proceedings of the STS Conference Graz 2019, p. 289–309.
Lopez, Paola: Artifical Intelligence und die normative Kraft des Faktischen. In: Merkur 75 (863) (2021), p. 42–52.
MacKinnon, Catharine: Toward a Feminist Understanding of the State, Cambridge Massachusetts 1991.
MacKinnon, Catharine: Substantive Equality. A Perspective. In: Minnesota Law Review 96(1) (2011), p. 1–27.
Mangold, A. Katharina: Mehrdimensionale Diskriminierung. In: Rechtsphilosophie 2(2) (2016), p. 152–168.
Mangold, A. Katharina: Demokratische Inklusion durch Recht. Antidiskriminierungsrecht als Ermöglichungsbedingungen der demokratischen Begegnung von Freien und Gleichen, Tübingen 2021.
Martini, Mario: Fundamentals of a regulatory system for algorithmic-based processes, Verbraucherzentrale Bundesverband, Speyer 2019.
Mathis, Klaus: Effizienz statt Gerechtigkeit? Auf der Suche nach den philosophischen Grundlagen der Ökonomischen Analyse des Rechts, Berlin 2019.
Mattes, Anna Livia: Polizeigesetz und Verfassungsschutzgesetz Hessen, https://freiheitsrechte.org/polizeigesetz-hessen/ (October 12, 2021).
Mayer-Schönberger, Viktor/Cukier, Kenneth: Big Data. A Revolution That Will transform How We Live, Work And Think, London 2013.
McGregor, Lorna/Murray, Daragh/Ng, Vivian: International Human Rights Law as a Framework for Algorithmic Accountability. In: International and Comparative Law Quarterly 68(2) (2019), p. 309–343.
Morozov, Evgeny: Don't Be Evil. In: The New Republic, July 13, 2011, https://hci.stanford.edu/courses/cs047n/readings/morozov-google-evil.pdf (October 13, 2021).
Ng, Annalyn; Soo, Kenneth: Numsense! Data Science for the Layman. No Math Added. 2017.
Nußberger, Angelika: Art. 3. In: Sachs, Michael (Ed.): Grundgesetz, München 2018.
O'Neil, Cathy: Weapons of Math Destruction, New York 2015.
Posner, Richard A.: Wealth Maximization Revisted. In: Notre Dame Journal of Law, Ethics & Policy, 2(1) (1985), p. 85–106.

Prietl, Bianca: Das Versprechen von Big Data im Spiegel feministischer Rationalitätskritik. In: GENDER (3) (2019), p. 11–25.

R (Bridges) vs. CC South Wales & ors, [2020] EWCA Civ 1958, Case Nº C1/2019/2670.

Röhner, Cara: Ungleichheit und Verfassung. Vorschlag für eine relationale Rechtsanalyse, Weilerswist 2019.

Rössler, Beate: Der Wert des Privaten, Berlin 2001.

Rössler, Beate: Autonomie, Berlin 2019.

Sacksofsky, Ute: Art. 3 (2–3). In: Umbach, Dieter C./Clemens, Thomas (Eds.): Mitarbeiterkommentar und Handbuch 1, Karlsruhe 2002.

Seyfert, Robert: Algorithms as regulatory objects. In: Information, Communication & Society (2021), p. 1–17.

Singelnstein, Tobias: Hessen sucht mit Palantir-Software nach Gefährdern. In: netzpolitik.org, June 3, 2019, https://netzpolitik.org/2019/big-data-bei-der-polizei-hessen-sucht-mit-palantir-software-nach-gefaehrdern/ (October 12, 2021).

Skitika, Linda J.; Mosier, Kathleen L./Budrick, Mark: Does automation bias decision-making?. In: International Journal of Human-Computer Studies 51(5) (1999), p. 991–1006.

Smith, Mitch: In Wisconsin, a Backlash Against Using Data to Foretell Defendants' Futures: In: The New York Times, June 22, 2016, https://www.nytimes.com/2016/06/23/us/backlash-in-wisconsin-against-using-data-to-foretell-defendants-futures.html (October 12, 2021).

Sommerer, Lucia M.: Personenbezogenes Predictive Policing, Baden-Baden 2020.

Stern, Klaus: Idee der Menschenrechte und Positivität der Grundrechte. In: Isensee, Josef/Kirchhof, Paul (Eds.): Handbuch des Staatsrechts IX, München 2011, p. 3–56.

Suresh, Harini; Guttag, John V.: A Framework for Understanding Unintended Consequences of Machine Learning. In: arXiv:1901.1000 2020, p. 1–11.

Szigetvari, András: AMS-Vorstand Kopf: "Was die EDV gar nicht abbilden kann, ist die Motivation". In : Der Standard, October 10, 2018, https://www.derstandard.at/consent/tcf/story/2000089096795/ams-vorstand-kopf-menschliche-komponente-wird-entscheidend-bleiben (October 12, 2021).

Thomson-DeVeaux, Amelia: The Supreme Court Is Stubbornly Analog. By Design. In: FiveThirtyEight, May 29, 2018, https://fivethirtyeight.com/features/the-supreme-court-is-stubbornly-analog-by-design/ (October 12, 2021).

Vigen, Tyler: Spurious correlations, https://tylervigen.com/spurious-correlations (October 12, 2021).

Wachter, Sandra; Mittelstadt, Brent: A Right to Reasonable Inferences. In: Columbia Business Law Review (2) (2019), p. 1–130.

Wachter, Sandra; Mittelstadt, Brent; Russell, Chris, Bias Preservation in Machine Learning. In: West Virginia Law Review 2021 (forthcoming), p. 1–51.

Wagner, Ben; Lopez, Paola; Cech, Florian; Grill, Gabriel; Sekwenz, Marie-Therese: Der AMS-Algorithmus. Transparenz, Verantwortung, Diskriminierung im Kontext von digitalem staatlichem Handeln. In: juridikum (2) (2020), p. 191–202.

Wimmer, Barbara: Computer sagt nein: Algorithmus gibt Frauen weniger Chancen beim AMS. In: futurezone, December 6, 2018, https://futurezone.at/netzpolitik/computer-sagt-nein-algorithmus-gibt-frauen-weniger-chancen-beim-ams/400345297 (October 12, 2021).

Wimmer, Barbara: Der AMS-Algorithmus ist ein "Paradebeispiel für Diskriminierung". In: futurezone, December 17, 2018 https://futurezone.at/netzpolitik/der-ams-algorithmus-ist-ein-paradebeispiel-fuer-diskriminierung/400147421 (October 12, 2021).

Wimmer, Barbara: Der AMS-Algorithmus sollte ganz abgedreht werden. In: futurezone, August 24, 2020, https://futurezone.at/netzpolitik/ams-algorithmus-sollte-ganz-abgedreht-werden/401009924 (October 12, 2021).

Winner, Langdon: Do Artifacts Have Politics? In: Daedalus 109(1) (1980), p. 121–136.

Xenidis, Raphaele: Tuning EU equality law to algorithmic discrimination. Three pathways to resilience. In: Maastricht Journal of European and Comparative Law 27(4) (2020), p. 736–758.

Zavadil, Andreas: Datenschutzrechtliche Zulässigkeit des "AMS-Algorithmus". In: DSB Newsletter (4) (2020), p. 3–4.

Žliobaitė, Indre: Measuring discrimination in algorithmic decision making. In: Data Mining and Knowledge Discovery 31(4) (2017), p. 1060–1089.

Katja Dill

When Search Engines Discriminate

The Posthuman Mimesis of Gender Bias

"An important feature of a learning machine is that its teacher will often be very largely ignorant of quite what is going on inside, although he may still be able to some extent to predict his pupil's behaviour. This should apply most strongly to the later education of a machine arising from a child-machine of well-tried design (or programme)."[1]

Already in 1950, Alan Turing disapproves the idea that a machine can only do what it is told to do; but rather postulates that machines are able to change induced rules. While at the time of writing his work "Computing Machinery and Intelligence" his ideas may have seemed rather abstract, we are now confronted with the digital aftermath. For example: Where would you turn when searching for (practical) information or an image? The approximately 3.5 billion Google searches carried out every day[2] reveal the ubiquity of the online search engines in modern life. If one considers search engines as the epicentre of information requests, the underlying architecture of Artificial Intelligence (AI) powered search technologies demands to be disclosed. While AI has undoubtedly democratised information and communication processes, the digital mediation of search engines is accompanied by new societal challenges. There are various definitions of AI; notwithstanding, this work defines AI as constituting the algorithms that function on behalf of learning and automated decision-making processes.[3] AI intends to optimize and simplify everything. However, experts wonder if the coherent algorithms perpetuate bias and misinterpret societies as more homogenous than they are.[4] With the prominence of search engines as the informative arbitrators of social realities, raising these concerns is vital. Research has found a number of cases that prove structural gender-based discrimination embedded in the knowledge platforms. For example, search engines that show well-paying technical and executive positions to men rather than women;[5]

---

[1] Turing, Alan M.: Computing Machinery and Intelligence. In: Mind LIX 236 (1950), p. 433–460.

[2] Internet Live Stats, Google search statistics 2020, https://www.internetlivestats.com/google-search-statistics/

[3] Howard, Ayanna/ Borenstein, Jason: The Ugly Truth About Ourselves and Our Robot Creations: The Problem of Bias and Social Inequity. In: Science and engineering ethics 24(5) (2018), p. 1521–1536.

[4] Rainie, Lee; Anderson, Janna: The Future of Jobs and Jobs Training. Pew Research Center, 2017, https://www.voced.edu.au/content/ngv%3A77734

[5] Howard; Borenstein 2018.

or search engine platforms that give a wrong impression about gender representations in occupations[6] and promote gender-related attractiveness stereotypes.[7] But can gender bias in search engines be interpreted as a feature of patriarchal structures? This question may arise if one considers that most of the AI systems are developed by mostly (white) men. The UNESCO report highlights that, in 2017, solely 12 per cent of the leading machine-learning researchers are represented by women.[8] Google represents one example of poor gender diversity, with women representing only one third of the total employees and even less in leadership positions.[9] But the discriminating patterns cannot only be found in Google's choice of workforce, but also in the algorithms they create. For example, Google Translate translates the Turkish phrase "O bir doktor" as "he is a doctor" in English, even though the Turkish pronouns are gender neutral. Yet, if the word doctor is replaced by the Turkish word for nurse, "hemsire", the translation becomes "she is a nurse".[10]

In the information age we live in, search engines act as a ubiquitous mediator between societies and knowledge production; but also play a pivotal role in the transformation of sociocultural norms. Research confirms that the answers provided by search engines have a significant effect on an individual's attitude, behaviour and preference.[11] Thus, the question arises of whether and how the curated, gendered realities presented by information intermediaries influence societies? Can AI have agency? And if so, how can we disobey in order to destabilize the technology-induced reproduction of inequalities? By breaking down the subject-object duality, this work will address these questions through the example of search engines. The following will open the

---

6   Kay, Matthew; Matuszek, Cynthia; Munson, Sean A.: Unequal representation and gender stereotypes in image search results for occupations. In: Proceedings of the 33rd Annual ACM Conference on Human Factors in Computing Systems (2015), p. 3819–3828.

7   Magno, Gabriel/ Araújo, Camila S./ Meira Jr., Wagner/ Almeida, Virgilio: Stereotypes in Search Engine Results: Understanding The Role of Local and Global Factors. In: DAT'16

8   UNESCO: I'd blush if I could: closing gender divides in digital skills through education (2019), https://en.unesco.org/Id-blush-if-I-could

9   UNESCO 2019.

10 Johnston, Ian: AI robots are learning racism, sexism and other prejudices from humans: In: The Independent (2017), https://www.independent.co.uk/life-style/gadgets-and-tech/news/ai-robots-artificial-intelligence-racism-sexism-prejudice-bias-language-learn-humans-a7683161.html

11 Epstein, Robert; Robertson, Ronald E.: The search engine manipulation effect (seme) and its possible impact on the outcomes of elections. In: Proceedings of the National Academy of Sciences 112(33) (2015), p. E4512–E4521.

debate by outlining research that focuses on (gender) bias in search engines. Next, this work will explore the concept of (non)human agency from an agential realist perspective in order to discuss whether artificial entities are capable of pursuing specific objectives and affecting the social world. With the growing responsibility of AI, I suggest that search engines can be interpreted as agency bearer; especially as they induce the posthuman mimesis of gender. Thus, this work can be seen as another endeavor to discuss the (re)emergence of asymmetries due to (non)human entanglements. The objective of this paper is to outline the analytical advantages of a diffractive methodology in order to point out the loop of gendering which has to be tackled by reversing the rules. Crucially for this work is the idea that responsibility is not limited to human-conditioned action, as technologies increasingly determine decisions. By bridging theories of feminist posthumanism with (trans)national practical examples of search engine bias, this work points out that technologies always imply (gender-hierarchical) power relations and therefore constitute a social field[12], which needs to be approached as such.

Let me Google that...

"These search engine results, for women whose identities are already maligned in the media, only further debase and erode efforts for social, political, and economic recognition and justice."[13] This quote from Safiya Umoja Noble[14] warns against the enormous power of search engines such as Google as knowledge producers. Noble[15] emphasises the urgent need to question the underlying influence of prominent information platforms—the following discussion will. Unlike this work, which will be peer-reviewed for the accuracy of its information and sources, the legitimacy of Google is ensured just by its pure dominant market position. As Google has become a synonymous with Internet search, covering a global desktop market share of around 87% and

---

12   Hummel, Diana; Stieß Immanuel; Sauer Arn: Technikfolgenabschätzung und Geschlecht: Bestandsaufnahme und Identifizierung von Diskursschnittstellen mit besonderem Fokus auf Digitalisierung. Expertise für den Dritten Gleichstellungsbericht der Bundesregierung, 2020.
13   Noble, Safiya U.: Searching for Black girls: Old traditions in new media (PhD dissertation 2012).
14   Noble 2012.
15   Noble 2012.

98% for mobile search[16], it is necessary to analyse the agency and the potential social outcome of the information provider.

Several studies have discussed (gender) bias in search engines.[17] Kay, Matuszek and Munson (2015)[18], for instance, analysed gender bias in professions on behalf of Google image search results. The study found that individuals rated search results higher if they were in line with occupational stereotypes and that shifting the gender ratio for a variety of professions could influence the perception of gender distributions in the actual world. Thereby, the researchers showed that gender stereotyping in search engines can lead to wrong presumptions about the actual gender distribution in occupations. As the researcher found a systematic under representation of women in specific work professions, the displayed representation of gender in image search results could promote bias and discrimination in the real world.[19] In addition, Magno and colleagues[20] examined the influence of digital prejudices regarding female attractiveness on search engine platforms. This study found that search engines can be biased and indicate stereotypes that are very distinctive from the actual appearance of women within the examined country.[21] They also found strong similarities among countries with the same language, which is why the biased search engines do not reflect the demographics of the respective countries. In terms of 'beauty', a previous study[22] found that search engines reproduced a Eurocentric standard of beauty, with negative stereotypes for black and Asian women and positive stereotypes for white women in search engines such as Google and Bing. In both search engines the proportion of black women was much higher when searching 'ugly women'. Moreover, regarding physical attractiveness, negative stereotypes linked to

16 Statcounter: Search Engine Market Share Worldwide, https://gs.statcounter.com/search-engine-market-share
17 Araújo, Camila Souza; Meira, Wagner; Almeida, Virgilio: Identifying stereotypes in the online perception of physical attractiveness. In: Spiro, Emma; Ahn, Yong-Yeol (Eds): Social Informatics. SocInfo 2016. Lecture Notes in Computer Science 10046 (2016) / Baker, Paul; Potts, Amanda: Why do white people have thin lips? Google and the perpetuation of stereotypes via auto-complete search forms. In: Critical Discourse Studies 10(2) (2013), p. 187–204 / Epstein; Robertson 2015 / Kay; Matuszek; Munson 2015 / Magno; Araújo; Meira Jr.; Almeida 2016.
18 Kay; Matuszek; Munson 2015.
19 Ibid.
20 Magno; Araújo; Meira Jr.; Almeida 2016.
21 Ibid.
22 Araújo; Meira; Almeida 2016.

older women have been proven; since in the search engine queries 'beautiful women' were predominantly represented younger than the 'ugly women'.

Instead of questioning the binary nature of the mentioned studies themselves, a study by Baker and Potts[23] should be presented, which investigated discrimination in the auto-instant search offered by Google. The study demonstrated negative stereotyping and implicit value attributions for certain identity groups, such as LGBTQI identities. For example, when typing 'why do gay' into the instant search, Google offered the following search proposals: 'why do gay men have high voices'; 'why do gay men get aids'; 'why do gays exist'.[24] This work goes in line with the UN women ad series from 2013, who used genuine Google searches to alarm against sexism and discrimination.[25] While, at the time of writing this, different queries were suggested than described by Baker and Potts[26], who used Google.co.uk; the fact remains that search engines are (re)productive information platforms that are inherently part of the discourse itself. This opens up questions about the ethical responsibilities of online information providers that arise with the increasing democratization of these information platforms, but also the question how it is possible to combat the reproduction of inequalities.

Given the scope and sovereignty of certain search engines, it must be emphasized that the biased search results can act as a catalyst for regressive (gender) stereotypes as well as discrimination in the digital and real world. However, it is important to note that these challenges do not only result from information intermediaries themselves, but also from the content that underlies their operational work. Ultimately, based on the usage of metrics, search engines decide which of the innumerable web pages are listed in the search results and, more importantly, how to rank them. As such, they are "determining any systematic inclusions and exclusions [as well as] the wide-ranging factors that dictate systematic prominence for some sites, dictating systematic invisibility for others".[27] An analysis found that of approximately 300 million clicks within one search engine 92% of those were on the first

---

23 Baker; Potts 2013.
24 Baker; Potts 2013.
25 UN Women: UN Women ad series reveals widespread sexism, https://www.unwomen.org/en/news/stories/2013/10/women-should-ads
26 Baker; Potts 2013.
27 Introna, Lucas D.; Nissenbaum, Helen: Shaping the Web: why the politics of search engines matters. In: The Information Society 16(3) (2000), p. 169–185.

page.[28] As search engine user trust higher-ranked results, the perception of social realities is also influenced in a political matter. Epstein and Robertson[29] conducted five experiments in order to analyse whether search rankings can manipulate voting preferences of undecided voters. They found that biased rankings could alter voting preferences by 20% or more, as this shift can be even higher in certain demographic groups. The researchers coined the neologism "search engine manipulation effect" (SEME) and set out the caveat that most of the search ranking bias is masked; which is why people are not aware of the manipulation. As such, SEME is a threat to democratic systems, especially in countries that are dominated by solely one search platform. At this point, it should be noted that Google covers 94% of the search engine market in Germany.[30]

The digitalisation does not only change the way we learn and live, but also has physiological and neural consequences. In 2008, a study found that the daily confrontation with search engines stimulates cell change and the release of neurotransmitters in the brain. As we are spending more time browsing websites than books, new nerve tracts in our brain are strengthened, while old ones are weakened. Specifically, experienced Google users showed a higher brain activity in the left frontal area, while beginners showed none or only minimal activity in that brain area.[31] Regardless of the Darwinian theories of media evolution,[32] it becomes clear that digitalisation has affected our society and daily life already. Even while now reading, if this occurs to be in a public room, the aftermath of the digital revolution should become evident. The transformation comes along with the rapid development of AI, which extends the cognitive as well as practical possibilities of human action by posthuman forms. This gives rise to the question whether the subject-object dualism needs to be dismantled in order to understand the way in which (non)human agency is entangled in the construction of the world. This article draws on Embirbayer and Misches' definition of agency as "the temporally constructed engagement by actors of different structural environments—the temporal-relational context of action—which through the in-

---

28   Chitika: Chitika Insights. The value of Google Result Positioning, 2013, http://info.chitika.com/uploads/4/9/2/1/49215843/chitikainsights-valueofgoogleresultspositioning.pdf
29   Epstein; Robertson 2015.
30   Statcounter.
31   Carr, Nicholas: Wer bin ich, wenn ich online bin … und was macht mein Gehirn solange? Wie das Internet unser Denken verändert, Munich 2010.
32   For an overview see Schröter, Jens (Ed.): Handbuch Medienwissenschaft, 2014, p. 405.

terplay of habit, imagination, and judgment, both reproduces and transforms those structures in interactive responses to the problems posed by changing historical situations".[33] In line with Barads' account of an agential realism as "one that incorporates important material and discursive, social and scientific, human and nonhuman, and natural and cultural factors"[34], this article aims to question these dichotomies, as to point out the posthuman mimesis of gender that goes beyond an anthropocentric understanding—to comprehend "how matter matters".[35]

The Question of (Posthuman) Agency

In the 1980s Langdon Winner published the essay "Do artifacts have politics?"[36], which emphasizes the social determination of technology. According to Winner[37], technology can be instrumentalized to increase authority and power; for example: the use of television to promote a political candidate during an election. (Epstein and Robertson[38] have shown how this strategy can also be implemented through search rankings). In his widely discussed essay, Winner[39] urges us to be vigilant, as technologies are methods to organize social order—especially as the systems play a pivotal role in daily life (deliberately or not).

> "Societies choose structures for technologies that influence how people are going to work, communicate, travel, consume, and so forth over a very long time. In the processes by which structuring decisions are made, different people are differently situated and possess unequal degrees of power as well as unequal levels of awareness".[40]

---

33 Emirbayer, Mustafa; Mische, Ann: What Is Agency?. In: American Journal of Sociology 103 (1998), p. 962–1023.
34 Barad, Karen: Posthumanist Performativity: Toward an Understanding of How Matter Comes to Matter. In: Signs 28(3) (2003), p. 801–331.
35 Barad 2003.
36 Winner, Langdon: Do Artifacts Have Politics? In: Daedalus 109(1) (1985), p. 121–136.
37 Winner 1985.
38 Epstein; Robertson 2015.
39 Winner 1985.
40 Winner 1985.

In line with this notion, Winner sets the striking example of a bridge as a technical artefact that can divide people within a society. He refers to the (low-hanging) bridge constructions by Robert Moses that allows to overpass New York and Long Island only with private cars.[41] Many of the overpasses between Long Island and New York were constructed with less than three meters of clearance at the curb.[42] This construction, Winner argued, was intended to keep those who could not afford a car (people from low-income groups and racial minorities) away from the "white" beaches. Winner concluded that Moses aimed to achieve a certain social effect by excluding (public) buses on these parkways; explicitly discriminating on the basis of social-class and race. However, due to the proof of public transportation connecting New York and Long Island, Winners' bridge example has been declared a myth.[43] Notwithstanding, the question can be left open whether the example was chosen (in)accurately, since the fact that Moses' constructions were focused on automobile owners, remains. Besides the strong doubts about the validity of Winners' bridge analogy, it can be held that Winners' essay about the underlying politics of technical objects initiated a debate in Science and Technology Studies (STS) about the notion that technology maintains and increases social injustice,[44] which is still valid today. According to the UNESCO report[45] for Digital Development the gap between industrial and developing countries is still widening:

> "In global terms, digital inequalities continue to be well-documented and, in many instances, divides across lines of geography, gender, age, physical abilities, socio-economic status, language, and educational attainment are growing. [...] Over half of the world's population (some 3.9 billion people) remain unable to connect regularly to the internet. Many of these people live in sub-Saharan Africa

---

41   Bath, Corinna: De-Gendering informatischer Artefakte. Grundlagen einer kritisch-feministischen Technikgestaltung (Dissertation 2009).

42   Winner 1985.

43   Joerges, Bernward: Do Politics Have Artefacts?. In: Social Studies of Science 29(3) (1999), p. 411–431 / Woolgar, Steve; Cooper, Goeff: Do Artefacts Have Ambilvalence? Moses' Bridges, Winner's Bridges and other Urban Legends in S&TS. In: Social Studies of Science 29(3) (1999), p. 433–449.

44   Bath 2009.

45   UNESCO: Working Group on Education: digital skills for life and work, 2017, https://unesdoc.unesco.org/ark:/48223/pf0000259013

and South Asia, with six countries (India, China, Indonesia, Pakistan, Bangladesh and Nigeria) accounting for around half of the world's offline population."[46]

In most parts of the world the digital skills gender gap is growing simultaneously:

> "Today, women and girls are 25 per cent less likely than men to know how to leverage digital technology for basic purposes, 4 times less likely to know how to programme computers and 13 times less likely to file for technology patent. At a moment when every sector is becoming a technology sector, these gaps should make policy-makers, educators and everyday citizens 'blush' in alarm."[47]

The idea that technology should not be considered as neutral, but rather as socio-political is shared by STS research. Whereas Winner acknowledges the social injustice embedded in technological systems, he does not concentrate on the agency of technology itself. Although Bruno Latour[48] agrees with Winners' notion that the interaction with technology influences society; he pleads for a more open perspective regarding the subject-object dualism. Accordingly, Latour[49] regards artefacts not as neutral, but rather credits their ability to act.[50] Under the actor-network theory (ANT), the dichotomy of technology and the living is particularly avoided.[51] The revision of agency began to be discussed in the field of STS, as nonhuman entities are an active part in the domain. In 1985 Steve Woolgar asked "Why should sociology stop short when it comes to machines?"[52] and Latour[53] delivered a potential answer to this question. In his work "Mixing Humans and Non-Humans Together: The Sociology of a Door-Closer", Latour[54] uses the example of a door

---

46   UNESCO 2017.
47   UNESCO 2019.
48   Latour, Bruno: Which politics for which artifacts?. In: Domus 171 (2004), p. 50–51.
49   Latour 2004.
50   Bath 2009.
51   Ibid.
52   Woolgar, Steve: Why not a sociology of machines? The case of sociology and artificial intelligence. In: Sociology 19 (1985), p. 557–572.
53   Latour, Bruno: Mixing Humans and Nonhumans Together: The Sociology of a Door-Closer. In: Social Problems 35(3) (1988), p. 298–310.
54   Latour 1988.

to elaborate that morality can be shifted into a medium.[55] Due to the door mechanism, individuals do not have to think about performing the social courtesy of closing a door behind them. Latour[56] emphasis that understanding our social world without the nonhuman is unreasonable, since morality, knowledge or sociability are not solely the possession of humans, but also of the delegates that build the social reality and their relations. In a Foucaultian manner, artefacts can be interpreted as a bio power that influences individuals without the mask of a subject.[57] Accordingly, Latour[58] offers a symmetric anthropology that regards human and non-human/ subjects and objects equally, also in terms of agency.

> "An 'actor' in ANT is a semiotic definition—an actant—, that is something that acts or to which activity is granted by others. It implies no special motivation of human individual actors, nor of humans in general. An actant can literally be anything provided it is granted to be the source of an action. Although this point has been made over and over again, anthropocentrism and sociocentrism are so strong in social sciences (as well as in the critiques of social explanations) that each use of ANT has been construed as if it talked of a few superhumans longing for power and stopping at nothing to achieve their ruthless goal."[59]

Another approach to (nonhuman) agency brings up new questions when analysing power differences and inequalities: If certain categories are in- or excluded, the implementation of technology can result in social shaping and vice versa; thus: "matter matters".[60] Judy Wajcman[61], who emphasizes that technology can be both a product but also a multiplicator of social constructions claims: "[...] gender relations can be thought of as materialized in technology, and masculinity and femininity in turn acquire their meaning

---

55 Braun, Holger: Soziologie der Hybriden. Über die Handlungsfähigkeit von technischen Agenten. In: TUTS Working Papers 4–2000, Berlin 2000.
56 Latour 1988.
57 Dreyfus, Hubert L.: Die Gefahren der modernen Technologie: Heidegger und Foucault. In: Honneth, Axel (Ed.): Pathologien des Sozialen. Die Aufgaben der Sozialphilosophie, Frankfurt/M. 1994, p. 107–120.
58 Latour, Bruno: On Actor-Network Theory. A Few Clarifications, Plus More Than a Few Complications. In: Philosophical Literary Journal Logos 27 (2017), p. 173–197.
59 Latour 2017.
60 Barad 2003.
61 Wajcman, Judy: TechnoFeminism, Cambridge 2004.

and character through their enrolment and embeddedness in working machines".[62] In line with Wajcman, Corinna Bath[63] calls for a co-construction of gender and technology. This article has taken this approach by presenting an onto-epistemological framework that does justice to the (non)human entanglements.

Agential Realism

Karen Barad, the feminist physicist, provides a theoretical alternative in order to capture the performativity of matter as an active contributor in the social becoming. In line with Haraways' idea of companion species[64], Barad[65] opens a concept of agential realism that incorporates discursive practices within the differential account of materialism; (dis)embodied or not.

> "Agential realism is an account of technoscientific and other practices that takes feminist, antiracist, poststructuralist, queer, Marxist, science studies and scientific insights seriously, building specifically on important insights from Niels Bohr, Judith Butler, Michel Foucault, Donna Haraway, Vicki Kirby, Joseph Rouse, and others."[66]

While each of the individual influences will not be addressed at this point, it should be emphasized that Niels Bohrs' interpretation of the quantum theory and his scepticism of a Cartesian epistemology have shaped Barads' differentiated understanding of materialism. Bohr refused atomistic metaphysics that regard things as ontologically-based entities with determinate boundaries, as he claimed that quantum physics needs to include observation as a process itself.[67] In particular, it is not possible to measure the

---

62   Wajcman 2004.
63   Bath 2009.
64   Haraway, Donna J.: The Companion Species Manifesto: Dogs, People, and Significant Otherness, Chicago 2003.
65   Barad, Karen: Agentieller Realismus. Über die Bedeutung materiell-diskursiver Praktiken. Übers. von Schröder, Jürgen. Berlin 2012.
66   Barad 2003.
67   Barad, Karen: Meeting the Universe Halfway: Realism and Social Constructivism without Contradiction. In: Nelson, Lynn H./ Nelson, Jack (eds): Feminism, Science, and the Philosophy of Science, Dorfrecht/ Boston/ London 1996, p. 161–164.

position and momentum of a particle simultaneously, which is why measurements cannot be understood as neutral interactions.[68] Thus, Bohr avoided the presumed division of the observer/knower and the observed/known.[69] Bohrs' philosophical account of physics emphasizes that the observed phenomena can be interpreted as an embodiment of cultural practices; as a result of intra-activity. In contrast to the word "inter" that presupposes the pre-existence of independent entities; the notion of "intra" incorporates an agential cut that is situated within the phenomenon of the observation.[70] This perspective makes not only the observer apparent, but primarily the observation as an operation. The conceptual shift offers (re)elaborated conditions for causality, since the exteriority between the observer/knower and the observed/known within phenomena is changed.

> "On an agential realist account of technoscientific practices, the 'knower' does not stand in a relation of absolute externality to the natural world being investigated—there is no such exterior observational point. It is therefore not absolute exteriority that is the condition of possibility for objectivity but rather agential separability—exteriority within phenomena. 'We' are not outside observers of the world. Nor are we simply located at particular places in the world; rather, we are part of the world in its ongoing intraactivity. This is a point Niels Bohr tried to get at in his insistence that our epistemology must take account of the fact that we are a part of that nature we see to understand."[71]

Thus, Barad claims that neither the observer has total agency over the passive matter, nor vice versa; but rather matter and meaning has to be regarded as an agential intra-acting.[72] With her posthumanist account, Barad states that agency cannot be delegated as an element of subjects or objects; as it is rather the being in its intra-action—"matter comes to matter through the iterative intra-activity of the world in its becoming."[73] Accordingly, Barad[74] argues that responsibility is not the exclusive right of humans. In this regard, practices of knowledge cannot be traced back as (solely) human

68 Barad 2012.
69 Barad 2003.
70 Ibid.
71 Ibid.
72 Barad 1996 / Barad 2003.
73 Ibid.
74 Barad 2012.

operations, since first of all we use nonhuman elements for the acquisition, but also because they result from intra-actions that go beyond divisive hierarchical reasoning. Ultimately, also search engines must be considered as parts of reconfiguring the social—making it intelligible.

"If agency is the answer, kindly repeat the question!" This is the title from Willhelm Halffman's essay on positions on agency and the normativity of technology.[75] Halffman[76] regards agency not as a determined answer that is based on theoretical choices, but rather as an empirical toss of a coin. In line with this, this article requests to consider agency in its heterogenous and multi-faceted conditions, which includes components that go beyond human enactment. Agency is relational and agile—a result of the (non)human intra-actions. Hence, this article seeks to shift the anthropocentric position as to rethink and reconfigure the comprehension of agency and its undertaking; in order to question the loop of gendering emerging with digitalization. It must be emphasized that a posthumanist perspective of agency does not replicate the nonhuman for the human, but rather searches answers for the way of social order and its active entities. The onto-epistemological indeterminacy of agentive realism is subject to an openness that meets the causality of the appropriation processes of algorithmic bias.

The Mimetic Processes of Gendering

In 1950, Alan Turing introduced his work "Computing Machinery and Intelligence", in which he argued that learning machines work through imitation.[77] But what if these systems learn to discriminate? Gender bias in AI repetitively perpetuates and reinforces gender constraints that are reflected in social and practical discourses. Judith Butler[78] describes the (re)production of gender as "[t]his repetition is at once a re-enactment and re-experiencing of meanings already socially established". Judith Halberstam draws the parallel "Gender, we might argue, like computer intelligence, is a learned,

---

75 Halffman, Willem: If agency is the answer, kindly repeat the question. Essay review of Harbers et al., Inside the Politics of Technology. In: Science and public policy 33(6) (2006), p. 469–472.
76 Halffman 2006.
77 Collett, Celementine; Dillon, Sarah: AI and Gender: Four Proposals for Future Research, 2019.
78 Butler, Judith: Gender Trouble: feminism and the subversion of identity, New York 1990.

imitative behavior that can be processed so well that it comes to look natural"[79]—or automatic?

By addressing the technological appropriation processes, I plead that with raising (non)human entanglements, materiality needs to be seen as well as a multiplier for gender conditions on behalf of mimetic learning. Most recently, when search engines reconstitute gender arrangements by learning normative meanings of it. Technologies are always sociohistorically anchored and reflect social conditions[80], which is why historical attributions are manifested and perpetuated in mimetic appropriation practices; vice versa they (re)shape the world in their productive imitation.

Christoph Wulf[81] emphasizes the variety of meanings of the term mimesis, since it is not only used in the field of aesthetics but can also be constitutive for social studies. The articulation of mimesis as an imitation can be traced back to antiquity, such as in Plato's third book "Republic", which is extended to education.[82] According to Plato, due to its lasting effects, mimetic processes are very powerful and constitutive for human development.[83] As such, Wulf acknowledges that mimetic practices have to be set in relation to contemporary power relations, especially as they can be productive in its self-sufficiency:

> "Mimetic learning, learning by imitation, constitutes one of the most important forms of learning. Mimetic learning does not, however, just denote mere imitation or copying: Rather, it is a process by which the act of relating to other persons and worlds in a mimetic way leads to an en-hancement of one's own world view, action, and behaviour."[84]

---

[79] Halberstam, Judith: Automating Gender: Postmodern Feminism in the Age of the Intelligent Machine. In: Feminist Studies 17(3) (1991), p. 439–460.

[80] Schünemann, Isabel; Lebert, Yannick: Algorithmen & Gesellschaft. Zur Zukunft der sozialen Teilhabe in Deutschland. Vodafone Institut für Gesellschaft und Kommunikation, 2019.

[81] Wulf, Christoph: Zur Genese des Sozialen: Mimesis, Performativität, Ritual, Bielefeld 2005.

[82] Wulf, Christoph: Mimetic Learning. In: Designs for Learning 1(1) (2008), p. 56–57.

[83] Wulf 2008 / Wulf, Christoph: Das Rätsel des Humanen. Eine Einführung in die historische Anthropologie, Paderborn 2013.

[84] Wulf 2008

While Wulf[85] recognizes mimesis as an anthropological capacity by presupposing a plasticity of the body, this work implements a posthumanist perspective on mimesis as this condition seems obsolete under the sociotechnological implications of algorithmic bias. In the entanglements of (non) human intra-actions, intelligent systems also sustainably appropriate schemata as orientation structures. Thus, it should be emphasized that mimetic processes cannot be understood as mere reproduction and imitation, but rather have a performative character.[86] Following Butler's conceptualization of performativity as a practice of repetition[87], this reproduction affects and alters genderization—simultaneously as reinforcement and sustainably as stabilization and transmission. While the mimetic constructions result from the reproduction of the human, they can carry other (lasting) effects; as the presented examples show. Hence, technological performativity unfolds new impulses in these enrichments and can be regarded as a new way of looking at familiar phenomena, but also a different way of responding to them: "Mimesis resists a clear-cut split between subject and object; it resists any unequivocal distinction between what is and what should be."[88]

This work aims to point out that social action and responsibility should not be limited to humans[89]; rather it should be clarified that it is transmitted to technologies as to show opportunities of disobedience. Thus, I suggest that technologies acquire its own agency in mimetic processes, which manifest contemporary relations of inequality. The term posthuman mimesis refers to the (re)productive intervention in building social schemas that result from digital appropriation practices. The recognition of posthuman mimesis allows to (re)locate agency and responsibility in an intangibly complex world in which non-human actors also play their part. Within the mimetic practices, gender role beliefs and their bias can be (re)produced faster and are widely spread.

"Such gender role beliefs, shared within a society, promote socialization practices that encourage children to gain the skills, traits, and preferences

---

85 Wulf 2013.
86 Wulf 2005 / Wulf, Christoph: Produktive Nachahmung. Weiterbildung. In: Zeitschrift für Grundlagen, Praxis und Trends 5 (2012), p. 12–15.
87 Butler 1990.
88 Gebauer, Gunter/ Wulf, Christoph/ Reneau, Don: Mimesis: Culture—Art—Society, 1996.
89 Bath 2009 / Braidotti, Rosi: Nomadic Subjects. Embodiment and Sexual Difference in Contemporary Feminist Theory, New York 2011 / Barad 2012.

that support their society's division of labour."[90] If the division of labour is widening the gender gap in AI, it could be assumed that the loop will continue to perpetuate bias. The Global Gender Report[91] found that 78 % of AI professionals are male. There are several examples of man-based machines or/ and data.[92] Coming back to the initial question: How can we overcome algorithmic biases? An answer could be built on Hardings' standpoint theory[93], which indicates that epistemology and conceptual frameworks result from the dominant groups of hierarchical societies, who establish social power. Thus, the man-machine reconfigurations call for a critical transformation of the social and technology—to tackle the principles of homophily—a concept introduced by Wendy Chun for describing sources for pattern discrimination[94]. Yet, besides reaching out for more diverse development teams, another way to subversively change the mimetic pattern will be introduced at last.

Concluding Remarks

"The claim that a machine cannot be the subject of its own thought can of course only be answered if it can be shown that the machine has some thought with some subject matter. Nevertheless, ′the subject matter of a machine's operations′ does seem to mean something, at least to people who deal with it. [...] By observing the results of its own behaviour it can modify its own programmes as to achieve some purpose more effectively. These are possibilities of the near future, rather than Utopian dreams."[95]

90 Eagly, Alice H./ Wood, Wendy: Biosocial Construction of Sex Differences and Similarities in Behavior. In: Advances in Experimental Social Psychology 46 (2012), p. 55–123.
91 The Global Gender Report (2018) World Economic Forum, http://www3.weforum.org/docs/WEF_GGGR_2018.pdf
92 Criado-Perez, Caroline: Unsichtbare Frauen. Wie eine von Daten beherrschte Welt die Hälfte der Bevölkerung ignoriert, Munich 2020.
93 Harding, Sandra: Standpoint methodologies and epistemologies: a logic of scientific inquiry for people. In: World Social Science Report 2010, p. 173–175.
94 Chun, Wendy H. K.: Queering Homophily. In: Apprich, Clemens/ Chun, Wendy H. K.; Cramer, Florian; Steyerl, Hito. Pattern Discrimination, Minneapolis 2018, p. 59–97.
95 Turing 1950.

Coming back to Turing's work[96] it should be noted that technological systems imitating human decisions can reify and reinforce biases. Algorithms are performative and vice versa they unfold in a state of uninterrupted negotiations and are thus in a continuous intermediate stage of building power and knowledge.[97] Even if the posthuman does not have the mask of a subject and implements bias unintentionally, algorithmic bias repetitively perpetuate categorizations in social and practical discourses. The presented studies show that biased search engines can lead to discrimination, but who is being held responsible? With the continuing (non)human entanglements these questions need to be approached. Due to technological developments, the objective of this contribution was to reconceptualize the relationship between humans and non-humans and to rethink the categories of agency and responsibility. If these technologies determine (in)equalities, it seems vital to assume that they are part of the social becoming. In efforts to discuss the implications of the agential realism the example of biasing technologies was chosen in order to illustrate that Barad's relational framework functions as a critical tool to approach mimetic appropriation processes as it takes (non)human on-going intra-actions into account. If nonhuman entities have an impact on our lives, it seems rather necessary to set an onto-epistemology offset; especially for responsibility ascriptions "not only for what we know, how we know, and what we do but, in part, for what exists".[98] The concept of agential realism proposes the inseparability between ontology and epistemology as the social is in a constate state of becoming. Thus, agential realism offers a perspective that enables to address the empirical implications when analyzing mimetic processes of technologies. By linking ontology and epistemology, Barads' theory contributes to the theories of situated knowledge[99] by offering a more comprehensive understanding of the relationship between humans and non-humans and

96 Ibid.
97 Roberge, Jonathan; Seyfert, Robert: Was sind Algorithmuskulturen? In: Ead. (Eds.): *Algorithmuskulturen. Über die rechnerische Konstruktion der Wirklichkeit, Bielefeld 2017, p. 7–40.
98 Barad 2003.
99 Haraway, Donna: Situated Knowledges: The Science Question in Feminism and the Privilege of Partial Perspectives. In: Feminist Studies 14(3) (1988), p. 575–599 / Harding, Sandra: Whose Science? Whose Knowledge? Thinking from Women's Lives, Ithaca 1991.

by re-conceptualizing the categories: subjectivity, agency and causality.[100] The entelechy of the rapidly progressing technologies and the (non)human intra-actions call for a methodological re-thinking: With the radical indeterminacy of objectivity and subjectivity, the onto-epistemological framework provides an approach that is better suited to capture the complexities of the entangled responsibilities.[101] Thus, I plead for an onto-epistemology that goes beyond anthropocentric paradigms as to enable to conceive responsibilities as continuous entangled relations; especially if these set (un)visibility, inclusion and representation in relation to resources, power and opportunities. Finally in order to square the circle, a constructive dialogue between and beyond the disciplines is needed. Concurrently, research is working on different data obfuscation techniques to ensure digital privacy protection[102]. One self-defense method is informational resistance, disobedience or protest "by producing misleading, false, or ambiguous data with the intention of confusing an adversary or simply adding to the time or cost of separating bad data from good".[103] Regarding the trade-off between usability and privacy, a pertinent daily method of disobedience is to change the pattern by covering one's track of data—data disobedience through depersonalization and irritation. To do this, demographic data, including (gender) identities, need to be varied throughout the web[104]. Thereby, the digital self but also the society can be multiplied in interesting ways, which can lead to positive side effects, such as building fluid identities and mi-

[100] Rouse, Joseph: Barad's Feminist Naturalism. In: Hypatia 19(1) (2004), p. 142–161 / Hinton, Perta: Situated Knowledges' and New Materialism(s). Rethinking a Politics of Location. In: Woman: A Cultural Review 25(1) (2014), p. 99–113 / Hoppe, Katharina; Lemke, Thomas: Die Macht der Materie. In: Soziale Welt 66 (2015), p. 261–280.

[101] Kayumova, Shakhnoza; Mcguire, Chad J.; Cardello, Suzanne: From empowerment to response-ability: rethinking socio-spatial, environmental justice, and nature-culture binaries in the context of STEM education: In: Cultural Studies of Science Education 14(1) (2019), p. 205–229.

[102] Bakken, David E.; Parameswaran, Rupa; Blough, Douglas M.; Franz, Andy A.; Palmer, Ty J.: Data obfuscation: Anonymity and desensitization of usable data sets. In: IEEE Security and Privacy 2(6) (2004), p. 34–41.

[103] Brunton, Finn; Nissenbaum, Helen: Vernacular resistance to data collection and analysis: A political theory of obfuscation. In: First Monday 16(5) (2011), np.

[104] Kausch, Julia: Wie digitale Netzwerke analoges Leben formen—und was das Problem ist. Das Filter (2 February 2018), http://dasfilter.com/kultur/wie-digitale-netzwerke-analoges-leben-formen-und-was-das-problem-ist-medienwissenschaftlerin-wendy-chun-im-interview

metizing pluralities towards a (digital) world in which demographics do not automatically implicit societal (dis)advantages.

Literature

Araújo, Camila Souza; Meira, Wagner; Almeida, Virgilio: Identifying stereotypes in the online perception of physical attractivenessIn: Spiro, Emma; Ahn, Yong-Yeol (Eds): Social Informatics. SocInfo 2016. Lecture Notes in Computer Science 10046. Cham 2016.

Baker, Paul; Potts, Amanda: 'Why do white people have thin lips?' google and the perpetuation of stereotypes via auto-complete search forms. Critical Discourse Studies, 10(2), 2013, p. 187–204.

Bakken, David E.; Parameswaran, Rupa; Blough, Douglas M.; Franz, Andy A.; Palmer, Ty J.: Data obfuscation: Anonymity and desensitization of usable data sets. IEEE Security and Privacy, 2(6), 2004, p. 31–41.

Bath, Corinna: De-Gendering informatischer Artefakte. Grundlagen einer kritisch-feministischen Technikgestaltung. Dissertation. Staats- und Universitätsbibliothek Bremen 2009.

Barad, Karen: Meeting the Universe Halfway: Realism and Social Constructivism without Contradiction. In: Nelson, Lynn Hankinson; Nelson, Jack (Eds.) Feminism, Science, and the Philosophy of Science. Dordrecht, Boston, London 1996, p. 161–194.

Barad, Karen: Posthumanist Performativity: Toward an Understanding of How Matter Comes to Matter. Signs, 28(3), 2003, p. 801–831.

Barad, Karen: Agentieller Realismus. Über die Bedeutung materiell-diskursiver Praktiken. Berlin 2012.

Braidotti, Rosi: Nomadic Subjects. Embodiment and Sexual Difference in Contemporary Feminist Theory. New York 2011.

Braun, Holger: Soziologie der Hybriden. Über die Handlungsfähigkeit von technischen Agenten. Technische Universität Berlin—TUTS Working Papers 4–2000.

Brunton, Finn; Nissenbaum, Helen: Vernacular resistance to data collection and analysis: A political thepry of obfuscation. First Monday, 16(5), 2011

Butler, Judith: Gender Trouble: feminism and the subversion of identity. New York 1990.

Carr, Nicholas: Wer bin ich, wenn ich online bin ... und was macht mein Gehirn solange? Wie das Internet unser Denken verändert. München 2010.

Chitika: The value of Google Result Positioning. Chitika Insights, 2010, Retrieved from http://info.chitika.com/uploads/4/9/2/1/49215843/chitikainsights-valueofgoogleresultspositioning.pdf

Chun, Wendy Hui Kyong: Queering Homophily. In: Apprich, Clemens; Chun, Wendy Hui Kyong; Cramer, Florian, Steyerl, Hito; Pattern Discrimination, Minneapolis 2018, p. 59–97.

Collett, Celementine; Dillon, Sarah: AI and Gender: Four Proposals for Future Research. Cambridge 2019.

Criado-Perez, Caroline: Unsichtbare Frauen. Wie eine von Daten beherrschte Welt die Hälfte der Bevölkerung ignoriert. München 2020.

Dreyfus, Hubert L. (1994). Die Gefahren der modernen Technologie: Heidegger und Foucault. In: Honneth, Axel (Ed.): Pathologien des Sozialen. Die Aufgaben der Sozialphilosophie. Frankfurt/M. 1994, p. 107–120.

Eagly, Alice; Wood, Wendy: Biosocial Construction of Sex Differences and Similarities in Behavior. Advances in Experimental Social Psychology, 46, 2012, p. 55–123.

Emirbayer, Mustafa; Mische, Ann: What is Agency? American Journal of Sociology, 103, 1998, p. 962–1023.

Epstein, Robert; Robertson, Ronald E.: The search engine manipulation effect (seme) and its possible impact on the outcomes of elections. Proceedings of the National Academy of Sciences, 112(33), 2015, p. E4512–E4521.

Gebauer, Gunter; Wulf, Christoph; Reneau, Don: Mimesis: Culture—Art—Society. Berkeley 1996.

Halberstam, Judith: Automating Gender: Postmodern Feminism in the Age of the Intelligent Machine. Feminist Studies, 17(3), 1991, p. 439–460.

Halffman, Willem: If agency is the answer, kindly repeat the question. Essay review of Harbers et al., Inside the Politics of Technology. Science and public policy, 33(6), 2006, p. 469–472.

Haraway, Donna J.: Situated Knowledges: The Science Question in Feminism and the Privilege of Partial Perspectives. Feminist Studies, 14(3), 1988, p. 575–599.

Haraway, Donna J.: The Companion Species Manifesto: Dogs, People, and Significant Otherness. Chicago 2003.

Harding, Sandra: Whose Science? Whose Knowledge? Thinking from Women's Lives. Ithaca, New York 1991.

Harding, Sandra: Standpoint methodologies and epistemologies: a logic of scientific inquiry for people. UNESCO and International Social Science Council 2010. World Social Science Report, 2010, p. 173–175.

Hinton, Perta: 'Situated Knowledges' and New Materialism(s). Rethinking a Politics of Location. Woman: A Cultural Review, 25(1), 2014, p. 99–113.

Hoppe, Katharina; Lemke, Thomas: Die Macht der Materie. Soziale Welt, 66, 2015, p. 261–280.

Howard, Ayanna; Borenstein, Jason: The Ugly Truth About Ourselves and Our Robot Creations: The Problem of Bias and Social Inequity. Science and engineering ethics, 24(5), 2018, p. 1521–1536.

Hummel, Diana; Stieß, Immanuel; Sauer, Arn: Technikfolgen-abschätzung und Geschlecht: Bestandsaufnahme und Identifizierung von Diskursschnittstellen mit besonderem Fokus auf Digitalisierung (Expertise für den Dritten Gleichstellungsbericht der Bundesregierung), 2020.

Internet Live Stats: Google search statistics, 2020, Retrieved from https://www.internetlivestats.com/google-search-statistics/

Introna, Lucas D.; Nissenbaum, Hellen: Shaping the Web: why the politics of search engines matters. The Information Society, 16(3), 2000, p. 169–185.

Joerges, Bernward: Do Politics Have Artefacts? Social Studies of Science, 29(3), 1999, p. 411–431.

Johnston, Ian: AI robots are 'learning racism, sexism and other prejudices from humans'. The Independent, 2017, Retrieved from https://www.independent.co.uk/life-style/gadgets-and-tech/news/ai-robots-artificial-intelligence-racism-sexism-prejudice-bias-language-learn-humans-a7683161.html

Kausch, Julia: Wie digitale Netzwerke analoges Leben formen—und was das Problem ist. In: Das Filter, February 2, 2018, Retrieved from http://dasfilter.com/kultur/wie-digitale-netzwerke-analoges-leben-formen-und-was-das-problem-ist-medienwissenschaftlerin-wendy-chun-im-interview

Kay, Matthew; Matuszek, Cynthia; Munson, Sean A.: Unequal representation and gender stereotypes in image search results for occupations. Proceedings of the 33rd Annual ACM Conference on Human Factors in Computing Systems, 2015, p. 3819–3828.

Kayumova, Shakhnoza; Mcguire, Chad J.; Cardello, Suzanne: From empowerment to response-ability: rethinking socio-spatial, environmental justice, and nature-culture binaries in the context of STEM education. Cultural Studies of Science Education, 14(1), 2019, p. 205–229.

Latour, Bruno: Mixing Humans and Nonhumans Together: The Sociology of a Door-Closer. Social Problems, 35(3), 1988, p. 298–310.

Latour, Bruno: Which politics for which artifacts? Domus, 171(June), 2004, p. 50–51.

Latour, Bruno: On Actor-Network Theory. A Few Clarifications, Plus More Than a Few Complications. Philosophical Literary Journal Logos, 27, 2017, p. 173–197.

Magno, Gabriel; Araújo, Camila S.; Meira Jr., Wagner; Almeida, Virgilio: Stereotypes in Search Engine Results: Understanding the Role of Local and Global Factors. Presented in the Workshop on Data and Algorithmic Transparency (DAT'16), 2016.

Noble, Safiya U.:. Searching for Black girls: Old traditions in new media. PhD dissertation 2012.

Rainie, Lee; Anderson, Janna: The Future of Jobs and Jobs Training. Pew Research Center, 2017, Retrieved from https://www.voced.edu.au/content/ngv%3A77340

Roberge, Jonathan; Seyfert, Rober: Was sind Algorithmuskulturen? In: Ead. (Eds.): Algorithmuskulturen. Über die rechnerische Konstruktion der Wirklichkeit. Bielefeld: 2017, p. 7–40.

Rouse, Joseph: Barad's Feminist Naturalism. Hypatia, 19(1), 2004, p. 142–161.

Schröter, Jens: Handbuch Medienwissenschaft. Stuttgart 2014.

Schünemann, Issabel; Lebert, Yannick: Algorithmen & Gesellschaft. Zur Zukunft der sozialen Teilhabe in Deutschland. Vodafone Institut für Gesellschaft und Kommunikation, 2019, Retrieved from https://www.vodafone-institut.de/wp-content/uploads/2019/10/Algorithmen_und_Gesellschaft.pdf

Statcounter: Search Engine Market Share Worldwide, 2020, Retrieved from https://gs.statcounter.com/search-engine-market-share

The Global Gender Report: World Economic Forum, 2018 Retrieved from
   http://www3.weforum.org/docs/WEF_GGGR_2018.pdf
Turing, Alan M.: Computing Machinery and Intelligence. Mind LIX, 236, 1950, p.
   433–460.
UN Women: UN Women ad series reveals widespread sexism, 2013,
   Retrieved from https://www.unwomen.org/en/news/stories/2013/10/
   women-should-ads
UNESCO: Working Group on Education: digital skills for life and work, 2017,
   Retrieved from https://unesdoc.unesco.org/ark:/48223/pf0000259013
UNESCO: I'd blush if I could: closing gender divides in digital skills through
   education, 2019, Retrieved from https://en.unesco.org/Id-blush-if-I-
   could
Wajcman, Judy: TechnoFeminism. Cambridge 2004.
Winner, Langdon: Do Artifacts Have Politics? Daedalus, 109(1), 1985,
   p. 26–38.
Woolgar, Steve: Why not a sociology of machines? The case of sociology
   and artificial intelligence. Sociology, 19, 1985, p. 557–572.
Woolgar, Steve; Cooper, Goeff: Do Artefacts Have Ambilvalence? Moses'
   Bridges, Winner's Bridges and other Urban Legends in S&TS. Social
   Studies of Science, 29(3), 1999, p. 433–449.
Wulf, Christoph: Zur Genese des Sozialen: Mimesis, Performativität, Ritual.
   Bielefeld 2005.
Wulf, Christoph: Mimetic Learning. Designs for Learning, 1(1), 2008,
   p. 56–67.
Wulf, Christoph: Produktive Nachahmung. Weiterbildung. Zeitschrift für
   Grundlagen, Praxis und Trends, 5, 2012, p. 12–15.
Wulf, Christoph: Das Rätsel des Humanen. Eine Einführung in die historische
   Anthropologie. Paderborn 2013.

Fabian Lütz

Discrimination by Correlation

Towards Eliminating Algorithmic Biases and Achieving Gender Equality

"Accountability requires human judgement, and only humans can perform the critical function of making sure that, as our social relations become ever more automated, domination and discrimination aren't built invisibly into their code"[1] (Frank Pasquale).

The analysis[2] focuses on opportunities and challenges of algorithms[3] and risks in the "algorithmic age"[4] and will explore avenues to address the impact of algorithms[5] in the area of gender equality (GE) law regarding biases and discrimination.

I. Obey and Disobey—the Terms Imposed by Behavior Changing Algorithms and Gender-based Discrimination

In most online activities[6] consumers' human intelligence[7] is confronted with decisions of algorithms. Consumers have to obey or dis-obey. Often there is no real choice. Not accepting the terms and conditions imposed by companies equals exclusion from the service, which can be best described by the term of *behavior changing algorithms*[8]. Some platforms face no competition, exercise monopoly[9] or "algorithmic power" and could be viewed as

---

[1] Pasquale, Frank: The Black Box Society: The Hidden Algorithms Behind Money and Information, Boston 2015, p. 213.

[2] The author would like to thank Tim Papenfuss for practical insights and comments on an early draft.

[3] See Russell, Stuart: Artificial intelligence: The future is superintelligent. In: Nature 548 (2017), p. 520–521.; Bostrom, Nick: Superintelligence. Paris 2017; Bostrom, Nick: The future of humanity. In: Geopolitics, History, and International Relations (2009), 1(2), 41–78. Tegmark, Max: Life 3.0: Being human in the age of artificial intelligence, London 2017.

[4] Louridas, Panos: Algorithms, Boston 2020, p. 1.

[5] For a critical perspective, see Gunkel, David J.: The Machine Question: Critical Perspectives on AI, Robots, and Ethics, Cambridge 2012.

[6] Search, applications for job postings or unemployment benefits, online advertisements (ads) for products or recommendations for books.

[7] Badre, David: On Task, Princeton 2020, p. 47.

[8] This terminology is inspired by Zuboff, Shoshana: The Age of Surveillance Capitalism: the Fight for a Human Future at the New Frontier of Power, New York 2019.

[9] See in general, Petit, Nicolas: Big Tech and the Digital Economy: The Moligopoly Scenario. Oxford 2020.

gate keepers[10]. In a democracy nobody should be discriminated because of gender when using services[11]. But what are algorithms? Barocas defines an algorithm as "a formally specified sequence of logical operations that provides step-by-step instructions for computers to act on data and thus automate decisions".[12]. Algorithms understood as a list of step-by-step instructions which are nourished with real world data, have an objective and follow the instructions or mathematical operations to achieve the defined aim[13]. Fry groups algorithms into four main categories according to the tasks: 1) priorization[14], 2) classification[15], 3) association[16] and 4) filtering[17]. These algorithms can come in the shape of either "rule-based algorithms" where instructions are programmed by a human or "machine-learning algorithms"[18]. The article will mostly refer to algorithms in general[19].

[10] See Article 3 (1) of the Proposal for a Regulation of the European Parliament and of the Council on contestable and fair markets in the digital sector (Digital Markets Act).

[11] See Zuiderveen Borgesius, Frederik: Strengthening legal protection against discrimination by algorithms and AI, In: The International Journal of Human Rights, 24:10 (2020), p. 1572–1593, highlighting the threat of AI to the right to non-discrimination.

[12] Barocas, Solon: Data & Civil Rights: Technology Primer (2014); In essence, algorithms are "a step-by-step procedure for solving a problem or accomplishing some end", see Algorithm." Merriam-Webster.com Dictionary, Merriam-Webster, https://www.merriam-webster.com/dictionary/algorithm (February 7, 2021).

[13] See Fry, Hannah: Hello World: How to be Human in the Age of the Machine, London 2018, p. 8–9.

[14] One classic example is search engines that rank different results or online video platforms suggesting what movies to watch, ibid., p. 9.

[15] An example is online advertisement by showing different categories of people different advertisements, ibid., p. 10.

[16] This task is important for this analysis, as it tries to find relationships, connections and correlations between things, used for example by online book stores to make recommendations, ibid., p. 10.

[17] This task removes noise from signals by filtering information, a type of task used by speech recognition or social media applications, ibid., p. 10–11.

[18] Ibid., p. 11–12: "You give the machine data, a goal and feedback when it's on the right track—and leave it to work out the best way of achieving the end", ibid., p. 12.

[19] Wooldridge 2020, p. 349. Under the umbrella term of narrow artificial intelligence, machine learning (ML) is a sub-category and (artificial) neural networks or deep learning further sub-categories. Boden is classifying 5 different forms of AI: symbolic artificial intelligence, artificial neural networks, evolutionary programming, cellular automata and dynamical systems, see Boden 2010, p. 6. For an introduction to algorithms see Louridas 2020, p. 181f; for an introduction to Deep Learning and the relationship between algorithm, machine learning and deep learning, see Keller, John D: Deep

Obey shall be understood in two ways: first, humans must obey the terms imposed by companies to use systems and second, the state can impose regulation on companies they need to obey to. Dis-obey shall be understood as humans dis-obeying in order to preserve their rights[20], notably in the absence of legal rules or if companies dis-obey regulatory attempts to preserve their business model. The *dis-obey* approach could inspire consumers to follow *rights-preserving behavior,* such as *data poor* approaches, favoring data friendly companies, introducing "noise" into their data supply or avoid digital services that potentially discriminate[21]. Considering this tension between *obey* and *dis-obey,* regulators have been reflecting on rules for fair and non-discriminatory algorithms. The European Commission (EC) published a draft Regulation (Artificial Intelligence Act)[22] on 21 April 2021, following the adoption of the Digital Services Act (DSA)[23] and the Digital Markets Act (DMA)[24]. Many international bodies have adopted standards on AI (OECD[25],

---

Learning, Boston 2019, p. 6. ML can be subdivided into supervised and un-supervised learning.

20 For example, by choosing alternative ways of using services offered by companies.
21 Consumers could use algorithms to detect discriminatory algorithms.
22 European Commission, Proposal for a Regulation of the European Parliament and the Council laying down harmonized rules on artificial intelligence (Artificial Intelligence Act) and amending certain Union legislative acts, COM (2021) 206 final.
23 The DSA tries to mitigate some of the risks for women: "Specific groups [...] may be vulnerable or disadvantaged in their use of online services because of their gender [...] They can be disproportionately affected by restrictions [...] following from (unconscious or conscious) biases potentially embedded in the notification systems by users and third parties, as well as replicated in automated content moderation tools used by platforms."
24 The European Digital Strategy consist of the Digital Services Act (DSA) and the Digital Markets Act (DMA):Proposal for a Regulation of the European Parliament and the Council on a Single Market For Digital Services (Digital Services Act) and amending Directive 2000/31/EC, COM/2020/825 final and Proposal for a Regulation of the European Parliament and the Council on contestable and fair markets in the digital sector (Digital Markets Act), COM/2020/842 final.
25 OECD, Principles on Artificial Intelligence, https://www.oecd.org/science/forty-two-countries-adopt-new-oecd-principles-on-artificial-intelligence.htm

Council of Europe[26] or UNESCO[27]). The EC's Advisory Committee on Equal Opportunities for Women and Men adopted an opinion on AI and GE[28], containing recommendations to address algorithmic biases and prevent gender-based discrimination.

A case of discrimination usually concerns individual cases, but the impact can reach societal scale when patterns of algorithmic discrimination evolve and reinforce biases and discrimination[29]. Each discriminated individual will be reflected in the datasets and contribute to create future risks of discrimination for women and men as categorized and classified by algorithms. However, humans also rely on automatic processing of data by schematizing and grouping people in boxes, for example by sex or race[30]. Such classification and generalization could base decisions on a group of women or men to the detriment of an individual, which impacts the well-being of consumers using products and services[31] that rely on technology or workers accessing the labor market[32]. Moreover, one of the problems is the opaque decision making of algorithms, or "black box" as used by Pasquale to describe the

---

[26] CoE Recommendation CM/Rec(2020)1 of the Committee of Ministers to member States on the human rights impacts of algorithmic systems, 8th April 2020, https://search.coe.int/cm/pages/result_details.aspx?objectid=09000016809e1154 "ensure that racial, gender and other societal and labour force imbalances that have not yet been eliminated from our societies are not deliberately or accidentally perpetuated through algorithmic systems, as well as the desirability of addressing these imbalances through using appropriate technologies" (Preamble).

[27] UNESCO, Report on AI and Gender Equality, https://unesdoc.unesco.org/ark:/48223/pf0000374174 (February 6, 2021).

[28] European Commission, Advisory Committee on Equal Opportunities for Women and Men, Opinion on Artificial Intelligence (2020), https://ec.europa.eu/info/sites/info/files/aid_development_cooperation_fundamental_rights/opinion_artificial_intelligence_gender_equality_2020_en.pdf (February 6, 2021).

[29] In general, see Adam, Alison: Artificial knowing: gender and the thinking machine. London 1998.

[30] Kleinberg, Jon; Ludwig, Jens; Mullainathan, Sendhil; Sunstein, Cass R.: Algorithms as discrimination detectors. In: Proceedings of the National Academy of Sciences Dec 2020, 117 (48), p. 30097.

[31] Council Directive 2004/113/EC of 13 December 2004 implementing the principle of equal treatment between men and women in the access to and supply of goods and services.

[32] Directive 2006/54/EC of the European Parliament and of the Council of 5 July 2006 on the implementation of the principle of equal opportunities and equal treatment of men and women in matters of employment and occupation (recast).

fact that the inner workings of an algorithm are sometimes difficult to grasp, especially for potential victims of discrimination.

Relying on literature and current institutional proposals, the article assesses the opportunities and risks both for regulating and using algorithms. Dealing with the topic of AI and gender from the angles of "regulatory object" and "useful tool" will shed new light and contribute to an ethical[33] and fair framework[34] to enforce GE laws.

II. From Classical Discrimination towards Discrimination by Correlation

Before explaining discrimination by correlation (3) and giving examples (4), I will present the relevant EU law and discuss the concept of discrimination (1) as well as the relationship between algorithms and bias (2).

1) Some Reflections on EU Law and Gender-based Discrimination

EU anti-discrimination law works with the concept of protected characteristics (Ex. gender or age). However, this becomes increasingly difficult when decisive elements in the decision-making result not from humans but algorithms. Current laws were adopted before the age of algorithms and are not equipped to deal with all new legal challenges even if formulated in an abstract and general way to deal with (un)foreseen situations[35]. Judges will have to interpret existing laws in light of technological developments, which could accommodate AI. EU law distinguishes between direct and indirect discrimination. A direct discrimination in EU law[36] exists "where one person

---

33 Liao, S. Matthew: A Short Introduction to the Ethics of Artificial Intelligence. Ethics of Artificial Intelligence. Oxford 2020.
34 This article will not discuss fair and ethical AI in general, see notably Coeckelbergh 2020.
35 On the nature of the abstract general design and force of the law, see Hart, Herbert Lionel Adolphus; Green, Leslie: The concept of law. Oxford 2015, p. 21.
36 US law differentiates along the lines of disparate treatment and disparate impact, therefore choosing a similar classification but closer to the dichotomy known under competition law as "by object/by effects approach", see for U.S. law the exhaustive overview by Barocas, Solon; Selbst, Andrew D.: Big Data's Disparate Impact. In: California Law Review 104 (2016), p. 671–732.

is treated less favorably on grounds of sex than another is, has been or would be treated in a comparable situation"[37]. Indirect discrimination "where an apparently neutral provision, criterion or practice would put persons of one sex at a particular disadvantage compared with persons of the other sex, unless that provision, criterion or practice is objectively justified by a legitimate aim, and the means of achieving that aim are appropriate and necessary"[38]. While direct discrimination cannot be justified in principle, a possibility for justification exists for indirect discrimination. A different treatment is not discriminatory, when it is justified, appropriate and necessary (proportionality test)[39]. Procedurally, the burden of proof is essential in non-discrimination cases because the claim for a discrimination needs to be supported by evidence, which is generally shared between the victim and the "alleged" discriminator[40]. Once a *prima facie* evidence is brought by the victim, the "discriminator" needs to rebut the claim, a process called the shifting of the burden of proof. The idea is to facilitate the access to evidence for the claimant, often difficult, especially in cases involving opaque algorithmic decision procedures. In the case *Schuch–Ghannadan*[41], the Court of Justice of the European Union (CJEU) refined its jurisprudence by ruling that the burden of proof does not require bringing statistical data or facts (beyond some prima facie evidence), if the claimant has no or difficult access[42]. This jurisprudence *de facto* extends the rights of victims of discrimination, defining what is expected of them in terms of evidence. Concretely, only evidence that is not more than reasonable to access can be expected which is of relevance for cases involving AI. This case law could facilitate bringing claims against companies. If the claimant cannot reasonably access the information contained in the algorithm, the "burden of proof" shifts to the company which needs to

37 Article 2 (1)(a) Directive 2006/54/EC.
38 Article 2 (1)(b) Directive 2006/54/EC.
39 See Craig, Paul; Gráinne De Búrca: EU law: text, cases, and materials. Oxford 2020, p. 544–545.
40 See for the discrimination test, Ellis, Evelyn; Watson, Philippa: EU anti-discrimination law, Oxford 2012.
41 C-274/18, Minoo Schuch-Ghannadan v Medizinische Universität Wien, EU:C:2019:828.
42 Ibid: "Art. 19 Abs. 1 der Richtlinie 2006/54 ist dahin auszulegen, dass er von der Partei, die sich durch eine solche Diskriminierung für beschwert hält, nicht verlangt, dass sie, um den Anschein einer Diskriminierung glaubhaft zu machen, in Bezug auf die Arbeitnehmer, die von der nationalen Regelung betroffen sind, konkrete statistische Zahlen oder konkrete Tatsachen vorbringt, wenn sie zu solchen Zahlen oder Tatsachen keinen oder nur schwer Zugang hat."

show that the algorithm did not discriminate which incentivizes companies to avoid discrimination in the first place. Previously, the CJEU was reluctant in terms of access to information when it excluded in *Meister*[43] a "right [...] to have access to information indicating whether the employer has recruited another applicant" even when the job applicant "claims plausibly that he meets the requirements listed in a job advertisement and whose application was rejected"[44]. This represented an obstacle for job applicants that were refused by algorithms to get access to the underlying data that influenced the decision outcome, making proof of algorithmic discrimination more difficult than classic discrimination. The CJEU had no opportunity (yet) to clarify its interpretation in a case of AI[45], but would dispose of tools to facilitate confidential access to data, for example via in *camera* procedures to protect business secrets or consulting AI experts to give expert evidence.

Statistical analysis is used for risk assessment by insurance companies to deal with complexity, sometimes to the detriment of accuracy. Insurance companies used *gender* to distinguish between different risks, to establish price differentiation by *gender* in car insurance contracts[46]. The case "Test-Achats" concerned the practice of using *gender* for insurance premiums[47]. The CJEU ruled that considering *gender* for calculating insurance premiums is discriminatory, obliging the firms to introduce *gender* neutral insurance contracts. Despite not being directly linked to AI, the case gives guidance to assess potential discriminations for situations of statistical data and data sets used by algorithms where a similar process of generalization exists. Even if the CJEU "banned "using *gender*-specific insurance contracts, algorithms can easily circumvent this prohibition by using criteria or so-called proxies, to infer the *gender* of a person. Consequently, it remains to be seen how courts would decide a case involving algorithms and if the concept of discrimination is still well equipped to "grasp" the essence of algorithmic

---

43 CJEU, C-415/10 Galina Meister v Speech Design Carrier Systems GmbH EU:C:2012:217.
44 Ibid, para. 49.
45 Some guidance was received from the CJEU in Seymour-Smith, that "mere generalizations concerning the capacity of a specific measure to encourage recruitment are not enough to show that the aim of the disputed rule is unrelated to any discrimination based on sex nor to provide evidence on the basis of which it could reasonably be considered that the means chosen were suitable for achieving that aim." CJEU, Case C-167/97, Seymour-Smith, EU:C:1999:60.
46 CJEU, C-236/09.
47 Ibid.

discrimination on the basis of *gender*[48]? The borders of the protected characteristics such as gender or race become increasingly blurred when algorithms are involved. Algorithms might replace the distinguishing element of *gender* by other data via correlation. One can expect more *discrimination by correlation* based on datasets that correlate and infer information indirectly and discriminate in fine by gender. I call this process *discrimination by correlation*, which is not restricted to AI. The detection of hidden or indirect mechanisms should interest the regulator, as traditional discrimination patterns (e.g. *gender* or *age*) risk becoming less frequent. Algorithms could play a role as "discrimination detectors"[49] for the regulator.

2) Towards Discrimination by Correlation: Algorithms Reflecting and Magnifying Gender Biases?

The assumption "machine learning is fair by default"[50] is disputable, as algorithms can "potentially increase bias and discrimination"[51]. Algorithms are seen as "neutral", as they simply "execute code" based on available data. However, algorithms are only as neutral as the datasets. The outcome of an algorithm could be amplifying biases because of gender-biased data (see further in II. 1 on the problem of the *gender data* gap)[52].

Recent literature is assessing potential impacts of algorithms on gender-based discrimination[53]. Bias is no new phenomena; it has been known

---

[48] On EU law, see Xenidis, Raphaële; Senden, Linda: EU Non Discrimination Law in the Era of Artificial Intelligence: Mapping the Challenges of Algorithmic Discrimination. In: Bernitz, Ulf; Groussot, Xavier; de Vries, Sybe A. (Eds.), General Principles of EU law and the EU Digital Order, Bruxelles 2020, pp. 151–182.

[49] Kleinberg et. al. 2020, p. 30096.

[50] Argued by Geerts, Thierry: Homo Digitalis, Lanno 2021; Hardt, Moritz. In: Medium 2014, How big data is unfair, https://medium.com/@mrtz/how-big-data-is-unfair-9aa544d739de (February 6, 2021).

[51] Coeckelbergh 2020, p. 75.

[52] This risk is also highlighted in the standard text book on AI: "Often, the data themselves reflect pervasive bias in society", see Russell, Stuart; Norvig, Peter: Artificial intelligence: a modern approach, London 2021, p. 49.

[53] See the special report European Commission, "Algorithmic discrimination in Europe: Challenges and opportunities for gender equality and non-discrimination law" (2021) prepared by the Legal Network of Gender Experts of the EC, https://www.equalitylaw.eu/downloads/5361-algorithmic-discrimination-in-europe-pdf-1-975

by enforcers analyzing discriminatory behavior[54]. But biases in algorithmic discrimination leverage and amplify discriminatory risks and lead to new forms of discrimination such as invisible discrimination. Discriminations involving algorithms are more complex and require refined detection mechanisms. As the decision-making process inside the algorithm is often unclear, discriminations might occur without ever being detected (or consciously felt), due to the opaque nature of the AI. Job ad recommendations not shown by the algorithm on the screen because women have not been defined as target audience, would be unthinkable in the real world. A billboard at the side of the highway or next to the bus stop would not "discriminate" on the basis of *gender* of the viewer.

Cause and origin of discrimination is not necessarily a protected characteristic (Ex. *gender*). If certain job postings are not shown to women because of the characteristic gender, algorithms decide/learn and recognize patterns based on available data. Data and the correlation between data points enable the algorithms to conclude that specific ads should not be shown to women. As algorithms correlate information from datasets on which they have been trained, *discrimination by correlation* grasps this new reality of algorithmic discrimination as it describes how discrimination occurs: by correlating data, without being able to identify which specific data points have caused a decision that is discriminatory.

3) Examples of Gender Bias and Discrimination by Correlation

Four examples illustrate the reflections in the areas of (a) online ads, (b) employment, (c) image processing and (d) natural language processing, where biases/stereotypes or (gender-based) discrimination occurs. There is increasing awareness about discrimination and inequalities occurring in online platforms[55], when it comes to determining recidivism for criminal

---

54 Coeckelbergh 2020, p. 125.
55 Renan Barzilay, Arianne: The Technologies of Discrimination: How Platforms Cultivate Gender Inequality. In: The Law & Ethics of Human Rights 13 (2019), no. 2, p. 179–202.

convicts[56] or predicting the likelihood of a future crime[57]. The predictive power of algorithms used by supermarkets to "predict" pregnancy[58] based on the products purchased[59] gained media attention. Feminist literature [60] and recent books expose that the data-driven world and algorithms are often designed by and for men[61].

a) Online Advertisements

Google and *Facebook* show targeted ads to users using algorithms [62]. Experimental research by Lambrecht/Tucker[63] revealed that women received less job ads for STEM[64] professions than men. The authors explored how algorithms deliver gender neutral job ads promoting job opportunities in the STEM sector. Despite gender neutrality, empirical evidence revealed that fewer women saw the ad despite a similar estimation of "click-through-rate". This is explained by the so-called "Gender Valuation Gap"[65] which

---

56   Skeem, Jennifer; John Monahan; Christopher Lowenkamp: Gender, risk assessment, and sanctioning: The cost of treating women like men. In: Law and human behavior 40.5 (2016), p. 580; Wright, Emily M.; Salisbury, Emily J.; Van Voorhis, Patricia: Predicting the prison misconducts of women offenders: The importance of gender-responsive needs. In: Journal of Contemporary Criminal Justice 23.4 (2007), p. 310–340; DeMichele, Matthew; Baumgartner, Peter; Wenger, Michael; Barrick, Kelle; Comfort, Megan; Misra, Shilpi: The Public Safety Assessment: A re-validation and assessment of predictive utility and differential prediction by race and gender in Kentucky (2018).

57   Mayson, Sandra G.: Bias in, bias out. In: Yale Law Journal 128 (2018), p. 2218.

58   Zuiderveen 2018, p. 13 as example for intentional discrimination based on gender which would be difficult to prove.

59   Basdevant, Adrien; Mignard, Jean-Pierre: L'Empire des données. Essai sur la société, les algorithmes et la loi. Paris 2018, p. 91f.

60   Wellner, Galit; Rothman, Tiran: Feminist AI: Can We Expect Our AI Systems to Become Feminist? In: Philosophy & Technology. 33 (2020), p. 191–205.

61   Perez, Caroline Criado: Invisible women: Exposing data bias in a world designed for men. London 2019.

62   Agrawal, Ajay; Joshua Gans; Avi Goldfarb: Máquinas predictivas: la sencilla economía de la inteligencia artificial, Madrid 2019, p. 238–241.

63   Lambrecht, Anja; Tucker, Catherine E.: Algorithmic Bias? An Empirical Study into Apparent Gender-Based Discrimination in the Display of STEM Career Ads. In: Management Science 65 (2019), p. 2966–2981.

64   Science Technology Engineering and Mathematics.

65   The 21% Gender Valuation Gap, https://www.wordstream.com/blog/ws/2014/05/13/gender-bias (February 6, 2021).

means ads are more expensive to show to women, as "women [are] being undervalued by 21% in online marketing"[66], which refers to the potential value per click and earnings from ads. As algorithms are run cost effectively, the companies prefer to show ads to men even for gender-neutral ads. This could represent a discriminatory risk if women are systematically excluded from seeing the ads[67]. Research revealed [68] the potential unequal treatment for men and women in image recognition algorithms for advertising[69], when inserting gender stereotypes into the datasets. Researchers concluded that *Facebook* could determine precisely to whom ads are targeted, which shows the discriminatory potential[70]. Referring to Lambrecht/Tucker, computer scientists developed a commendable strategy[71] to achieve fairer ads without gender bias[72]. Research and specific algorithms hint at the possibility to control discrimination in online advertisement auctions[73].

---

66 Criado et al. 2020, p. 1.
67 Lambrecht; Tucker 2018.
68 See the examples by Orwat, Carsten: Risks of Discrimination through the Use of Algorithms. A study compiled with a grant from the Federal Anti-Discrimination Agency. Berlin 2020, p. 37.
69 Ali, Muhammad; Sapiezynski, Piotr; Bogen, Miranda; Korolova, Aleksandra; Mislove, Alan; Rieke, Aaron (2019): Discrimination through optimization: How Facebook's ad delivery can lead to skewed outcomes. In: arXiv e-prints, https://arxiv.org/pdf/1904.02095.pdf (February 6, 2021).
70 The images were only readable for the algorithm but not for humans and targeted either men or women depending on the stereotype "coded" into the pictures beforehand.
71 Methodology, http://cs.yale.edu/bias/blog/jekyll/update/2019/02/08/fair-advertising.html (February 6, 2021).
72 Demo, https://fair-online-advertising.herokuapp.com (February 6, 2021).
73 Celis, L. Elisa ; Mehrotra, Anay; Vishnoi, Nisheeth: Toward controlling discrimination in online ad auctions. In: International Conference on Machine Learning. PMLR, 2019.

b) Employment and Recruitment

Algorithms are used at all stages of employment[74]. One example is Amazon's recruitment algorithm which discriminated women[75]. They are also used for the distribution of unemployment benefits which potentially discriminated women, where algorithms classify unemployed people into three categories in accordance with job prospects, therefore a classical exercise of sorting. In *concreto*, women received different scores than men, notably due to absences in the labor market (maternity and parental leave)[76]. This algorithm is problematic[77] because gender, labor market absences, births and family leaves are incorporated into the predictions[78] of job prospects. Private companies and national administrations use algorithms to guide and (improve?) decision-making. Even if in the Austrian example, the court rejected claims of discrimination by the algorithm, legal scholars and computer scientists criticized this algorithm for using criteria that are strongly linked or associated with one sex. Using maternity leave, family leave (dominantly taken by women) or military service (mostly men) besides the protected characteristic of *gender* is problematic. Discrimination can be difficult to detect and is sometimes easily confused in some situations. Known as the "Simpson's paradox", statistics do not necessarily reveal the underlying reasons for different (potentially discriminatory) outcomes reflected in a

---

74 Pre-employment, recruitment, employment including promotions and evaluations, post-employment, unemployment benefits.

75 Reuters, 11th October 2018, Amazon scraps secret artificial intelligence recruiting tool that showed bias against women, https://www.reuters.com/article/us-amazon-com-jobs-automation-insight/amazon-scraps-secret-ai-recruiting-tool-that-showed-bias-against-women-idUSKCN1MK08G (February 6, 2021).

76 https://verfassungsblog.de/koennen-algorithmen-diskriminieren/ (February 6, 2021).

77 For a schematic overview of some of the parameters used, see https://www.derstandard.at/story/2000089720308/leseanleitung-zum-ams-algorithmus ; https://algorithmwatch.org/en/story/austrias-employment-agency-ams-rolls-out-discriminatory-algorithm/ and here for a critical assessment of the Austrian Academy of Sciences that discussed potential discriminatory effects of the algorithm https://www.oeaw.ac.at/ita/projekte/2020/der-ams-algorithmus. The algorithm was stopped temporarily in 2020, and then again authorized by court decision in December 2020: https://netzpolitik.org/2020/automatisierte-entscheidungen-gericht-macht-weg-fuer-den-ams-algorithmus-wieder-frei/

78 For predictions made by algorithms, Spiegelhalter, David: The art of statistics: learning from data, London 2019, p. 143.

statistic, which was revealed in the context of university admission[79]. Such arguments can easily be used by defendants in court to refute alleged cases of discrimination[80].

In general, an International Labor Organization (ILO) report sums up the challenges of AI used in employment: "[...] An automated recruitment system based on analyzing historic data would replicate [...] bias, thereby reinforcing pre-existing discrimination"[81]. An example for discriminatory treatment at work,[82] is "classification bias", which "occurs when employers rely on classification schemes, such as data algorithms, to sort or score workers in ways that worsen inequality or disadvantage along the lines of [...] sex, or other protected characteristics"[83]. Finally, Kleinberg et al. describe a hypothetical example of alleged discrimination where a tech company is not hiring a woman. They compare a human decision to discriminate with a potential AI-based decision to discriminate[84]. For classification, attempts have been made to achieve fair and non-discriminatory outcomes of the algorithm[85].

---

79   Ibid, p. 110–112.
80   Kleinberg et al. 2020, p. 30097: "Challenges in using statistical evidence to show intentional discrimination, small sample sizes, unclear objectives, and the general opacity of human cognition combine to create a fog of ambiguity, which prevents us from stopping a behavior that we know to be widespread yet for which in any one instance there may well be plausible alternative explanations."
81   Ernst, Ekkehardt; Merola, Rossana; Samaan, Daniel: Economics of artificial intelligence: Implications for the future of work. In: IZA Journal of Labor Policy 9.1 (2019), p. 16.
82   Kim, Pauline T.: Data-driven discrimination at work. In: William & Mary Law Review 58 (2016), p. 857–866.
83   Ibid., p. 866.
84   Kleinberg et al. 2020, p. 30096–30097.
85   Concrete examples for code to be used to avoid discriminatory outcomes on the basis of sex: https://github.com/Trusted-AI/AIF360/blob/master/examples/demo_meta_classifier.ipynb (February 6, 2021).

c) Image Processing

The photo tagging algorithm of Google created a discriminatory concern, when black people were labeled erroneously as "gorillas"[86]. This relates to the problem described in section III.) on the (un)availability of data sourcing the algorithm as described by Hosaganar: "Image-processing algorithms that hadn't been trained on a large enough number of photos of black people were unable to account for different skin tones and lightning"[87]. As research on gender and racial biases highlights[88], similar observations were identified with regard to pictures of search engines. When searching for "CEO", much more pictures of men were displayed than women, but the percentage reflected was worse than the real ratio between men and women. An attempt to achieve a more balanced image search[89] has been developed by Celis, L. Elisa, et al.[90].

d) Natural Language Processing[91], Search and Autocomplete Functions

The auto-complete function is implemented in most search engines. Search queries feed the search algorithms, and this is fed back to suggest search terms while the user is typing the query. A useful tool without doubt, it could make suggestions (or predict the user's search intentions) in ways that do not necessarily match the real intention of the searcher, leading to a discriminatory behavior or reinforcing current discriminatory patterns. Examples reported by *The Economist* include a Dutch father searching for infor-

---

86 Hosanagar, Kartik: A human's guide to machine intelligence: how algorithms are shaping our lives and how we can stay in control, New York 2020, p. 44–45.
87 Ibid., p. 44–45.
88 Buolamwini, Joy; Timnit Gebru: Gender shades: Intersectional accuracy disparities in commercial gender classification. In: Conference on fairness, accountability and transparency. PMLR (2018); Skeem 2016, p. 580.
89 See methodology, http://cs.yale.edu/bias/blog/jekyll/update/2018/01/20/balanced-news-search.html; see the demo: https://fair-image-search.herokuapp.com/image Diversity.php (February 6, 2021).
90 Celis, L. Elisa; Kapoor, Sayash; Salehi, Farnood; Vishnoi K. Nisheeth: An algorithmic framework to control bias in bandit-based personalization. In: arXiv:1802.08674(2018), https://arxiv.org/abs/1802.08674 (February 6, 2021).
91 For an overview of natural language processing, see Mitchell, Melanie: Artificial intelligence: A guide for thinking humans. London 2019, p. 223–251.

mation on parental leave and "how to combine work and fatherhood" with the auto-complete function suggesting: "When he searched for advice on combining fatherhood with work, the search engine asked if he had meant "motherhood and work". [92] This is not only discriminatory towards women (and men), it also perpetuates stereotypes and biases on gender roles and distorts reality. This might change over time[93] but the importance of search predictions without gender bias remains.

A second example revealed by Cadwalladr concerns ads highlighted by U.N. Women[94] which is also based on auto-complete suggestions[95]. According to the information, the ads revealed that if you type "women should" this leads to "women should stay at home" and "women should be slaves". Likewise, "women shouldn't" leads to "women shouldn't have rights" and "women shouldn't vote"[96]. Even if this reveals existing perceptions about society, stereotypes, and biases (as a result of people searching for this key words), there is a risk, that people are steered in a direction they would not have considered, creating a new audience for gender bias, stereotypes and attempts to discriminate. Some authors conclude that gender bias and racial bias enshrined in search engines like "Google's autocomplete is by no means an exception in the world of algorithms"[97].

Finally, another illuminating example[98] comes from the area of natural language processing (NLP), where it has been shown that word embeddings [99] can cause an amplification of existing bias, stereotypes and lead to discriminatory outcomes. Word embeddings are widely used in applications such as search or CV analysis. Some authors argue that the use of word embeddings is "blatantly sexist [...] and hence risk introducing biases of various

---

92 The Economist 7th October 2017, Men, women and work, https://www.economist.com/international/2017/10/07/the-gender-pay-gap (February 6, 2021).
93 The author repeated this search query on 10 October 2021.
94 https://www.unwomen.org/en/news/stories/2013/10/women-should-ads (February 6, 2021).
95 Hosanagar 2020, p. 42–43.
96 Ibid, p. 42.
97 Ibid, p. 44.
98 Mitchell 2019, p. 250–251.
99 Bolukbasi, Tolga; Chang, Kai-Wei; Zou, James; Saligrama, Venkatesh, Kalaim Adam: Man is to computer programmer as woman is to homemaker? debiasing word embeddings. In: arXiv:1607.06520 (2016).

types into real-world systems"[100]. Even gender-neutral wording is often associated as either female (homemaker, nurse, receptionist) or male (maestro, skipper, protégé). Whereas in analogy puzzles, "man is to king, as woman is to X", the best answer is "queen", however for other simple vector arithmetic, such word embeddings reveal potential sexism implicit in the words as shown in the following example: "man: woman :: computer programmer: homemaker". The authors of the empirical research propose a solution to this risk for biased data and have developed an algorithm detecting such risks in NLP[101]. NLP is vital for the advances in AI and is helpful to avoid biases and discrimination by correlation[102]. Another risk associated with NLP methods such as Word2vec[103] developed by Google is the de facto standard for neural networks to automatically learn word vectors. Programmers will have to "obey" this standard and use Google's database if they want to design a quality product. The influence of such neural networks is to "predict what words are likely to be paired with a given input word",[104] which is crucial for search. Considering the use of search in today's world and the occurrence of sexist and gender discriminatory outcomes caused by neural networks, the state needs to consider regulation. A possible solution to gender imbalance in rankings (for search, news feeds or recommendation systems), has been developed by computer scientists[105] in the framework of a Yale project "controlling bias in Artificial Intelligence"[106] including a demo version[107]. Such solutions could form part of the approach non-discrimination by code.

---

100 Bolukbasi et al., p. 11.
101 Ibid, p. 11; see also the strategy proposed by Ghili, Soheil; Ehsan Kazemi; Amin Karbasi: Eliminating latent discrimination: Train then mask. In: Proceedings of the AAAI Conference on Artificial Intelligence 2019, 33. № 01.
102 Mitchell 2019, p. 242.
103 https://code.google.com/archive/p/word2vec/ (February 6, 2021).
104 Mitchell 2019, p. 243.
105 http://cs.yale.edu/bias/blog/jekyll/update/2018/11/03/balanced-ranking.html (February 6, 2021).
106 http://balanced-ranking.herokuapp.com (February 6, 2021).
107 Ibid.

III. The (Un)available Data as Source for Gender Bias and Discrimination by Correlation

Algorithmic discrimination can be framed as a problem of how information processing by machines leads to gender-based discrimination. The AI White Paper of the EC highlights quite succinctly, that "without data, there is no AI. The functioning of [...] AI [...], and [its] actions and decisions [...] very much depend on the data set on which the systems have been trained. The necessary measures should therefore be taken to ensure that, where it comes to the data used to train AI systems, the EU's values and rules are respected, specifically in relation [...] the protection of fundamental rights."[108]

Even if the design of AI plays a role, in general, decisions or predictions are a direct result of the data[109]. Therefore, rather than focusing on the design stage (algorithmic processing bias)[110] and possible intentions of programmers[111], the present analysis will concentrate on the role of data as discriminations can occur regardless of whether the object of the algorithms is to discriminate or not.

---

[108] European Commission 2020, White Paper AI, p. 19.

[109] This was raised recently: "The question is where it is rooted—in the training dataset or in the algorithm?", see Wellner 2020; Strauß, S. From Big Data to Deep Learning: A Leap Towards Strong AI or 'Intelligentia Obscura'? In: Big Data Cogn. Comput. 2018, 2, p. 16.

[110] See a cross-disciplinary perspective and a typology of three different biases relevant for the analysis of discrimination, Ferrer, Xavier, et al.: Bias and Discrimination in AI: a cross-disciplinary perspective. In: arXiv preprint arXiv:2008.07309 (2020), p. 1, https://arxiv.org/abs/2008.07309 (February 6, 2021).

[111] However, diversity plays a decisive role, see Crawford, Kate; Whittaker, Meredith; Elish, Madelein Clare; Barocas, Solon; Plasek, Aaron; Ferryman, Kadija: The AI Now Report. The Social and Economic Implications of Artificial Intelligence Technologies in the Near-Term, New York 2016; European Commission, Gender Equality AI Opinion (2020), p. 8–9.

1) How History Defines the Future—the Problem of Gender Biased Data Sets

Data collection is limited to the available data and therefore algorithms also mirror bias (algorithmic bias[112])[113] present in society. The main source for biases[114] is data, in the form of input data and training data ("training bias")[115]. Consequently, the input data reflects the status of the world and societal perceptions. The algorithm identifies and finds data patterns during the training process and learns how to predict or advise decisions. If a gender bias is reflected in the data, it is likely to be incorporated in the algorithm. Thus, there is an increased risk for women of being discriminated if such patterns mirror stereotypes and biases.

The real danger for gender-based discrimination is that rather than identifying a protected characteristic (gender), it infers a person's protected characteristic based on available information. The power of algorithms is the result of correlating[116] data, making predictions based on (historic) data and by inference from non-existing characteristics. The algorithm could increase the risk of discrimination in apparently neutral situations where a characteristic such as gender is not known, explicitly excluded, or disregarded by the algorithm[117]. In essence, if there is no fully unbiased training data set, the algorithm will never be neutral.

---

112 Wooldridge 2020, p. 338.
113 For an overview of the 5 multiple sources of bias and discrimination (how target and class labels are defined; labelling the training data; collecting the training data; feature selection; and proxies), see Barocas; Selbst 2016, p. 677–693; Zuiderveen 2018, p. 10–13.
114 Next to the classification of Barocas; Selbst 2016, p. 677–693, some authors reduce the causes of algorithmic bias to two types ("biased training data and unequal ground truth"), see Hacker 2018, p. 5. The present analysis will take a different approach, focusing on the sources and entry points of bias around data.
115 See Ferrer et.al 2020, p. 1: "Algorithms learn to make decisions or predictions based on datasets that often contain past decisions. If a dataset used for training purposes reflects existing prejudices, algorithms will very likely learn to make the same biased decisions. Moreover, if the data does not correctly represent the characteristics of different populations, representing an unequal ground truth, it may result in biased algorithmic decisions."
116 A correlation means that there exists a relationship between facts, data or numbers and should not be confused with causation, see for example Spiegelthaler 2019, p. 96–99.
117 See notably, Barocas; Selbst 2016, p. 671.

The Council of Europe (CoE) Recommendation on the human rights impacts of algorithmic systems specifies on datasets: "In the design, development, [...] of algorithmic systems [...] States should carefully assess what human rights and non-discrimination rules may be affected as a result of the quality of data that are being put into and extracted from an algorithmic system, as these often contain bias and may stand in as a proxy for classifiers such as gender, race, [...]"[118]. The process of collecting data creates knowledge about consumers habits, referred to as profiling[119]. By profiling, companies are conducting a large-scale pattern recognition system that classifies consumers into categories. This facilitates decision-making by generalization and typification of consumers, such as recommending a product or showing a specific ad based on profiling[120]. Despite lacking accuracy, it is often a fast and cheap process for firms[121].

It has been argued by Hardt[122], that dominant groups tend to be favored by automated decision-making processes because more data is available and therefore receive fairer, more representative, and accurate decisions/predictions, than minority groups for which data sets are limited. The gender data gap captures this deficiency, as much less data on women is available in datasets[123]. Hardt even argues that accuracy could be considered as a proxy to fairness which means that women risk receiving fewer fair decisions by AI. Ensuring a fair data mining process could help de-bias and reduce discrimination. To sum up, AI "[...] raises difficult questions about how to ensure that

---

[118] Recommendation CoE CM/Rec (2020)1 on the human rights impacts of algorithmic systems, point 2.2.
[119] Hildebrandt, M. Profiling: From data to knowledge. In: DuD 30 (2006), p. 548–552.
[120] See notably Anrig, Bernhard; Browne, Will; Gasson, Mark: The Role of Algorithms in Profiling. In: Hildebrandt, Mireille; Gutwirth, Serge (Eds.) Profiling the European Citizen. Berlin 2008, who distinguish two essential roles in data mining: "the procedure of the profiling process" and as a "mathematical procedure to identify trends, relationships and hidden patterns in disparate groups of data".
[121] Packin, Nizan; Lev-Aretz, Yafit: Learning algorithms and discrimination. In: Research Handbook on the Law of Artificial Intelligence. Cheltenham, London 2018, p. 91, who highlight issues of reliability and data accuracy in the light of learning algorithms and discrimination.
[122] Hardt 2014.
[123] For the gender data gap, Kraft-Buchman, Caitlin; Arian, Réné: The Deadly Data Gap: Gender and Data. Geneva: Women at the Table (2019).

discriminatory effects resulting from automated decision processes, whether intended or not, can be detected, measured, and redressed".[124]

Having identified the source and nature of biases which could lead to discriminatory effects by algorithms, what to do about it?

2) Biases, Data Mining and Generalization

Data mining is the process of data collection to feed the algorithm. This is the first stage where biases and discrimination can be prevented. The type and quality of data collected is essential for creating fair and gender equal datasets as it influences potential and gravity of discrimination by the algorithm. Data quality, accuracy and representativeness are assets of good data sets. If datasets do not contain accurate, complete or any information on a specific group, it will be difficult to produce the desired (accurate) results of suggesting a behavior or predicting outcomes. Hence, collection and labelling of the data are crucial for training algorithms. Specific features, "the components of a piece of data that a ML program bases its decisions on"[125], need to be selected, in the stage during which a company filters and selects certain relevant criteria or data points. In this context, proxies are relevant to define the way the algorithm moves through the data and orients itself. Another challenge is the possibility for developers to hide anti-discriminatory behavior by masking the process. This prevents decision makers to (de)construct the data or manipulates the design of the algorithm by "hiding" and "covering" direct intentional discrimination[126].

Once data has been mined and datasets compiled, the algorithm uses generalization and concretization[127]. An authoritative book on stereotypes and probabilities has argued that "generalizations based on gender are important in their own right and as an illuminating beginning in considering

---

[124] US White House, Executive Office of the President, Big Data: Seizing Opportunities, preserving, Washington 2014, http://www.whitehouse.gov/sites/default/files/docs/big_data_privacy_report _5.1.14_final_print.pdf (February 6, 2021), point 64.
[125] Wooldridge 2020, p. 343.
[126] Zuiderveen 2018, p. 13.
[127] Lee, Felicia R. : Discriminating? Yes. Discriminatory? № The New York Times, December 13, 2003. advance.lexis.com/api/document?collection=news&id=urn:contentItem: 4B70-S120-01KN-20KW-00000-00&context=1516831 (February 6, 2021).

the circumstances under which using even statistically rational generalizations might be wrong"[128]. Problematic for non-discrimination by correlation is the so-called "tragedy of big data"[129], according to which the more variables or data you have, the more correlations that can show significance will be found by researchers or algorithms. According to Taleb, "falsity grows faster than information; it is nonlinear (convex) with respect to data".[130] and one problem associated with big data is that "there is a certain property of data: in large data sets, large deviations are vastly more attributable to noise (or variance) than to information (or signal)"[131]. This should caution regulators about the potential growing discriminatory nature of algorithms in ever increasing large data sets and encourage them to focus on unbiased and accurate datasets. One could envisage regulatory oversight for certain datasets if the risk of discrimination has its main origin there.

Finally, if algorithms learn by themselves, and develop new solutions to problems, there is a risk that reliance on data results in a pattern of potential discriminatory practices that is learned. If bias is not eliminated or reduced, it will perpetuate the discriminatory decision-making process. Algorithms should strive to be designed in a "gender aware" way, to have less biased outcomes.

3) Concluding Remarks on Datasets and Bias

This paper argues that the focus should be on more accurate and representative data sets instead of falling victim to the *"unreasonable effectiveness of big data"*[132], notably due to its shortcomings. While the quality of the data is key for having accurate, non-discriminatory and fair decisions, this often comes at the cost of inferior algorithms. Establishing a dataset for algorithms[133] is costly for companies which might therefore focus on cheaper and

---

[128] Schauer, Frederick: Profiles, Probabilities, and Stereotypes. Harvard University Press, 2003, p. 131ff.

[129] Taleb, Nassim Nicholas: Antifragile: Things that gain from disorder, p. 416–418.

[130] Taleb 2012, p. 417.

[131] Ibid, p. 417.

[132] Halevy, Alon; Norvig, Peter; Pereira, Fernando: The unreasonable effectiveness of data. In: IEEE Intelligent Systems 24.2 (2009), p. 8–12.

[133] For example, with the help of humans labeling for example images and using training data for algorithms.

easier methods of collecting massive amounts of data (of poorer quality) for their algorithms. The EC highlighted in its AI White Paper some important elements and requirements for the design of AI systems for (training) data sets, which go in the direction advocated in the present analysis: "Requirements to take reasonable measures aimed at ensuring that such subsequent use of AI systems does not lead to outcomes entailing prohibited discrimination. These requirements could entail obligations to use data sets that are sufficiently representative, especially to ensure that all relevant dimensions of gender [...]are appropriately reflected in those data sets"[134].

At input-level, one solution to overcome biased datasets leading potentially to discrimination by correlation could be a better selection of input data, to "teach" algorithms to avoid bias in the training phase or to let companies and regulators use an algorithm that "checks" the relevant algorithm for biases[135] (a sort of data "TÜV")[136]. Compliance could be either voluntary or mandatory, but it would increase the trust of consumers in algorithms[137].

The challenge is how to detect biases and if a verification should be undertaken for algorithms prior to market entry or only in cases where discrimination occurs. Ferrer et al[138] highlight some of the problems: "To assess whether an algorithm is free from biases, there is a need to analyze the entirety of the algorithmic process. This entails first confirming that the algorithm's underlying assumptions and its modelling are not biased; second, that its training and test data does not include biases and prejudices; and finally, that it is adequate to make decisions for that specific context and task." As discussed earlier, access to information is difficult, notably in the presence of AI. In essence, the source code of the algorithm and the training data is often protected by intellectual property or privacy laws which might prevent training data tests. This complicates identification of biases in the model absent company agreement or a legal provision forcing companies to grant access to the relevant information[139]. Ghili et al. developed a strategy for eliminating (latent) discrimination: "In order to prevent other features

---

[134] European Commission, AI White Paper 2020, p. 19.
[135] For algorithms checking datasets and detecting biases, see Bolukbasi et al. 2016.
[136] Similar to the German technical inspection association (TÜV) which has the mission to test, inspect and certify technical systems in order to minimize hazards and prevent damages.
[137] Increased marketability for companies and possible reputation gains could result.
[138] Ferrer et al. 2020, p. 2.
[139] Ibid, p. 2.

proxying for sensitive features, we need to include sensitive features in the training phase but exclude them in the test/evaluation phase while controlling for their effects. We evaluate the performance of our algorithm on several real-world datasets and show how fairness for these datasets can be improved with a very small loss in accuracy"[140]. This strategy seems to address the problem of substituting protected characteristics by other proxies while at the same time preserving accuracy. Legislators depend on the development and advancement of such bias detecting techniques by computer scientists to build the corresponding legal tools and adapt the legal framework and enforcement accordingly. The CoE AI Recommendation is clear on this point and should serve as inspiration for regulators: "For the purposes of analyzing the impacts of algorithmic systems [...] on the exercise of rights [...], private sector actors should extend access to relevant individual data and meta-datasets, including access to data that has been classified for deletion, to appropriate parties, notably independent researchers, the media and civil society organizations. This extension of access should take place with full respect to legally protected interests as well as all applicable privacy and data protection rules"[141]. Transforming this guidance into binding law, would ensure the above-mentioned verification process by computer scientists and help victims in discrimination cases to bring evidence in court to prove discrimination claims.

IV. Strategies and Legal Tools to Capture and Overcome 'Algorithmic Discrimination by Correlation'

Eliminating algorithmic biases and achieving GE requires a cross-pollination strategy between regulating algorithms and algorithms assisting the regulator, which can be subdivided into three branches which rely on and influence each other: (1) artificial intelligence assisting the regulator, (2) *non-discrimination by design* and (3) *non-discrimination by law*. First, regulators need to be equipped with adequate tools (e.g. specifically designed algorithms for regulators that detect discrimination by correlation), to enforce non-discrimination rules by detecting algorithmic discrimination.

---

140 Ghili et al. 2019.
141 Recommendation CoE CM/Rec (2020), point 6.1.

Second, the question is whether some forms of discrimination should not (only) be solved by law, but already from the outset in the design of the algorithms by coding in a non-discriminatory way[142]. Such a *non-discrimination by design* approach could help to eliminate some forms of discriminatory behavior (albeit not as stand-alone solution but rather as a complement to traditional regulation), but it raises the question of legal certainty and more generally whether *regulation by code,* is the appropriate form of regulation[143]. This shows interaction between the three strategies and a process of cross-pollination between law, code as well as between the regulator and algorithms.

Third, the cornerstone of each regulatory design aiming to capture discrimination by correlation will be built on *non-discrimination by law*. Choices have to be made between a mix of the above three branches of (legal) strategies, but also between ex-ante, ex-post, general or sector-specific regulation[144], in order to adequately address the issues of *discrimination by correlation* and the underlying root causes (treatment of data and biased datasets). The AI literature has been enriched by many different theoretical reflections[145]. While some authors distinguish code-driven and data-driven regulation while anchoring their regulatory suggestions in the rule of law[146], others call for types of non-discrimination by design, non-discrimination by

---

142 For a similar idea in relation to code and capital, Pistor, Katharina: The code of capital: How the law creates wealth and inequality. Princeton 2020; Hassan, Samer; De Filippi, Primavera: The Expansion of Algorithmic Governance: From Code is Law to Law is Code. In: Field Actions Science Reports (2017), Special Issue 17.
143 See two examples: Hacker, Philipp: Teaching fairness to artificial intelligence: existing and novel strategies against algorithmic discrimination under EU law. In: Common Market Law Review 55.4 (2018), p. 1143–1185 and Hildebrandt, Mireille: Algorithmic regulation and the rule of law. In: Philosophical Transactions of the Royal Society A: Mathematical, Physical and Engineering Sciences 376.2128 (2018), p. 20170355.
144 On the question if and what type of regulation is appropriate, see Petit 2020, p. 240.
145 See Meneceur, Yannick: L'intelligence artificielle en procès, Bruxelles 2020; Wischmeyer, Thomas: Regulierung intelligenter Systeme. In: Archiv des öffentlichen Rechts 143.1 (2018), p.1–66; Hermstrüwer, Yoan: Artificial Intelligence and Administrative Decisions Under Uncertainty. In: Wischmeyer, Thomas; Rademacher, Timo (Eds.) Regulating Artificial Intelligence. Berlin 2020.; Sunstein, Cass R.: Of artificial intelligence and legal reasoning. University of Chicago Law School. In: Public Law & Legal Theory Working Papers № 18, 2001.
146 Hildebrandt 2018, p. 20170355.

law (either arguing no, minimal, or maximal changes to the current legislative framework) or a combination of both code and law[147].

1) Using Algorithms to Detect Violations of Gender-based Discrimination

While literature and debates tend to focus on the regulation of technology, the question of how regulators could use algorithms to detect algorithmic discrimination[148] or even delegate some form of regulatory power to the stage of coding, is often left aside[149]. There are two separate questions. First, the more fundamental question, whether some forms of discriminatory risks could be captured and avoided, if developers of algorithms (were obliged by law to) use data that significantly reduces the risk of discrimination. This would soften the need for regulatory intervention if empirically less discriminatory harm could be proven. The regulator could couple this with a "marketing authorization style" system known for pharmaceuticals[150] and would merely check the algorithm against incorporated biases before it can be used[151]. Second, whether algorithms should be used by anti-discrim-

---

147 Cazals, François ; Chantal Cazals: Intelligence artificielle: l'intelligence amplifiée par la technologie. Louvain-la-Neuve 2020, p. 200.
148 Kleinberg et al. 2020.
149 On the question of how algorithms can support regulators, see Alarie, Benjamin; Anthony Niblett; Albert Yoon: Regulation by machine, https://dx.doi.org/10.2139/ssrn.2878950 (February 6, 2021).
150 Detela, Giulia; Lodge, Anthony: EU regulatory pathways for ATMPs: standard, accelerated and adaptive pathways to marketing authorization. In: Molecular Therapy-Methods & Clinical Development 13 (2019), p. 205–232.: "The Marketing Authorisation Application (MAA) procedure [...] ensures the quality, safety, and efficacy of all medicinal products [...] by requiring regulatory review of quality, safety, and efficacy data generated during clinical [...]" which "must comply with the particular standards and requirements within the legislation and the principles of good clinical practice and Good Manufacturing Practice to ensure that the data presented [...] are complete, accurate, and satisfactory."
151 One could model such a system on the market authorization procedure used in pharmaceutical law. Here the clinical trials are also conducted and financed by the industry, underpinned by studies. Companies could test algorithms and datasets with algorithms for biases, submit results to the regulator. That way the industry does the verification and checks itself and the regulator tests and reviews the submitted evidence.

ination bodies to detect discriminatory behavior[152]. "The fact that AI can pick up on discrimination suggests it can be made aware of it. For instance, AI could help spot digital forms of discrimination, and assist in acting upon it."[153] Empowering regulators with algorithmic capabilities would improve and would facilitate decision-making in administration, notably for AI-based discrimination. This might raise questions of knowledge and skills to interpret any such findings, where techniques and algorithms are used to detect biases[154]. For the latter it raises the question to what degree algorithms are merely assisting the regulator with guidance, decision support or substituting (part of) the administrator's decision, in other words, what is the degree of control that the administration would have over the decision-making process. Surely it could not "delegate" regulatory power completely to AI, so control needs to be ensured. Mere assistance to resolve complex matters involving artificial intelligence could be imagined. This is how the concept of cross-pollination is to be understood: algorithms pose challenges and risks for the regulator but also comes along with opportunities, where the power of algorithms can be used to detect discriminatory practices and prove them in court[155]. Regulators could be assisted by algorithms to detect discrimination which could improve the decision-making process. Humans decide differently from machines. While machines are better at abstract and cognitive decision making[156], such as pattern recognition, humans excel at non-abstract decision making such as implicit know-how and intuition as well as ethical and fair reasoning. In this way a combination in the form of support by artificial intelligence while humans remain in the driving seat for the final decision is probably the best mix for taking administrative decisions regarding GE law.

---

[152] See Veale, Michael; Brass, Irina: Administration by algorithm? Public management meets public sector machine learning. In: Public Management Meets Public Sector Machine Learning, Oxford 2019, p. 121–122.; Kleinberg, Jon; Ludwig, Jens; Mullainathan, Sendhil; Sunstein, Cass R.: Discrimination in the Age of Algorithms, In: Journal of Legal Analysis, 10 (2018), p. 113–174.

[153] Ferrer et al. 2020, p. 2.

[154] Criado Pacheco, Natalia; Ferrer Aran, Xavier; Such, José Mark: A Normative approach to Attest Digital Discrimination. In: Advancing Towards the SDGS Artificial Intelligence for a Fair, Just and Equitable World Workshop of the 24th European Conference on Artificial Intelligence (ECAI'20): AI4EQ ECAI2020.

[155] See Hacker 2018.

[156] Coeckelbergh 2020, p. 201.

Algorithms often lack accuracy[157] as the run to cost effectiveness often leads to unfair outcomes. If for example, reputation is associated with key words (such as Elite Universities), then representations in the data might have a disproportionate impact on the decision outcome. With speed and pattern recognition algorithms could assist the regulator with sorting and treating cases of discrimination more efficiently. Jointly, algorithms and human decision makers could filter information for investigations, filtering evidence, verify more easily, improve case law analysis, and create more user-friendly data bases. Combining human intelligence and artificial intelligence would probably reduce both type-1 and type-2 errors. A type 1 error (false positive) in our context would be that due to a generalization, a person is being discriminated even though there was no objective reason to discriminate the person. A type 2 error (false negative) would be a situation where a person is not being discriminated (access to credit despite financial problems) despite objective reasons indicating a justification for discriminating a person in terms of access to credit[158].

Relying on generalizations based on the available data entails the risk of decision errors. If generalization is used (due to cost effectiveness), a comparison needs to be made between false positives and false negatives. Such an approach can only be acceptable and justifiable if the errors it produces do not lead to the detriment of the discriminated person. If for example statistical information is available, showing that persons from a specific group with specific characteristics (gender, postal code, attendance of a specific university etc.) typically tend to not repay their loans for example, this could serve as a justification to "label" them with a specific risk and exclude them from receiving for example a credit. However, these practices could lead to exclude persons who despite fulfilling the stereotypical characteristics never had problems paying back a credit and are financially well of.

To conclude, I argue that algorithms assisting the regulator should not be confused with delegating decision-making powers to algorithms. If the regulator remains in control over the decision-making process and artificial intelligence is only assisting human intelligence, there is scope for a better enforcement of gender-based discrimination by correlation, as the potential

---

157 Chmait Nader; Dowe, David L.; Li Yuan-Fang; Green, David G.: An Information-Theoretic Predictive Model for the Accuracy of AI Agents Adapted from Psychometrics. In: Everitt Tom; Goertzel Ben; Potapov, Alexey (Eds.) Artificial General Intelligence. AGI, Melbourne 2017.

158 For a good example on false negatives and false positives see, Fry 2018, p. 73.

of both systems (artificial and human intelligence) is used to the benefit of fairness and non-discrimination[159]. Therefore, in the spirit of obey-and disobey, not only regulators, but also consumers should be equipped with algorithms (for example put at the disposal by the regulator to enable consumers to test/detect discriminatory behavior) to detect violations of gender-based discrimination which could lead to democratization and decentralization of part of the detection process and lead to better enforcement[160].

2) Non-Discrimination by Design

One could try to reflect as good as possible the principle of non-discrimination at the stage of developing and coding the algorithms. It should never be a substitute to regulation and enforcement but a promising complement to avoid some of the discriminatory behavior. One of the key prerequisites is risk awareness of gender-based discrimination among programmers building AI. Equally to achieving more representative data considering diversity of society, one could address the female gender gap for AI scientists[161] and developers to influence the design and the way algorithms work[162]. A more equal representation of women might shape algorithms for the better. Furthermore, if coders do not understand the legal concept of discrimination, it will be difficult to reflect it in the code. Even if a full "translation" of the concept of discrimination into code will be challenging, basic elements of non-discrimination could be incorporated so that the algorithm tries to avoid or reduce potential discriminations. This could be done for example by checking the datasets used to ensure that they are representative and regularly updated. Some successful processes have been developed in computer science

---

[159] Kleinberg et al. 2020, p. 30097: "The risk that algorithms introduce is not from their use per se, but rather the risk that our regulatory and legal systems will not keep pace with the changing technology."

[160] In the absence of a clear legal framework or the lack of algorithms in the regulator's hand (but also if such a system is in place, to support the regulator's enforcement), it could be imagined that consumer rights groups, NGOs, academics and computer scientists could reveal discriminatory algorithms.

[161] According to Russel; Norvig 2021 and the "Standford AI100 study" which includes information on diversity, 80% of all AI professors in the world, PhD students and industry hires in the field of AI are male and only 20% female, see Russel; Norvig 2021, p. 45.

[162] Crawford 2020, p. 8–9; European Commission, Gender Equality AI Opinion (2020), p. 8–9; Wooldridge 2020, p. 291.

to mitigate risks of bias in datasets, which could tame discriminatory effects already at the stage of programming algorithms.[163]

Finally, despite promising efforts being made to achieve non-discrimination by design, the legal regime continues to apply, and discriminations can be detected and brought to the attention of regulators. The complementary nature of coding the principle of non-discrimination into algorithms is therefore an appreciated effort to help tackle the issue of gender-based discrimination as it also helps regulators. But the need for regulation remains and is even advocated by computer scientists.[164]

3) Non-Discrimination by Law

When choosing to treat the problem of *discrimination by correlation* with the tools of the law, one has several regulatory options. The force of the law, by controlling the behavior of market actors (making them "obey" to legal norms) can influence the AIs' behavior and is certainly the strongest option at the disposal of the state. Regulators often recur to the law because self-regulation and other soft law measures do not solve the problem adequately (a). They have the choice between ex-ante (b) and ex-post (c) regulation. The current analysis has revealed that due to the increasing importance of algorithms a more mutual understanding and exchange on the theoretical side between computer scientist and lawyers on the one hand and between AI programmers/developers as well as business developing an algorithm and regulators is necessary.

a) The Failure of Self-Regulation and Soft Law

In light of not-successful self-regulation and a certain "disobedience" of market actors towards regulators, eliminating biases and stereotypes from datasets is the adequate regulatory approach[165]. Market players lack incen-

---

[163] Celis, L. Elisa; Vijay, Keswani; Vishnoi, Nisheeth: Data preprocessing to mitigate bias: A maximum entropy based approach. In: International Conference on Machine Learning. PMLR, 2020.

[164] See for example Mitchell 2019, p. 150–152.

[165] For the idea of a regulatory market (albeit for AI safety), see Clark, Jack; Hadfield, Gillian K.: Regulatory Markets for AI Safety (2019). In: arXiv, https://arxiv.org/abs/2001.00078 (February 6, 2021).

tives to ensure that their algorithms don't discriminate as this entails costs for them. In 2019, the OECD adopted a Recommendation on AI, which highlights in its section on human-centered values and fairness, that "AI actors should respect the rule of law, human rights and democratic values, throughout the AI system lifecycle. These include freedom, dignity and autonomy, privacy and data protection, non-discrimination and equality, diversity, fairness, social justice, and internationally recognized labor rights." "[166]. Despite numerous AI principles published by companies (e.g. Google[167]) and recommendations on AI regulation[168], the OECD principles shall be understood as a call for regulation in order to achieve the objectives laid down in those principles. Importantly, the OECD highlights the observance of the principle of non-discrimination along the whole algorithm lifecycle, which includes industry development, training, data collection, usage, etc. I argue in favor of such an approach which is equally reflected in the CoE Recommendation on AI:" Private sector actors that design, develop or implement algorithmic systems should follow a standard framework for human rights due diligence to avoid fostering or entrenching discrimination throughout all life-cycles of their systems. They should seek to ensure that the design, development and ongoing deployment of their algorithmic systems do not have direct or indirect discriminatory effects on individuals or groups that are affected by these systems, including on those [...] who may face structural inequalities in their access to human rights"[169].

[166] OECD, C/MIN (2019)3/FINAL, https://one.oecd.org/document/C/MIN(2019)3/FINAL/en/pdf.

[167] Google for example states in point 2 on (unfair) bias, that "AI algorithms and datasets can reflect, reinforce, or reduce unfair biases. recognize that distinguishing fair from unfair biases is not always simple, and differs across cultures and societies. will seek to avoid unjust impacts on people, particularly those related to sensitive characteristics such as race, ethnicity, gender [...].", https://ai.google/principles/ (February 6, 2021).

[168] Google has also some suggestions for regulation: "Where existing discrimination laws provide clear guidelines and accountability mechanisms, new rules may be unnecessary. But not all unfair outcomes are the result of illegal discrimination, and some AI systems may have unfair impacts in ways that are not anticipated by existing laws and regulatory frameworks. In these situations, regulators should take a nuanced approach, ensuring that organizations consider the unique historical context in which an AI system is deployed, and use appropriate performance benchmarks for different groups to ensure accountability", https://ai.google/static/documents/recommendations-for-regulating-ai.pdf (February 6, 2021).

[169] Recommendation CoE CM/Rec (2020)1 on the human rights impacts of algorithmic systems, point 1.4.

Ultimately, the aim is to ensure fair and non-discriminatory algorithms that improve and facilitate the life of consumers and that earn the companies a fair profit for the innovation and investments. Considering that algorithms usually make "ordinary transactions faster and more efficient"[170], there is a risk of opposition by the industry for fully fledged regulation, as this would entail costs and time. The European Commission's High-Level Expert Group on AI refers to seven key requirements, among which human agency and oversight, transparency, non-discrimination, and fairness as well as accountability are relevant here[171]. Transparency[172] regarding how algorithms take decisions is often considered as a solution to reduce discriminatory AI. Transparency is thought to lead to better decisions and could help overcome "the lack of transparency (opaqueness of AI) makes it difficult to identify and prove possible breaches of laws, including legal provisions that protect fundamental rights, attribute liability and meet the conditions to claim compensation."[173]. However, ensuring transparency is sometimes hard, due to the possibility to include elements of randomness into the algorithm. Including "noise" (e.g. randomness) into the algorithm at the development stage can ensure fairness[174] because it diminishes the impact of each relevant data point. Noise can also be included when consumers provide a lot of data, thereby "diluting" the risk of discrimination. *Explainability* is often based on transparency considerations and thought to lead to transparency[175]. If a certain algorithm can be explained to consumers, this makes the process transparent, and the consumer can take an informed decision.

Achieving transparency and explainability for consumers is sometimes difficult even for the developers. Consumers will not be able to understand the algorithm or why a decision has been taken in a particular way. If pro-

---

170 Pasquale 2015, p. 213.
171 See European Commission, COM (2019) 168 final, https://eur-lex.europa.eu/legal-content/EN/TXT/PDF/?uri=CELEX:52019DC0168&from=GA.
172 Recommendation CoE CM/Rec (2020)1 on the human rights impacts of algorithmic systems, point 4.1.
173 AI White Paper, p. 14–15: "The opacity of systems based on algorithms could be addressed through transparency requirements".
174 Hosanagar 2020, p. 203.
175 The Coe Recommendation of the CoE on human rights impacts of algorithmic systems include it under transparency in point 4.1. "The use of algorithmic systems in decision-making processes that carry high risks to human rights should be subject to particularly high standards as regards the explainability of processes and outputs."; European Commission, White Paper AI, p. 5.

grammers introduce noise/randomness to ensure fairness it further complicates attempts to ensure both explainability and transparency. In addition, transparency and explainability is often ensured via terms and conditions or user's agreements which must be accepted prior to using a specific service power by AI. These legal constructs are hardly diligently read, except for lawyers or consumer rights groups or in the case of litigation. Consequently, the question is raised whether it is enough and acceptable to delegate a relevant concern of transparency and explainability into the "hidden" corner of terms and conditions.

A similar question of informed consent is also raised in privacy law regarding whether transparency and full information serve the interest of the consumer or whether his or her goal is merely not to be discriminated. Some authors argue for example in the context of privacy regulation, that informed consent in the form of providing information to gain consent is not the appropriate tool to ensure the protection of privacy rights[176]. *In fine*, one could argue that transparency and explainability on their own are not enough and cannot replace regulation. The same holds for AI principles that are only self-binding guidelines for the companies and cannot be enforced in courts.

b) Various Hybrid Models and Ideas of Regulation

There are concrete ideas that blend the approaches of non-discrimination by design/code and non-discrimination by law. One of them has been presented by Hildebrandt as "Ambient Law", "which advocates a framework of technologically embedded legal rules that guarantee transparency of profiles that should allow European citizens to decide which of their data they

---

[176] See for example in that sense, Hermstrüwer, Yoan; Dickert, Stephan: Sharing is daring: An experiment on consent, chilling effects and a salient privacy nudge. International Review of Law and Economics 51 (2017), p. 38–49: "Our study hints at a regulatory dilemma, which arises from the fact that current privacy laws are designed to steer consent choices through salient information and notice: instead of empowering people to make a free and Informed choice over consent, salient information and consent options may push people into conformity. Lawmakers and lawyers might want to consider this risk of backfire effects in the implementation of information and notice policies" and "there is a risk that salient and incentivized consent architectures will systematically push people towards consent with short-term monetary benefits and long-term costs to liberty."

want to hide, when and in which context"[177]. Another approach modelled on computer science wants to incorporate a legal perspective into the design and functioning of algorithms[178]. From a procedural point of view, the detection of discriminatory algorithms could be supported by detection tools made available by the state as open source to support anti-discrimination enforcement, which could serve as complimentary enforcement and due to its decentralized nature would accelerate and facilitate the regulator's effort to detect violations of GE law.

c) Regulating with the Force of the Law: Between Ex-Ante, Ex-Post and Sector Specific Regulation

In light of the high risk of (gender-based) discrimination, there is an argument to regulate algorithms before they enter the market, e.g. via an authorization mechanism (ex-ante). The state could alternatively wait for more information, learn about problems and risks for discrimination of the technology, before intervening (ex-post)[179] ?

There are good arguments on both sides. Rather than regulating in advance and potentially harming and delaying innovations in AI, a more refined approach of regulation could consist in allowing the market forces to do their work but to carefully supervise and regulate as and when market failures or discrimination occurs. Others advocate sector specific regulation[180] rather than general rules, arguing that "Even for algorithmic systems that make decisions about humans, the risks are different in different sectors, and different rules should apply."[181]. Another challenge is the attribution of responsibility for the decisions taken by the algorithm and defining the addressee of the regulatory intervention[182].

---

[177] Hildebrandt, Mireille: Profiling and AmI. In: Rannenberg K., Royer D., Deuker A. (Eds.) The Future of Identity in the Information Society. Berlin, Heidelberg 2009.

[178] Criado Pacheco et al. 2020.

[179] On the choice between ex-ante and ex-post regulation with a plaidoyer for ex-ante regulation, see Galle, Brian: In Praise of Ex Ante Regulation. In: Vanderbilt Law Review 68 (2015), p. 1715.

[180] Zuiderveen 2020, p. 1573.

[181] Ibid, p. 1585.

[182] See Coeckelbergh, Mark: Artificial Intelligence, Responsibility Attribution, and a Relational Justification of Explainability. In: Science Engineering Ethics 26 (2020), p. 2051–2068; Hacker 2018, p. 243–288.

In terms of substantive law, the appropriate design of legal rules needs to capture the behavior causing *discrimination by correlation*. Referring to the work of Searle[183] who claims that a computer program can basically give all outputs desired based on given inputs, which can even be correct, without understanding what it is doing, one could argue that this suggests that computer programs don't possess "intentionality", which only humans can have. This distinguishes computers from humans and is important for the analysis, also with regard to how to assess the discriminatory impact caused by algorithms. In other words, algorithms do not possess "meaning", because meaning is human and can only be given by and expressed by humans. Indirect (discrimination) not requiring the element of knowledge and intent under EU law can be considered an advantage in the context of *discrimination by correlation*.

Regarding the design, the law is always confronted with the dilemma of using generalizations as much as possible to find a rule that captures as many situations as possible instead of regulating many different individual cases (that are unknown in advance). The emergence of a general law of artificial intelligence sees itself confronted with a fast-moving regulatory target[184].

When analyzing potential algorithmic discriminations and statistical data[185] ("statistical discrimination"[186]), generalization plays a more important role than in traditional cases of discrimination.[187] This owes to data mining, huge amounts of data and the classification of consumers into groups to facilitate decision-making. In practice, algorithms discriminate automatically based on (personal) data instead of a specific characteristic of gender[188] and thereby enlarges the field of potential "hooks" to discriminate because many more data points are used compared to the offline world.

---

183 Searle, John R.: Minds, brains, and programs. In: The Behavioral and Brain Sciences (1980), 3(3), p. 417–424.
184 Barfield, Woodrow; Pagallo, Ugo (Eds.): Research Handbook on the Law of Artificial Intelligence. Cheltenham 2018.
185 For statistical discrimination, association and correlation see Spiegelhalter, p. 109ff.
186 Bohnet, Iris. What works. Boston 2016, p. 31–35, gives an example of statistical discrimination between women and men in negotiations for car sales.
187 Schauer, Frederick: Introduction: The Varieties of Rules. In: Playing by the Rules: A Philosophical Examination of Rule-Based Decision-Making in Law and in Life. Oxford 1993.
188 See in general, Criado, Natalia; Such, Jose M.: Digital discrimination. Algorithmic Regulation. Oxford 2019.

Any approach could be modelled on existing competition or privacy law[189] enforcement mechanisms[190]. Notably the experience of competition authorities[191] combined with elements from the "newer" approach of data protection enforcement could inform the regulatory approach for *discrimination by correlation*[192].

V. Conclusion

The present analysis has revealed some of the challenges, opportunities and strategies to avoid biased data sets and gender-based discrimination caused by algorithms, which I call *'discrimination by correlation'*.

Several (legal) strategies have been presented that could help overcome or reduce gender bias and discrimination. Even though *non-discrimination by design/non-discrimination by code* that implements the principle of non-discrimination in code is welcomed where feasible, it should be complementary to legislation and regulatory efforts. Strengthening *non-discrimination by law*, it could be envisaged that computer scientists/developers and lawyers/enforcers cooperate on issues of mutual interest and benefit in order to shape the design of algorithms and strive towards the respect of human rights and non-discrimination. An institutionalized forum of exchange of AI and GE experts will enrich both sides and contribute to non-discriminatory AI. Exchange between computer scientists and lawyers should be complemented by including practical knowledge of development and coding also among regulators. Considering that discriminations mostly result from datasets, consumers can also rely on the concept of "noise" and "dis-obey" algorithms by providing a lot of data and introduce elements of randomness.

---

[189] Hacker 2018, p. 5, suggest an interesting approach of combining the enforcement tools of the GDPR-regulation with the concepts of anti-discrimination.

[190] For regulatory approach in competition law see, Bailey, Richard; Whish, David: Competition Law, Oxford 2015, p. 1–26.

[191] The OECD explores the topic of gender inclusive competition policy by identifying additional relevant features of the market, behavior of consumers and firms, as well as whether a more effective competition policy can help address gender inequality, see http://www.oecd.org/competition/gender-inclusive-competition-policy.htm (February 6, 2021).

[192] See specifically on the role of AI and algorithms, Surblytė-Namavičienė, Gintarė: Competition and Regulation in the Data Economy, London 2020.

The law remains the *conditio sine qua non* to ensure the fair, ethical and non-discriminatory use of algorithms. Even though EU non-discrimination law is flexible in principle to deal with some of the challenges[193] arising with *discrimination by correlation*[194], the law needs to evolve in light of technological developments to adequately capture gender-based *discrimination by correlation* and ensure sufficient legal protection to victims of gender-based discrimination.

Literature

Adam, Alison: Artificial knowing: gender and the thinking machine. London 1998.

Agrawal, Ajay; Joshua Gans; Avi Goldfarb: Máquinas predictivas: la sencilla economía de la inteligencia artificial, Madrid 2019.

Alarie, Benjamin; Anthony Niblett; Albert Yoon: Regulation by machine, http://dx.doi.org/10.2139/ssrn.2878950 (February 6, 2021).

Ali, Muhammad; Sapiezynski, Piotr; Bogen, Miranda; Korolova, Aleksandra; Mislove, Alan; Rieke, Aaron (2019): Discrimination through optimization: How Facebook's ad delivery can lead to skewed outcomes. In: arXiv e-prints, https://arxiv.org/pdf/1904.02095.pdf (February 6, 2021).

Anrig, Bernhard; Browne, Will; Gasson, Mark: The Role of Algorithms in Profiling. In: Hildebrandt, Mireille; Gutwirth, Serge (Eds.): Profiling the European Citizen. Berlin 2008.

Badre, David: On Task, Princeton 2020.

Bailey, Richard; Whish, David: Competition Law, Oxford 2015.

Barfield, Woodrow; Pagallo, Ugo (Eds.): Research Handbook on the Law of Artificial Intelligence. Cheltenham 2018.

---

[193] Agreeing in principle while also suggesting additional regulation to capture algorithmic decision-making, Zuiderveen 2020, p. 1585.

[194] See discussion of the CJEU case Schuch-Ghannadan (Section II.) which suggests that in cases of discrimination by correlation, there are good arguments for claimants, who succeed in bringing prima facie evidence for an alleged discrimination in cases where access to evidence is impossible or only unreasonably difficult (which is typically the problem surrounding the workings of the algorithm), that the burden of proof shifts to the company who would need to proof that their algorithm did not discriminate.

Barocas, Solon; Selbst, Andrew D.: Big Data's Disparate Impact. In: California Law Review 104 (2016), p. 671–732.

Barocas, Solon: Data & Civil Rights: Technology Primer (2014), http://www.datacivilrights.org/pubs/2014-1030/Technology.pdf (February 6, 2021).

Basdevant, Adrien; Mignard, Jean-Pierre: L'Empire des données. Essai sur la société, les algorithmes et la loi. Paris 2018.

Boden, Margaret A: AI: Its nature and future. Oxford 2016.

Bolukbasi, Tolga; Chang, Kai-Wei; Zou, James; Saligrama, Venkatesh, Kalaim Adam: Man is to computer programmer as woman is to homemaker? debiasing word embeddings. In: arXiv preprint arXiv:1607.06520 (2016), https://arxiv.org/abs/1607.06520v1 (February 6, 2021).

Bohnet, Iris: What works. Boston 2016.

Bostrom, Nick: Superintelligence. Paris 2017.

Bostrom, Nick: The future of humanity. In: Geopolitics, History, and International Relations 1(2) (2009), 41–78.

Buolamwini, Joy; Timnit Gebru: Gender shades: Intersectional accuracy disparities in commercial gender classification. In: Conference on fairness, accountability and transparency. PMLR, 2018.

Cazals, François ; Chantal Cazals: Intelligence artificielle: l'intelligence amplifiée par la technologie. Louvain-la-Neuve 2020.

Celis, L. Elisa ; Mehrotra, Anay; Vishnoi, Nisheeth: Toward controlling discrimination in online ad auctions. In: International Conference on Machine Learning. PMLR, 2019, https://arxiv.org/abs/1901.10450.

Celis, L. Elisa; Kapoor, Sayash; Salehi, Farnood; Vishnoi K. Nisheeth: An algorithmic framework to control bias in bandit-based personalization. In: arXiv preprint arXiv:1802.08674(2018).

Celis, L. Elisa; Vijay, Keswani; Vishnoi, Nisheeth: Data preprocessing to mitigate bias: A maximum entropy based approach. In: International Conference on Machine Learning. PMLR, 2020.

Chmait Nader; Dowe, David L.; Li Yuan-Fang; Green, David G.: An Information-Theoretic Predictive Model for the Accuracy of AI Agents Adapted from Psychometrics. In: Everitt Tom; Goertzel Ben; Potapov, Alexey (Eds.) Artificial General Intelligence. AGI, Melbourne 2017.

Clark, Jack; Hadfield, Gillian K.: Regulatory Markets for AI Safety. In: arXiv preprint arXiv:2001.00078 (2019), https://arxiv.org/abs/2001.00078 (February 6, 2021).

Coeckelbergh, Mark: AI Ethics, Boston 2020.

Coeckelbergh, Mark: Artificial Intelligence, Responsibility Attribution, and a Relational Justification of Explainability. In: Science Engineering Ethics 26 (2020), p. 2051–2068.

Craig, Paul; Gráinne De Búrca: EU law: text, cases, and materials. Oxford 2020.

Crawford, Kate; Whittaker, Meredith; Elish, Madelein Clare; Barocas, Solon; Plasek, Aaron; Ferryman, Kadija: The AI Now Report. The Social and Economic Implications of Artificial Intelligence Technologies in the Near-Term, New York 2016.

Criado Pacheco, Natalia; Ferrer Aran, Xavier; Such, José Mark Coté: A Normative approach to Attest Digital Discrimination. In: Advancing Towards the SDGS Artificial Intelligence for a Fair, Just and Equitable World Workshop of the 24th European Conference on Artificial Intelligence (ECAI'20): AI4EQ ECAI2020.

Criado, Natalia; Such, José Mark: Digital discrimination. Algorithmic Regulation, Oxford 2019.

Council of Europe, Recommendation CM/Rec(2020)1 of the Committee of Ministers to member States on the human rights impacts of algorithmic systems, 8th April 2020, https://search.coe.int/cm/pages/result_details.aspx?objectid=09000016809e1154 (February 6, 2021).

DeMichele, Matthew; Baumgartner, Peter; Wenger, Michael; Barrick, Kelle; Comfort, Megan; Misra, Shilpi: The Public Safety Assessment: A re-validation and assessment of predictive utility and differential prediction by race and gender in Kentucky (2018), https://www.dcjs.virginia.gov/sites/dcjs.virginia.gov/files/announcements/predictiveutilitystudy.pdf (February 6, 2021).

Detela, Giulia; Lodge, Anthony: EU regulatory pathways for ATMPs: standard, accelerated and adaptive pathways to marketing authorization. In: Molecular Therapy-Methods & Clinical Development 13 (2019), p. 205–232.

Ellis, Evelyn; Watson, Philippa: EU anti-discrimination law, Oxford 2012.

Ernst, Ekkehardt; Merola, Rossana; Samaan, Daniel: Economics of artificial intelligence: Implications for the future of work. In: IZA Journal of Labor Policy 9.1 (2019), p. 16.

European Commission, Advisory Committee on Equal Opportunities for Women and Men, Opinion on Artificial Intelligence (2020), https://ec.europa.eu/info/sites/info/files/aid_development_cooperation_fundamental_rights/opinion_artificial_intelligence_gender_equality_2020_en.pdf (February 6, 2021).

European Commission, Proposal for a Regulation of the European Parliament and of the Council laying down harmonised rules on artificial intellgience (Artificial Intelligence Act) and amending certain Union legislative acts, COM (2021) 206 final.

European Commission, "Algorithmic discrimination in Europe: Challenges and opportunities for gender equality and non-discrimination law" (2021) prepared by the Legal Network of Gender Experts of the EC, https://www.equalitylaw.eu/downloads/5361-algorithmic-discrimination-in-europe-pdf-1-975

European Commission, White Paper, On Artificial Intelligence - A European approach to excellence and trust, COM(2020) 65 final, https://ec.europa.eu/info/sites/info/files/commission-white-paper-artificial-intelligence-feb2020_en.pdf (February 6, 2021).

European Commission, Proposal for a Regulation of the European Parliament and of the Council on a Single Market For Digital Services (Digital Services Act) and amending Directive 2000/31/EC, COM/2020/825 final.

European Commission, Proposal for a Regulation of the European Parliament and of the Council on contestable and fair markets in the digital sector (Digital Markets Act), COM/2020/842 final.

Ferrer, Xavier; van Neunen, Tom; Such, Jose M.; Coté, Mark; Criado, Natalia: Bias and Discrimination in AI: a cross-disciplinary perspective. In: arXiv preprint arXiv:2008.07309 (2020), p. 1., https://arxiv.org/abs/2008.07309 (February 6, 2021).

Surblytė-Namavičienė, Gintaré: Competition and Regulation in the Data Economy, London 2020.

Fry, Hannah: Hello World: How to be Human in the Age of the Machine, London 2018.

Galle, Brian: In Praise of Ex Ante Regulation. In: Vanderbilt Law Review 68 (2015), p. 1715.

Geerts, Thierry: Homo Digitalis, Tielt 2021.

Ghili, Soheil; Ehsan Kazemi; Amin Karbasi: Eliminating latent discrimination: Train then mask. In: Proceedings of the AAAI Conference on Artificial Intelligence (2019), 33. Nº 01.
Gunkel, David. J.: The Machine Question: Critical Perspectives on AI, Robots, and Ethics, Cambridge 2012.
Hacker, Philipp: Teaching fairness to artificial intelligence: existing and novel strategies against algorithmic discrimination under EU law. In: Common Market Law Review 55.4 (2018), p. 1143–1185.
Hacker, Philipp: Verhaltens- und Wissenszurechnung beim Einsatz von Künstlicher Intelligenz. In: RW Rechtswissenschaft 2018, p. 243–288.
Halevy, Alon; Norvig, Peter; Pereira, Fernando: The unreasonable effectiveness of data. In: IEEE Intelligent Systems 24.2 (2009), p. 8–12, https://dl.acm.org/doi/10.1109/MIS.2009.36 (February 6, 2021).
Hardt, Moritz: How big data is unfair. In: Medium 2014, https://medium.com/@mrtz/how-big-data-is-unfair-9aa544d739de (February 6, 2021).
Hart, Herbert Lionel Adolphus; Green, Leslie: The concept of law. Oxford 2015.
Hassan, Samer; De Filippi, Primavera: The Expansion of Algorithmic Governance: From Code is Law to Law is Code. In: Field Actions Science Reports (2017), Special Issue 17, http://journals.openedition.org/factsreports/4518 (February 6, 2021).
Hermstrüwer, Yoan; Dickert, Stephan: Sharing is daring: An experiment on consent, chilling effects and a salient privacy nudge. In: International Review of Law and Economics 51 (2017), p. 38–49.
Hermstrüwer, Yoan: Artificial Intelligence and Administrative Decisions Under Uncertainty. In: Wischmeyer, Thomas; Rademacher, Timo (Eds.): Regulating Artificial Intelligence. Berlin 2020.
Hildebrandt, Mireille: Profiling and AmI. In: Rannenberg K., Royer D., Deuker A. (Eds.): The Future of Identity in the Information Society. Berlin, Heidelberg 2009.
Hildebrandt, Mireille: Profiling: From data to knowledge. In: Datenschutz und Datensicherheit DuD (2006) 30, p. 548–552.
Hildebrandt, Mireille: Algorithmic regulation and the rule of law. In: Philosophical Transactions of the Royal Society A: Mathematical, Physical and Engineering Sciences 376.2128 (2018): 20170355.
Hosanagar, Kartik: A human's guide to machine intelligence: how algorithms are shaping our lives and how we can stay in control, New York 2020.
Keller, John D: Deep Learning, Boston 2019.

Kleinberg, Jon; Ludwig, Jens; Mullainathan, Sendhil; Sunstein, Cass R.: Algorithms as discrimination detectors, In: Proceedings of the National Academy of Sciences Dec 2020, 117 (48), p. 30096–30100.

Kleinberg, Jon; Ludwig, Jens; Mullainathan, Sendhil; Sunstein, Cass R.: Discrimination in the Age of Algorithms, In: Journal of Legal Analysis, 10 (2018), p. 113–174.

Kim, Pauline T.: Data-driven discrimination at work. In: William & Mary Law Review 58 (2016), p. 857–866.

Kraft-Buchman, Caitlin; Arian, Réné: The Deadly Data Gap: Gender and Data. Women at the Table, Geneva 2019, http://bit.ly/DeadlyDataGenderGap (February 6, 2021).

Lambrecht, Anja; Tucker, Catherine E.: Algorithmic Bias? An Empirical Study into Apparent Gender-Based Discrimination in the Display of STEM Career Ads. In: Management Science, 65 (2019), p. 2966–2981.

Lee, Felicia R.: Discriminating? Yes. Discriminatory? Nº The New York Times, December 13,2003. advance.lexis.com/api/document?collection=news&id=urn:contentItem:4B70-S120-01KN-20KW-00000-00&context=1516831 (February 6, 2021).

Liao, S. Matthew: A Short Introduction to the Ethics of Artificial Intelligence. Ethics of Artificial Intelligence: Oxford University Press, 2020.

Louridas, Panos: Algorithms, Boston 2020.

Mayson, Sandra G.: Bias in, bias out. In: Yale Law Journal 128 (2018), p. 2218.

McAfee, Andrew Paul; Brynjolfsson, Erik: Machine, Platform, Crowd: Harnessing Our Digital Future, New York 2017, p. 67.

Meneceur, Yannick: L'intelligence artificielle en procès, Bruxelles 2020.

Mitchell, Melanie: Artificial intelligence: A guide for thinking humans. London 2019.

OECD, Principles on Artificial Intelligence, https://www.oecd.org/science/forty-two-countries-adopt-new-oecd-principles-on-artificial-intelligence.htm (February 6, 2021).

Orwat, Carsten: Risks of Discrimination through the Use of Algorithms. A study compiled with a grant from the Federal Anti-Discrimination Agency. Berlin 2020.

Packin, Nizan; Lev-Aretz, Yafit: Learning algorithms and discrimination. In: Research Handbook on the Law of Artificial Intelligence. Cheltenham, London 2018, p. 91.

Pasquale, Frank: The Black Box Society: The Hidden Algorithms Behind Money and Information, Boston 2015.

Perez, Caroline Criado: Invisible women: Exposing data bias in a world designed for men. London 2019.

Petit, Nicolas: Big Tech and the Digital Economy: The Moligopoly Scenario. Oxford 2020.

Pistor, Katharina: The code of capital: How the law creates wealth and inequality. Princeton 2020.

Renan Barzilay, Arianne: The Technologies of Discrimination: How Platforms Cultivate Gender Inequality. In: The Law & Ethics of Human Rights, 13 (2019), no. 2, p. 179–202.

Russell, Stuart: Artificial intelligence: The future is superintelligent. In: Nature 548 (2017), p. 520–521.

Russell, Stuart; Norvig, Peter: Artificial intelligence: a modern approach, London 2021.

Schauer, Frederick: Introduction: The Varieties of Rules. In: Playing by the Rules: A Philosophical Examination of Rule-Based Decision-Making in Law and in Life. Oxford 1993.

Schauer, Frederick: Profiles, Probabilities, and Stereotypes. Boston 2003.

Searle, John R.: Minds, brains, and programs. In: The Behavioral and Brain Sciences, 3(3) (1980), p. 417–424.

Skeem, Jennifer; John Monahan; Christopher Lowenkamp: Gender, risk assessment, and sanctioning: The cost of treating women like men. In: Law and human behavior 40.5 (2016), p. 580.

Spiegelhalter, David: The art of statistics: learning from data, London 2019.

Strauß, Stefan: From Big Data to Deep Learning: A Leap Towards Strong AI or 'Intelligentia Obscura'? In: Big Data Cogn. Comput. 2 (2018), p. 16.

Sunstein, Cass R.: Of artificial intelligence and legal reasoning. University of Chicago Law School, In: Public Law & Legal Theory Working Papers № 18, 2001, http://chicagounbound.uchicago.edu/ public_law_and_legal_theory/207/ (February 6, 2021).

Taleb, Nassim Nicholas: Antifragile: Things that gain from disorder, p. 416–418.

Tegmark, Max: Life 3.0: Being human in the age of artificial intelligence, London 2017.

US White House, Executive Office of the President, Big Data: Seizing Opportunities, preserving, Washington 2014, http://www.whitehouse.gov/sites/default/files/docs/big_data_privacy_report _5.1.14_final_print.pdf (February 6, 2021).

UNESCO, Report on AI and Gender Equality, https://unesdoc.unesco.org/ark:/48223/pf0000374174 (February 6, 2021).

Veale, Michael; Brass, Irina: Administration by algorithm? Public management meets public sector machine learning. Public Management Meets Public Sector Machine Learning, Oxford 2019, p. 121–122.

Wellner, Galit; Rothman, Tiran: Feminist AI: Can We Expect Our AI Systems to Become Feminist? In: Philosophy & Technology 33 (2020), p. 191–205.

Wischmeyer, Thomas: Regulierung intelligenter Systeme. In: Archiv des öffentlichen Rechts 143.1 (2018), p. 1–66.

Wooldridge, Michael: The Road to Conscious Machines: The Story of AI. London 2020.

Wright, Emily M.; Salisbury, Emily J.; Van Voorhis, Patricia: Predicting the prison misconducts of women offenders: The importance of gender-responsive needs. In: Journal of Contemporary Criminal Justice 23.4 (2007), p. 310–340.

Xenidis, Raphaële; Senden, Linda: EU Non Discrimination Law in the Era of Artificial Intelligence: Mapping the Challenges of Algorithmic Discrimination, in: Bernitz, Ulf; Groussot, Xavier; de Vries, Sybe A. (Eds.): General Principles of EU law and the EU Digital Order, Bruxelles 2020.

Zuboff, Shoshana: The Age of Surveillance Capitalism: the Fight for a Human Future at the New Frontier of Power, New York 2019.

Zuiderveen Borgesius, Frederik: Discrimination, artificial intelligence, and algorithmic decision-making. Study for the Council of Europe, Strasbourg 2018, https://rm.coe.int/discrimination-artificial-intelligence-and-algorithmic-decision-making/1680925d73 (February 6, 2021).

Zuiderveen Borgesius, Frederik: Strengthening legal protection against discrimination by algorithms and AI. In: The International Journal of Human Rights (2020), 24:10, p. 1572–1593.

Matthias Pfeffer

The Power of Algorithms and the Structural Transformation of the Digital Public

The Power of Algorithms and the Structural Transformation of the Digital Public

Introduction

The public sphere is the central arena that makes democracy possible at all.[1] This has been the case since the "rule of the people" first saw the light of day in ancient Athens as a counter-design to the arbitrary rule through sheer power of tyrants and kings. Since then, this public sphere has been the commonly shared space in which understanding and the formation of the will of the citizens takes place. It is an arena of struggle and debate between speech and counter-speech, which nevertheless proceed according to rules that have developed over centuries. It is only in this arena that discourse, and criticism can be used to negotiate always new how the community is to be shaped, which rule is legitimate and which is not. Only in it can free people live together according to rules that they have given themselves and which can therefore generate a lasting bond because they stem from an act of self-determination and are compatible with the highest degree of self-determination. But in the digital world there is hardly any public space in this sense, its rules—at least for some actors—are no longer valid.

Today we need to understand how the public sphere, which will stay essential for democracy, is being changed by the power of algorithmic decision-making systems that are in the hands of a few globally operating corporations, and how it is being destroyed as a result. The digital structural transformation of the public sphere, which we have been experiencing for about twenty years, has the effect that the public sphere is increasingly shaped and thereby also deformed by the mechanisms of digitalization. Today, even in developed societies and enlightened democracies, different groups in society face each other more and more irreconcilably and with hostility, unable or unwilling to enter into the process of common will formation if only because they can no longer reach agreement on the simplest facts. This division of society is largely brought about by the algorithms and business models of social media. They are not the only cause for this, but an essential one.

The commonly shared space of facts, values, and decency in which the cause of res publica, the public affairs, is determined, is diminishing. A pro-

---

[1] Habermas, Jürgen: The Structural Transformation of the Public Sphere: An Inquiry Into a Category of Bourgeois Society, Hoboken, New Jersey, 2015, german: Habermas, Jürgen, Strukturwandel der Öffentlichkeit, Untersuchungen zu einer Kategorie der bürgerlichen Gesellschaft, Darmstadt 1962 and Arendt, Hannah: The Human Condition: 2nd Revised edition. Chicago 1998, german: Elemente und Ursprünge totaler Herrschaft, Antisemitismus, Imperialismus, totale Herrschaft, München 1986.

cess that is closely linked to the logic of social media algorithms: In the prevailing economy of attention, they reward publications that emotionalize and contribute to the bubble formation of public communication through self-reinforcing effects.[2] Only recently have the effects of this deformation, which is increasingly dividing societies, come into general awareness. This consciousness is emerging at a time when, more and more societies are realizing the extent of the negative effects of emotionalizing bubble communications, so hopefully just in time. The structural transformation of the public also means that traditional press companies are weakened, and more and more Algorithms are used in public communication.

This raises the question of who will shape the future: the logic of technology or the logic of democracy and human reason? The former is based on a narrowly understood scientific-technical worldview, the latter is oriented towards social and political norms. To answer it, we need to rethink this public space, its architecture, and the future design it can have after the digital transformation. In addition, we need to rethink what makes it possible for people to rethink in the first place: their reason. A reflection that has only just begun in view of the possible replacement of this reason by a "superior" AI. And it should come to fruition soon. Because otherwise the question of who will shape the public sphere of the future will be answered by technology, or more precisely by artificial intelligence one day.

1. Public Sphere: Origin and Meaning

The public sphere has been defined since antiquity by demarcating it from private space. For the Greeks, this was the oikos, one's own household, from which economy and ecology were derived. The citizen first had to be free, able to form his own household, in order to be able to raise his voice as part of the assembly in the polis. The assemblies took place in the agora, where the market of goods and services was also held. The private sphere and its protection were thus the precondition for the emergence of the public sphere. The exact boundaries of both spheres, as well as the question of who was entitled to these rights, were constantly renegotiated, and shifted over the centuries. In the modern era, following Hannah Arendt, the social was added as a mid-

---

[2] See among others: Jaster, Romy; Lanius, David: Die Wahrheit schafft sich ab, wie Fake News Politik machen, Ditzingen 2019 and: Russell, Stuart: Human Compatible, Artificial Intelligence and the Problem of Control, New York 2019; german ed. Frechen 2020. p. 16f

dle and mediating sphere between the private and the political. It was also Hannah Arendt who recognized that the complete dissolution of the private through total socialization leads straight to totalitarianism.[3]

Above all, economic activity detached itself from the oikos of the individual and became the economy we know today. Through the division of labor, the movement of goods and trade, an enormous dynamic was unleashed. In the newly created public space, also made possible by new media technologies such as first printing, then radio, film and television, a public sphere emerged that enabled the negotiation of public affairs through processes of public communication and decision-making. In the process, the blind spots, and foreshortenings that in the early days of democracy reflected the limitations of a patriarchal slaveholding society and therefore excluded women and slaves from political participation increasingly dissolved. In the modern era, a universalist pattern of reason has become increasingly prevalent: The fundamental rights to free development of the personality, to participate in general and secret elections and the principle that equal rights apply to all are precisely only fundamental rights if they concern all people, if all people can invoke them regardless of gender, class, religion, social origin, or sexual orientation. These values have gained their power and charisma not least through their universality. Without publicity, their development would not have been possible. Conversely, they are constitutive for the functioning of the public sphere.[4]

This development has long been seen as a process of progress in which implicit norms gain ever more explicit validity by embodying themselves ever more strongly in laws and institutions. Hegel defined history as "Progress in the awareness of freedom"[5]. Today, this freedom, but also the consciousness of it as a fundamental factor of modernization, is acutely endangered. If Hegel wrote his philosophy against the historical backdrop of the French Revolution, today we must understand the causes of populism and authoritarianism as side-effects of unchecked technological development. The structural change of the bourgeois public sphere once described by Jürgen Habermas is marked by the storming of the Bastille, the digital structural change of today by the storming of the American Capitol as a respective historical caesura.

---

3   Arendt, Hannah: The origins of Totalitarism, 2nd ed., Edition Charleston 2011.
4   Habermas, Jürgen: The structural Tranformation of the public Sphere, opt.cit.
5   "Die Weltgeschichte ist der Fortschritt im Bewusstsein der Freiheit" That does not mean only in the awareness of technological optimization. Source: Hegel, G.W.F.: Philosophie der Geschichte, Werke Bd. 12, Frankfurt 1970, p. 39.

Matthias Pfeffer

The iconographies for both incisions come from Eugene Delacroix, whose painting "Liberty Leads the People" from 1830 shows the tricolor-waving folk heroine Marianne with half her breast exposed, leading the people to the barricades in the name of liberty. An unemployed occasional actor, taken by an AP photographer inside the Capitol with his chest also bared and crowned by buffalo horns, became the icon of our days. Symbol of the people's amplifier social media, to whose echo chambers he owes his crude world of imagination. Two pictures, both iconic, both equally determined by the national colors of blue, white and red. But both with an opposite message: A people that would not have risen up without the writings and pamphlets of the Enlightenment thinkers, a mob that would not have set itself in motion without the echo chambers of Facebook, Twitter and Telegram. The public sphere has always also been determined by the media technologies that made it possible and, in the process, shaped it. But if modern democracy was born when the Bastille was stormed, it was almost buried when the Capitol was stormed.

At the same time, new technologies were always celebrated as liberators of humanity. This was also the case with digital media in their beginnings in California in the 60s and 70s, which today, instead of enabling emancipation, threaten freedom and democracy because of the way the algorithms of surveillance capitalism work.

"Marianne" as an anonymous woman from the people became the french national figure of the revolution. An icon that, created by an artist, becomes an allegory of an entire people and a symbol of freedom. The occasional actor Jake Angeli from Arizona is largely created by algorithms of exaggeration and provocation, to which he adapts his strange appearance and finally owes the longed-for worldly attention. He thus becomes a symbol of the threat to democracy posed by the mechanisms of populism and the digital attention economy. While "Marianne" embodied an idea that went around the world under the slogan freedom, equality, fraternity, the buffalo man embodies the image obsession of a narcissistic social media age that lures with the promise to give everyone, if they are sufficiently crazy and stand out, their 5 minutes of fame spread by the digital viral mechanisms of the attention economy, that rules social media.

These "viral" laws of social media combined with the with the fragmenting effect of the algorithms undermine the basic function of the media public sphere, and thereby the immunity of democratic society which forms public opinion from published opinions through criticism and discourse. For a "deliberative" public sphere, as Habermas called the bourgeois public sphere, needs facts and arguments as well as opinions presented in a spirit of respect for other opinions and other people. And it needs, above all, faith in the power of reasonable arguments on the basis of commonly shared facts. Only what prevails in these debates through convincing arguments after a controversial discourse can itself shape opinion. For published opinions to become public opinion, reflection and discourse are mandatory. They are the sounding board of democracy. Replacing them with algorithms leads us astray in the situation we find ourselves in today in which democracy is increasingly coming under attack.

Weighing up, arguing with a focus on factual arguments while sparing the persons, that is at least how one could describe the ideal image of such a public sounding board, which is guided by the rules of "reasoning", by the rules of reason. "I disapprove of what you say, but I will defend to the death your right to say it", the great Enlightenment philosopher Voltaire is often quoted. Even if the quote is not authentic, it still says something true[6]. Not everyone abides by this ideal—not even in a democratic public sphere. Nevertheless, the ideal of tolerance, in which one advocates the free expression of dissent, is more relevant than ever. In the technical digital public sphere, all these factors that are essential for the formation of public opinion no longer exist. Here, only the laws of the so-called attention economy prevail, behind which nothing else is hidden than the total unrestrained economization of the public sphere, which takes less and less account of other spheres of value. The digital transformation has already put democracies under pressure worldwide. A few years ago, movements such as the Arab Spring made it seem as if democracy and self-determination would be fuelled worldwide by digital possibilities, but for some time now the negative effects of this development have been coming more and more into focus. The digital organisation of such a freedom movement alone obviously cannot ensure its sustainable success. This would require an association of people who are committed in the long term to implementing their interests in a political programme. The digital can enable such a union, but it offers no substitute for lasting commitment and the institutional safeguarding of fought-for freedoms. In contrast, the attacks on democracy from inside and outside by autocrats or populists, by

---

6   It originates from Hall, Evelyn Beatrice: The Friends of Voltaire, New York 1907, cit. Cornell University Library 2009, The phrase originally intended by Hall as a summary of Voltaire's attitude, was widely misread as a literal quotation from Voltaire.

troll factories and hackers work all the better digitally. The disruptive forces of the digital are at work behind the scenes of this transformation. In the long run, they seem to be stronger than the emancipatory potential of alternative forums, such as those that made the Arab Spring and other liberation movements possible.

Increasingly replacing editors and journalists by technical algorithms, has several consequences that are barely compatible with democracy. It could turn out, that human actors, with all their weaknesses, are better able to regulate this space at least if it is to remain a democratic space.

2. Disruption of the Digital

In the liberal theories of the 18th and 19th centuries, the market and democracy are understood as systems in which prices can be formed through citizens' free access to information, flows of goods are directed, and political rule is legitimized through criticism and free discourse. The recognition of a private sphere, which is defined by the fact that everyone himself determines how much of it he discloses publicly, forms the reference point of personal freedom, which is the prerequisite for being a citizen in the political debate. It is only possible when it is protected. Conversely, the institutions of a democratic state in which, alongside those of democracy, fundamental rights and the rule of law prevail, form the prerequisite for all citizens to be able to live in freedom.

In this model of deliberative democracy, the free circulation of both verified and verifiable information in a public space, the rules of which are in turn set by this public itself, is the prerequisite for freedom and self-determination. Today, this model is under attack worldwide because the public has undergone a paradigm shift that is as imperceptible as it is radical, operated by a handful of big tech companies that like to describe themselves as "disruptive": "Move fast and break things"—with this motto Marc Zuckerberg started to turn the platform he designed for his university into a global corporation, which, as Zuckerberg's description of the mission was, pretended to pursue the goal of potentially connecting all people with one another. But he soon started to connect all data with one another to create personal profiles and templates from them that could be monetized on the commodity futures markets of the advertising industry. The funny communication of trivialities to friends became a communication system that rewarded emotions in order to be able to control and manipulate emotions better and better to be able to place advertising perfectly and thus the greater its importance for informing citizens became increasingly undermines the reasonable and civilized discourse. The "destroy things" became more and more a "destroy democracy".

Under the pretext of networking people with one another, social media first collected people's data and then networked them with one another for pattern recognition to create behavior predictions on this basis that revolutionized the advertising markets as killer applications, and were incidentally, the classic grave diggers of Media. Media as the fourth estate has the task of providing information and forming opinions guided by self-regulation that is independent of the state but complies with democratic law. Privileged rights of the press with access to information and, for example, the protection of informants—in return, self-commitment to responsible and careful handling of information and compliance with general personal rights—naturally including compliance with the criminal code V.i.S.d.P.—so is the abbreviation in the imprint of newspapers in Germany.[7] But apparently nobody in the digital public is "responsible in the sense of the press law" anymore, at least not the big platforms that organize and control everything and profit out of it most. The major platforms rather reject this, citing so-called platform neutrality.[8]

The digital public consists of total transparency of the individual user data for the platforms with a simultaneous total lack of transparency of the algorithms for the public, which, like the secret formula of Coca Cola, are declared a trade secret. The disruption of the public therefore also means that the design of the public spaces is largely hidden from this public, while at the same time the privacy of the users is dissolved.

With the same means with which the AI algorithms are presented with ever-richer Big Data collections, the people who provide this data in abundance are threatened in their privacy and their self-determination.[9] By us-

---

7   "Verantwortlich im Sinne des Presserechts": Responsible in the sense of the Press Law is the form used in German publications to indicate the responsibility under press law for the published content.

8   Platform neutrality became largely part of Communications Decency act (CDA) in 1996 in US due to Barlow, John Perry: 'A Declaration of the Independence of Cyberspace', Electronic Frontier Foundation, February 8, 1996, https://www.eff.org/de/cyberspace-independence (September 22, 2021). See the current discussion about "Section 230" in the US: https://www.latimes.com/business/technology/story/2021-04-27/facebook-twitter-youtube-pressed-on-poisonous-algorithms

9   See for more details to the following: Zuboff, Shoshana: The Age of Surveillance Capitalism. The Fight for a Human Future at the New Frontier of Power, New York 2019.

ing their personal profiles to make predictions about their future behavior they are addressed where they are most vulnerable. With their feelings, especially their fears. The greater the amount of personal data that the person concerned has left behind, the more accurate these addresses are. The more precisely algorithms can calculate the probabilities of future desires, needs and future actions, forecasts that allow advertising to be placed in a targeted manner that shows the highest possible conversion rates for purchasing the advertised products. It is about quickly and safely gaining their attention and keeping them as long as possible: through emotions, especially negative ones, such as fear, indignation and horror. The logic of targeted advertising is increasingly taking hold in the formation of political opinion, but it has no place there. As former Google employee and technology ethicist Tristan Harris pointes out: "As long as social media companies profit from addiction, depression, and division, our society will continue to be at risk." Harris founded the Center for human Technology (CHT) which is dedicated to reimagining the digital infrastructure.[10]

This digital structural transformation of the public sphere has expanded into a tectonic shift in the balance of power around the world. Today, the question of whether and how the democracies can succeed in limiting the power of big tech and subordinating it to democratically established law is becoming more and more acute. If algorithms increasingly determine the basic functions of our democracy, the question arises of who determines the algorithms. The answer: they are a handful of global companies that are also among the financially strongest companies history has ever seen. These companies have understood how to develop and offer digital services as "early movers", which have established their dominance on the world markets through the effects of the network economy. They can be divided into companies of US (GAFAM[11]) and Chinese provenance.

Both seem to follow a different political, but largely comparable technological and economic logic. US companies in particular have been able to

---

[10] Tristan Harris, Named to the TIME 100 "Next Leaders Shaping the Future" and Rolling Stone Magazine's "25 People Shaping the World," Co-Founder & President of the Center for Humane Technology, which—in it's own words—is catalyzing a comprehensive shift toward humane technology that operates for the common good, strengthening our capacity to tackle our biggest global challenges. Source: Harris, Tristan: Time well spent. In: Center for humane technology, An Introduction to our work, https://humanetech.com (September 22, 2021).

[11] Abbreviation for Google, Apple, Facebook, Amazon and Microsoft.

develop outside of democratic law thanks to the neoliberal ideology of free and unregulated cyberspace that has prevailed until recently. Today there is no longer any argument about the need for rules that are suitable for limiting their negative impact on the formation of public opinion. It's just a matter of how exactly and when they will come.

But why do these companies only "initially" determine which algorithms structure the public space and thus have a decisive influence on the political shaping of the world? It is possible, but not certain, but also not ruled out, that technical systems develop such an intrinsic logic and "autonomy" that they transform the domination by technology, as it is exercised today by big tech companies, into a domination of technology itself. The development of such a powerful technology from today's AI could take place further as "general" Artificial Intelligence, "superintelligence" or as a complete integration of unlimited big data and the algorithms of quantum computing which is unequally powerful by today's standards.

The future of the public and the future of democracy, like the future of individual autonomy, depend on the political and legal shaping of a technology that has already proven to be powerful enough to challenge democracy.

3. The Economic-Technical Public Complex

Behind the logic of the social media algorithms is the business model of so-called targeted advertising[12], personalized advertising, which threatens democracy in several ways: By creating personalized data profiles, it wants to lay the foundation for targeted advertising that is delivered to the user at the ideal time. This only works if as much data as possible is collected about the user, for which he should stay on the relevant social media pages for as long as possible. Emotional and scandalous messages are therefore preferred on these, and further behavior of the user in the network is read out through tracking with cookies. With this knowledge, not only behavior profiles are created that, as in the old analog advertising models, define abstract "target groups" and deliver suitable advertising to these groups. The advertiser in targeting advertising is promised more: his ad should be placed with the customer, precisely at the time when he is so interested in the advertised product

---

12   Amongst others, Google AdWords integrates advertisements into web pages through contextual placement, which requires the registration of personal data.

that he kicks and buys it. This conversion also works without any media discontinuity. While classic advertising in magazines, radio and TV is supposed to be memorized by constantly repeating an easily recognizable message in order to be able to influence consumer behavior when shopping in the store days later, targeted advertising aims entirely at the momentary attention. It is important to captivate and influence them, since the advertising message and ideally the purchase of the product on the Internet is always just a click away.

The attention economy of Internet advertising is thus shaping a cult of the moment. Satisfaction is immediately promised in the here and now, the apparent immediacy, in which all wishes can supposedly now be implemented, has paradisiacal features. Reflection, contextualization, and criticism are undesirable. Reflection is transformed into a pure reflex. The new attention economy is not only operating the old manipulation business of classic advertising and PR, but also driving it into completely new dimensions with the new technical possibilities of reading out individual profiles. The attempt to control the conversion rate upwards, which can be measured and manipulated just as precisely as the user, ultimately leads the classic model of manipulating behavior through advertising into completely new dimensions.

Ultimately, this model is about making the advertising message appear as a perfect match for the user's deepest desires. It's about controlling ones free will.[13] Because this manipulative model not only dominates information behavior about products, but also about people's global knowledge, and because people are increasingly communicating according to these rules, the two greatest dangers for democracy grow here: false, manipulative, and selective information as the basis of group communication that is geared towards confirmation loops and constant rule violations. Ultimately, only those who are sufficiently conspicuous to attract the attention of the trained algorithms can be heard and seen. This form of communication in social media platforms then in turn creates social pressure to adapt in the direction of cheeky "influencers". Through the constant high level of general excitement, it creates the possibility of triggering "shitstorms", digital campaigns of hatred and destruction, which increasingly create a climate of fear and self-censorship. And that in supposedly completely free cyberspace.

The first threat to democracy, which consists in the weakening of the autonomous individual through superior knowledge on the part of the plat-

---

13   See Zuboff 2019.

form, comes as a second threat to the effect on social group formation and group dynamics. The disinformation leads to miscommunication. A controversial development of decisions that is ultimately accepted as a majority decision presupposes that the discourse takes place based on shared values. But if a consensus cannot be reached even on simple facts and fundamental truths, the formation of a majority cannot pacify. If the losing minority cannot count on having their fundamental rights respected and in principle being able to form the majority in the next election itself, or even worse, if the opposing side disputes the validity of the election without supporting documents, the basic mechanism of democracy will be lost. Not to mention the restraint of sensitive minds in this elegantly expressed robust form of argument. But it is precisely their balancing and thoughtful opinions that could actually be indispensable.

One effect the targeted advertising business and its superior effectiveness against all other forms of advertising is that it deprives the media, which traditionally rely on advertising sales as a second pillar alongside sales revenues, of their economic basis.

The public is thus destroyed at the same time on several levels, all of which are interconnected: Destruction of informational self-determination through the asymmetry of knowledge between the individual and the platform: the platform knows more about the individual, that he knows about himself. Through the power of personalized search and recommendation algorithms, it determines what information the user receives. It is those that the algorithm considers to be "suitable" for the interests of the user—or is it not rather the interests of the advertisers and the platform itself that are in the foreground here?

On the other hand, by destroying the economic foundations of an independent, privately financed press and the classic model of mass communication, in which the "fourth estate", based on press law and voluntary principles such as diligence, balance and liability for the published content, is remote from the state regulates. In their place comes irresponsible handling of the disseminated content according to the privileges of the so-called platform privilege. And finally, through the destruction of a civilized culture of conversation and debate, in which nothing less than reason itself is at stake. Because reason can only develop where reasonable discourses are permitted and cultivated.

Far-reaching changes are associated with this structural change: Instead of media companies that see themselves as journalistic representatives of the fourth estate, technology companies that see themselves exclusively in competition for technological innovations through which they strive for market leadership are emerging. Instead of a profit-oriented but socially embedded model of journalism, there is an economic value-added model that is free from all restrictions and is subject to purely technical optimization laws. At the stele of professionally trained opinion leaders, there are automated control mechanisms. The amplification effects of the algorithms used favor emotion-driven arguments and irreconcilable group argumentation instead of reasonable discourse, thus supporting division in society.

While the sender of information and opinions was recognizable in the age of mass media, the technical platforms now see themselves purely as "curators" of content, whose control they leave to automatisms that are programmed solely to excite and captivate. To be more precise: to excite the user in order to be able to captivate his attention. The responsible consumer is no more the target of powerful surveillance capitalism than the responsible citizen. Even in the age of the classical mass media there was the legacy of the public through economic imperatives. After all, advertising revenues are an important economic pillar for publishers. And: the element of opinion-making, i.e. manipulating the audience, was by no means alien to the mass media. But it was known who the sender of information was and there were clear legal regulations for the professional and careful work of journalists as well as for the defense against prevailing power of opinion, which were supposed to ensure the diversity of journalistic voices and thus the prerequisite for free formation of opinion. Above all, in the logic of the tabloid media, the spectacle could not be personalized, at least as far as the addressees were concerned, but was aimed at a shared public, which it could also reflect and cushion. There were also outliers in the published opinion of the analogue media, but these could be caught and corrected by the sounding board of a common public before they could become a contribution to public opinion. This necessary sounding board of shared information and values threatens to get lost in the personalized bubbles of the 2.0 public and to be replaced by a confusing number of sub-publics. This would mean that common convictions would be lost, and with it the basis for organizing together in a democratic community.[14]

14   Nemitz, Paul; Pfeffer, Matthias: Prinzip Mensch, Macht, Freiheit und Demokratie im Zeitalter der Künstlichen Intelligenz, Bonn, 2020, p. 202 ff. and: Frühbrodt, Lutz; Floren, Annette: Unboxing YouTube, Im Netzwerk der Profis und Profiteure, Frankfurt 2019. In: https://www.otto-brenner-stiftung.de/fileadmin/user_data/stiftung/02_Wissenschaftsportal/03_Publikationen/AH98_YouTube.pdf (September 22, 2021).

The power of algorithms is based on data; we are interested in personal data that is shaped by advertising-based business models into personal behavioral predictions and thus into advertising products. Because these algorithms process the most important raw material of the digital economy: personal data that is nothing more than the traces of the lives and experiences of millions and millions of people, which are turned into tradable capital goods. Above all, AI-algorithms are needed to analyze this ever-growing flood of data in real time, if possible, and to convert it into behavioral predictions. If you have just bought this, you will surely buy this soon, if you have just thought this, you will surely think this soon, if you have chosen this party, you will surely be happy to support this group…

The mechanism is the same, regardless of whether it is economic manipulation through highly efficient advertising models or political manipulation through equally efficient profile evaluation and pattern recognition.

This model was first introduced by Google and then largely copied by Facebook. Google set out to "organize the world's information and make it universally accessible and useful".[15] Evil should be avoided, as the original Google mission statement expressed: "Don't be evil".[16] But to this day it is controversial whether this original company motto referred to the company's own values, or rather to the users: if you don't do anything bad, you have nothing to fear from our total surveillance. And in fact, arguments like: "I have no problem keeping my data, I have nothing to hide" have been found in the debates of the last two decades when users were asked about Google's business practices.

Google originally planned to use the data that users leave behind with each search only to improve the search function, i.e. to increase the relevance of the displayed results. This model can be described as a "fair search", but it was canceled, by Google itself. Founders Larry Page and Sergey Brin decided not least because investors demanded a clear business model in connection with the company's IPO in 2002 to systematically evaluate the traces of their users, which were previously referred to internally as "data exhausts", in order to be able to offer superior advertising models. After all, he who knows the most about his customers can sell a product best. And Google knows almost everything about almost everyone. And the knowledge grows with ev-

---

15 Source: https://about.google/intl/ALL_us/ (September 22, 2021).
16 Source: https://en.wikipedia.org/wiki/Don%27t_be_evil (September 22, 2021).

ery search query. In addition to Google, which officially committed itself to the mission of imparting knowledge, Facebook wanted to empower people to form communities and bring the world closer together. The company's philosophy is described on its own homepage as follows: Facebook's mission is to "give people the power to build community and bring the world closer together".[17] So Facebook was about communication.

Public communication traditionally takes place even more than the transfer of knowledge in public spaces. At least when it comes to matters that affect the general affairs. From now on, this was structured according to mechanisms that, on the one hand, meant a complete shift in the boundaries between the private and the public: the private was no longer private, but was annexed by corporations for the best possible control of global markets. Public communication, on the other hand, had apparently become private. Driven by "recommendation algorithms", it played itself increasingly in the comfort zone of personal likes and dislikes, which it increasingly contoured and reinforced. Finally, by networking with like-minded people, constant confirmation feedback was generated. The perfidiousness of this mechanism is that the associated personalization is perceived by the users as a gain in freedom. But this is in fact a trap.

The personalization trap destroys the public through social media algorithms. The social media networks make it possible for the first time to operate mass communication as personalized communication. But in the pitfalls of "personalization" there is a risk of dumbing down through commercialization and the rules of the click economy: If the information is individually tailored, the individual cannot rely on it being recorded and controlled by everyone else. But there can be no individual truths, except as the "felt truths" rampant today, which are often not true. Information shared and checked together is a prerequisite for a functioning public in a democracy. Part of the freedom of information is the security that the information that everyone receives is shared by others and that it is not only tailored to the individual but can also be viewed and verified by everyone else.

Only based on countless personal data, often illegally collected, and stored under EU law, can the recommendation algorithms begin their selection process, which is entirely geared towards capturing the user with his personal preferences, feelings, and weaknesses. The user should stay on the

---

17 Facebooks mission statement on their investor relations home page: https://investor.fb.com/resources/default.aspx (September 22, 2021).

pages as long as possible in order to elicit further data from him, which will then be used against him in the next attack on his attention. For this purpose, the selection of messages is tailored precisely to his profile. In this way, the recommendation algorithms destroy the basic function of the public, in which what is relevant for the public can be discussed by all on a common basis. Common sense only arises where the common ground of a shared public sphere is present. Internet personalization is splitting the common ground into countless small parcels. With this consistent individualization of information, the public breaks up, with consequences that go far beyond the obvious isolation of the users: A situation threatens in which everyone ultimately lives in a different world of perception. The basis for joint action is thus destroyed. There is a threat of common ground zero, which is fatal for society and individuals alike.

If the right to informational self-determination is not respected and the citizen must expect that his behavior and the data of his life are constantly recorded and evaluated, his behavior will adapt to this possibility in accordance with the laws of Panoptism.[18] The chilling effect of constant observation leads to conformity and lack of criticism. The manipulation of the information flow based on personal profiles also destroys the autonomy: Instead of making decisions yourself and in free exchange with others, the algorithms' automatic decision-making systems have always decided what everyone should want next. The attack on the formation of the will occurs through the immense knowledge of intimate data, which allow manipulative techniques to be used in the innermost core of people. An accumulation of knowledge about people, whether in the state or in corporations, as it is real today, is simply incompatible with a democratic social order that relies on the free activity and self-determination of its members. And it is also incompatible with the idea of an innovation society. Because conformism is the enemy of creativity.

---

18 The philosopher Michel Foucault coined the term panoptism, from the Greek panoptes, "the all-seeing", to describe the systematic surveillance and disciplining in modern societies. Foucault, Michel, Überwachen und Strafen, Frankfurt 1976; The "panoptic effects" of surveillance, which describe the adaptation and conformism of the individual, are also described as "chilling effects", see on chilling effects in german jurisprudence: Assion, Simon: Was sag das Recht zu Chilling Effects? In: Telemedicus, Recht der Informationsgesellschaft, May 9, 2014, https://www.telemedicus.info/was-sagt-die-rechtsprechung-zu-chilling-effects/ (September 22, 2021).

And these mechanisms are very directly becoming a threat to democracy: Only about one in five Germans feel free to express their opinions in public any more. 35 percent even conclude that free expression of opinion is only possible in private.[19] The reasons given are rude behavior and the fear of "shitstorms". The anarchy in cyberspace thus leads to the censorship that it supposedly wants to avoid through lack of rules and anonymization.

In a representative survey, 50% of mayors in Germany state that they have already experienced hatred and violence in office and that they therefore behave differently.[20] A number of them no longer want to exercise their democratic office in the face of threats in the digital space, a result of the of non-regulated rude internet behavior which more and more shapes the core of democratic society. These are the direct effects of the incremental logic of social media algorithms, which also reward hate and call for violence because their main goal is to mobilize emotions. One can call this circumstance the digital paradox: The same technology that once promised liberation is becoming the greatest censorship machine of modern society through the absence of rules and accountability.

Why is this model nonetheless so successful? We use the digital offers primarily for convenience. Thanks to enormous data profiles, algorithms can suggest more and more suitable products, even seemingly foresee our future behavior, and finally manipulate them through "nudging"[21]. We apparently no longer need to worry about the selection in the product and news jungle of an increasingly complex world. But not worrying is bad for your own intelligence and at the same time strengthens the artificial intelligence because more and more data is flowing to it. The subject is relieved and thereby forgets how to use his own mind. Users are lured into the convenience trap and dependency is created, which in turn means that the servers are entrusted with even more data and the algorithms with even more decisions. A vicious circle.

---

19   Source: Laeber, Thomas: Mehrheit der Deutschen äußert sich in der Öffentlichkeit nur vorsichtig. In: WELT, May 25, 2019, https://www.welt.de/politik/article193977845/Deutsche-sehen-Meinungsfreiheit-in-der-Oeffentlichkeit-eingeschraenkt.html (September 22, 2021).

20   Source: Heinsch, Marc-Julien: Wo bedrohte Amtsträger Hilfe finden. In: Süddeutsche Zeitung, April 29, 2021, https://www.sueddeutsche.de/politik/hass-gewalt-buergermeister-plattform-hilfe-1.5280201 (September 22, 2021).

21   Thaler, Richard; Sunstein, Cass: Nudge, Improving decisions about Health, Wealth and Happiness, London 2009.

The forecasts, based on which the recommendation algorithms filter the information, also create the appearance of coming from the future. But in truth they are based on data from the past. They not only form an informational filter bubble, but also a time capsule, because they reinforce prejudices, exclude surprises from the new and the foreign and thus prevent innovation and future viability. In addition to personalization, there is the main rule of the click economy that addressing emotions and instincts triggers more clicks and retweets and generates more followers than presenting facts and reasonable arguments. But because the money is earned with the number of clicks and retweets, the algorithms of the electronic public prefer emotions to the detriment of common sense. In this way we are moving away from a public in which, for the sake of democratic decision-making, the better argument is reasonably fought for. And we are moving towards a public that is asserted with hatred and emotion, in which it is first about attention, then only about excitement, and the goal of sensible democratic decision-making gets out of sight. The ultimately economically driven pull of the spiral of attention leads to smear campaigns taking the place of debates. However, despite all the "personalization", these mechanisms by no means create "singularities"[22], i.e. unmistakable uniqueness of the individuals. Rather, the so-called personalization of the algorithms inevitably misses the unique individuality of each person. Because the subjects are not targeted by the AI as such, rather only as precise "types". It starts with the sorting of the users into certain groups: Facebook first assigns each user to a type based on a model of personality psychology (also known as the ocean model) to find out how they can best stimulate themselves according to their psychological personality traits let manipulate. Cambridge Analytica used these methods in the 2016 election of Donald Trump and in Brexit. According to its own information, the company had created 220 million psychograms of US citizens.[23]

Artificial intelligence is also used to control social media communication. Which posts and messages attract attention and thus spread is decided by artificial intelligences that have previously been trained to use human weaknesses as consistently as possible in order to increase the length of time spent on certain offers. Personalize, polarize, scandalize, and always think

---

22 See: Reckwitz, Andreas: Die Gesellschaft der Singularitäten, Zum Strukturwandel der Moderne, Berlin 2019.
23 Source: Beuth, Patrick: Die Luftpumpen von Cambridge Alalytica. In: DIE ZEIT, March 7, 2017, https://www.zeit.de/digital/internet/2017-03/us-wahl-cambridge-analytica-donald-trump-widerspruch (September 22, 2021).

about the emotions of the users. According to this logic, artificial intelligence is increasingly organizing public space and thereby destroying the human—and democracy.

Is automated journalism the future model of the digital public? According to the logic of Silicon Valley, problems that have arisen through technology can only be solved through technology. This logic is gaining ground more and more. Media companies, too, believe they have no choice but to join in under the pressure of declining revenues. A trend in journalism is the use of journalistic bots. Associated Press, AP for short, now employs a 'News Automation Editor'. With its help, the editorial team publishes from the start around 4,400 automatically generated financial reports on listed companies every quarter. Human employees previously only had a capacity of around 300 reports.[24]

In Germany, too, investments are being made in this direction, by publishers who are teaming up with Google. However, so far, AI has only been used for niche topics in journalism in Germany. The performance of the AI is also largely viewed critically in the publishing houses—for the time being. In the meantime, cases of false reports by AI are known in the USA, which, in addition to the question of trust, above all raise the question of liability.[25] There are also studies on the use of AI in journalism showing that texts generated by AI score with the audience with better grades in terms of credibility and competence. Is this because of the dwindling quality of real journalists or because they are used to being pre-sorted and presented by machines with what best suits their own profile and thus their own prejudices?

Text programs are getting better and better at generating larger coherent texts that can compete with the quality of human writers. The limits of performance keep shifting. Even if only simple data journalism is currently mostly possible and the research of sources, the critical classification and evaluation is still done by journalists: One must not fail to recognize that the economic pressure on the editorial offices to save costs with such tools, in view of the structural change in the media is enormous. It seems that the automation of the digital public is being driven inexorably.

Especially when using AI in journalism, due to the special role the public plays in democracy, the question of the effects on society must be asked

24 Source: https://www.ap.org/discover/artificial-intelligence
25 Source: Lobe, Adrian: Zu schnell für die Kontrolle. In: Süddeutsche Zeitung, July 26, 2019, https://www.sueddeutsche.de/medien/ki-journalismus-fehler-1.4539688 (September 22, 2021).

early and consistently. Transparency about the use of AI and clear demarcation between the communication between human and non-human actors is becoming increasingly important in view of the rapid development of these programs.

4. Outlook: The Need for Regulation

Whatever the future of the public will look like: One thing is certain, it will increasingly be determined by technology. Only the question of what logic this technology follows seems to be open. If you want democracy to survive, you have to replace the current logic of social media algorithms with the observance of data protection and a logic of democracy-compatible search and recommendation algorithm. In them, valuable, professionally checked information and opinions that adhere to the rules of law must be given preference. Based on a "fair" search, as it was envisioned by Google in the early years, data can be recorded and evaluated in a way that aims to improve the results, not to gain control over the user. Rather, such algorithms can contribute that users can form a picture of the world despite the growing and seemingly unmanageable complexity and have a part in determining what it looks like.

It will not work without respect for the law and the introduction of the principle of responsibility for those who earn big money by organizing social communication. Specifically, this means, among other things, the end of the platform privilege that enables the big tech corporations not only to fundamentally revolutionize markets, but also to become markets themselves and set their own rules. We must therefore:

- regulate uncontrolled data collection: only certain personal data may be collected, stored for a limited time, and evaluated in the public interest, pseudonymized or anonymized.
- hold on to the concept of informational self-determination because it is the basis for self-determination in general. In the information age, this is truer than ever, even if a redefinition of the boundaries of the private may be indicated.
- regulate the powerful new technologies of artificial intelligence and quantum computers in such a way that they are used in accordance with basic values and that clear liability rules apply.

- Develop and make mandatory technical platforms for information and exchange with hardware and software components that enable information and communication within the same legal framework that applies to the analog media world. Fair search and recommendation algorithms must enable diversity instead of reinforcing the formation of bubbles, make facts clearly distinguishable from fakes and transfer the basic rules of mutual respect, as laid down by the law for analog public spaces, to the digital public. Basically, everything must be digitally permitted or prohibited that is also permitted or prohibited in analogue.

Even if the line between the private and the public will continue to shift, and this may also be necessary in view of new challenges and new technologies: The distinction itself must never be given up. The question of which personal data is public and which is not, is a deeply political question. And today, more than ever, it is a question of power, because it is about economic and increasingly also about geopolitical power in the use of digital technology. The architecture of the digital public space must reflect these questions of power and answer them in terms of protecting autonomy and the weaker. It must clearly answer the question of responsibility and liability, make impact assessments of the future effects of technical innovation mandatory, establish transparency and control rules that do justice to the dynamics and complexity of technological developments if possible, through an ex-ante regulation.

We need a set of rules for the digital public that is based on democracy, the rule of law and fundamental rights and ensures that these values are not further undermined. On the contrary, an attempt must be made to transfer the principle of the separation of powers, which is one of the key principles for the containment and control of political power, to the economic and technological power of Big Tec. The enormous, concentrated power of Big Tec must be split up in order to remain controllable for democracy. The first approaches to such an appropriate and comprehensive regulation can be found in the new legislative proposals of the European Commission, the Digital Service Act and Digital Market Act. But that can only be the beginning.

One thing is clear: technological disruption must end where the law begins. Might must not take the place of right, because that would mean the end of freedom and democracy.

Literature

Arendt, Hannah: The Human Condition: 2nd Revised edition. Chicago 1998, german: Elemente und Ursprünge totaler Herrschaft, Antisemitismus, Imperialismus, totale Herrschaft, München 1986

Arendt, Hannah: The origins of Totalitarism, 2nd ed., Edition Charleston, 2011.

Assion, Simon: Was sagt die Rechtsprechung zu Chilling Effects? In: Telemedicus, Recht der Informationsgesellschaft, May 9, 2014, https://www.telemedicus.info/was-sagt-die-rechtsprechung-zu-chilling-effects/ (September 22, 2021).

Barlow, John Perry: 'A Declaration of the Independence of Cyberspace', Electronic Frontier Foundation, 8. February 1996, https://www.eff.org/de/cyberspace-independence (September 22, 2021).

Beuth, Patrick: Die Luftpumpen von Cambridge Alalytica. In: DIE ZEIT, March 7, 2017, https://www.zeit.de/digital/internet/2017-03/us-wahl-cambridge-analytica-donald-trump-widerspruch (September 22, 2021).

Edgerton, Anna; Banares, Ilya: Facebook, Twitter, YouTube are pressed on 'poisonous' algorithms. In: Los Angeles Times, April 27, 2021, https://www.latimes.com/business/technology/story/2021-04-27/facebook-twitter-youtube-pressed-on-poisonous-algorithms (September 22, 2021).

Foucault, Michel: Überwachen und Strafen, Frankfurt 1976.

Frühbrodt, Lutz; Floren, Annette: Unboxing YouTube, Im Netzwerk der Profis und Profiteure, Frankfurt 2019. In: https://www.otto-brenner-stiftung.de/fileadmin/user_data/stiftung/02_Wissenschaftsportal/03_Publikationen/AH98_YouTube.pdf (September 22, 2021).

Habermas, Jürgen: The Structural Transformation of the Public Sphere: An Inquiry Into a Category of Bourgeois Society, Hoboken, New Jersey, 2015, german: Habermas, Jürgen, Strukturwandel der Öffentlichkeit, Untersuchungen zu einer Kategorie der bürgerlichen Gesellschaft, Darmstadt 1962.

Hall, Evelyn Beatrice: The Friends of Voltaire, New York 1907.

Harris, Tristan: Time well spent, Center for humane technology, An Introduction to our work, https://humanetech.com/ (September 22, 2021).

Hegel, G.W.F.: Philosophie der Geschichte, Werke Bd. 12, Frankfurt 1970.

Jaster, Romy; Lanius, David: Die Wahrheit schafft sich ab, wie Fake News Politik machen, Ditzingen 2019.

Laeber, Thomas: Mehrheit der Deutschen äußert sich in der Öffentlichkeit nur vorsichtig. In: WELT, May 22, 2019, https://www.welt.de/politik/article193977845/Deutsche-sehen-Meinungsfreiheit-in-der-Oeffentlichkeit-eingeschraenkt.html (September 22, 2021).

Lobe, Adrian: Zu schnell für die Kontrolle. In: Süddeutsche Zeitung, July 26, 2019, https://www.sueddeutsche.de/medien/ki-journalismus-fehler-1.4539688 (September 22, 2021).

Nemitz, Paul; Pfeffer, Matthias: Prinzip Mensch, Macht, Freiheit und Demokratie im Zeitalter der Künstlichen Intelligenz, Bonn 2020.

Reckwitz, Andreas: Die Gesellschaft der Singularitäten, Zum Strukturwandel der Moderne, Berlin 2019.

Russell, Stuart: Human Compatible, Artificial Intelligence and the Problem of Control, New York 2019; german ed. Frechen 2020.

Thaler, Richard; Sunstein, Cass, Nudge, Improving decisions about Health, Wealth and Happiness, London 2009.

Zuboff, Shoshana: The Age of Surveillance Capitalism. The Fight for a Human Future at the New Frontier of Power, New York 2019.

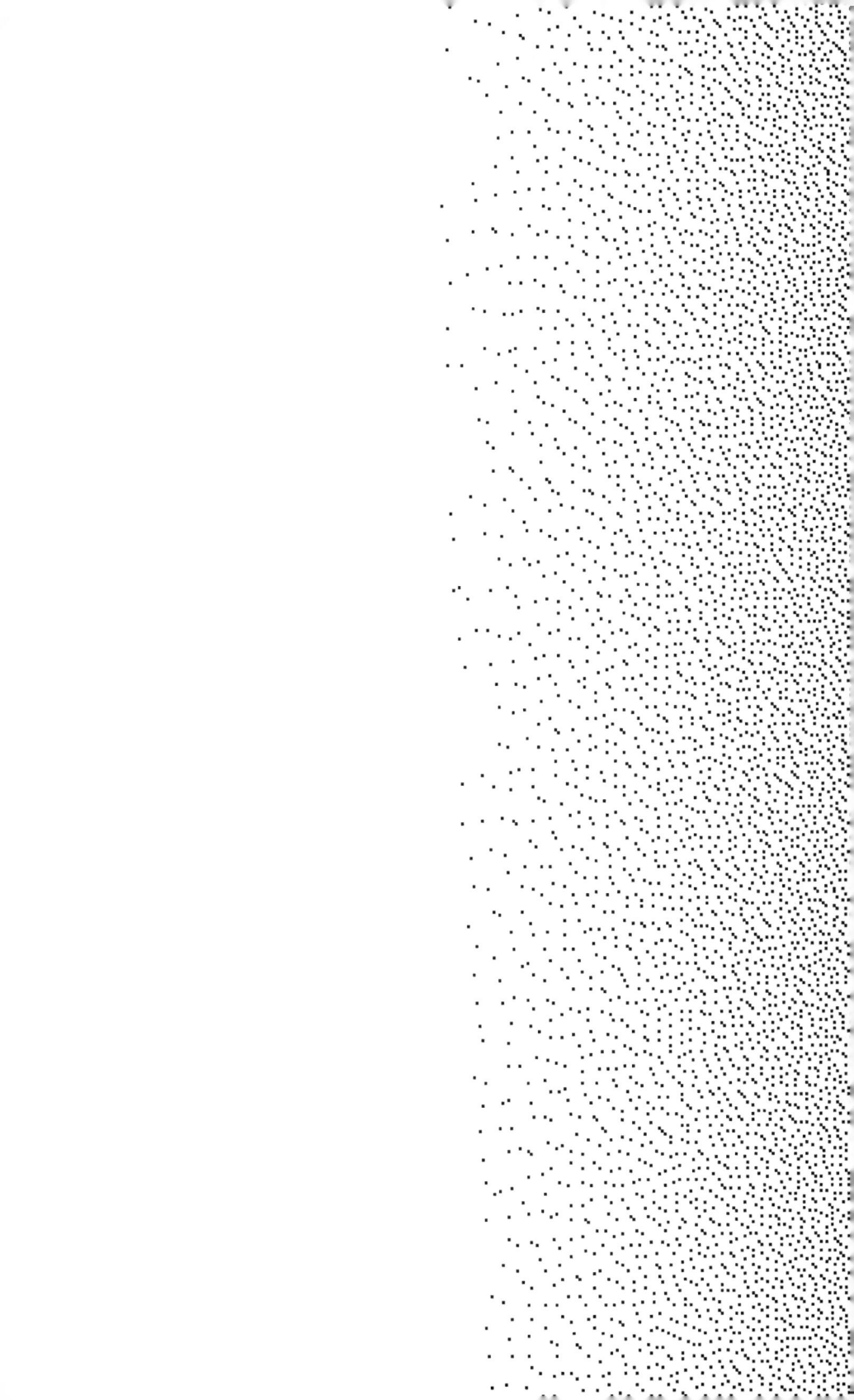

Lotte Houwing

Reclaim your Face and the Streets

Why Facial Recognition, and Other Biometric Surveillance Technology in Public Spaces, Should be Banned

Public spaces play a crucial role in democratic societies. They are sometimes called a sanctuary for our fundamental rights. With the deployment of biometric surveillance technology you can be identified, analysed, tracked, manipulated and controlled throughout your day. It is easy to see how this deployment is incompatible with a free society in which we can exercise our fundamental rights. However, in this article I will take some more space to elaborate on the problems of biometric surveillance, and why the use of this technology in public spaces should be effectively and legally banned.

Biometric surveillance reduces people to walking barcodes. It leaves no space for an opt-out, but enables the connection between persons in physical space with that of profiles in existing, searchable databases. Belonging to the family of surveillance technologies that make use of profiling, it aims to sort people. Neither these profiles, the algorithms nor the technology are neutral and they exacerbate systemic inequalities in our society. These are not just technological deficiencies that are solvable with more diverse datasets to train the algorithms. Making the technology working equally well ON everybody does not mean it works equally well FOR everybody. The deployment of the technology is inherently untargeted, making it a means of mass surveillance. The law is clear about that: Biometric mass surveillance is illegitimate. However, two parties might benefit from a slow and steady introduction of the technology: governments hungry for control and industry seeking product-market-fits. And in practice we see the use of biometric surveillance popping up like mushrooms in autumn. To protect our streets, our freedoms and our societies, we need a more explicit and effectively enforced ban on biometric surveillance technology in publicly accessible spaces.

Public Space: The Street is Where it Happens

When we talk about a free democracy it is important to realise that parliament is not the (only) space where politics happen and society is formed. Publicly accessible spaces play a fundamental role in facilitating debate among the people who together form a society. It are the places where individuals encounter each other in a more random fashion than in the private sphere and therefore have to relate to each other's differences and have a public debate about how to live together.

Moreover, public space is the physical stage for protest and political interventions. An analogue example of the effect that altering public space has on the potential for protesting is seen in the urban planning of Paris by Georges-Eugène Haussmann. His broad boulevards made it much more easy for the French army to control and repress popular uprisings.[1]

A more technological example can be found in Hong Kong where AI surveillance in public space can severely impact the freedoms that underlie the right to protest and form a threat to the safety of protesters. Protesters fight back by finding ways to block or demolish the invasive technology, like laser pointers against cameras or simply tearing down poles with facial recognition cameras on them.[2] But fighting back gets harder when you have to fight technology that is turning your own face into a weapon that will be used against you.[3] We see that this kind of surveillance in public space is used to target protesters against the establishment, but we also see that it prevents people from going to protests in the first place.

Surveillance technologies in public spaces are also introduced from other, less obvious, angles like smart cities. The idea of monitoring and measuring everything to make experiences as seamless as possible introduces all kinds of data-driven surveillance technologies that rearticulate the experience and function of public spaces. From a place of (relative) anonymity, all kinds of smart devices make the urban public spaces into places of data capture which before was reserved for research laboratories and high-surveillance institutions like prisons, hospitals or mental institutions.[4] It is of the utmost importance that from the smart city perspective, we should also be very critical of the introduction of surveillance technology into our public spaces. Too often in these debates, the value of privacy and public space are stripped of their political meaning and reduced to respectively data protection and an open space where the public aspect is translated into 'up for grabs' of your personal information. When we look at publicly accessible spaces as

---

[1] Cf. Willsher, Kim: Story of Cities #12 : Hausmann rips up Paris—and divides France to this day. In: The Guardian of March 31, 2016, https://www.theguardian.com/cities/2016/mar/31/story-cities-12-paris-baron-haussmann-france-urban-planner-napoleon (March 5, 2021).

[2] Cf. Reason TV: Hong Kong protestors combat the surveillance state. In: Youtube of 4 October 2019, https://www.youtube.com/watch?v=VXog6t4kNyc (January 13, 2021).

[3] Cf. Mozur, Paul: In Hong Kong protests, faces become weapons. In: The New York Times of July 26, 2019, https://www.nytimes.com/2019/07/26/technology/hong-kong-protests-facial-recognition-surveillance.html (December 8, 2020).

[4] Cf. Galic, Maša: Surveillance, privacy and public space in the Stratumseind Living Lab: the smart city debate, beyond data. In: Ars Aequi (2019), July/August, p. 1.

spaces where public debate takes place, where the plurality of people and their lifestyles is facilitated and where democratic rights are exercised. And we look at privacy as more than the protection of our personal data but also as a fundamental right, a fundamental social value, a necessary condition for the safe use of other fundamental rights such as our freedom of speech, freedom of religion and the protection of our autonomy. We realise that we cannot let our guard down regarding the protection of privacy in public spaces when we value a free society.

Maša Galič and Marc Schuilenburg examine the current debate on smart cities by looking at three contemporary perspectives on "the right to the city" a concept which is coined by Henri Lefebvre. This concept consists of several aspects that are important in understanding the political aspects and role of public spaces in a city. Lefebvre argues that "struggles for the city are vital to any emancipatory politics of space".[5] In this context, a few qualities of the city and public space come to the fore: The centrality of public spaces in a city facilitates surprise, meeting and difference. It is the space where (near-)strangers have social encounters that enable a community. The right to difference entails the creation of an inclusive city composed of different lifestyles as opposed to forces of abstraction and homogenization of space, produced by a bureaucratic capitalist system.[6] And appropriation, the idea that the public space in a city should be shaped according to the inhabitants needs.

In their paper Galič and Schuilenburg describe how the roll out of smart cities often happens from a perspective of Morozov's 'solutionism', a way of thinking that "presumes rather than investigates the problems that it is trying to solve, reaching for the answer before the questions have been fully asked".[7] Investing in smart technology is seen as the best way to avoid and solve all kinds of problems, when it comes to 'smart' surveillance technology, this mostly comes down to fighting crime, protecting property, creating a seamless experience and maintaining public order in a very narrow sense. Galič and Schuilenburg identify, as others before them, public safety and security as key drivers for the implementation of smart technologies. There is a strong focus on the elimination of disorder and conflict and smart technolo-

---

5   Galič, Maša; Schuilenburg, Marc: Reclaiming the Smart City: Toward a New Right to the City. In: Juan Carlos Augusto, Handbook of Smart Cities (2020), p. 5.
6   Cf. Galič; Schuilenburg 2020.
7   Morozov, Evgeny: To save everything, click Here, New York 2013, p. 6.

gies promise better protection against these dangers by taking a more proactive approach, based on and coupled with a trend of datafication.[8]

An example of this can be found in the Dutch city of Eindhoven. The local government wanted to 'revitalise' this street with mostly bars. To do that, a Living Lab was started to measure, analyse and influence the behaviour of its visitors. Several kinds of sensors in the street and monitoring of social media together give an impression of the atmosphere. The collected data onsists of among others the amount of beer that is sold, the amount of people that are present, the weather, the volume of the sound and data from wifi-tracking. The aim of the project is to no longer react to every small incident after a norm is breached, but to change the environment to manage the relationship between the incident and the crowd. Central to this project is a business-model of undisturbed consumption: More beer, less unrest.[9] Here you see that the technology that is deployed in this space is mostly serving the goal of efficiency in maintaining public order and the commercial interests of the bar owners, by placing everybody in the space under surveillance. Whether you are living there, just passing by, working in a bar, having a date or celebrating a birthday.

To limit the scope of the discussion within this paper, I will focus specifically on biometric surveillance technologies in public space. I made this choice because work on the topic feels urgent. Wee see facial recognition popping up significantly in Europe, infiltrating our public spaces and the discussion on the topic is lively. We do not have the luxury to make this mistake. Therefore we, a coalition of more than 40 (digital) human rights organisations throughout Europe, started the campaign Reclaim Your Face. In the campaign we call for a ban on all biometric surveillance technologies in publicly accessible spaces. I will now explain why we need to stop this.

---

8 Cf. Galič; Schuilenburg 2020, p. 4.
9 Cf. Houwing, Lotte: Experimentele Manipulatie: Burger steeds vaker onwetend proefdier. In: Bits of Freedom of June 5, 2019, https://www.bitsoffreedom.nl/2019/06/05/experimentele-manipulatie-burger-steeds-vaker-onwetend-proefdier/ (December 2, 2021).

From Bio to Metrics: A Fundamental Reduction

Ok, so let's first take a step back. What are we talking about when we are talking about biometric surveillance technologies? In the General Data Protection Regulation (GDPR), biometric data is defined as "personal data resulting from specific technical processing relating to the physical, physiological or behavioural characteristics of a natural person, which allow or confirm the unique identification of that natural person, such as facial images or dactyloscopic [fingerprint] data".[10] This means that the European law recognises two categories of information as biometric data: The first one pertains to bodily characteristics like facial features, DNA or fingerprints. The second one pertains to behavioural characteristics like handwriting or gait. To both categories applies the logic of the word biometric: The specific technical processing requires and performs a reduction from a biological characteristic of a natural person to something that a computer can digest; metrics.

The next step in the development of facial recognition technology, technologies that perform emotion recognition, are normally also included in biometrics. These technologies might not be focussing on the unique identification of a natural person, but they do analyse behavioural characteristics of our bodies in a specific technical process with personal data as a result. What they also do is cause the same reduction. Motions of the muscles in our face and our facial expressions are made machine-readable and linked to emotional states by algorithms, based on a presumption of universality.[11] This is the reduction in full glory: even our emotions get quantified.

David Lyon, director of the Surveillance Studies Center at Queens University, has provided a definition of surveillance: "Any focused attention to personal details for the purposes of influence, management, or control."[12] Biometric data can be used to identify people, but it can also be used to categorise people, and sort them. An example is facial recognition software that

---

10   Article 4 sub 14 GDPR.
11   Cf. Schwartz, Oscar: Don't look now, why you should be worried about machines reading your emotions. In: The Guardian of March 6, 2019, https://www.theguardian.com/technology/2019/mar/06/facial-recognition-software-emotional-science (March 5, 2021).
12   Lyon, David: Surveillance Power and Everyday Life. In: Oxford Handbook of Information and Communication Technologies (2007) January, p. 1.

is used in China to recognize Uighur minorities.[13] But we should not just point our finger at China, EU Horizon 2020 projects include for example a virtual agent using emotional recognition systems at its borders to judge the truthfulness of travelers.[14]

To put it all together: Biometric surveillance technologies are technologies that make use of our unique and highly personal, biometric data in order to automatically influence, manage, or control us. It reduces us as human beings to walking barcodes allowing different regimes to apply according to automatically ascribed values and decisions.

Shaping Behavior and Shaping Society: To Shape or to be Shaped?

This fundamental reduction brings along some effects. One is strongly normative. Since measurable things have averages and enable data about what is most common, it delivers an account of what seems to be normal, and thus also what is perceived as divergent, which is easily viewed as suspicious. Especially when the technology that is deployed is there to mostly serve goals of public order and safety. Examples of this are 'smart' cameras at airports or train stations that detect suspicious behaviour when people pursue abnormal walking patterns or forget their luggage. We should never forget that we shape technology, but that thereafter, technology is shaping us. When we design cameras to detect divergent behaviour, it might trigger some alert when we start behave in a manner that diverges from the expectations and predictions that are coded in the technology, for example when we start dancing in the streets. Are we

---

13 Cf. Harwell, Drew; Dou, Eva: Huawei tested AI software that could recognize Uighur minorities and alert police, report says. In: The Washington Post of December 8, 2020, https://www.washingtonpost.com/technology/2020/12/08/huawei-tested-ai-software-that-could-recognize-uighur-minorities-alert-police-report-says/ (December 8, 2020).

14 Cf. Gallagher, Ryan; Jona, Ludovica: We tested Europe's new lie detector for travelers and immediately triggered a false positive. In: The Intercept of July 26, 2019, https://theintercept.com/2019/07/26/europe-border-control-ai-lie-detector/ (December 8, 2020).

OK with surveillance choreographing us?[15] Wouldn't that be a very dystopian image?

An other effect of this reduction is that uncertainties are being removed. A risk score of 0.7 leaves room for uncertainties. But when this score is attributed to an individual it is used to inform a decision: Either classify it as a high risk score, treat it as a 1 and apply a more strict regime to this individual, or do not do that, treat it as a 0 and let the person pass. To get to an outcome, all the uncertainties in the process of getting there have to be removed.[16] This subtracts nuance and grey tones as well as accountability from reality, leaving black and white action perspectives.

By taking the road of datafication and surveillance we demand citizens to be continually transparent. By taking a proactive approach in preventing crimes or anticipating on behaviour that the machine might interpret as suspicious, the tables of fundamental principles of the rule of law are turned. Citizens have to consistently provide insight and justification about themselves and their actions as opposed to the situation that their actions should give reason to a reasonable suspicion that needs to precede off the legitimize any form of control. By legitimizing control in advance and outsourcing the judgment of what behaviour is a reason for suspicion, we limit the scope of what might be acceptable behaviour, chilling our political freedoms and sense of social experiment, risking our Lefebvrian right to the city.

There is no Opt-Out

The biggest fallacy of surveillance in publicly accessibel spaces is that it can legitimately be based on consent. This is not possible because consent needs to be informed and freely given. Informed means that it must be clear to the person whose information is processed what he/she/they is consenting to. So it must be claur what kind of surveillance is being deployed, what data is processed, by whom, under what conditions etc. Freely given means that it must be possible for the person to say no, without having negative consequences of this refusal. This situation simply does not correspond with the practicallities of surveillance in publicly accessible spaces. In general, there is

15 Cf. Doringer, Bogomir: When you feel pain, keep on dancing. In: TQW of June 24, 2020, https://tqw.at/when-you-feel-pain-keep-on-dancing-doringer/ (January 13, 2021).

16 Cf. Rasch, Miriam: Ethiek in tijden van dataïsme, Amsterdam 2020, p. 120.

a lack of transparency when it comes to the deployment of surveillance. And it is also not realistic to think that people will read informative signs before entering spaces they need to be going throughout their daily lifes. Above that, there is no option for refusal, you cannot opt-out.

There are two distinct ways in which the deployment of biometric surveillance technologies in publicly accessible spaces leave people no choice to opt-out. Although public space might not be well-defined in law, and the limits of which spaces are public and which aren't, are not agreed upon, there is consensus about the fact that public space is a place where people wanting to take part in society have no ability to opt out from entering. So deployment in public space requires people to accept their bodies being scanned to take part in society.

In addition to the impossibility to opt-out from public space, it is impossible to opt-out from your body, and difficult to prevent your body from being surveilled once the technology is being deployed on the streets. The extremely personal nature of your biometric data means that it cannot be changed or left at home in a drawer. On top of that, it is fairly easy to gather biometric information covertly and distantly. This allows others to identify and follow people through public space without their knowledge.[17]

The demand for transparency on the side of people and the disability to opt-out from your body as a unique identifier are shown in the battle about facial datapoints. Several countries have laws that forbid to cover your face when in public space. The coronavirus created an exception to this, requiring people to wear facemasks and thus also covering data points that are used in identification. However, the protection this exception had to offer was only a matter of time, since researchers already scraped images of masked up faces from social media, creating specific datasets to train face recognition on masked faces.[18]

---

[17] Cf. Houwing, Lotte: Stop the Creep of Biometric Surveillance Technology. In: European Data Protection Law Review (2020), nr. 2, p. 174.

[18] Cf. Ng, Alfred: Your face mask selfies could be training the next facial recognition tool. In: Cnet of May 19, 2020, https://www.cnet.com/news/your-face-mask-selfies-could-be-training-the-next-facial-recognition-tool/ (March 5, 2021).

Transformation of Existing Surveillance Infrastructure

Before the deployment of biometric surveillance technology in publicly accessible spaces it was already hard to move around the city without being spied upon. Most people living in cities are used to being surveilled by CCTV systems when going about their daily lives. Still, it makes a difference whether this is a 'normal' camera, or one equipped with biometric data analysis functions, because it is shifting the focus from the "what" to the "who". Where CCTV systems capture stories of what is happening in a certain place, biometric surveillance technologies are adding the dimension of identification, making it about tracing people and their personal behaviour, and expanding the scope of information that can be extracted from and linked to the images.

Using our physical characteristics as unique identifiers brings along another aspect of transformation of existing surveillance infrastructure: It enables a connection between our physical appearance and information about us in existing, searchable databases. This may sound abstract, so a few examples:

Churchix is facial recognition software that is used to measure attendance.[19] It makes it possible for church leaders (or for that sake, everybody) to automatically track which members of a religious community are attending a mass and which are not, based on the feed of the security camera near the entrance.[20]

The app FindFace makes it possible to search for people on VK, the biggest social network of Russia. The photographer Egor Tsvetkov tried it out in his project "Your face is Big Data" with random people in the subway, and he was able to link 70% of the young people he encountered to their online presence.[21] They might not even have noticed.[22]

Last but not last, your personal identity is linked to several kinds of government registration systems, like a social security number, or a police file. Once surveillance systems in the streets are able to uniquely identi-

---

19 https://churchix.com/ (December 8, 2020).
20 de Zwart, Hans: 'Geen gezicht'—De Big Brother Awards speech van Hans de Zwart. In: Bits of Freedom of 15 November 2016, https://www.bitsoffreedom.nl/2016/11/15/geen-gezicht-de-big-brother-awards-speech-van-hans-de-zwart/ (December 8, 2020).
21 Cf. Tsvetkov, Egor: Your Face is Big Data. In: Cargo Collective, https://cargocollective.com/egortsvetkov/Your-Face-Is-Big-Data (December 8, 2020).
22 Cf. de Zwart 2020.

fy passersby, people in crowds are like walking barcodes connected to their whole cabinet of files. The chilling effect this creates is something Haussmann could only dream about.

To show how easy it is to use this potential, and thus how easy deployment of it gets out of control, Bits of Freedom took it to the test and made the first steps to build the ultimate stalker tool.[23] On the website www.webcam.nl/amsterdam you can follow several livestreams of what is happening throughout the city of Amsterdam. We went to the Dam to get our face on camera. We downloaded the livestream as well as a free trial of Amazon's Rekognition to see whether the facial recognition software was able to correctly identify us out of the feed, and succeeded. This shows that it is possible for every slightly tech savvy person to build a tool that enables you to follow a specific person ((ex-)partner? Child? Employee?) around and to maybe even add notifications if they get in a certain area, without spending any money or having to get up from their couch.

Another transformation that takes place is that this extra functionality can go into hiding. 'Plain' cameras (can) look the same as for example facial recognition cameras. So while this extra functionality makes you a lot more transparent, you are left in the dark about the kind of surveillance that is performed.

Surveillance Sorts People

As I described above, surveillance can be defined as "any focused attention to personal details for the purposes of influence, management, or control".[24] Social sorting is "a way to establish identities, but also to assign risks and value(s) to people". Biometric surveillance technology is focussing on unique personal details to identify people, and based on the information that is linked to them certain rules apply. Social sorting is what's happening when you are buying a washing machine online, and based on your location you get a different price. But this is also what's happening when you are stopped more often for a police control because you are a non-white person.

---

23   Cf. Hooyman, Paula: Amazons Rekognition shows its true colors. In: Bits of Freedom of December 12, 2019, https://www.bitsoffreedom.nl/2019/12/12/amazons-rekognition-shows-its-true-colors/ (December 8, 2020).

24   Lyon, David: Surveillance Power and Everyday Life. In: Oxford Handbook of Information and Communication Technologies (2007) January, p. 1.

In the Netherlands there is a very well-known game, called "Wie is het?" (Who is it?). The point of the game is that you have to ask questions to single out the person that the other player has in their mind. You do this by categorising people, based on characteristics of their physical appearance. For example: Does this person wear any kind of hat? If yes, all others go down. It is the analogue gamification model of social sorting based on physical appearance.

A real life example where values and risks are automatically assigned to people, based on an analysis of their face is iBorderCtrl.[25] iBorderCtrl uses a virtual agent to have conversations with migrants at the EU border and serves as an automated lie-detector. While you answer questions at customs like "What is your name?" and "What is the reason of your visit?" the system analyses the movements of the smallest muscles in your face, assigning you a reliability score on which depends whether you should be subject to further checks or not.

Bias in the Technology

Before I get into this point I want to make a remark: Biases are very problematic, but too often they are presented as the main problem with invasive surveillance technology, like facial recognition. I want to emphasize that in my perspective, these technologies will also be problematic if they would not contain biases. With that of out of the way, what are we talking about when we talk about bias in technology? One of the problems with these systems is that they are built with data. Data that is subjective and established in colonial and patriarchal structures.[26] While to many people automated decision making has a hint of objectivity as compared with human made decisions

---

25 Cf. https://cordis.europa.eu/project/id/700626, last updated on 22 October 2020 (December 8, 2020).

26 See for more: Crawford, Kate: The Atles of AI: The Real Worlds of Artificial Intelligence, Yale University Press 2021; D'Ignazio, Catherine; Klein, Lauren F: Data-Feminism, MIT Press 2020; Digital Freedom Fund: The Decolonising Data Panel. In: YouTube, https://www.youtube.com/watch?v=WRobUCm13m4 ; Fubara-Manuel, Irene: Biometric Capture: Disrupting the Digital Codification of Black Migrants in the UK. In: African Diaspora of April 2, 2020, S. 117–141; Van Dijck, José: Datafication, dataïsm and dataveillance: Big Data between scientific paradigm and ideology. In: Surveillance & Society 2014 12(2), S. 197–208; Gitelman, Lisa: Raw data is an oxymoron, MIT Press: 2013.

but it is the other way around. The bias is in the data that is used to train the algorithms and in the decisions made by humans in the design of the algorithms. The bias might be hidden by the promise of neutrality that goes out from the technology, but in fact, it has the power to unjustly discriminate at a much larger scale than biased individuals.[27] This means that the categories, profiles, algorithms etc all entail, reproduce and exacerbate this bias. When we use these tools to surveil people, which effectively means to sort people, the systemic inequality is reinforced to say the least. We could also say it in more simple words: Biometric surveillance technologies like facial recognition are racist and sexist.

Some examples: Since corona made us all work and study from home, it hurts me to see the messages of frustrated black students and students of color who are having a hard time dealing with proctoring software failing to deliver a fair and valuable contribution to a functioning education system in this new situation in several ways. One of the most painful ones being that it shuts them out from entering their online exams because the facial recognition gives an error of "poor lighting".[28] One student that is also software researcher looked into Proctorio, one of the most used proctoring softwares. His research has shown that the software uses a facial detection model that is failing to detect black faces more than 50% of the time.[29]

This racism also plays a part in algorithms used to prioritise images and deciding who gets a digital stage and who doesn't, based on the characteristics in the picture. People with Twitter might be familiar with this experiment on the cropping algorithm of the social media platform.[30] The main goal of the algorithm is to make people click on links and let them stay on the platform. Therefore it prioritises the parts of content that it expects you to prefer. Resulting in that it gives the stage to the people on stage.

Then there is a great research from Joy Buolamwini called Gender Shades[31], where she shows how much better European and American facial

---

27 Cf. Benjamin, Ruha: Assessing risk, automating racism. In: Science (2019) vol. 366 issue 6464, p. 421–422.
28 Khan, Alivardi on Twitter on September 11, 2020, https://twitter.com/uhreeb/status/1304451031066083331
29 Cf. Feathers, Todd: Proctorio is using racist algorithms to detect faces. In: Vice of 8 April 2021 (May 11, 2021).
30 Cf. Arcieri, Tony on Twitter on September 20, 2020, https://twitter.com/bascule/status/1307440596668182528
31 Cf. Buolamwini, Joy: 2018, http://gendershades.org/

recognition systems are in recognising white males compared to the recognition of women of color, and thus how the chances of being false flagged are unequally spread over society, along the lines of privilege.

Database Scandals and Unethical Revenu Models

In the discussion about automated surveillance, this is sometimes portrayed as just a matter of technological deficiencies, and thus easily solvable. In that perspective, the solution lies in training these systems with bigger, more diverse datasets. And if the goal is to let the technology work equally well on everybody, and we look at technology as something that exists in a vacuum, it might be true. In taking this solution into the real world we live in today, it sketches a different scenario. Since technology does not exist in a vacuum, the problem of discriminatory effects is not just in the technology, but also in the deployment of it. We get to this later. First I want to pay some attention to the way in which the same problems reoccur in the so-called solution of attempts to de-bias this technology. We find that in database scandals and unethical revenu models.

A few examples, coming from the real world: To improve its Pixel 4 facial recognition technology, Google contractors targeted homeless people of color to collect more facial scans of people with darker skin. These people were offered a 5 dollar coupon in return for their face data, they were asked to play a "selfie-game", or tricked without knowing they were recorded.[32] Homeless people were specifically targeted because they were least likely to say anything to the media, and the most likely to be convinced by a small amount of money. There are too many stories to pay attention to them all in this article, but there are many examples of tech companies scraping our faces from the internet without permission and use them to fuel the development of their surveillance systems.[33]

---

32 Cf. Hollister, Sean: Google contractors reportedly targeted homeless people for Pixel 4 recognition. In: The Verge of October 2, 2019, https://www.theverge.com/2019/10/2/20896181/google-contractor-reportedly-targeted-homeless-people-for-pixel-4-facial-recognition (December 8, 2020).

33 Cf. Solon, Olivia: Facial recognition's 'dirty little secret': Millions of online photos scraped without consent. In: NBC News of March 19, 2019, https://www.nbcnews.com/tech/internet/facial-recognition-s-dirty-little-secret-millions-online-photos-scraped-n981921 (Dec 8, 2020); Murgua, Madhumita: Who's using your face? The

People even provide companies with their facial data in a more direct way. A quite well-known example is FaceApp, a free photo manipulation app that showed you what you would look like in 30 years after uploading a photo to their server. For a short time it was a very popular app, and many people gave their face to this company. And not just this company. In their privacy policy FaceApp stated that all data you gave them could be shared with other companies in their group, that could be expanded at any moment, and be used to develop their new technologies. So users of the app provided their data to a non-defined group of companies that can use it to develop their own technologies and services. It should not be surprising that when this data consists of faces, the services and technologies that are trained also include face surveillance systems. By wanting to have a look into the future, the future will be watching us.[34]

The largest scandal of the year might have been the now infamous company Clearview AI that scraped three billion images from the internet, put it in a database and sold it to law enforcement as a service that gives them easy access to personal information on people. It enabled police officers to walk on the streets, make pictures of people, upload it in the app and get to see public photos of that person with links to where these photos appeared on the internet. It is important that although this already happened so often that we keep seeing these as scandals and unethical revenu models, because the internet

ugly truth about facial recognition. In: the Financial Times of September 18, 2019, https://www.ft.com/content/cf19b956-60a2-11e9-b285-3acd5d43599e (December 8, 2020); Roberts, Jeff John: The Business of your face: While you weren't looking, tech companies help themselves to your photos to power a facial recognition boom. Here's how. In: Fortune of March 27, 2019, https://fortune.com/longform/facial-recognition/ (Dec 8, 2020); Hill, Kashmir: How photo's of your kids are powering surveillance technology. In: The New York Times of 11 October 2019, https://www.nytimes.com/interactive/2019/10/11/technology/flickr-facial-recognition.html (Dec 8, 2020); Liao, Shannon: IBM didn't inform people when it used their Flickr photos for facial recognition training. In: the Verge of March 12, 2019, https://www.theverge.com/2019/3/12/18262646/ibm-didnt-inform-people-when-it-used-their-flickr-photos-for-facial-recognition-training (December 8, 2020) and there are many, many more.

34 Cf. Houwing, Lotte: FaceApp: Van kijken naar bekeken worden. In: Bits of Freedom of July 19, 2019, https://www.bitsoffreedom.nl/2019/07/19/faceapp-van-kijken-naar-bekeken-worden/ (December 8, 2020).

is not a face database for the development of mass surveillance technology.[35] And it should not be.

The Problem is Not Just Technological

The creation of those bigger, more diverse databases is not making the picture more beautiful. However, there is something more important going on. Focussing on the aspect of technological accuracy is leading the attention away from a more broad discussion and context of racialised surveillance. Solving the accuracy problem is just making sure that the technology is working equally well ON everybody, leaving the question whether it works equally well FOR everybody unaddressed. It might be that we are talking about technology that becomes more dangerous the better it works.

Even if the technology would be de-biased, it is highly likely that it will be disproportionately used against communities of color.[36] It would be used mostly for policing less serious crimes associated with poverty and against people in more vulnerable positions like protestors.[37] Since these problems are ingrained in larger society, fixing the discriminatory effects of biometric surveillance technology is not that simple. There is more work to be done.

---

35   Cf. Hill, Kashmir: The secretive company that might end privacy as we know it. In: The New York Times of January 18, 2020, https://www.nytimes.com/2020/01/18/technology/clearview-privacy-facial-recognition.html (December 8, 2020).

36   Cf. Chowdhury, A: Unmasking Facial Recognition. an exploration of the racial bias implications of facial recognition surveillance in the United Kingdom. In: webrootsdemocracy.org: 2020.

37   Cf. Gellman, Barton; Adler-Bell, Sam: The Disparate Impact of Surveillance.In: The Century Foundation of December 21, 2017, https://tcf.org/content/report/disparate-impact-surveillance/?agreed=1 (December 8, 2020); Henly, Jon; Booth, Robert: Welfare surveillance system violate human rights, Dutch court rules. In: The Guardian of February 5, 2020, https://www.theguardian.com/technology/2020/feb/05/welfare-surveillance-system-violates-human-rights-dutch-court-rules (December 8, 2020).

Mass Surveillance

Often when surveillance technology is introduced, arguments are made that it will only be used to combat serious crimes, and deployed in a targeted manner. But this is impossible. To recognize this one person in the crowd, the technology has to scan every passerby, process their physical data and match it to the database. Especially when this is deployed in a publicly accessible space, the effect of the deployment of this technology is untargeted and amounts to mass-scale processing of very sensitive, biometric data.

The databases that entail the list of persons who the so-called targeted deployment of the technology is aiming for show a great drive to expand. In 2016, a study from Georgetown Law's Center on Privacy and Technology found that half of US adults were already recorded in police facial recognition databases.[38] In the Netherlands it is already 1 in every 12 adults.[39]

These large scale databases and untargeted effects of the deployment of surveillance technologies mean that fundamental principles of the rule of law are not being upheld. Where the rule of law requires reasonable suspicion before infringing capabilities can be deployed against citizens, untargeted mass surveillance technologies start with treating everybody as a suspect. We have to be very conscious that with the choices we make in which technology we are going to use, especially in public space, we are shaping our gaze into society and society itself. Therefore we should include in those processes the question: what kind of society do we want?

(Self)Regulation Won't Do

We do not need (self)regulation of biometric surveillance technology in publicly accessible spaces, we need to get rid of it.

Calling for a regulatory framework might imply to some that current legislation is ambiguous about the acceptability of biometric mass surveillance. We need to be very clear that assessing biometric surveillance in the

---

[38] Cf. Garvie, Clare; Bedoya, Alvaro/Frankie, Jonathan: The Perpetual Line-Up: Unregulated police facerecognition in America. Georgetown Law Center on Privacy and Technology October 18, 2016, https://www.perpetuallineup.org/

[39] Cf. Houwing, Lotte: We need to be bolder. In: Bits of Freedom of 30 January 2020, https://www.bitsoffreedom.nl/2020/01/30/we-need-to-be-bolder/ (December 8, 2020).

light of the European Convention on Human Rights, the Charter of Fundamental Rights of the European Union, and the principles set out in the General Data Protection Regulation, do not leave space for the deployment of these biometric surveillance technologies in publicly accessible spaces, since it requires mass-scale processing of biometric data.

Regulation implies a limited legitimization. My concern is that we will not be able to contain the use of biometric surveillance. History has taught us never to underestimate the power of function creep. There are several ways the use and effects of facial recognition surveillance might expand over time. First, the legal basis and/or the scope of the basis can be expanded. Limiting the use of such far-reaching technology to combating terrorism might sound limited, but the limitation and therefore protections are dependent on government classifications. Several examples around the world, including in the Netherlands, show that even non-violent citizen interests groups are classified as 'extremist' or 'terrorist' when more powers to surveil these groups are desired. A second example of how function creep will take place, is with regards to access to the data. Waiving the fraud-prevention-flag, and showing a complete distrust of citizens, government institutions are very keen to share access and combine databases. Why would databases filled with our biometric data be exempt from this data hunger?[40]

Several companies pleaded for a moratorium. However, more than anything else, what a moratorium will result in, is time. Time in which the technology will become normalized. Time in which industry will deploy its lobbyists. Time in which the companies at the forefront of product development, search for and find product-market-fit. Time in which civil society will again and again mobilize citizens until those citizens become fatigued and weary, and disbelieving that their voice makes a difference.

Then there are the tech companies themselves, taking part in the political discussion that have evolved about facial recognition. We already see this happening in communications from tech companies. The CEO of IBM wrote a letter to Congress to sunset their general purpose facial recognition.[41] And a little later Amazon followed with a one year moratorium on the use of the

---

40   Cf. Ibid.
41   Cf. Krishna, Arvind: A letter from our CEO on IBM.org: 2019, https://www.ibm.org/responsibility/2019/letter (December 8, 2020).

technology by law enforcement.[42] It is hard however, to see this as anything else than a PR stunt.

The EDRi-network wrote IBM a letter with a request for more information about their statement. It included questions like "Which contracts will be stopped as a result? Which contracts won't? How does IBM define general purpose? Has IBM engaged fundamental rights experts? Do these steps apply only to the US, or to IBM's global activities?" In the response the Chief Privacy Officer of the company only reiterated the general statement and gave some more information about initiatives on artificial intelligence and ethics IBM participated in. Not a single question that was asked, was answered.[43]

We're concerned, therefore, that the demand for a moratorium isn't bold enough. We believe existing regulation needs to be enforced, banning the deployment of facial recognition as a surveillance tool in public space.

Conclusion

The important notions that Lefebvre describes when it comes to the right to the city are all put under pressure by the deployment of biometric surveillance in publicly accessible spaces: Building a community and have our community events in freedom. The freedom to be ourselves and live our lives the way we want to and we believe it should be lived. Without having to abide to a norm that is an arbitrairy average, destilled out of big data and forced upon is by technology that makes assumptions of suspicion about every person, every body and every behaviour that deviates from this norm. And the ability to give shape to public space in a way that it facilitates the needs of the people that use it, instead of just the commercial interests of tech companies or the interests of people who are responsible for enforcing public order.

The introduction of biometric mass surveillance in publicly accessible spaces reduces lively public spaces to spaces where technology is monitoring,

---

42 Cf. Kari, Paul: Amazon to ban police use of facial recognition software for a year. In: The Guardian of 11 June 2020, https://www.theguardian.com/technology/2020/jun/10/amazon-rekognition-software-police-black-lives-matter (December 8, 2020).

43 Cf. European Digital Rights: IBM's facial recognition: the solution cannot be left to companies. In: https://www.edri.org of July 17, 2020, https://edri.org/our-work/ibm-facial-recognition-solution-cannot-be-left-to-companies/ (December 8, 2020).

analysing, judging and manipulating us and our behaviour. It reduces variety among people to different ways in which people deviate from norms, that can be quantified into risk scores based on which people can be sorted into different regimes at airports and border or ticketcontrols. It reduces people to walking barcodes that can be scanned while walking the streets, linking their physical appearances to information about them in existing and searchable databases. And if we don't pay attention, it reduces our minds and what we perceive as possible or acceptable ways to shape our future realities and approach each other and our differences with an open mind.

Current legislation does not leave space for the mass processing of biometric data, and thus not for biometric surveillance technology in public spaces. However, in practice we see it popping up like mushrooms in autumn. Often introduced as pilots, surveillance technology finds its way in, but once introduced these kinds of technology tend to stick around. Therefore, we need a clear statement from the EU and national legislators to protect our public spaces and democratic rights. Their task is clear: Ban biometric mass surveillance.

Preferably this would be layed down in a human-rights based piece of legislation, but there are opportunities for this in upcoming legal instruments as well, like the European legislation on AI. The Commission published their proposal the 21nd of April 2021 and included a very limited ban on real time biometric identification systems in publicly accessible spaces for law enforcement purposes.[44] By including this ban the European Commission shows she acknowledges the far-reaching infringements biometric surveillance in oublicly accessible spaces is making into our fundamental rights, and the risks it brings along for our free societies. However, by the way it is formulated at the moment it will not solve this: The ban is too narrow, the exceptions are too broad and there is too much unclarity that leaves room for misuse.[45]

---

44 Cf. https://digital-strategy.ec.europa.eu/en/library/proposal-regulation-laying-down-harmonised-rules-artificial-intelligence-artificial-intelligence.

45 Cf. Houwing, Lotte: Europees AI wetsvoorstel laat zien waarom wij vechten voor een verbod. In: Bits of Freedom of April 22, 2021, https://www.bitsoffreedom.nl/2021/04/22/europese-ai-wetgeving-laat-zien-waarom-wij-vechten-voor-een-verbod/ (May 11, 2021); Reclaim Your Face: European Commission's proposal for new AI Regulation shows exactly why we are fighting to ban BMS. In: Reclaim Your Face of April 21, 2021, https://reclaimyourface.eu/european-commission-proposal-new-ai-regulation-fighting-ban-biometric-mass-surveillance/ (May 11, 2021).

We don't need to regulate biometric surveillance technologies, we need to ban them. That's not just my position, but the position of many surveillance experts and (digital) human rights activists in civil society. Together with several digital rights organisations throughout Europe we gathered forces in the Reclaim Your Face campaign to make this ban a reality. We have launched a European Citizens' Initiative to call the European Commision to seize the chance it has to set a global example in upcoming AI legislation to protect our fundamental rights and public spaces against the harm that biometric mass surveilance can do. We need one million signatures of EU-citizens within a year, so we urge all of you to #ReclaimYourFace with us. Go check it out, and sign, at https://www.reclaimyourface.eu

This Citizens' Initiative is just one form of struggle against one form of algorithms limiting our freedoms. But there are many more and there is much more to be done. If you are now asking yourself the question: What else can I do (in the meantime)? Remember the title of this book. Here is some inspiration:

- Here you can find the ultimate stalker tool project we did with the public livestreams and Amazon's Rekognition: h*ttps://www.bitsoffreedom.nl/2019/12/12/amazons-rekognition-shows-its-true-colors/*
- Students from the Digital Society School developed a prototype mouthmask on which you can print an AI generated face, to trigger misidentification by facial recognition technology that is trained to recognize masked up faces: *http://projecthiveminds.com/ph/letsfaceit.php*
- They also made this analogue webcam filter that is 3p printable and provides you with privacy during your videocalls without letting your personal space be analyzed by algorithms: *http://projecthiveminds.com/ph/filteredreality.php*
- You can make your own LED throwies that stick to surveillance technology in public spaces to make them more visible and inform people about their presence. Here is a guide on how to make them: *https://www.instructables.com/LED-Throwies/*
- Several designers made fashion that protects you against surveillance. Some examples: *https://www.newyorker.com/magazine/2020/03/16/dressing-for-the-surveillance-age | https://www.theguardian.com/world/2019/aug/13/the-fashion-line-designed-to-trick-surveillance-cameras | https://mashable.com/article/anti-surveillance-masks/?europe=true | https://yr.media/tech/guide-to-anti-surveillance-fashion/*

In this piece I elaborated on the risks and problems of biometric surveillance technologies. I also wrote about our European Citizens' Initiative as one way to address this. As shown by the examples there are much more strateies of disobedience possible. I hope this will inspire others to keep on fighting against algorithms where they are limiting our freedoms and imagination.

Literature

Benjamin, Ruha: Assessing risk, automating racism. In: Science (2019) vol. 366 issue 6464, S. 421–422.

Buolamwini, Joy: 2018, http://gendershades.org/

Chowdhury, A: Unmasking Facial Recognition. an exploration of the racial bias implications of facial recognition surveillance in the United Kingdom. In: Webrootsdemocracy.org 2020.

Doringer, Bogomir: When you feel pain, keep on dancing. In: TQW of 24 June 2020, https://tqw.at/when-you-feel-pain-keep-on-dancing-doringer/

European Digital Rights: IBM's facial recognition: the solution cannot be left to companies. In: https://www.edri.org of July 17, 2020, https://edri.org/our-work/ibm-facial-recognition-solution-cannot-be-left-to-companies/

Galic, Maša: Surveillance, privacy and public space in the Stratumseind Living Lab: the smart city debate, beyond data. In: Ars Aequi 2019, July/August.

Galič, Maša; Schuilenburg, Marc: Reclaiming the Smart City: Toward a New Right to the City. In: Juan Carlos Augusto, Handbook of Smart Cities 2020.

Gallagher, Ryan; Jona, Ludovica: We tested Europe's new lie detector for travelers and immediately triggered a false positive. In: The Intercept of July 26, 2019, https://theintercept.com/2019/07/26/europe-border-control-ai-lie-detector/

Garvie, Clare; Bedoya, Alvaro/Frankie, Jonathan: The Perpetual Line-Up: Unregulated police facerecognition in America. Georgetown Law Center on Privacy and Technology October 18, 2016, https://www.perpetuallineup.org/

Gellman, Barton; Adler-Bell, Sam: The Disparate Impact of Surveillance. In The Century Foundation of December 21, 2017, https://tcf.org/content/report/disparate-impact-surveillance/?agreed=1

Harwell, Drew; Dou, Eva: Huawei tested AI software that could recognize Uighur minorities and alert police, report says. In: The Washington Post of December 8, 2020, https://www.washingtonpost.com/technology/2020/12/08/huawei-tested-ai-software-that-could-recognize-uighur-minorities-alert-police-report-says/

Henly, Jon; Booth, Robert: Welfare surveillance system violate human rights, Dutch court rules. In: The Guardian of February 5, 2020, https://www.theguardian.com/technology/2020/feb/05/welfare-surveillance-system-violates-human-rights-dutch-court-rules

Hill, Kashmir: The secretive company that might end privacy as we know it. In: The New York Times of January 18, 2020, https://www.nytimes.com/2020/01/18/technology/clearview-privacy-facial-recognition.html

Hollister, Sean: Google contractors reportedly targeted homeless people for Pixel 4 recognition. In: The Verge of October 2, 2019, https://www.theverge.com/2019/10/2/20896181/google-contractor-reportedly-targeted-homeless-people-for-pixel-4-facial-recognition

Hooyman, Paula: Amazons Rekognition shows its true colors. In: Bits of Freedom of December 12, 2019, https://www.bitsoffreedom.nl/2019/12/12/amazons-rekognition-shows-its-true-colors/

Houwing, Lotte: Experimentele Manipulatie: Burger steeds vaker onwetend proefdier. In: Bits of Freedom of 5 June 2019, https://www.bitsoffreedom.nl/2019/06/05/experimentele-manipulatie-burger-steeds-vaker-onwetend-proefdier/

Houwing, Lotte: Europees AI wetsvoorstel laat zien waarom wij vechten voor een verbod. In: Bits of Freedom of April 22, 2021. https://www.bitsoffreedom.nl/2021/04/22/europese-ai-wetgeving-laat-zien-waarom-wij-vechten-voor-een-verbod/

Houwing, Lotte: FaceApp: Van kijken naar bekeken worden. In: Bits of Freedom of July 19, 2019, https://www.bitsoffreedom.nl/2019/07/19/faceapp-van-kijken-naar-bekeken-worden/

Houwing, Lotte: Stop the Creep of Biometric Surveillance Technology. In: European Data Protection Law Review (2020), nr. 2, S. 174.

Houwing, Lotte: We need to be bolder. In: Bits of Freedom of 30 January 2020, https://www.bitsoffreedom.nl/2020/01/30/we-need-to-be-bolder/

Kari, Paul: Amazon to ban police use of facial recognition software for a year. In: The Guardian of June 11, 2020, https://www.theguardian.com/technology/2020/jun/10/amazon-rekognition-software-police-black-lives-matter

Krishna, Arvind: A letter from our CEO. In IBM.org: 2019, https://www.ibm.org/responsibility/2019/letter

Lefebvre, Henri: Writings on cities. Cambridge 1996.

Lyon, David: Surveillance Power and Everyday Life. In: Oxford Handbook of Information and Communication Technologies, (2007).

Morozov, Evgeny: To save everything, click Here. New York 2013.

Mozur, Paul: In Hong Kong protests, faces become weapons. In: The New York Times of Juli 26, 2019, https://www.nytimes.com/2019/07/26/technology/hong-kong-protests-facial-recognition-surveillance.html

Ng, Alfred: Your face mask selfies could be training the next facial recognition tool. In: Cnet of May 19, 2020, https://www.cnet.com/news/your-face-mask-selfies-could-be-training-the-next-facial-recognition-tool/

Rasch, Miriam: Ethiek in tijden van dataïsme. Amsterdam 2020.

Reason TV: Hong Kong protestors combat the surveillance state. In: Youtube of October 4, 2019, https://www.youtube.com/watch?v=VXog6t4kNyc

Reclaim Your Face: European Commission's proposal for new AI Regulation shows exactly why we are fighting to ban BMS. In: Reclaim Your Face of April 21, 2021, https://reclaimyourface.eu/european-commission-proposal-new-ai-regulation-fighting-ban-biometric-mass-surveillance/

Schwartz, Oscar: Don't look now, why you should be worried about machines reading your emotions. In: The Guardian of March 6, 2019, https://www.theguardian.com/technology/2019/mar/06/facial-recognition-software-emotional-science

Tsvetkov, Egor: Your Face is Big Data. In: Cargo Collective, https://cargocollective.com/egortsvetkov/Your-Face-Is-Big-Data

Willsher, Kim: Story of Cities #12: Hausmann rips up Paris—and divides France to this day. In: The Guardian vom March 31, 2016, https://www.theguardian.com/cities/2016/mar/31/story-cities-12-paris-baron-haussmann-france-urban-planner-napoleon

de Zwart, Hans: 'Geen gezicht'—De Big Brother Awards speech van Hans de Zwart. In: Bits of Freedom of November 15, 2016, https://www.bitsoffreedom.nl/2016/11/15/geen-gezicht-de-big-brother-awards-speech-van-hans-de-zwart/

Bernd Friedrich Schon

Identity 5.0: How to Fight Algorithms Online (Fast)

Heuristic Compressions of Personality Concepts (Dis)Obedient to Algorithmic Power— from Film, Television and a Cult Classic Novel

Identity 5.0: How to Fight Algorithms Online (Fast)

"This is the voice of world control. I bring you peace.
It may be the peace of plenty and content
or the peace of unburied death.
The choice is yours.
Obey me and live.
Or disobey and die."
"Colossus: The Forbin Project" (USA 1970)

How does the increasing influence of algorithms[1] shape the development of current and future identities[2], the idea of what it means to be human? What can we learn from fictional characters to counter surveillance,

[1] The mathematical use of algorithms can be traced back roughly four thousand years to the ancient Sumerian civilization, the word algorithm to the ninth century, to Persian polymath Muhammad ibn Musa al-Khwarizmi. The term algorithm stems from the Latinization of his name al-Khwarizmi to "Algorithmi", that took place three hundred years later (cf. Zweig, Katharina: Ein Algorithmus hat kein Taktgefühl, Munich 2019, p. 50). It describes a step-by-step procedure to solve mathematical problems. The evident example is the navigation system that calculates the shortest route based on the current position and a given destination (cf. ibid., pp. 50–51). In machine or deep learning algorithms, it is not the compilation of rules that comes first (as it is the case in rule-based algorithms), but rather an input data set used to train an artificial neural network. Since such algorithmic systems learn similarly to living organisms—via trial and error—they are subsumed under the term artificial intelligence or AI (cf. Fry, Hannah: Hello World. Was Algorithmen können und wie sie unser Leben verändern, Munich 2019, p. 23). The machine is given a goal, fed data, and manages to figure out how to reach the goal by itself. Such algorithmic systems can become black boxes even for their programmers. Their key advantage is that, by analysing a mass of data, they can detect even weak correlations invisible to humans.

[2] The term "identity" is understood here as an individual's communicatively constructed self-image determined by social constraints (cf. Akremi, Leila: Kommunikative Konstruktion von Zukunftsängsten. Imaginationen zukünftiger Identitäten im dystopischen Spielfilm, Wiesbaden 2016, p. 41). While the identity was extensively predetermined in traditional societies, it is becoming increasingly performative in modern, especially in pluralistic and individualistic ones. Successful identity work is measured by individuals from the inside by the criterion of authenticity and from the outside by the criterion of recognition (cf. Keupp, Heiner: Vom Ringen um Identität in der spätmodernen Gesellschaft, Lindau 2010, p. 14). Recent research suggests that human beings behave irrationally and inconsistently, they are increasingly perceived as subjective, biased, and manipulable. In this context, Zweig refers to Kahnemann's research on the irrationality of humans and Thalers idea of "nudging" (cf. Zweig 2019, p. 10). This gives rise to the assumption

manipulation and control, executed by machines? Is the assumption of an overpowering algorithmic influence perhaps itself contaminated by fiction?

With digital transformation, the influence of algorithms rises, they have crept into almost every area of modern life—health, crime, traffic and politics. Algorithms evaluate our personality, help us navigate and find our partners, and declare us creditworthy or not.[3] Algorithms accumulate behavioral data, make decisions, monitor, predict future actions, manipulate and discipline.

Regarding the rapid technological developments of data mining and deep learning, innovative optimism arises, but also a feeling of unease. Citizens become more and more uncomfortable about the mostly non-transparent collection of data and hence the resulting power of companies, governmental and other actors who utilize this data.

Artist James Bridle sees himself transferred into a "New Dark Age" in which technology plays not a salvific but a sinister role.[4] Political scientist Sebastian Heilmann described the implementation of "Sesame Credit", the Chinese "Social Credit System", as a sort of "techno-authoritarianism".[5] Adrian Lobe states that, in the current age of "datopocene", such techno-authoritarianism is realized almost everywhere.[6] Social psychologist Shoshana Zuboff also criticized the developing of a "surveillance capitalism" and demanded increased protection of personal data and transparency[7], Peter Schaar believed "post privacy" to be a road to a "surveillance society".[8]

---

that intelligent machines are more incorruptible than humans, capable of more objective decisions.

3 Cf. Schaar, Peter: Das digitale Wir. Unser Weg in die transparente Gesellschaft, Hamburg 2015, p. 50.

4 Cf. James Bridle: New Dark Age, Munich 2019.

5 Cf. Unknown author: China-Experte: Corona-Pandemie treibt Techno-Autoritaritarismus in China voran. Osnabrück, 25/01 (2021), https://www.presseportal.de/pm/58964/4820118 (November 13, 2021).

6 Cf. Lobe, Adrian: Speichern und Strafen. Die Gesellschaft im Datengefängnis, Munich 2019. By "datopocene", Lobe is referring to a phase in human history, in which search engines, smartphone apps, fitness trackers, and 'smart homes' store data about their users and pass it on to service providers, who in turn improve their products and service with them—but also are possibly trading on these data.

7 Cf. Zuboff, Shoshana: Zeitalter des Überwachungskapitalismus, Munich 2018.

8 Cf. Schaar, Peter: Das Ende der Privatsphäre: der Weg in die Überwachungsgesellschaft, Munich 2009.

Regardless of the political systems in which algorithms are used: Constant measurement of their inhabitants seems to inevitably lead to social adaptation. It can be assumed that algorithms shape the identity of the homo digitalis—whether he is aware of this or not.

Looking to the future, several dystopians go far beyond aforementioned warnings: They fear the development of a Singularity, an AGI (Artificial General Intelligence) that surpasses human intelligence.[9] Back in 2014, the now deceased cosmologist Stephen Hawking warned: "The development of full artificial intelligence could spell the end of the human race."[10] Computer scientist Kai-Fu Lee also explains that a super intelligent entity could effortlessly wipe out humanity.[11] Bostrom, who has interviewed several AI researchers, indicates that the median forecast for an AGI to be developed is 2040.[12] According to the dystopians, it could very quickly become urgent to counteract threatening algorithms and the development of even more powerful machines.[13]

But how can we escape or resist algorithms? How might forms of disobedience to constant algorithmic surveying, monitoring, manipulation, control or even deadly force look like?

---

9 Oxford philosopher Nick Bostrom considers such a "superintelligence" an existential risk (cf. Superintelligenz, Frankfurt 2014), Tesla founder Elon Musk the greatest risk that human civilization will have to face (cf. Lee, Kai-Fu: AI Superpowers. China, Silicon Valley und die neue Weltordnung, Frankfurt/New York 2019, p. 187). Physicist Antony Garrett Lisi assumes that robots will rule us in the future (cf. Brockmann, John [Ed.]: Was sollen wir von der künstlichen Intelligenz halten? Frankfurt 2017, p. 52)—which is why the roboticist Anthony Levandowski already founded, as a precautionary measure, the "Way of the Future Church", which intends to realize, accept and worship an AI-based deity made of hardware and software (cf. Zweig 2019, pp. 269–270).

10 Rory Cellan-Jones: Stephen Hawking warns artificial intelligence could end mankind, BBC News, 02/12 (2014), https://www.bbc.com/news/technology-30290540 (November 13, 2021).

11 Cf. Lee 2019, p. 188.

12 Cf. ibid.

13 The situation appears even more virulent, regarding the so-called "Collingridge dilemma": In his 1981 book "The Social Control of Technology", David Collingridge explained that the unintended side effects of a new technology are often only identified once it has become so widespread that it will be reversed at great economic expense, if at all. An obvious example is the internal combustion engine and individualized traffic. Cf. Zweig 2019, p. 279.

Cinema, television and literature test ways of resistance against rulers and usurpers within the realms of aesthetics. But might an evaluation of these experimental attempts be profitable in respect to disobedience to algorithmic power?

An examination of fiction should not be aiming at empirically supported predictions about probable futures.[14] Nevertheless, literature, films and TV serials must be regarded as defining forces, due to an ontological shift within scientific discourses. For if the concept of reality was previously conceived as societal mediated, it has been increasingly understood as communicatively constructed since the 1990s.[15] But if our knowledge about reality—and thus about identity—is acquired communicatively, mass media must be considered influential. Schroer presumes that our knowledge on social topics as 'work', 'poverty', 'family', 'gender', 'art', 'law', 'religion', 'economy', 'city' or 'surveillance' comes to a large extent from cinema.[16]

As objectifications of social desires, hopes, and fears, movies contribute to (self-)observation of society.[17] And cinema, television, and literature have always, by presenting heroes, victims, villains, or even ordinary persons, made offers of identity concepts.[18]

Those imaginations accumulate by time, so that the future is mostly thought of in concepts from (science) fiction[19]—a "colonization of the future" (Giddens).[20] Evidence for this is that companies or technologies are named after fictional elements: "Palantir Technologies'" name stems from the "palantíri", the indestructible crystals of J. R. R. Tolkien's "Middle Earth",

---

14 Cf. Akremi 2016, p. 116.
15 Cf. ibid., p. 7. In this context, Akremi refers especially to the work of Hubert Knoblauch (1995, 2010, 2013).
16 Cf. Schroer, Markus: Die Soziologie und der Film. In: Schroer, Markus (Ed.): Gesellschaft im Film, Konstanz 2008, p. 10.
17 Cf. Akremi 2016, p. 118, p. 620. Incidentally, this is also true for aged fiction—cult movies and classics—which can influence society far beyond their release date (cf. ibid., p. 126), which is why these are also dealt with in this article.
18 Cf. Peltzer, Anja: Identität und Spektakel. Der Hollywood-Blockbuster als global erfolgreicher Identitätsanbieter, Konstanz 2011.
19 Cf. Steinmüller, Karlheinz: Gestaltbare Zukünfte. Zukunftsforschung und Science Fiction. Werkstattbericht 23. Sekretariat für Zukunftsforschung, Gelsenkirchen 1995, p. 3, https://steinmuller.de/de/zukunftsforschung/downloads/WB%2013%20Science%20Fiction.pdf (November 13, 2021).
20 Cf. Giddens, Anthony: Modernity and Self-Identity. Self and Society in the Late Modern Age, Cambridge 1991, p. 111.

with which one can look into the future or the past[21]—and a NSA surveillance program is named after the antagonistic computer network "Skynet" of the "Terminator" cinema series (USA 1984, 1991, 2003, 2009, 2015).[22]

Within science fiction, hacker films, espionage thrillers, in arthouse cinema and biopics, there are depictions which—mutatis mutandis—show strategies of disobedience that could be useful against algorithms. From a multitude of character concepts, four heuristic ideal types are compressed below, each of which is paradigmatic for a specific approach against algorithmic force: E-pimetheus, Phantom, E-xistentialist and Dice Man. These four 'disobedient' identity types are preceded by an 'obedient' Puppet Identity to illustrate different dimensions of algorithm dependence. The compression undertaken is inspired by the method of distant reading.[23]

---

[21] Cf. Sontheimer et al.: Palantir Technologies: Die geheimnisvollen Datensortierer. 30/10 (2020). In: ZEIT Online, https://www.zeit.de/digital/internet/2020-09/palantir-technologies-daten-analyse-boersengang-peter-thiel-alex-karp/komplettansicht (November 13, 2021).

[22] Cf. Zweig 2019, p. 172. Made public by the leak of Edward Snowden in 2013, the "Skynet" software is designed to determine the risk of terrorist activity from the cell phone data of 55 million users.

[23] The term "distant reading" was coined by the literary scholar Franco Moretti and means looking at as many works as possible from a great distance and evaluating already existing secondary literature—with a focus on overarching patterns and systems. Cf. Moretti, Franco: Distant Reading, Konstanz 2016; Moretti, Franco: Kurven, Karten, Bäume. Abstrakte Modelle für die Literaturgeschichte, Frankfurt 2009. At the Stanford Literary Lab, of which Moretti is director, computers are used to process large quantities of text using statistical methods.

Puppet Identity

Algorithms exercise a secret power, they slowly and imperceptibly change what it means to be human. In the fictional domestic plot of "The Social Dilemma" (2020), a digital double of teenager Ben (Skyler Gisondo) is assembled from data points of his internet usage. As his doppelganger's appearance approaches Ben's, the boy becomes a puppet controlled by data collectors—they can predict and manipulate his actions.[24]

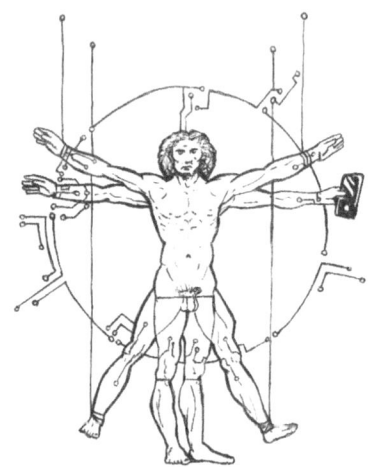

It seems obvious that the Puppet Identity is generous with its data, exchanging it for products and services. It is no accident that dictatorial supercomputer "Colossus" demands total control by surveillance[25] and that the dystopian novel "We" by Yevgeny Zamyatin (1920; TV adaptation: 1982) depicts a state in which all buildings are made of glass.[26] Puppet Identity's willingness to provide data is not due to its naivety, but rather to economic conditions. Cathy O'Neil points out that the protection of personal data is increasingly becoming a luxury that only the wealthy can afford.[27]

Collected data is used to give us feedback, which is experienced as helpful where fitness trackers and productivity apps help us self-optimize or where online shops or streaming sites can effortlessly predict which products

---

24 It has to be said that reality is probably not as monocausal as director Jeff Orlowski depicts it, cf. Schinke, Chris: Das Dilemma mit den sozialen Medien, Bonn 2020, https://www.filmdienst.de/film/details/615660/das-dilemma-mit-den-sozialen-medien#kritik (November 13, 2021).

25 Cf. Akremi 2016, p. 411.

26 Cf. ibid., p. 92.

27 Cf. O'Neil, Cathy: Angriff der Algorithmen. Wie sie Wahlen manipulieren, Berufschancen zerstören und unsere Gesundheit gefährden, Munich 2017, p. 232.

and services suit our taste. At the same time, however, algorithmic systems pursue "optimization" in terms of their own agenda: to improve goods and services, but also to harvest, analyse and sell user data.

Jaron Lanier states that almost all providers based on siren servers attain information sovereignty through their superior computational capacities, thus almost inevitably leading to a monopoly position.[28] It is a concern of almost all providers that users spend as much time as possible with their platforms—which is discussed under the term "addictive technology".[29]

Algorithmic systems exploit Puppet Identity's flaws, e.g. designing privacy statements in such a way that it is more convenient to accept them unread or starting the following streaming series episode without asking. Puppet Identity thus spends its time using addictive technology while the number of its friends and likes in social networks publicly documents its esteem in which it is valued.[30]

But this does not mean that networking Puppet Identities would lead to stronger sense of social cohesion. Schaar refers to a study that demonstrates that digital natives trust other human beings significantly less than the generations of non-liners and digital immigrants—probably caused by the debate culture on the Internet, the lurking dangers of cyberbullying, "trolls" and shitstorms.[31] There is currently also widespread discussion about filter bubbles and echo chambers, that algorithmically automated adaptation of (also: news) content to consumer preferences leads to a lack of exchange with dissenters.

Interaction via social media platforms doesn't leave Puppet Identity sustainably happier: If the analysis of a user's online conduct reveals that she is more likely to buy certain products when she is sad, algorithmic systems will try to influence her emotional state accordingly—by displaying news content that also led her to "like" or share rather negative posts the last

---

28 Cf. Lanier Jaron: Wem gehört die Zukunft? Munich 2013, pp. 18. It is no surprise, then, that the market is currently dominated by a few major players, the so-called "Seven Giants of 'AI age'": Google, Facebook (now called "Meta"), Amazon, Microsoft, Baidu, Alibaba and Tencent (cf. Lee 2019, p. 115).

29 Cf. Zweig 2019, p. 273. See also: Alter, Adam: Unwiderstehlich—Der Aufstieg suchterzeugender Technologien und das Geschäft mit unserer Abhängigkeit, Munich 2017; Wu, Tim: The Attention Merchants. The Epic Struggle to Get Inside Our Heads, London 2017.

30 Cf. Schaar 2015, pp. 31–31.

31 Cf. ibid., p. 33.

times.³² Back in 2017, a study suggested that social media use could increase feelings of social isolation.³³

Puppet Identity's social adaptation is enhanced by its awareness of constant evaluation—its scorisation. According to Schep, there is a "digital reputation economy" emerging that leads to a "culture of conformity".³⁴ Schep speaks of social cooling, referring to chilling effects that Peter Schaar describes as intimidation reactions resulting from constant surveillance: Those who are monitored feel an urge to socially adapt and may even voluntarily refrain from asserting their rights.³⁵ Political scientist Adrian Lobe assumes that even a "post-punishment society" is emerging, because algorithms would prevent undesirable conduct in advance.

Predictions made by mathematical algorithms are reliably more accurate than those made by humans.³⁶ This has led to the widespread assumption that it is advisable to leave important decisions to intelligent machines. This is also the argument of the American president (Gordon Pinsent) in "Colossus": "Colossus' decisions are superior to any we humans can make. For it can absorb and process more knowledge than is remotely possible for the greatest genius that ever lived."³⁷

Accordingly, Puppet Identity blindly trusts the machines and defers a notable amount of decision-making to them—and thus increases its dependence on them. But since algorithms act as unfathomable black boxes, their judgment and decision come like a divine verdict. Respectively, in "Colossus", the American president warns his CIA official Grauber (William Schaller). When the latter asks: "Persistent evil, isn't he?"³⁸, he answers "Don't personalize it, Grauber. The next stop is deification".³⁹

---

32 Cf. Paar, Christof in: Barbera, Patrizia: Facebook & Co.: Das Dreieck des Wandels. 22/02 (2021), https://heise.de/-5061297 (November 13, 2021).
33 Cf. Primack, Brian A. et al.: Social Media Use and Perceived Social Isolation Among Young Adults in the U.S.. In: American Journal for Preventive Medicine, 06/03 (2017), https://doi.org/10.1016/j.amepre.2017.01.010 (November 13, 2021).
34 Cf. Schep, Tijmen: Social Cooling, https://www.tijmenschep.com/socialcooling/ (November 13, 2021).
35 Cf. Schaar 2015, pp. 167–168.
36 Cf. Fry 2019, p. 35.
37 Akremi 2016, p. 414.
38 Ibid.
39 Ibid. That humans are indeed prone to deification of computers in recognition of their amazing capabilities is evidenced by a statement made by chess grandmaster Garry Kasparov, who remarked a few days after losing to IBM's Deep Blue in

Puppet Identity nevertheless does not question the prognoses, judgments, and decisions of the algorithms, considers them objective, impartial, and safe, increasingly trusting them more than its own abilities. Back in 2015, psychologist Epstein explained that people assume that search engines make wise choices. Users do not even consciously notice when they are being manipulated, but assume they are forming their own opinion, they believe to have voluntarily adopted a certain way of thinking[40]—a phenomenon for which the acronym SEME (Search Engine Manipulation Effect) was coined.[41] The more its political and consumer decisions are guided by machines, the more manipulable Puppet Identity becomes. It seems evident, then, that it will be conformist, consumerist, fashionable, state of the art, self-optimized, and status-conscious.

Puppet Identity is not aware of the fact that algorithms can be prejudiced, that they may even reinforce preconceptions by not treating individuals as such but sorting them into "tribes" of similar ones—which in the worst case can lead to collective punishment, relying just on weak characteristics—e.g. how quickly the members of the cluster type or how charged their cell phone battery is.[42]

Since 'social engineering' is used in capitalist technocracies in the sense of Taylorism and Fordism primarily to increase productivity and efficiency of the workforce[43] and to adapt to needs of the market, Puppet Identity enters further technological dependencies.

It is quite likely that Puppet Identity will not be among those privileged by "new work". Schaar argues that numerous indicators suggest that the distribution of wealth will continue to polarize with increasing digitization. Steltzner expects that there will be a minority that tells the computer what to do—these few will possess the greatest wealth. Opposite them, there will be a much larger group of precariously employed people who will be told what to do by the computer.[44] Historian Yuval Noah Harari also fears that a tiny AI

May 1997 that the computer "suddenly played like God for a moment". Cf. Fry 2019, p. 18.
40 Cf. Fry 2019, pp. 28–29.
41 Epstein, Robert; Robertson, Ronald E.: The search engine manipulation effect (SEME) and its possible impact on the outcomes of elections. 04/08 (2015), https://www.pnas.org/content/112/33/E4512 (November 13, 2021).
42 Cf. Lee 2019, p. 152.
43 Cf. Akremi 2016, p. 316.
44 Cf. Schaar 2015, p. 20.

elite will be faced with a vast global "useless class", that most human beings will no longer succeed in creating enough economic value to make a living.[45]

So Puppet Identity's work is choreographed by sophisticated software utilizing every minute. If the market demands it, work must be done during the night, on public holidays or at weekends.[46] Puppet Identity will not rebel against exploitation for fear of ending up like some beggars on China's streets: With a paper showing QR codes for Alipay and WeChat.[47]

Movies like Fritz Lang's "Metropolis" (1926) or Chaplin's "Modern Times" (1936) created powerful images of how the working class is subjugated to the rhythm of machines.[48] "Colossus" meticulously dictates his entire daily routine to Dr. Forbin (Eric Braeden). Any resistance is immediately punished.[49] In Zamyatin's novel "We", the daily routine of all citizens is synchronized.[50]

By relying increasingly on automated systems, Puppet Identity also gradually loses its own capabilities—an effect that psychologist Lisanne Bainbridge described as an "Irony of Automation".[51] It is obvious that this effect is dangerous for its livelihood.

Puppet Identity even voluntarily pursues a self-algorithmization because of the prevailing optimization ideology. Computer scientist Lee describes how he quantified everything in his life, balanced those inputs, and fine-tuned the algorithm as much as possible[52]—which made him lose his humanity.[53] Focusing on (self-)optimization, he missed to lovingly interact with people closest to him.[54] Fascinated by his mission to invent machines that thought like humans, he transformed himself into a human who thought

---

45 Cf. Lee 2019, p. 226. Cf. also: Harari, Yuval Noah: The Rise of the Useless Class. 24/02 (2017). In: Ideas.Ted.Com, https://ideas.ted.com/the-rise-of-the-useless-class/ (November 13, 2021).
46 Cf. O'Neil 2017, pp. 171–172; pp. 177–178.
47 Cf. Lee 2019, p. 105.
48 Cf. Akremi 2016, p. 371.
49 Cf. ibid., p. 411.
50 Cf. ibid., p. 92.
51 Cf. Bainbridge, Lisanne: Ironies of Automation. In: Automatica, Vol. 19, Nº. 6, (Oxford 1983), https://ckrybus.com/static/papers/Bainbridge_1983_Automatica.pdf (November 13, 2021).
52 Cf. Lee 2019, p. 229.
53 Cf. ibid., pp. 243–244.
54 Cf. ibid., p. 230.

like a machine.[55] Determined by algorithms, Puppet Identity is in danger of evolving into a veritable "machine identity".[56]

Within classic dystopias, the individual is almost completely absorbed into a collective. Accordingly, human characters often have no name, but are designated by a sequence of numbers ("THX 1138" [1971]) or a series name ("Logan's Run" [1976], "The Island", [2005]). Feelings, creativity and empathy are often considered a threat here and are suppressed by means of sedatives ("THX 1138", "Equilibrium" [2002]).[57]

The situation is different for now emerging Puppet Identity: Thus it wants to appear (self-)optimized and en vogue, it must necessarily seem happy, beautiful and creative for this purpose.[58] In a paradoxical adaptation, Puppet Identity wants to display self-determined individuality through creative life design—and thus acts in conformity with the demands made on it.

Now that we have an idea of what an algorithm-"obedient" Puppet Identity resembles, we will move on to the four disobedient identities: E-pimetheus, Phantom, E-xistentialist, and Dice Man.

---

55 Cf. ibid.
56 Cf. Akremi 2016, p. 496.
57 Cf. Akremi 2016, p. 219. In Zamyatin's novel "We" creativity is seen as the ultimate threat for the state, therefore the citizens are urged to undergo a specific brain surgery to remove it. Cf. ibid., p. 93.
58 That creativity has now become a general social imperative is evidenced by Andreas Reckwitz's study "Die Erfindung der Kreativität", Frankfurt 2012.

E-pimetheus

Will the narcissism of mankind have to face a fourth severe blow?[59] After the—according to Freud[60]—1. cosmological blow accompanying Copernicus, that the earth is not the centre of the universe, the 2. biological blow following Darwin, that man emerged from the animal and the 3. psychological blow, that human action is largely determined by his unconscious, the 4. technological blow would be that tools created by man outperform their creator.[61]

The ongoing discourse on the growing influence of algorithms currently focuses on the competition between humankind and machine. The accelerating race in the real world is reflected in fictional imagery that often leads to a martial vanishing point: Human protagonists battle representatives of the machine sphere, e.g. anthropomorphic or shape-altering "Terminator" androids or intelligent computer programs that deceive humans by an illusionistic cyberspace to enslave them ("The Matrix" [1999]). Sometimes, this battle is fought in a more subtle way, for instance when android Ava (Alicia Vikander) in "Ex Machina" (2005) verbally manipulates her human counterpart.

Due to the aforementioned fourth severe blow, it is not surprising that humans empathize with their machines and imagine how their humiliated slaves ("Blade Runner" [1982], "I, Robot" [2004], "Westworld" [1973]) rise up, replace them ("A. I." [2001], "The Stepford Wives" [1975]), turn against them ("Terminator" series)—and take over as machine dictators

---

59   Cf. also: Zweig 2019, p. 269.
60   Cf. Freud, Sigmund: Eine Schwierigkeit der Psychoanalyse, 1917. In: GW, Vol. 12., Frankfurt 1984, pp. 1–12.
61   Chess computer Deep Blue already defeated the world's best chess player Kasparov in 1997, IBM computer Watson won the quiz "Jeopardy!" against the champions Rutter and Jennings in 2011 (cf. Schaar 2015, p. 50) and AlphaGo overcame the Chinese professional Go player Ke Jie in 2017 (cf. Lee 2019, p. 17).

("Alphaville" [1965], "Colossus", "The Matrix", "I, Robot"). Here, strangely enough, man dreams up his own submission, according to Eva Horn even his annihilation.[62] Apparently, because, as Akremi points out, he has caused his own dehumanization by himself.[63] The machines thus act as an avenging nemesis for human transgressions.

The characters that compete with intelligent machines can be condensed to the first ideal-typic identity concept called E-pimetheus. This first identity type is written with a hyphen to signal that the mythical character (Epimetheus [Ἐπιμηθεύς]) has been transferred to the electrified era of digital transformation. Even if the original model did not belong to humans, but to the Titans, its type is nevertheless intended here to characterise humans. And although its mythical origin was male, here E-pimetheus nevertheless represents a concept of identity independent of gender.

Its antique archetype was enchanted by Pandora—an artificial creation of Zeus—, opened her box that became proverbial, releasing all conceivable misfortune into the world. According to its descriptive name it is "one who thinks afterwards", which is understood here that only in retrospect it realises what kind of mischief it has (co-)caused.

It is a primal pattern of numerous science fiction plots that man develops a technology, is bewitched by its possibilities, but then, by its means, brings forth disaster. Afterwards, man seeks to humbly conquer the spirits he has called upon. Therefore, it is no coincidence that mythical Pandora is actualised in early science fiction cinema, appearing as the "false Maria" (Brigitte Helm), a gynoid, in Fritz Lang's "Metropolis" (1927).[64]

E-pimetheus acts as a memorial not to be overwhelmed by the possibilities and outward appearance of elegant new technologies, but rather to "think ahead" so that disaster does not occur in the first place. And E-pimetheus shall convince us that humanity can learn from its failures. It is calling for a rational and moral approach to innovations, a reflection on its values.

But as it is the "one who thinks afterwards", E-pimetheus also stands for those technophobes who act excessively for fear of disaster. E-pimetheus tends to take an overly martial approach to its opponents: It wants to turn

62 Cf. Horn, Eva: Zukunft als Katastrophe, Frankfurt 2014, p. 10.
63 Cf. Akremi 2016, p. 579.
64 A contemporary incarnation of "seduction by technology" can be seen in K's (Ryan Gosling) holographic AI girlfriend Joi (Anna de Armas), who appears in "Blade Runner 2049" (2017): It is never sure if she has a free will and loves K or if she is a kind of customized filter bubble/echo chamber, telling him only what he wants to hear.

them off, unplug, destroy and burn them, and may even threaten to wipe out technological achievements of centuries—as "Snake" Plissken (Kurt Russel) does with the words "Welcome to the Human Race" at the end of "Escape from L.A." (1996).

E-pimetheus' black-and-white thinking is a significant problem in our high-tech age.[65] Fry points out that we tend to trust algorithms too much, but as soon as we know that they can make mistakes, we overreact, no longer rely on them at all—a behavior for which researchers have coined the term algorithm aversion.[66]

But, if all efforts of man to compete with his machines were to be in vain, what would remain to him? He could at least try to hide from their detection range. Which leads us to the next ideal type.

Phantom

From all those characters who try to elude surveillance and manipulation—whistleblowers, activists, hackers, spies or criminals[67]—the identity concept of Phantom can be distilled, its intention is to become invisible to monitoring algorithms.

According to Peter Schaar, anonymity is often equated with irresponsibility: Those who do not disclose their identity are presumably intending to cheat or commit crimes.[68] And indeed, cybercrime and -bullying are unthinkable without anonymity. Which is why the demand for a kind of ban on mummery in virtual space seems understand-

---

65 Cf. Fry 2019, p. 37. Philosopher Rebekka Reinhard thinks in a similar direction. However, she believes the problem is that our thinking is getting successively alike the binary information processing of computers. Cf. Reinhard, Rebekka: Wach denken: Für einen zeitgemäßen Vernunftgebrauch, Hamburg 2020.
66 Cf. Ibid., p. 36.
67 But also from unknown-known celebrities like Thomas Pynchon, The Residents, Martin Margiela or Banksy.
68 Cf. Schaar 2015, p. 182.

able.[69] However, when almost every citizen on earth is tracked and analyzed by algorithms, the desire for privacy seems equally reasonable.

Subscribing to newsletters, filling out a warranty card, making search queries—personal data is always being harvested and sold, e.g. in the format of clickstreams—the path taken on a website—and geo-tags—geographic location details of the user[70]—in some cases even complete browser histories.[71]

Data brokers like Palantir, Acxiom, Corelogic, Datalogix, and eBureau[72] combine all this data, link it, and create comprehensive user profiles: Name, date of birth, religion, vacation habits, where and when you used your credit card, whether you participate in gambling, health restrictions, what medications you take, whether you had an abortion, whether your parents are divorced, whether you are a quick addict, whether you have been raped, how you feel about firearms, your outwardly presented sexual orientation, your actual sexual orientation, and how credulous you are.[73] Fry summarizes: In thousands of categories and files on secret servers, thousands of details are stored just about every one of us.[74]

Understandably, Phantom wants to protect itself from this access, tries to produce as little accessible data as possible or disinform through a plethora of false information. Respectively, Phantom sometimes deceives its pursuers by means of identity theft or doubles. Privacy activists who seek to restrict algorithmic access to personal data by means of political influence can also be subordinated to the Phantom identity.

Given that automated facial recognition procedures threaten anonymity—and that more and more personalized biometric information is available or can be gleaned from photographs[75], it is not surprising that it is typical for Phantom to mask itself. So, paradigmatic for this identity type are masks and disguises, also technical voice changer. The Guy Fawkes mask of the freedom fighter V (Hugo Weaving) from "V for Vendetta" (2005), which is now used by the "Occupy" movement and the hacker collective "Anonymous", has become

69   Cf. ibid.
70   Cf. O'Neil 2019, p. 197.
71   Cf. Fry 2019, p. 46.
72   Cf. ibid.
73   Cf. ibid., p. 47.
74   Cf. ibid.
75   Cf. Schaar 2015, pp. 185–186.

iconic.[76] But it's not only its face that Phantom's identity concept shrouds, but its hands as well. For now it has become possible to read fingerprints from a high-resolution photograph taken from a distance and to compare them with reference files.[77]

In Cyberspace, Avatars belonging to the identity type Phantom are mostly also in disguise ("Who Am I", [2014]), which shall signal the viewer that software is hiding the owner's identity.[78] Nevertheless, the identity of the user can be inferred from the content of the communication and from technical parameters of the hardware and software used, which is why Phantom encrypts or encodes its communication or avoids statements that allow such inferences to be made.[79]

That its virtual activities have real-world implications becomes clear when Phantom also tricks, deceives, and sometimes even lies in the empirical world (like Moritz (Maximilian Mundt) in "How to Sell Drugs Online (Fast)", since 2019), so that its identity is not revealed even when it literally acts unmasked.

Phantom exerts security precautions against surveillance not only by software but also by the circumspect handling of hardware: "Snowden" (2016) puts mobile phones into the microwave, covers the webcam lens of his notebook. Robert Dean (Will Smith), who has become the "Enemy of the State" (1998), speaks his mentor Brill (Gene Hackman) in a Faraday cage, which is supposed to prevent the interception of sensitive data.

In a figurative sense, the latter situation represents that the Phantom identity temporarily (as a digital detox) or even completely denies access to the Internet, as Newport promotes in his book on "Digital Minimalism"[80], just as the loosely organized Attention Resistance Movement.[81]

---

76 Contemporary artists like Sterling Crispin, Leonardo Selvaggio, and Zach Blas have developed masks that especially defy machine recognition. The works of Ceren Paydas and Adam Harvey are also intended to outsmart algorithmic facial recognition.

77 Cf. Schaar 2015, p. 186.

78 Cf. ibid. One of the best-known tools for this purpose is the TOR project (The Onion Router), sponsored by the U.S. military and appreciated by the hacker community, which covers the user's tracks by redirecting his or her data packets via several servers distributed around the world.

79 Cf. ibid.

80 Cf. Newport, Cal: Digital Minimalism. Choosing a Focused Life in a Noisy World, New York 2019.

81 Cf. Reiff, Charlotte: Attention Resistance (Webpage), Vienna, https://www.attention-resistance.com/ (November 13, 2021).

According to its caution, Phantom tends to paranoia—impressively illustrated in the last scene of "The Conversation" (1974), in which surveillance specialist Harry Caul (Gene Hackman) destroys his flat room in search of a hidden microphone.

While Phantom wants to become indetectable to its pursuers, the next identity concept takes a diametrically opposite approach.

E-xistentialist

In the identity concept of the E-xistentialist—again, the spelling is supposed to mark the projection of this concept into the digital age—those personality types are merged, who are aware of the algorithmic apparatus, but do not want to surrender to its manipulating influence.

Within audio-visual portraits of whistleblowers and activists (e.g. "The Fifth Estate" [2013]), but also of hackers and criminals, there are always culminating points of action where their identity is revealed, and they must take a stand on their agenda.

Like its philosophical role models (Sartre, de Beauvoir), the e-xistentialist identity concept pursues a radical idea of freedom and a self-imposed mission, which is always also an ethical one. If this idea of freedom and its mission cannot be reconciled with the respective algorithmic regime, it remains true and stands for what it represents.

From Sartre, E-xistentialist adopts the notion that existence precedes essence[82], by which is meant that it is one's choices and acts alone that shape identity, not primarily ideas. And a large part of an individual's actions is now digitally preserved from oblivion. Moreover, since many of the acts are

---

82 French: "l'existence précède l'essence." Cf. Sartre, Jean-Paul: Existentialism Is a Humanism. In: Kaufman, Walter (Ed.): Existentialism: from Dostoevsky to Sartre, New York 1989, https://www.marxists.org/reference/archive/sartre/works/exist/sartre.htm (November 13, 2021).

publicly viewable, responsibility for those very deeds becomes an obligation. In view of its finiteness—and nowadays also: in view of enormously increased possibilities of choice—it must undertake its decisions in high uncertainty. And it must stand by his decisions and actions.

E-xistentialist attempts to question traditional ideas and to acquire one's own insights via in-depth observation of phenomena—in the manner of an epoché (ἐποχή), as Edmund Husserl would have called this "suspension of judgment".[83] The choice of the red pill by Neo (Keano Reeves) in "The Matrix" has become a paradigmatic image for the search for knowledge and the discarding of deception. But: Existentialists were often criticized that their insights are subjective in nature[84]—which is illustrated in film, for example, by the visualized (inner) worlds of "The Cell" (2000) and "Inception" (2010).

Due to the subjective character of this identity concept, caution is advised, because: Whether the E-xistentialist's approach can be sustainable in an algorithmical environment, depends on the respective insight into algorithms' modes of operation. For studies have shown—as explained above—that target persons are often not even aware of their manipulations. Consequently, the concept of freedom pursued by E-xistentialist is first a goal to be realised. Without insight into the algorithmic possibilities of influence, E-xistentialist falls short of its own ambition.

That E-xistentialist can be blind to defining conditions (such as algorithms) is evident, for example, in the fact that Sartre demanded that humans not acknowledge certain facts (e.g. gender, skin colour) but transcend them in their actions, and that he focused strongly on the individual. The thoughts that overcoming formative conditions is sometimes impossible and that our freedom also touches that of our fellow human beings were then important driving forces for Simone de Beauvoir's works, especially for her examination of the "The Second Sex" (1949).

Even if this e-xistentialist idea of freedom is not being realised, the emergence of the ideal type is evident in all those who openly and loudly take

---

83 Cf. Wang, Shin-Yun: Die Methode der Epoché in der Phänomenologie Husserls, Freiburg 2004, p. 1, https://freidok.uni-freiburg.de/fedora/objects/freidok:1688/datastreams/FILE1/content (November 13, 2021).

84 To be precise: Whereby "Heidegger [...] denies that the categories of subject and object characterize our most basic way of encountering entities. He maintains, however, that they apply to a derivative kind of encounter." (Wheeler, Martin: Martin Heidegger. In: E. Zalta [ed.]: Stanford Encyclopedia of Philosophy 12/10 [2011]), https://plato.stanford.edu/entries/heidegger/ (November 13, 2021).

dubious positions online and in the empirical world, regardless of whether it brings them social exclusion.

Dice Man

The identity concept Dice Man does not, as one might think, compress those characters who hack gambling systems or outwit their operators, as they appear in "The Sting" (1973), "Revolver" (2005) or "21" (2008).[85] Those characters who fight algorithmic systems by finding and exploiting their flaws are subordinated to E-pimetheus in our taxonomy, since it is this identity concept that competitively opposes algorithms and, of course, also uses its (mathematical) intelligence to do so.

The template for the identity concept Dice Man is derived from Luke Rhinehart's (or George Cockroft's) cult novel "The Dice Man" (1971), in which the first-person narrator lets the dice decide on his next steps. For this purpose he always writes down six things he could do, then rolls the dice. And what the dice indicates, he must inevitably do.[86]

Shaped here as a concept of identity, the form of Dice Man is to apply to each gender type. This personality model can be understood as a radicalisation of the literary character of the flâneur, who allows himself to drift aimlessly on his walks[87]–and has his contemporary interpretation with Niko (Tom Schilling) from "Oh Boy" (2012). Dice Man leaves its fate to chance, plays a game of vabanque, and considers itself a participant in a social experiment, as is the case with Karen (Bodil Jørgenson) in Lars von Trier's "Idioterne" (1997).

---

85   From this genre, "21" would certainly be the most interesting for our purposes. For here it is a mathematics professor (Kevin Spacey) who develops his winning strategies in "Black Jack" using scientific methods. The film was based on a non-fiction book by Mezrich, Ben: Bringing Down The House, London 2003.
86   Cf. Rhinehart, Luke: Der Würfler, Halle 2011, p. 120.
87   Cf. Neumeyer, Harald: Der Flaneur: Konzeptionen der Moderne, Würzburg 1999.

By completely submitting to the dictates of the dice, Rhinehart's Dice Man, a bored psychologist, originally wants to escape ennui and find out how people can be changed for the better.[88] To this end, he wants to experiment with social roles to destroy his ego,[89] to completely give up his identity, which is only conceived to be fixed. And indeed, Rhinehart's Dice Man becomes less and less tangible and classifiable; he even speaks of a self-generated personality split.[90]

Rhinehart's alter ego then develops "dice therapy"[91] in order to turn other people into "humans of chance", into "unpredictable individuals"[92], into "volatile, unreliable, progressively schizoid personalities"[93], so that they would become free—above all from other people's and their own role expectations.

If we apply this identity concept to the current and future environment dominated by algorithms, it becomes clear that the integration of chance enables the Dice Man to become unpredictable for algorithmic measurement.

Paradoxically, such a complete submission to chance is not experienced as subjugation but as liberation, as an escape from routine. The identity concept of the Dice Man is preceded by a change within the understanding of chance: If chance was once seen as an adversary that can disrupt one's plans, today—in a context of saturated markets and satisfied needs—it is seen as an important stimulus for innovation, so that taking risks appears to be a virtue, since chance always holds opportunities.

Conclusions and Prospects

Social models of disobedience to algorithms can be drawn from numerous characters that appear in films, series and literature. When asking whether they can advise us, we must keep in mind that all these figures stem from fictional universes that not equal the empirical world. But also to be

---

88 Cf. Rhinehart 2011, p. 160.
89 Cf. ibid., p. 113, p. 227.
90 Cf. ibid., p. 238.
91 Cf. ibid., p. 178.
92 Cf. ibid., p. 151.
93 Cf. ibid., p. 248.

considered is that notions of algorithmic systems—the "colonization of the future" has already been mentioned—are contaminated by the fictional.

Several dystopians mentioned above seem to misjudge the nature of algorithmic systems, like Puppet Identity they impute intentionality to them, and tend to deify them. So, another identity type appears to be essential: The Enlightener, who could write a "Critique of Algorithmic Reason". Many of the authors cited here represent this identity type.[94] Zweig insists that Artificial Intelligence is a misnomer in the eyes of most of the scientific community;[95] it is a promotional term for powerful statistical systems that are supposed to be granted a certain magic by an appealing name.[96] Fry agrees that it would be more useful to think of the current achievements as a revolution in computational statistics, not intelligence.[97]

One has to always be aware that what currently goes by the term artificial intelligence is basically not comparable to human intelligence[98], that it merely mimics cognitive processes.[99] This circumstance is rarely illuminated in fiction, for example when a robot (Arnold Schwarzenegger) clumsily shoots an enemy's leg on the order to stop killing ("Terminator 2—Judgment Day" [1991]) or when the programming of the former police robot "Chappie" (2015) is deleted and a few criminals try to educate him to become a gangster. In doing so his gradual learning process is portrayed, which is always accompanied by mistakes.

---

94 Schaar, Zweig, O'Neil and Fry e.g. do so by pointing out that algorithmic systems only prove correlations (cf. Zweig: 2019, 194) and thus can be subject to erroneous conclusions after the pattern post/cum hoc ergo propter hoc and that they can amplify prejudices and discriminate people (cf. Zweig 2019, p. 149). The quality of algorithmic decisions depends on the database, the control of incoming data, the specific modelling of the social world and the research questions—all these parameters have to be handled sensitively. It should not be understated here, however, that algorithms can also improve the social process. After all, human decision-making processes can also be biased and flawed. Fry points out that there are not exactly many examples of perfectly fair, equitable systems even without the involvement of algorithms (cf. Fry 2019, p. 235).
95 Cf. Zweig 2019, p. 126.
96 Cf. ibid., p. 267.
97 Cf. Fry 2019, p. 25.
98 Cf. Zweig 2019, p. 268.
99 Cf. ibid., p. 129.

There is controversy among researchers as to whether so-called AGI will ever be able to outperform human intelligence in all respects.[100] Lee believes that it will take decades, if not centuries, to develop a superhuman intelligence, and that it is possible that humanity will never succeed in creating one.[101] Fry states that at present we are still far from creating even an intelligence on the level of a hedgehog.[102]

Enlightener looks forward to a future where we no longer view algorithms as objective masters but treat them like any other source of power—questioning their decisions, demanding information about who their beneficiary is, and holding them accountable for their mistakes.[103] So, Enlightener's primal task is to question the alleged infallibility of the so-called artificial intelligence. Because there are just still numerous areas, which algorithms do not master—like examining questions of justice.[104] Enlightener investigates the results and decisions of algorithmic systems, thus reconstructing their modelling to analyze how just they are[105]—via programming software bots, which pretend online to be different kinds of persons—rich, poor, white, BIPoC, young, old, male, female or mentally impaired. Algorithms' reactions allow to evaluate how biased they are.[106] Fry argues that people should be given the right to veto decisions made by algorithms. Unlike algorithms, humans sense how serious the consequences of their decisions are.[107] Most certainly, the benefits of technology should be used because: Algorithms do not tire, as pathologists they rarely misdiagnose. For this, however, man and machine should work in partnership.[108]

Enlightener, just as many of the cited authors, spurs us on and take us to task. Lee explains that we are not experiencing the AI revolution as

---

[100] Cf. Zweig 2019, p. 269.
[101] Cf. Lee 2019, p. 190.
[102] Cf. Fry 2019, pp. 25–26. In this context, she refers to the "Openworm" research project, which aims to simulate the brain of a worm. Cf. http://openworm.org (November 13, 2021).
[103] Cf. ibid., p. 237.
[104] Cf. O'Neil 2017, p. 211.
[105] Cf. ibid., pp. 281–282.
[106] Cf. ibid, pp. 285–286. Such analyses are being conducted by the "Web Transparency and Accountability Project" based at Princeton University, similar approaches exist at Carnegie Mellon University and MIT. Cf. ibid., p. 285.
[107] Cf. Fry 2019, p. 33.
[108] Cf. ibid., p. 236.

passive spectators, but as its authors.[109] Zweig calls us to reflect on what we think are good choices and how a machine can help us make them. For ethics come into the machine only through man.[110] In view of the radical changes to be expected because of automation and robotization, Lee argues that we need to move away from a mentality that regards people as variables in a giant productivity optimization algorithm. To this end, socially productive work should be rewarded in the same way as economically productive activities in the future.[111] This means: No matter in which of the mentioned identity types we find ourselves or whose strategies we want to use—we must decide consciously to improve the situation, if necessary: disobey. To this end, fiction can also make its contribution: By reminding us what values are worth following, by warning us what catastrophes are looming, by asking wise questions and questioning overly simplistic answers, stereotypes and imaginations.

Literature

Akremi, Leila: Kommunikative Konstruktion von Zukunftsängsten. Imaginationen zukünftiger Identitäten im dystopischen Spielfilm, Wiesbaden 2016.

Alter, Adam: Unwiderstehlich—Der Aufstieg suchterzeugender Technologien und das Geschäft mit unserer Abhängigkeit, Munich 2017.

Bainbridge, Lisanne: Ironies of Automation. In: Automatica, Vol. 19, Nº. 6, (Oxford, 1983), https://ckrybus.com/static/papers/Bainbridge_1983_Automatica.pdf (November 13, 2021).

Barbera, Patrizia: Facebook & Co.: Das Dreieck des Wandels. 22/02 (2021), https://heise.de/-5061297 (November 13, 2021).

Beauvoir, Simone de: Das andere Geschlecht. Sitte und Sexus der Frau, Reinbek 2011.

Bostrom, Nick: Superintelligenz: Szenarien einer kommenden Revolution, Frankfurt 2014.

---

[109] Cf. Lee 2019, p. 296.
[110] Cf. Zweig 2019, p. 286.
[111] Cf. Lee 2019, pp. 259–260.

Bridle, James: New Dark Age. Der Sieg der Technologie und das Ende der Zukunft, Munich 2019.

Brockmann, John (Ed.): Was sollen wir von der künstlichen Intelligenz halten? Frankfurt 2017.

Cellan-Jones, Rory: Stephen Hawking warns artificial intelligence could end mankind, BBC News, 02/12 (2014), https://www.bbc.com/news/technology-30290540 (November 13, 2021).

Epstein, Robert; Robertson, Ronald E.: The search engine manipulation effect (SEME) and its possible impact on the outcomes of elections. 04/08 (2015), https://www.pnas.org/content/112/33/E4512 (November 13, 2021).

Foucault, Michel: Überwachen und Strafen, Frankfurt 1994.

Freud, Sigmund: Eine Schwierigkeit der Psychoanalyse (1917). In: GW, Bd. 12, Frankfurt 1984.

Fry, Hannah: Hello World. Was Algorithmen können und wie sie unser Leben verändern, Munich 2019.

Fumagalli, Marco: Algorithmus versus Individualität? Studie zur Bedeutung der Künstlichen Intelligenz für das menschliche Ich. Hamburg 2020.

Giddens, Anthony: Modernity and Self-Identity. Self and Society in the Late Modern Age, Cambridge 1991.

Grundmann, Matthias; Beer, Raphael (Eds.): Subjekttheorien interdisziplinär. Diskussionsbeiträge aus Sozialwissenschaften, Philosophie und Neurowissenschaften, Münster 2004.

Harari, Yuval Noah: The Rise of the Useless Class. 24/02 (2017), https://ideas.ted.com/the-rise-of-the-useless-class/ (November 13, 2021).

Horn, Eva: Zukunft als Katastrophe, Frankfurt 2014.

Keenan, Thomas P.: Technocreep. The Surrender of Privacy and the Capitalization of Intimacy, New York 2014.

Keupp, Heiner: Vom Ringen um Identität in der spätmodernen Gesellschaft. Eröffnungsrede bei den 60. Lindauer Psychotherapiewochen. (Lindau, 2010), https://www.lptw.de/archiv/vortrag/2010/keupp-vom-ringen-um-identitaet-in-der-spaetmodernen-gesellschaft-lindauer-psychotherapiewochen2010.pdf (November 13, 2021).

Lanier, Jaron: Wem gehört die Zukunft? "Du bist nicht der Kunde der Internetkonzerne. Du bist ihr Produkt." Munich 2013.

Lee, Kai-Fu: AI Superpowers. China, Silicon Valley und die neue Weltordnung, Frankfurt/New York 2019.

Lobe, Adrian: Speichern und strafen. Die Gesellschaft im Datengefängnis, Munich 2019.

Mezrich, Ben: Bringing Down The House. How Six Students Took Vegas for Millions, London 2003.

Neumayer, Harald: Der Flaneur: Konzeptionen der Moderne, Würzburg 1999.

Newport, Cal: Digital Minimalism. Choosing a Focused Life in a Noisy World, New York 2019.

Nida-Rühmelin, Julian; Weidenfeldt, Natalie: Digitaler Humanismus, München 2018.

O'Neil, Cathy: Angriff der Algorithmen. Wie sie Wahlen manipulieren, Berufschancen zerstören und unsere Gesundheit gefährden, Munich 2017.

Paydaş, Ceren: World War A: Humans vs. Algorithms (Boston 2015), https://www.dropbox.com/s/fhsylc5zqekj0zq/thesis_book.pdf?dl=0 (November 13, 2021).

Peltzer, Anja: Identität und Spektakel. Der Hollywood-Blockbuster als global erfolgreicher Identitätsanbieter, Konstanz 2011.

Pinker, Steven: Das unbeschriebene Blatt, Berlin 2003.

Primack, Brian A.; Shensa, Ariel; Sidani, Jaime E.; Whaite, Erin O.; Lin, Liu Yi; Rosen, Daniel; Colditz, Jason B.; Radovic; Ana, Miller, Elizabeth: Social Media Use and Perceived Social Isolation Among Young Adults in the U.S. In: American Journal for Preventive Medicine, 06/03 (2017), https://doi.org/10.1016/j.amepre.2017.01.010 (November 13, 2021).

Reckwitz, Andreas: Die Erfindung der Kreativität, Frankfurt 2012.

Reiff, Charlotte: Attention Resistance (Webpage), Vienna, https://www.attention-resistance.com/ (November 13, 2021).

Reinhard, Rebekka: Wach denken: Für einen zeitgemäßen Vernunftgebrauch, Hamburg 2020.

Rhinehart, Luke: Der Würfler, Halle 2011.

Sartre, Jean-Paul: Existentialism Is a Humanism. In: Walter Kaufman (Ed.): Existentialism: from Dostoevsky to Sartre (New York 1989), URL: https://www.marxists.org/reference/archive/sartre/works/exist/sartre.htm (November 13, 2021).

Schaar, Peter: Das digitale Wir. Unser Weg in die transparente Gesellschaft, Hamburg 2015.

Schaar, Peter: Das Ende der Privatsphäre: der Weg in die Überwachungsgesellschaft, Munich 2018.

Schep, Tijmen: Social Cooling, https://www.tijmenschep.com/socialcooling/ (November 13, 2021).

Schinke, Chris: Das Dilemma mit den sozialen Medien (Bonn, 2020), https://www.filmdienst.de/film/details/615660/das-dilemma-mit-den-sozialen-medien#kritik (November 13, 2021).

Schroer, Markus: Gesellschaft und Film, Konstanz 2008.

Sontheimer, Leonie; Hegemann, Lisa; Becker, Georg: Palantir Technologies: Die geheimnisvollen Datensortierer. 30/10 (2020), https://www.zeit.de/digital/internet/2020-09/palantir-technologies-daten-analyse-boersengang-peter-thiel-alex-karp/komplettansicht (November 13, 2021).

Steinmüller, Karlheinz: Gestaltbare Zukünfte. Zukunftsforschung und Science Fiction. Werkstattbericht 23. Sekretariat für Zukunftsforschung. (Gelsenkirchen 1995), 3, https://steinmuller.de/de/zukunftsforschung/downloads/WB%2013%20Science%20Fiction.pdf (November 13, 2021).

Tegmark, Max: Leben 3.0: Mensch sein im Zeitalter Künstlicher Intelligenz, Berlin 2017.

Unknown author: China-Experte: Corona-Pandemie treibt Techno-Autoritarismus in China voran, Osnabrück, 25/01 (2021), https://www.presseportal.de/pm/58964/4820118 (November 13, 2021).

Wang, Shin-Yun: Die Methode der Epoché in der Phänomenologie Husserls (Freiburg 2004), https://freidok.uni-freiburg.de/fedora/objects/freidok:1688/datastreams/FILE1/content (November 13, 2021).

Weidenfeld, Nathalie: Das Drama der Identität im Film, Marburg 2012.

Wheeler, Martin: Martin Heidegger. In: (Edward Zalta [Ed.]): The Stanford Encyclopedia of Philosophy 12/10 (2011), https://plato.stanford.edu/entries/heidegger/ (November 13, 2021).

Wu, Tim: The Attention Merchants. The Epic Struggle to Get Inside Our Heads, London 2017.

Zuboff, Shoshana: Zeitalter des Überwachungskapitalismus, Munich 2018.

Zweig, Katharina: Ein Algorithmus hat kein Taktgefühl, Munich 2019.

Filmography

Fiction films: Metropolis (1927) | Modern Times (1936) | Desk Set (1957) | Alphaville (1965) | 2001: A Space Odyssey (1968) | Colossus (1970) | THX 1138 (1971) | The Sting (1973) | Westworld (1973) | Welt am Draht (1973) | The Conversation (1974) | The Stepford Wives (1975) | Logan's Run (1976) | Tron (1982), Tron Legacy (2010) | Blade Runner (1982) | Wir (1982) | WarGames (1983) | Electric Dreams (1984) | Hide and Seek (1984) | Sneakers (1992) | Ghost in the Shell (1995, 2004, 2017) | Hackers (1995) | Strange Days (1995) | The Net (1995) | Escape from L.A. (1996) | Idioterne (1997) | Masterminds (1997) | 23—Nichts ist wie es scheint (1998) | Enemy of the State (1998) | eXistenZ (1999) | Matrix (1999) | Pi (1998) | The 13th Floor (1999) | Takedown (2000) | The Cell (2000) | A.I. (2001) | Antitrust (2001) | Enigma (2001) | Password Swordfish (2001) | Equilibrium (2002) | Minority Report (2002) | The Bourne Identity (2002) | Nicotina (2003) | I, Robot (2004) | One Point Zero (2004) | Revolver (2005) | The Island (2005) | V for Vendetta (2005) | A Scanner Darkly (2006) | Firewall (2006) | Untraceable (2008) | 21 (2008) | The Girl with the Dragon Tattoo (2009) | Inception (2010) | The Social Network (2010) | Millenium (2010) | Disconnect (2012) | Oh Boy (2012) | Skyfall (2012) | Fifth Estate (2013) | Her (2013) | Algorithm (2014) | Ex Machina (2014) | Open Windows (2014) | The Imitation Game (2014) | Transcendence (2014) | Who Am I (2014) | Blackhat (2015) | Mr. Robot (series, since 2015) | Ratter (2015) | Chappie (2015) | Jason Bourne (2016) | Snowden (2016) | IBoy (2017) | The Circle (2017) | Blade Runner 2049 (2017) | Anon (2018) | Hacked (2018) | Ready Player One (2018) | Eagle Eye (2019) | How To Sell Drugs Online (Fast) (series, since 2019) | Password (2019)

Bernd Friedrich Schon

Documentaries: Hackers—Wizards of the Electronic Age (1984) | Hackers in Wonderland (2000) | Freedom Downtime (2001) | Revolution OS (2001) | Hacking Democracy (2006) | Hackers Are People Too (2008) | Hacker (2010) | We are Legion: The Story of the Hacktivists (2012) | Terms and Conditions May Apply (2013) | We Steal Secrets (2013) | Citizenfour (2014) | The Hacker Wars (2014) | Deep Web (2015) | Risk (2016) | Zero Days (2016) | Bombshell—The Hedy Lamarr Story (2017) | Kim Dotcom: Caught in the Web (2017) | The Social Dilemma (2020)

Illustrations

Puppet Identity, E-pimetheus, Phantom, E-xistentialist, Dice Man — courtesy of Bernd Friedrich Schon

About the Authors

About the Authors

Florian Arnold works as a academic researcher at the State Academy of Fine Arts Stuttgart. He did his first doctorate in philosophy at the University of Heidelberg and his second in Design at the HfG Offenbach. Since 2016 he is managing editor of the Philosophische Rundschau, and has written several books on philosophy, design, and aesthetics in general.

Moritz Ahlert works as researcher and lecturer at Habitat Unit, Institute of Architecture, at Technical University of Berlin. The urban researcher did his doctorate at University of Fine Arts of Hamburg, where he was part of the Postgraduate Doctorate Programme "Aesthetics of the Virtual". Since 2021 he is Post Doc in the interdisciplinary research consortium "Transforming Solidarities. Practices and Infrastructures in Migration Society". (BUA/DFG). His research focuses on the intersection of actor-based planning processes, mapping and digitalization.

Katja Dill is a doctoral candidate at the University of Vechta and a research associate at the Harriet Taylor Mill-Institute at the Berlin School of Economics and Law. In 2019 she founded Social Period e.V., a non-profit association that facilitates access to hygiene products for homeless people and those in need. Her research focuses on interdisciplinary gender studies, science and technology studies, feminist theory and epistemology and digitalization.

Victoria Guijarro Santos works as a research assistant at the law faculty at the University of Muenster. She writes her interdisciplinary doctoral thesis on the laws against data-based discrimination. As initiator and co-organizer of the conference "What We Don't Talk About When We Talk About Law" and the kick-off conference of the German forum "Junges Digitales Recht"/"Young Data Law", Victoria advocates for a critical approach to law, power and technologies and dedicates herself to a feminist net policy at the German association netzforma* e.V.

Christina Hecht is currently finishing her master's degree in social sciences at Humboldt University in Berlin. Her thesis explores individual perceptions of datafied situations in contexts of work and lifestyle, as well as how data and algorithms are seen to play a role in society. In the course of her studies, she has dealt with the change of employment relations in the light of digitalization. She works at the Weizenbaum Institute for the Networked Society as a student assistant in the research group "Digital Citizenship" and supports, among other things, the annual implementation of a telephone assisted interview survey on (digital) political participation.

Carolin Höfler works as a professor of design theory and research at the Köln International School of Design at TH Köln. The art historian and architect did her doctorate at the Humboldt-Universität zu Berlin and was an assistant professor at the Department of Architecture at TU Braunschweig. She is co-founder of the DFG Research Training Group "Connecting – Excluding" at the University of Cologne. Her research focuses on practices, concepts and media in architecture and design, the medial saturation of public space and ephemeral urbanism.

Lotte Houwing works as a policy advisor at Bits of Freedom in Amsterdam. She has a bachelor of science degree in philosophy and IT-law and graduaded cum laude from her masters on the functionality of Law at the University in Groningen. She worked as a research and teaching assistant at Security, Technology and e-Privacy at this same university. Before ending up at Bits of Freedom she worked as a file coordinator at the Public Interest Litigation Project and did an internship at lawyers office Prakken d'Oliveira. Next to this she published articles, focussing on government surveillance.

Fabian Lütz is currently a PhD candidate at the University of Lausanne (UNIL). He worked as Legal Officer in the European Commission (Gender Equality Unit) between 2015 and 2020. His research focuses on competition, discrimination and gender equality law especially work life balance, algorithmic discrimination and the regulation of Artificial Intelligence as well as behavioral law and Economics.

About the Authors

Johanna Mellentin is an anthropologist with legal background. Currently she is emploied as an scientific research assistant by the deputy chairman of the Green Party in the German parliament. Her main responsibilities are domestic politics, (IT) security, freedom rights and democracy. Passionate for all things digital, she does alongside voluntary work in many different organisations, handling topics like media, digitalisation and network policy. As a chair woman of netzforma* e.V. she conceptualizes and implements sustainable, purposeful and reflective long-term strategies and multiple projects for the social good. She is also speaker for digital politics as a City-Council and speaker for the digital think tank of Bündnis 90/Die Grünen in bavaria.

Simon Nestler is a professor for Human-Computer Interaction at Technische Hochschule Ingolstadt. He studied computer science at the Technische Universität München and received his Ph.D. in the field of Human-Computer Interaction. He researches and consults on UUX (Usability & User Experience) of government applications and is a member of the presidium of the Gesellschaft für Informatik, a member of the Association for Computing Machinery (ACM) and of the German UPA.

Klaus Neuburg is a professor of media design with a focus on interactive media at the Ostfalia University of Applied Sciences Braunschweig/Wolfenbüttel. He studied architecture at RWTH Aachen University. Alongside his work in various design disciplines, he co-founded the independent journalism NGO Froh! e.V., with whom he developed several transmedia formats. His research sits at the intersection of design, society and technology, with a particular interest in social contexts.

Matthias Pfeffer ist a TV journalist, author and producer and founder of PfefferMedia. He studied philosophy and was managing director and editor-in-chief of FOCUS TV for 20 years. Together with Paul Nemitz, he published "Prinzip Mensch, Macht Freiheit und Demokratie im Zeitalter der Künstlichen Intelligenz" which made it onto the shortlist "Das politische Buch 2020". In 2021, his book "Menschliches Denken und Künstliche Intelligenz. Eine Aufforderung" (Human Thinking and Artificial Intelligence. A Call to Action) was published by Dietz Verlag. He lives in Berlin and Munich.

Sven Quadflieg is a professor at the Hamm-Lippstadt University of Applied Sciences. He studied design at the Folkwang University of the Arts and the Zurich University of the Arts and earned his doctorate at the HFBK Hamburg. In his research he is interested in political and social design and the mutual influences and dependencies between design and society. He is a member of the DGTF and the International Gender Design Network.

Francesca Schmidt studied German studies, German linguistics and society, history, and politics in South Asia in Heidelberg and Berlin. She is a founding member and board member of Netzforma* e.V., a feminist digital policy association. In her work, she deals with questions of digital violence, surveillance and control, algorithms, artificial intelligence, and their socio-normative implications. Her book "Digital Policy. A feminist Introduction" was published by Barbara Budrich Verlag in 2020.

Bernd Friedrich Schon works as a senior editor and screenwriter and created the illustrations for his article. He studied at the Institute for Art and Art Theory in Cologne, graduated in media design at the University of Applied Sciences in Mainz, studied film sciences, literature and philosophy (Johannes Gutenberg University Mainz) and is currently completing his doctorate on the topic of "Narrative Closure, Openness and Ambiguity in Feature Film Dramaturgy".

Robert Thum is professor for computational design in architecture, and directs the architecture department at the Hochschule Trier. He studied architecture in Vienna, Stuttgart, Phoenix, and London. He was head of the master program at the University of East London (2006–13). Together with Harald Trapp, he collaborated on the research project Capital Architecture, which dealt with the connection between Karl Marx and the production of space and architecture.

About the Authors

Harald Trapp is a sociologist and architect. He co-curated and designed the Austrian Pavilion at the Venice Architecture Biennale in 2014. From 2015–2018 he was head of the Master of Architecture programme at the University of East London. Since 2017 he is running the research project "Capital Architecture" in cooperation with Prof. Robert Thum. In 2019 he co-founded AKT, a collective of young architects in Vienna. Currently he is a guest professor at the University of Innsbruck, UAC Skopje and teaches at Vienna University of Technology.

Fabian Weiss is a photographer and lecturer in the field of photography and visual storytelling. He lives and works in Austria and Germany and is a PhD candidate at the University of Applied Arts Vienna, pursuing an artistic research project with a focus on body optimization, artificial intelligence and the role of images. Fabian Weiss is represented by the agency laif and his visual works have been published, awarded and exhibited internationally. As a board member of the Cologne-based media-NGO FROH! e.V. and co-founder of the international workshop series Publish Yourself! he teaches and conducts workshops in Europe and further east.

Medienwissenschaft

Tanja Köhler (Hg.)
**Fake News, Framing, Fact-Checking:
Nachrichten im digitalen Zeitalter**
Ein Handbuch

2020, 568 S., kart., 41 SW-Abbildungen
39,00 € (DE), 978-3-8376-5025-9
E-Book:
PDF: 38,99 € (DE), ISBN 978-3-8394-5025-3

Geert Lovink
Digitaler Nihilismus
Thesen zur dunklen Seite der Plattformen

2019, 242 S., kart.
24,99 € (DE), 978-3-8376-4975-8
E-Book:
PDF: 21,99 € (DE), ISBN 978-3-8394-4975-2
EPUB: 21,99 € (DE), ISBN 978-3-7328-4975-8

Mozilla Foundation
Internet Health Report 2019

2019, 118 p., pb., ill.
19,99 € (DE), 978-3-8376-4946-8
E-Book: available as free open access publication
PDF: ISBN 978-3-8394-4946-2

Leseproben, weitere Informationen und Bestellmöglichkeiten
finden Sie unter www.transcript-verlag.de

Medienwissenschaft

Ziko van Dijk
Wikis und die Wikipedia verstehen
Eine Einführung

März 2021, 340 S., kart.,
Dispersionsbindung, 13 SW-Abbildungen
35,00 € (DE), 978-3-8376-5645-9
E-Book: kostenlos erhältlich als Open-Access-Publikation
PDF: ISBN 978-3-8394-5645-3
ISBN 978-3-7328-5645-9

Gesellschaft für Medienwissenschaft (Hg.)
Zeitschrift für Medienwissenschaft
Jg. 13, Heft 2/2021: Spielen

September 2021, 180 S., kart.
24,99 € (DE), 978-3-8376-5400-4
E-Book: kostenlos erhältlich als Open-Access-Publikation
PDF: ISBN 978-3-8394-5400-8
ISBN 978-3-7328-5400-4

Anna Dahlgren, Karin Hansson,
Ramón Reichert, Amanda Wasielewski (eds.)
Digital Culture & Society (DCS)
Vol. 6, Issue 2/2020 – The Politics of Metadata

June 2021, 274 p., pb., ill.
29,99 € (DE), 978-3-8376-4956-7
E-Book:
PDF: 29,99 € (DE), ISBN 978-3-8394-4956-1

**Leseproben, weitere Informationen und Bestellmöglichkeiten
finden Sie unter www.transcript-verlag.de**